W9-DDT-443

MAC OS
Web Server Handbook
X

ISBN 0-13-032715-8
90000
9 780130 327154

MAC OS X Web Server Handbook

David L. Hart

Prentice Hall PTR
Upper Saddle River, New Jersey 07458
www.phptr.com

Library of Congress Cataloging-in-Publication Data

Hart, David L.
Mac OS X Web server handbook / David L. Hart.
p. cm.
Includes bibliographical references and index.
ISBN 0-13-032715-8
1. Mac OS. 2. Operating systems (Computers) 3. Macintosh (Computer) 4. Web servers. I. Title.

QA76.76.O63 H3555 2001
004.67'8--dc21 2001021341

Editorial/production supervision: *Jane Bonnell*
Cover design director: *Jerry Votta*
Cover design: *Anthony Gemmellaro*
Manufacturing buyer: *Maura Zaldivar*
Acquisitions editor: *Michael Meehan*
Editorial assistant: *Linda Ramagnano*
Marketing manager: *Debby van Dijk*

Prentice-Hall, Inc.
Upper Saddle River, New Jersey 07458

Prentice Hall books are widely used by corporations and government agencies for training, marketing, and resale.
The publisher offers discounts on this book when ordered in bulk quantities. For more information, contact Corporate Sales Department, Phone: 800-382-3419; FAX: 201-236-7141;
E-mail: corpsales@prenhall.com
Or write: Prentice Hall PTR, Corporate Sales Dept., One Lake Street, Upper Saddle River, NJ 07458.

Printed in the United States of America
10 9 8 7 6 5 4 3 2 1

ISBN 0-13-032715-8

Prentice-Hall International (UK) Limited, *London*
Prentice-Hall of Australia Pty. Limited, *Sydney*
Prentice-Hall Canada Inc., *Toronto*
Prentice-Hall Hispanoamericana, S.A., *Mexico*
Prentice-Hall of India Private Limited, *New Delhi*
Prentice-Hall of Japan, Inc., *Tokyo*
Pearson Education Asia Pte. Ltd.
Editora Prentice-Hall do Brasil, Ltda., *Rio de Janeiro*

Contents

PREFACE

This book hits the shelves almost three years after its predecessor, the *Mac OS 8 Web Server Cookbook,* and it's interesting to consider how things—especially the Internet—have changed in that span of time. For starters, the Web has truly come of age and has become an integral part of daily life rather than a gee-whiz accessory for university or high-tech communities. While the Web is still experiencing some growing pains and has not yet settled into its final niche in the media spectrum, it has affected how people communicate, publish information, shop, and gather information.

Another major change has seen Apple rebound from a period in which its future was often called into question by all but the most die-hard proponents to a profitable three-year run (only recently interrupted by a slight downturn along with much of the personal computer industry). The past few years have seen the introduction of the iMac, such as the graphite iMac DV Special Edition on which this book was written, the iBook, the G4 processor, and the Titanium PowerBook. And of course, there's Mac OS X.

Mac OS X marks a significant shift in the operating system that most Mac users have come to know and love. The "Classic" Mac OS—from System 7 to Mac OS 8 and Mac OS 9—has long been simultaneously adored by advocates for its ease of use and condemned by others for certain shortcomings really understood only by those who have a background in the intricacies of computer operating systems. For everyone else, these shortcomings are most evident in the annoying need to manually adjust the memory allocation assigned to Mac OS applications.

After several years of fits and starts, Apple has accomplished a fairly amazing feat. It has taken an industrial-strength UNIX foundation, renovated the graphical Mac OS interface to shield most users from the technicalities of this UNIX-based environment, granted access to the UNIX underpinnings for the technically adept, *and* provided a migration path that ensures backwards compatibility with the Classic Mac OS.

For Mac adherents who want to use their Macs to join the World Wide Web, Mac OS X represents yet another leap forward. Mac OS X merges the Web serving tools that have evolved with attention to the ease of use of the Mac OS and the tools (both free and commercial) that have been developed for UNIX, the dominant operating system of Web serving computers.

So the three years since this book's predecessor have seen major changes in the landscape of Mac Web serving, and it was clear to me that an update to the *Mac OS 8 Web Server Cookbook* was in order. And that update soon became a wholesale rewrite of the book. There are some similarities, and I carried over those portions that had stood the test of time, but the organization and selection of software and Web resources has been completely reconstructed. I hope you find my efforts useful.

The Book for You

If you have decided it's time to serve some information, either to the whole world via the Web or to a single organization via an intranet, this may be the book for you. My first job is to turn that "may" into a yes or a no. If you want a succinct road map for establishing an Internet server, complete with Web server and a full suite of enhancements, read on. What you'll find here is everything you need to get started. If you really wanted software documentation for whatever piece of software you're having trouble with at the moment, then you need a different book.

This road map was assembled for three groups of people:

- Mac addicts who will use a Mac for their Internet server even if they have to write the code themselves,
- Users who are considering Macs for their Internet server but aren't sure if Macs are up to it, and
- Webmasters, regardless of platform, who might be seeking some information about the potential of Mac OS X for their servers.

To the Mac addicts, I'd like to say: Relax. Setting up a solid, secure Mac OS X Internet server is just as easy as installing any Mac application. It might take as little as three mouse clicks. (See Chapter 7.)

To those of you considering a Mac OS X Web server, I'll just say: If you want an Apache Web server that takes about 30 minutes to set up and can handle just as many hits as any other operating system, you might want to look closely at Mac OS X. If you want a Web server running on an operating system that requires years of training to administer, go with UNIX or Windows.

To webmasters using UNIX and Windows systems: Regardless of the operating system you're using for your Web servers, the steps to establish your server and the results your visitors see are all about the same. You might find this book useful in many respects, and you might learn a thing or two about Mac OS X in the process.

Scope

Let's make sure you understand the scope of the material presented in this book.

Emphasis on Information Servers, Not Clients. Downloading a file with FTP, sending e-mail, or surfing the Web are *client* activities. Setting up a secure FTP server, redistributing an incoming message to a mailing list, or making a Web home page available are *server* activities. Most Internet-related books deal only with the client side of the Internet. This is not a book about using Web browsers like Netscape Navigator or Internet Explorer, nor is it a book of "cool" sites. Having said that, Chapter 6 helps you install and configure client software so you can review the information on your own server.

Not Just the Web. Of the books available that do describe how to set up an Internet server, the focus is almost always on a Web server. This book is about designing and maintaining a server to support FTP, mailing list servers, search engines, forums, e-commerce sites, and databases as well as the Web.

Establishing a Mac OS X–based Information Server. Many of the principles in this book apply to servers using any of the UNIX and Microsoft Windows variants, as well as to Mac OS servers. However, this book will have much shorter chapters on installing software, configuring the system, and administering the server than a comparable book about non-Mac operating systems.

The Handbook Format

As a handbook, this book doesn't spend time on too many details. You can think of the book as a road map. With a road map, you begin with something that covers a large area and shows you how to get from Point A to Point B on regional highways and major surface streets before homing in on the specifics. This handbook mentions hundreds of different software applications; there's no way I can present complete documentation on all of them. All I can do is point you in the right direction and give you the tools you need to find the rest of the information you need.

At this level, my road map helps you answer questions about the route you want to take to get to the Web server of your dreams: Should I use a database? How do I support online communities? Should I stream video clips? What's the difference between a Java applet and a Java servlet?

In one of the most significant changes from the previous version of this book, I've steered clear of the details of creating HTML pages. You won't find definitions of the various tags and attributes, although there are some examples here and there. I made this change for two reasons. First, there are many books out there that do the job more completely and thoroughly. (The fact that describing HTML fills a book is another reason not to give it short shrift in this book devoted to other purposes.)

Second, this book discusses not only HTML, but also XML, SMIL, XHTML, CSS, and other markup languages. In fairness to all the other languages, there was no clear reason to detail HTML alone. Finally, advances in Web page editing tools have made it much less necessary to understand the nuances of HTML to create your Web pages. I heartily recommend that you *do* learn about HTML if you have anything to do with creating Web pages, but you'll need a different book to help you with that.

Prerequisites

You don't need years of experience with Mac OS X to make use of this book, which is lucky, since Mac OS X has only recently been available to the public. However, this book does assume you have some knowledge of using a Macintosh. In some cases, some familiarity with UNIX will come in handy, but it's not absolutely necessary.

Degree of Macintosh Proficiency. In setting up a Macintosh server, you need a basic familiarity with configuring and operating the Mac OS. For example, you should understand the basics of folders and files, and using the mouse to open items or make selections from menus. If you can perform these tasks, you can run an Internet server.

Familiarity with HTML and Web Languages. I have assumed that you have some passing familiarity with HTML and related Web markup languages. I expect that you won't be baffled by the basic structure of an HTML file and that you know about tags and attributes. If you know that the bulk of a Web page is put between the <body> and </body> tags and that you can display text in boldface by putting it between <b> and </b> tags, then you should be fine.

Established Local Area Networks. For those wishing to set up an Internet server on a local-area network (LAN), this book assumes the LAN has already been established. This book does not discuss how to set up Macintosh networks, although some pointers for further information are provided. For the most part, I provide instructions only for connecting a single Macintosh (from a home or business) to the Internet.

Software Disclaimer

I also want to issue a disclaimer. This whole book was written during the public beta release of Mac OS X, just in time for the final release to appear as the publisher had the "final" manuscript. Many frantic, last-minute changes were made to ensure that the descriptions in this book coincide with what you see in the final release of Mac OS X. This book is as accurate as I could make it based on the software available. However, not all developers produced Mac OS X–compatible versions of their software during the public beta release, so I was not always able to run the software in question. In fact, many applications were not yet available for the public beta of Mac OS X. Many developers were understandably hesitant to release beta software on a beta operating system.

However, because of Apple's efforts to make it easy for developers to port Classic Mac OS applications to Mac OS X, this book assumes that most Classic Mac OS applications will become available for Mac OS X at its final release or shortly thereafter. I did my best to confirm that the applications featured prominently in this book, and to a lesser degree those listed in the tables, would be available for Mac OS X, but that was not always possible. I also tried to note in the text those applications for which I made this assumption.

In any event, I tried to list as many Mac OS applications as possible to recognize the efforts of Mac software developers in general. You might also find that a few UNIX-native applications will become available for Mac OS X soon after its release. I hope all this doesn't cause too much confusion.

Conventions

Throughout this book, I've used some conventions as shorthand for items that would otherwise take too long to explain each time that they occurred. I've included a list in the table on the following page.

For example, because of the predominance of the Web, I've omitted almost every occurrence of the *http://* prefix from Web URLs. I realize this may offend purists, but maybe it'll save some ink and a tree or two. In general, if you see a computer host-name in italics—usually but not always beginning with *www*—try visiting that location with your Web browser.

Another common convention is the use of a file-name extension to denote files of a certain type. For example, I'll often refer to text files that contain

HTML markup commands as *.html* files. GIF images are often described as *.gif* files. This shorthand serves both to identify the file type and to remind you about the Web's naming conventions. These conventions are usually required for your Web server to work, so it pays to adhere to them.

Finally, you'll also see an occasional UNIX command. As a rule, type in the commands exactly as shown, with all the spaces and punctuation, and finish by pressing the Return key. And I've abbreviated the system prompt as the "%" character; Mac OS X uses a different default prompt for the Terminal command line, but the exact text may vary.

Conventions Used in This Book

Convention	Definition
www.apple.com *hart-mac.sdsc.edu*	Shorthand URLs for a Web site or page. The *http://* prefix is omitted for brevity.
http://www.sdsc.edu/Cookbook/	A complete URL for finding information on the Web.
ftp://ftp.sdsc.edu/pub/cookbook/	A URL beginning *ftp://* indicates a resource to be accessed using anonymous FTP.
www.your-company.com	A placeholder domain name. You should replace such occurrences with your own domain name.
hart-mac.sdsc.edu/Cookbook/webcam/ *webcam.html*	URLs spanning more than one line may be broken following a slash (/). Hyphens located in a URL are part of the URL.
`% cd /Library/WebServer` `% chmod 775 file.cgi`	Commands to be entered at the command line of the Terminal application. The "%" represents the system prompt, which may vary. Each command is ended with a carriage return. Spaces and punctuation are significant.
.gif, .html, .mov	File-name extensions denoting files of a certain type.
<textarea name="{name}" rows="{size}" cols="{size}"> {optional text} </textarea>	HTML tag. The curly braces { } enclose material to be entered by the user and are not present in the actual tag. Lowercase is used for tags and attribute names to conform with the XHTML standard.

INTERNET-ENHANCED BOOK

While this book offers a concise description of building and maintaining an Internet information server, it cannot hope to stay current for long, given the speed at which the Internet is evolving. Providing a CD-ROM with a book sometimes helps because it provides more information than the book, but in this case it would become dated too quickly. Instead, this book is "Internet-enhanced." In effect, I've used the Internet as a book supplement, which can be updated continuously and made available to you long after the book has been published.

The book itself summarizes the reasons to establish an information server and shows how to establish and maintain that server. It contains many pointers—in the form of Web resources—to additional sources of information and to software that you will need. Those pointers are also available on a Web server at the San Diego Supercomputer Center (SDSC), a national laboratory for computational science and engineering. This Web site serves two purposes.

First, you don't have to type these URLs each time you wish to visit a site. You just have to add a single pointer to your Web browser's bookmarks list:

http://hart-mac.sdsc.edu/Handbook/

From there you can locate the Web pointer you need.

Second, and more important, I can keep this Web-based list of pointers current. Thus, while a pointer in this book is considered the best reference at the time of writing, it may not be the best reference at the time of reading. However, you can get the current reference simply by connecting to the SDSC server. This is important, since Internet technology is changing more quickly than new editions of a book can be produced. Through the information server, I can regularly supplement the book with current information.

Why don't I put the whole book online and update that? Maybe that will work for future generations, but for now many folks, including me, like the feel of a book in our hands and are comfortable navigating that medium. If you are reading this in the bookstore, or from someone else's copy, at this point you may be thinking: Why buy the book when I can jot down the pointer above and read the Web site? You are welcome to do that, of course. However, the combination of book and Internet server will provide the most useful and usable information.

You may also be thinking: How will Dave keep all the pointers to pertinent information and software current? In part, the answer is that you will help. There is a Reader's Corner accessible on the server for you to report pointers to sites that you think should be included in the handbook. I'll review these suggestions and, if appropriate, add them to the server.

Involving readers in the material they are reading, to the point where they begin to make their own contributions, is a very good use of the Internet. In fact, the Internet has supported many such projects, such as Perl, Mozilla, and others, not to mention the community of Mac OS shareware developers. The Internet has provided a communication channel between reader and author to enhance the quality and longevity of the book. In other words, the book is "Internet-enhanced."

So Finally...

The Web has come a long way in a short time from its origin as a way for physicists to distribute experimental results and papers. While it may not be the greatest innovation since sliced bread, neither is it completely without its advantages. The Web has a lot of growing up to do, a lot of growing pains to overcome, and everyone who participates has a chance to guide its growth. I hope this book helps you make your contribution to the Web's future.

Acknowledgments

Although it may have seemed so at the start of this endeavor, with a blank computer screen and a sketchy table of contents staring me in the face, no book is created completely from scratch. Especially this book, which follows the lead of the *Mac OS 8 Web Server Cookbook*. Through their responses to that book, many people have contributed indirectly, if not directly, to this book. And others have contributed to this new effort.

For the *Mac OS 8 Web Server Cookbook*, I would like to reiterate my thanks to those who helped with that project. I would like to thank Phil Bourne for publishing the original UNIX version of the *Cookbook* and giving me the chance to co-author the Mac version. Without that foot in the door, the *Mac OS 8 Web Server Cookbook*, my subsequent *Cross-Platform Mac Handbook*, and this book would not have happened.

Many thanks also go to Mike Meehan at Prentice Hall PTR for taking a chance with yet another Mac book, sticking with it through the uncertain Mac OS X release schedule, and shepherding the book through the publishing house from proposal to production to print. Thanks to Jane Bonnell and Lisa Iarkowski at Prentice Hall PTR for helping my computer files see the light of day as an actual book. And thanks to the nameless copyeditor and proofreaders who performed the thankless task of finding the typos and grammatical clinkers in my original manuscript.

I want to extend my heartfelt thanks to my wife, Casey, who put up with more than a year of me spending my early mornings, evenings, and weekends holed up in our spare bedroom working on this book. If there's an award for supportive spouses, then I'd like to nominate her for it.

I also want to extend my thanks to Steve Jobs and the folks at Apple for some great years at Apple, for the iMac, and for putting some excitement back in the Mac world. Most significantly, they managed to complete Mac OS X—whether you love it or loathe it. It represents a major technological achievement and makes the Mac a much more appealing and powerful Web serving platform.

Lastly, I have to thank the many people who have contributed to this book and don't even know it. The information and software at the many URLs cited in this book required a great deal of time and energy to develop. In many cases I'm sure the effort was in no way related to the developer's job requirements but was done as a community service. Thanks to you all.

CHAPTER 1

THE BIG PICTURE

This chapter introduces the levels you need to consider in establishing a fully functional Mac OS X Internet information server. This book considers the most common types of Internet services in use today—starting from a plain vanilla Web server to an interactive Internet community with e-commerce, file downloads, mailing lists, forums, and custom Web applications. To reach the widest possible audience, you should be prepared to support services such as FTP and e-mail in addition to the basic Web service.

Figure 1-1 summarizes the levels even further. From top to bottom, each box in Figure 1-1 lists a level in the process. The numbers in the boxes represent the chapters that encompass each of the levels. The types of information you will encounter are shown on the left of the boxes and the types of software tools on the right.

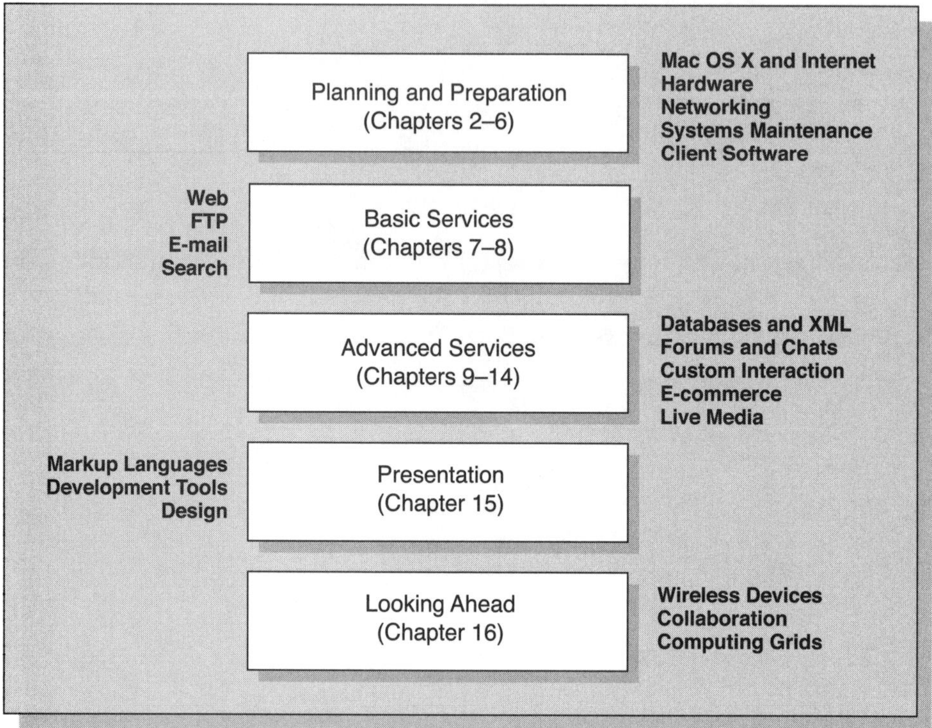

Figure 1-1. The Big Picture.

I've learned the hard way that you should progress through the Big Picture levels in roughly the order suggested to get the best results when installing and maintaining these services. Let's take a quick look at each of these levels.

PLANNING AND PREPARATION

Chapters 2–5: Background and Planning. If you can resist the urge to jump straight from taking your new Mac out of the box to issuing your initial public offering, you and your visitors will benefit from a little time spent devising a plan of attack. You'll want to assess the human, hardware, and networking resources you'll need for your server.

You have to decide first who your audience is, then what information you are going to provide to your audience, and then how you will provide it. Supporting sound and video, for example, requires additional server software and also will place heavy demands on your server. Planning will help you address these sorts of potential downfalls and make informed software choices from the available programs for each of the servers—file transfer protocol (FTP), list server, and Web.

Obviously, the most important piece of planning for an Internet server is getting Internet access. I'll discuss briefly how to obtain Internet access, if you do not already have it, and how to manage it on your Mac OS machine once you are connected. You also need to consider the demands a Web server will place on a computer. The most immediate concern is likely to be sufficient disk space to store all the information. If your server becomes popular, you need to ensure that memory, file transfers, network bandwidth, and processor power don't limit the rate at which you can serve information. I'll step through what these demands are and when in the development cycle they are likely to occur.

You then might want to think about "housekeeping"—these details will help you keep your Internet site up and running. For the most part, this involves the same tasks that you already know you *should* be doing for your computer—backups, disk management, security, server maintenance, and virus protection, for example—but that you've been putting off. And then you should consider how you want your intended audience to interact with your Web server. Whether you plan to phase in services or unleash them all at the same time, your first steps can put you on the easiest route to your eventual destination—or put you on a road potholed with a lot of reengineering and sleepless nights.

Chapter 6: Client Software. With the planning done and hardware selected, you are almost ready to start building your information server. First, however, you need to install the client software for the services you'll be providing on your server. As the first visitor to your server, you'll need to test whether the server functions as expected and whether the information is presented the way you want. I'll briefly discuss installing client software, including a Web browser such as Netscape Navigator or Microsoft Internet Explorer.

BASIC SERVICES

Chapter 7: Web Servers. Your choice of Web server will affect many future decisions, so you'll want to spend some time considering the options. Some Web server suites include an FTP server, a search engine, and mail services. Others may include integrated databases or e-commerce functions. Performance, extensibility, and administration may also factor into your decision.

In this book, I'll provide an overview of the major and minor options—yes, there are quite a few Mac OS options. Next, the book will focus on few popular options, including Apache and iTools, WebSTAR, and Web Server 4D. All but the most casual Web servers will probably want to analyze their servers' traffic, and I'll talk about log analysis tools, too.

Chapter 8: FTP, E-Mail, and Search Engines. If you choose a Web server that does not provide FTP, e-mail, or search capabilities, or if your traffic demands dedicated computers and software for these services, you can provide these functions separately. Of course, let's not forget that you may not need a Web server at all. This chapter will look at commercial and shareware options for FTP servers for file exchange, mail servers for individual e-mail accounts, list servers for reaching groups of subscribers, and search engines for crawling, indexing, and searching Web sites.

Advanced Services

Chapter 9: Databases and XML. Once you have established a Web server for delivering basic Web pages, your next step will be to extend the capabilities of your site with dynamic information features. A database is a common and critical step, and Chapter 9 describes options ranging from adding tab-delimited spreadsheet tables to integration with high-end relational database management systems. Many further extensions build on this choice of database. You may also want to prepare your site for the Extensible Markup Language (XML), which is rapidly growing in popularity.

Chapter 10: Guestbooks, Forums, and Chats. There are many other types of interaction and media content that you may want to provide to your audience. This chapter will look at community building software to establish guestbooks, forums, and chat rooms.

Chapters 11–12: Scripting and Web Applications. These chapters present your options for creating your own custom Web applications, from forms and Common Gateway Interface (CGI) scripts to dynamic server applications, to Java and JavaScript options. These are advanced topics, and in a single book, I can't teach you everything you need to know about the programming languages I'll mention. But as is true of all discussions in this book, I'll get you started and point you to reference material available on the Internet.

Chapter 13: E-Commerce. In today's electronic marketplace, you may also want your server to handle retail transactions. This chapter walks you through the requirements and software for hanging up your e-commerce shingle, and what you need to exchange goods for money electronically. I'll take you through adding encrypted transactions to protect your customers' information, filling up your online catalogs, providing electronic shopping carts, and processing credit card purchases.

Chapter 14: Live and Streaming Media. Finally, we will discuss delivery of live media through streaming audio and video and Web cams. If your goal with your Web site is to entertain as well as inform your audience, live media can keep your visitors coming back for more.

PRESENTATION

Chapter 15: Development and Design. Now that you've established a fully functional server, you need to give it some information to serve. Creating the information you want to serve could take a couple of hours to several months, depending on the complexity of the information. For this step, you need a different set of tools.

In a change from the first edition of this book, I won't be going into great detail on the syntax of the HyperText Markup Language (HTML). There are a multitude of tutorials and examples on the Web, created and updated by major sites targeting Web developers. I will discuss the basics of HTML, as well as the basics of related markup languages.

As the amount of information on your server grows, how you organize the various types of information becomes important. The tricks are to avoid duplication, provide easy file retrieval, and provide a suitable path for growth as your Internet server evolves. Yes, this requires more planning. (Sound familiar?) How you organize your server's information so it is accessible, readable, useful, and easily maintainable is critical. Anyone can provide a server with little effort—even if it doesn't appear so from what we've said; however, usability and value to the intended audience of the server require work.

The Web has advanced far enough that these tasks—creating Web pages and organizing your content—have been made much easier by improved software tools. For basic sites, you might still choose to use SimpleText to write Web pages from scratch or use Web and graphics editors and format converters to turn existing documents into Web pages. If you are going to provide sound and video, you will need tools for producing, editing, and browsing these formats. At the professional end of the spectrum, there are tools that also help you manage your files and keep track of your site's organization.

LOOKING AHEAD

Chapter 16: Future Web. Internet information servers involve rapidly changing technology, and you need to keep abreast of developments that may affect your server. I don't claim to be a psychic who can predict the future, but some technologies have progressed to the point that they will be common components of Web servers in just a few years. This chapter will point out a few promising technologies to watch.

Appendices. At this point, you have just about everything you need to know to set up a fully featured Mac OS X Web server. The appendices will point you to some sources of information on Mac OS X and general Web development resources.

CHAPTER 2

MAC OS X AND INTERNET BASICS

Just to make sure we're all starting from the same perspective, this chapter runs through some basic information and background you'll need to know about Mac OS X and the Internet. In the process, I'll talk about why Mac OS X is so appealing as a Web serving platform.

MAC OS X

Even though you're already using a Macintosh, a few words about Mac OS X as an Web server are in order: Mac OS X changes everything. Prior to Mac OS X, even die-hard Mac users often wondered whether a Mac could put in a strong showing as an Internet server. Convincing a Windows NT or UNIX supporter to go with a Mac was an even tougher sell. Security has been and continues to be the strong suit of the Mac OS; Web server performance for versions of the Mac

OS up through Mac OS 9 was not. Mac OS X has modifications under the hood that make it a Web serving powerhouse.

If you are running a Web server under an older version of the Mac OS, the question isn't really *why* you should switch to Mac OS X, but *how quickly* you can.

Overview and Basic Features

In late 1996, Apple acquired NeXT Software, the developers of NeXTStep. Rechristened OpenStep, NeXTStep allowed Apple to accelerate its timeline for producing a so-called modern and high-performance operating system. The original plan described a dual operating system future: an operating system code-named Rhapsody for the high-end server market and the Mac OS for the consumer market. However, developers really wanted it all—the modern, high-performance benefits of Rhapsody and the familiar, installed user base of the Mac OS. Enter Mac OS X.

In the technically driven world of operating systems, it's important to remember that "modern" refers to low-level issues "under the hood" and not to a system's modern user interface and ease of use. "High performance" describes the performance of system tasks and not the day-to-day productivity of the system's users.

However, as an organization's Web serving needs grow, performance issues take on greater importance. Ideally, then, what you would like is an operating system that combines the Mac OS ease of use with the low-level performance of UNIX. With a UNIX-like kernel as its base and a Mac-like graphical user interface on the surface, Mac OS X has the potential to open an express lane to your Web server.

The Mac OS Advantage

There are many reasons to use a Mac OS X system as a Web server. First and foremost, if you are a Mac user already, it doesn't make much sense to learn the ins and outs of Windows or UNIX just to run an Internet server—a chore that some people spend years learning. In the Windows and UNIX world, these people are called system administrators. A Mac office might need a network administrator, who typically can support far more computers than his or her UNIX

Table 2-1. The Mac OS Advantage

Location	Description
www.maccentral.com/news/0004/24.dual.shtml	"Dual Platform Issues, Part 1: Total Cost of Ownership," *MacCentral Online,* April 24, 2000.
macweek.zdnet.com/2000/04/16/0419welch.html	"Analysis: Avoiding the Standardization Blues," MacWeek.com, April 21, 2000.
www.netcraft.com/survey	The Netcraft surveys poll known Web servers to determine the server software.
www.apple.com/smallbusiness/networking/101 *www.apple.com/education/k12/networking*	Blueprints for building wired and wireless Mac OS networks.
www.vision.net.au/~apaterson/index_computer.htm	A compilation of Mac advantages by Australian Alex Paterson.

or Windows counterparts, but if you can add or remove system extensions and adjust a control panel, you've already mastered the skills of a Mac administrator.

Because maintaining a Web server requires effort above and beyond that required in normal desktop operation, the Mac's ease of use and ease of maintenance also provide a distinct advantage. With a Mac, running a Web server doesn't have to be any more complicated than running your word processor or desktop publishing software.

For those of you who need more convincing, Table 2-1 provides a list of sites where you can find more reasons to use a Mac as your Internet server. According to the July 2000 Netcraft survey, WebSTAR is the tenth most popular Web server software, and Macs account for approximately 1 percent of servers. The introduction of Apache with Mac OS X could change this balance.

The Aqua Interface

Mac OS X sports a redesigned interface look called Aqua. While maintaining many of the interface conventions of prior Mac OS versions, Aqua adds a new level to the way Mac OS X uses color, depth, transparency, and motion. You'll notice the difference in such elements as the glowing colored buttons on semi-transparent dialog boxes and the window frames.

Icons have also come of age. Instead of being confined to 32 pixels square, icons can now be up to 128 pixels square with full color. These larger icons allow easier viewing and better document previews. Icons for folders, applications, documents, storage devices, minimized windows, QuickTime movies, digital images, and links to Web sites are stored in the Dock at the bottom of the screen. The Dock expands to fill the bottom of the screen, and once it's filled, more additions cause all the icons to shrink.

Along with the interface, the Finder has gotten an overhaul in Mac OS X. In a significant change, the Finder is now contained within a single window that can be manipulated as in other applications. Large buttons in the Finder window give you quick access to your applications, documents, favorites, and people with whom you often communicate. You still use the Finder to navigate through your hierarchy of files and folders, and you can still get list and icon views. The Finder adds a column view that displays the path you've taken through your file system or through networks. Figure 2-1 shows a screen shot of the Mac OS X Aqua interface.

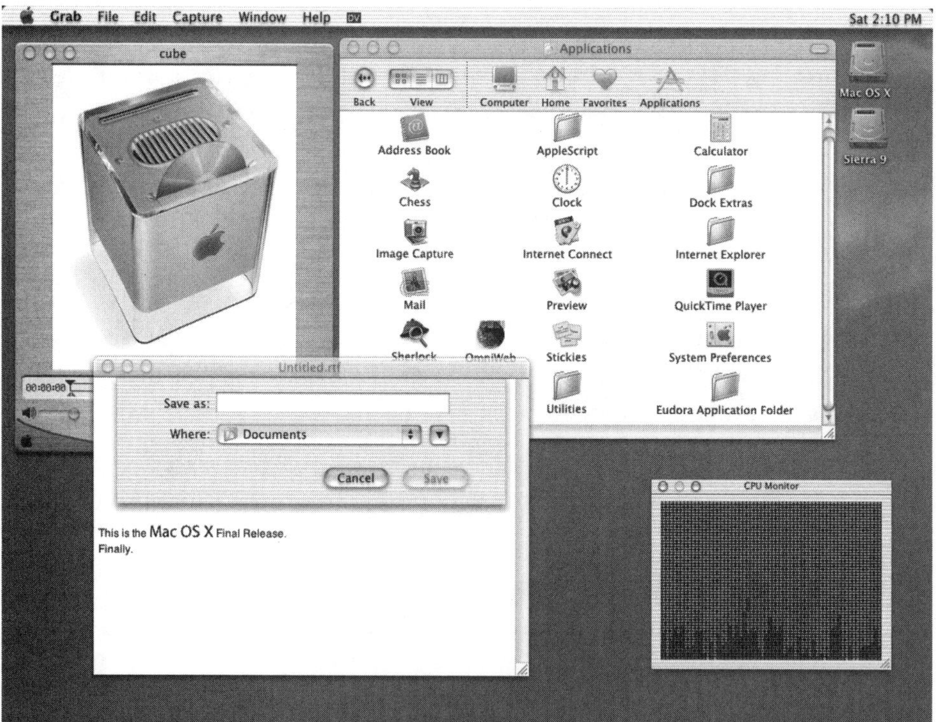

Figure 2-1. The Mac OS X Aqua Interface.

Since this book is focusing on the server aspects of Mac OS X, we won't go into detail about the basics of navigation. Suffice it to say that the interface has many new elements, but enough continuity that Mac users comfortable with the Mac OS 9 (or earlier) interface should be able to find their way around.

System Administration

Mac OS X presents two faces as far as system administration goes: one for Joe or Jane User, and another for command-line aficionados. For a typical user, Mac OS X permits most system functions and preferences to be controlled through Aqua's graphical interface. But it is possible for expert users to access the UNIX underpinnings of the Darwin kernel. Mac OS X, like UNIX, is an inherently multiuser operating system. A computer running Mac OS X has an all-powerful administrator, while most users of the system operate with far fewer privileges than the administrator has.

The person who installs Mac OS X establishes an administrator account. For businesses, this allows technical support personnel to restrict the ability of users to alter sensitive system settings. The administrator can standardize an organization's Mac OS X environment. As an individual, however, you may be the primary user as well as the administrator, but you do not need two separate accounts. Most administrator settings require you to enter the administrator password, so you will not inadvertently change system settings you've worked so hard to get right. In fact, it is possible to "become" temporarily the administrator within a less privileged account by authenticating yourself with the administrator password to unlock and adjust some settings.

I'll refer you to Appendix A for sources of more information on administering Mac OS X. But for the purposes of this book, I'll lay out some basic terms and features that will crop up throughout subsequent chapters. In doing so, I'll draw some parallels and contrasts to the Mac OS 9 terms and features you may be familiar with.

Mac OS X and the Classic Environment. If you are using Mac OS X, it is possible to continue using Mac OS 9 applications within the Classic compatibility environment. The Classic environment essentially lets you run Mac OS 9.1 as an application within Mac OS X, and Classic Mac OS applications run within that application, with access to the hard drive as usual. In fact, Classic applications retain the Platinum appearance among your Aqua-based Mac OS X applications—a rather surreal effect. However, applications in the Classic environment cannot take advantage of the modern features of Mac OS X. Nevertheless, the Classic environment paves a smooth transition path as you wait for developers to create Mac OS X versions of their products.

The Classic environment has one feature missing: the Finder. You always use the Mac OS X Finder and Desktop to start Classic Mac OS applications and locate files.

Desktop and Finder. These features of Mac OS 9, which have been carried into Mac OS X, continue to perform roughly the same jobs. Obviously, both now sport the new Aqua look, but there are further differences at a more technical level. For example, in the classic Mac OS, the Finder is the main system application and the Desktop is the primary screen that the Finder presents while you're using it. In Mac OS X, these roles are reversed. The Desktop is now the main system application, which lets you switch between applications, displays the primary screen, and manages the Dock, while the Finder is an application that lets you navigate the Mac OS X file system. This distinction may be a bit esoteric for typical users. If you find the distinction confusing, you can probably ignore it and safely assume that the Desktop and Finder together perform functions similar to their Mac OS 9 counterparts.

The Finder and the File System. There is one important difference between the Classic Mac OS Finder and the Mac OS X Finder. The classic Finder presents pretty much a direct view of the contents of your hard drive (hidden files notwithstanding). The Mac OS X Finder definitely does not permit users to access the file system directly. Instead, it presents a "sanitized" view that allows a typical user to avoid staring at the underlying proliferation of files.

In particular, Mac OS X introduces the concept of *bundles*. At the file system level, bundles are special types of folders that contain related files. But if you're looking at a bundle through the Finder, a bundle appears to be a single file. For example, the executable code for a Mac OS X application is actually a bundle of all the pieces—code, images, sounds, and so on—needed to start an application. If you look at the bundle from the Terminal command line, you can see all of the pieces. But in the Finder, the bundle looks like a single file, and double-clicking on that "file" starts the application. In fact, Mac OS X requires file-name extensions in many cases, unlike the Classic Mac OS. The Finder, though, often hides these extensions from users.

System Preferences and Control Panels. The functionality provided by Control Panels in the Classic Mac OS is now handled by the System Preferences application, as shown in Figure 2-2. The preference panels themselves are stored as bundles within the */System/Library/Preferences* folder. And because Mac OS X is a multi-user system, some System Preferences can be modified only after entering the administrator password.

System Library and Extensions. The expandability provided by Extensions in the Classic Mac OS is handled in Mac OS X through a wide variety of system files. Although there is a */System/Library/Extensions* folder, many of the folders within the */System/Library* folder perform the same type of services as the Classic Mac OS Extensions. Mess with the */System/Library* at your own risk.

Installing Applications. Apple has managed to make installing applications on a UNIX-like operating system very similar to installing them in the Classic Mac OS. (At least, Apple has made it possible for developers to make their applications easy to install.) As usual, you must first download and uncompress the application file from the Internet. (As in the Classic Mac OS, Aladdin Systems' StuffIt Expander is available for Mac OS X.)

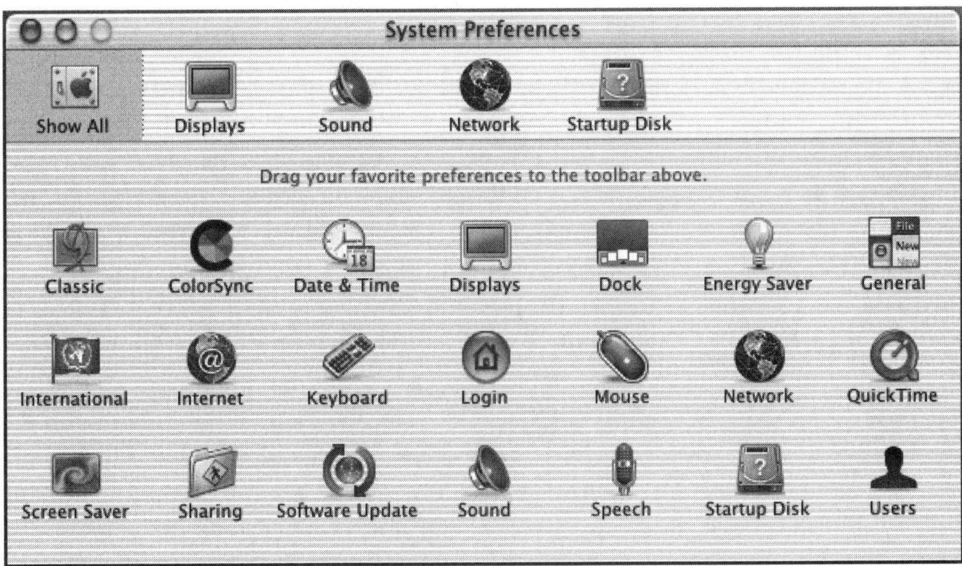

Figure 2-2. Mac OS X System Preferences.

Double-clicking on the application's uncompressed installer package opens Mac OS X's Installer utility, which takes care of installing all the bundles and files. You can then move the installed application or folder to its final location.

Application Compatibility

Apple plans to help users make the transition from Mac OS 9 to Mac OS X over 12 months. To make the transition process as gentle as possible, Mac OS X supports three application environments, called Classic, Carbon, and Cocoa. Mac webmasters can take advantage of these environments to move gradually to Mac OS X.

The first step in the transition is the ability to install Mac OS X and run your current applications in the Classic environment. Classic lets you run existing Macintosh applications "as is." Your old applications will run as they do on Mac OS 9, even using the familiar Platinum interface, but they won't be able to take advantage of Mac OS X's modern components under the hood (described in the next section). I don't recommend doing this with your Web server, simply because you'll want critical applications such as your server running as a native application (whether in Mac OS 9 or Mac OS X). You might, however, choose to run some server extension software as a Classic application while your server runs as a Mac OS X application.

Once developers have introduced Mac OS X–native versions of your Web applications, you can move to the next stage of the transition. The first native Mac OS X applications will take advantage of the Carbon development environment, which gives applications access to the modern Carbon applications programming interface and all the great features under the hood. You should not have long to wait for Mac OS X–native applications, since most developers have been preparing for this stage with Carbon-compatible applications for Mac OS 8 and 9. In fact, Mac OS X has a native version of Apache built-in, and other current Web servers will likely be available along with the final release.

Note that Carbon-compliant Mac OS 9 applications still require further preparation and new installation methods before they are released as Mac OS X applications. However, a properly created Mac OS X application will also run directly as a Mac OS 9 application.

Finally, as Mac OS X becomes established, you will begin to see new applications developed for Mac OS X from the ground up using the Cocoa interface, an advanced object-oriented programming environment. Cocoa gives developers a whole new toolbox for building the next generation of applications. It remains to be seen what will emerge.

Advanced Features

While the Aqua interface gives Mac OS X a superficially new look, the most significant changes for Mac webmasters are the changes under the hood. Although Mac OS X runs Mac OS 9 applications without changes, only modified software can take advantage of Mac OS X's modern high-performance features, which give Mac OS X the horsepower to run a high-performance Web server. These features—including preemptive multitasking, memory protection, and dynamic memory allocation—are so fundamental to its operation that chances are, you will never have to do anything to or for them. But it's nice to know they're there.

The Darwin Kernel

An operating system's *kernel* handles most of the interaction between the operating system and the hardware. The Mac OS X kernel, called Darwin, is based on Mach 3.0 from Carnegie Mellon University and FreeBSD 3.2 (derived from the University of California, Berkeley's BSD 4.4), two highly regarded core technologies from modern UNIX operating system projects.

Another interesting aspect of Darwin is that it is being developed as an open source project. Even as Mac OS X hits the streets, early steps are being taken to compile Darwin on the Intel platform. However, much development remains before we'll see Mac OS X on Intel-based systems.

Mac OS X has a close kinship to other flavors of UNIX, at least at its foundation. Darwin incorporates the BSD networking stack. UNIX-like BSD networking is the basis of the vast majority of TCP/IP implementations on the Internet today. For Mac webmasters, this means increased network performance, which translates to the ability to handle more Web requests per second. (But Mac OS X still supports AppleTalk, so you won't have to reengineer existing Macintosh networks.)

Preemptive Multitasking

In a nutshell, *preemptive multitasking* describes an operating system with a scheduler that can automatically switch between running applications, so that each gets its turn for access to the processor. In contrast, Mac OS 9 and earlier versions have *cooperative multitasking*, in which applications must be coded to give up the processor to another application.

Both forms of multitasking let your computer perform more than one task at a time. However, with cooperative multitasking, background applications have fewer opportunities to use the processor and must run more slowly. It also means that switching between applications takes a few moments longer. And when you're running a Web server, those few moments can mean the difference between keeping or losing a visitor to your Web site. Preemptive multitasking also handles several different tasks at once, giving priority to your primary application, but still giving other background jobs a fair shake.

The Darwin kernel makes this possible. It works like an air traffic controller, watching over your computer's processor—prioritizing tasks and ensuring that every task gets the resources it needs. When a higher-priority task is awakened by data that comes along, such as a network request, the Darwin scheduler prioritizes it over other waiting tasks.

Protected Memory

Memory protection describes a system by which the operating system prevents one process from corrupting the memory of any other. UNIX and Windows NT have strong memory protection, while Microsoft Windows 3.1, Windows 95, and the Mac OS do not, although Mac OS 8 and 9 offer a limited form of protection.

Protected memory essentially walls off applications from each other, and Mac OS X includes a protected memory architecture that allocates a unique address space for each application or process running on the computer.

When applications are isolated in their own memory space, they can't interfere with each other if one crashes, and you don't need to restart your computer after an application crash. The computer shuts down the offending application and its memory space, letting you continue without interruption.

Along with protected memory, Mac OS X provides a virtual memory manager so you no longer have to worry about how much memory an application like Adobe Photoshop needs to open large files. When an application needs memory, the virtual memory manager automatically allocates the necessary amount of memory.

Security

In addition to being easier to troubleshoot and resuscitate from system failures, Mac OS X systems continue the Mac OS tradition as more secure Internet servers than their Windows and UNIX counterparts. The U.S. Army became one highly publicized convert to the Classic Mac OS when the Army moved its main Web page to a Mac server, stating security reasons explicitly. So far, despite attacks on other Army servers, the main Army Web site has successfully repelled would-be intruders.

However, because Mac OS X has more in common with UNIX, it will likely also have more opportunities for security problems. Mac OS X adds standard services such as a Web server, telnet, and FTP, allowing easy operability with UNIX systems and applications, but also introducing potential entry points. While these features don't make the operating system inherently insecure, Mac OS X webmasters should pay careful attention to security updates and announcements as they are released.

Apple's approach to security in Mac OS X includes a default installation that leaves most networking services turned off. Administrators should then follow the general rule of thumb for maximizing security that recommends leaving off any networking services that aren't absolutely necessary. For example, if you are not using telnet or FTP services on a particular machine, they should be turned off. Careful configuration of Mac OS X—or any operating system—makes a system secure, while careless configuration can make any operating system as full of holes as Swiss cheese. Table 2-2 has additional links to Mac OS X security resources.

The Command Line and "Root"

For most Mac users, the most disconcerting feature of Mac OS X may be that, for the first time, the Mac OS has a command-line interface in addition to the

Table 2-2. Mac OS X Internet Security

Location	Description
www.maccentral.com/news/0006/23.macosx.shtml	"Road to Mac OS X: Security and OS X," by Dennis Sellers at *MacCentral Online.*
www.securemac.com	Macintosh security site from StaticUsers.net.

graphical user interface Mac users know and love. For most common tasks, the Aqua interface and Finder hide the complexity of the UNIX operating system underlying Mac OS X. However, to unleash some of the features of Mac OS X, advanced users, including most webmasters, will have to venture to the command line at some point. Because this book regularly describes UNIX commands that must be issued to perform certain tasks, I thought I'd introduce the command-line interface briefly here.

You access the command-line interface through the Terminal application, which you will find in the */Applications/Utilities* folder. Starting the Terminal application will cause a window to open and display the system prompt, which by default shows the current directory and your user name.

As an average user, UNIX prevents you from reading, deleting, or overwriting files, such as critical system files, that average users shouldn't be mucking about with. If you created the first account on this Mac OS X system, however, you are more than an average user. You are an "admin" user, which means you have the ability to configure settings for network connections and other system functions. But there are core parts of the operating system that are still beyond your reach. The all-powerful user on a system is the super user, which is also called "root" by convention. To enable some features of Mac OS X, you need to issue commands as "root." In UNIX-speak, you need to have root access.

By default, Mac OS X is installed with the root account disabled. There is no root password and you can't login as root, but there are two ways to gain root access. In the simpler option, you must first be logged in as an admin user. Open a Terminal window and enter the following command:

```
% sudo –s
```

This is short for "superuser do." You will be asked for your password; enter the password for this admin user (usually the password you created when installing Mac OS X). Note that your command-line prompt has changed. You now have root access.

The other way to gain root access is to enable the root account. Start the NetInfo Manager in the */Applications/Utilities* folder. Under the Domain menu, select Security, then Authenticate. Enter the password for your admin account. Next, under the Domain menu, select Security, then Enable Root Account. NetInfo Manager will complain that there is no root set yet. Select Okay, and enter a new password (different from your admin password). Your root account is now enabled. At a Terminal command-line, you can enter the following command to log in as root:

```
% su
```

When asked for a password, enter the password you created for the root account. As "root," you now have the ability to customize Mac OS X at the most fundamental level. You can also do serious damage, including deleting every file on your Mac OS X drive with as few as eight keystrokes. Be sure to use the utmost care when you have root access.

Before we end this section, I thought I'd point you to the hidden part of Mac OS X. From the Terminal command line, enter these two commands:

```
% cd /
% ls
```

Mac OS X lists ("ls") the files and folders at the top-most level of the file system hierarchy. You can see the folders that you could see through the Finder, which begin with capital letters. You can also see the directories, such as *bin, etc, usr,* and so on that are hidden by the Finder. We'll return to these hidden directories in later chapters to configure various Web serving elements of Mac OS X.

Switching from Mac OS 9

As with any significant change to your current Web server, it makes sense to compare the costs of switching from Mac OS 8 or 9 to Mac OS X versus the costs of *not* switching. The advantages of not switching, of course, are the time, money, and effort you save from not upgrading your operating system software, and most likely some or all of your Web server software. If you are now running a Mac Web server—particularly one with lots of extensions, plug-ins, or custom interaction—and that server is handling the traffic to your site, then you may decide that you don't yet need to make the switch to Mac OS X. You may want to wait until your server's traffic begins stressing the capacity of your server, or until your current suite of applications have all made the transition to Mac OS X.

On the other hand, if you haven't yet created your Mac-based Web server or if you want to wring every last drop of performance from your machine, then switching to Mac OS X will probably pay off for you. The advanced features of

Mac OS X, described in the previous section, substantially increase the speed of network communication, the stability of applications, and the speed of switching between applications, all of which help your Web server perform better.

THE INTERNET

Just to make sure that we're all starting from the same place, I want to clarify the definitions of some terms that will be appearing throughout the book, specifically, the term "Internet" and related words. Since you are exploring how to set up your own Web server, it seems safe to assume that you have probably been using the Internet for some time—downloading files, sending mail, or surfing the Web. If so, then much of this may be familiar.

The Internet, Intranets, and the Web

Attempting to answer the question "What is the Internet?" leads to a variety of detailed discussions, some technical, some philosophical. You can find examples of these discussions, as well as some background on the Internet, at the sites listed in Table 2-3.

The Internet. For our purposes, it is enough to know that the Internet is a conglomeration of computer networks. While size, accessibility, management, and so on can vary within these networks, they all communicate via a common set of *protocols,* or structured languages, known collectively as the transmission control protocol and Internet protocol (TCP/IP). Without getting technical, this means these networks can all communicate with each other, creating a vast global network, and can put a user on any Internet computer in contact with the information and resources on your soon-to-be-established Web server. Worldwide accessibility to vast quantities of information at very low cost is changing the dynamics of our society—in government, education, commerce, and elsewhere. You will soon be contributing to that change.

Intranets and Extranets. The term "intranet" came into vogue as people realized that the same technology that enabled information sharing on the Internet could be used to share information within an organization, whether that organi-

Table 2-3. History of the Internet

Location	Description
www.isoc.org	A detailed discussion of Internet philosophy and history.
www.pbs.org/internet/timeline	The Web site accompanying the PBS series *Life on the Internet.*
www.supercomp.org/sc97/inet_history97	"History of the Internet," an exhibit from the SC97 conference.
www.w3.org/People/Berners-Lee/FAQ.html	A history of the Web, according to Tim Berners-Lee.

zation occupies a few offices, an entire building, or the facilities of a multinational corporation.

In essence, an *intranet* is a private section of the Internet, accessible by only the intended audience. If you establish a TCP/IP-based network in your office but allow only computers in your office to communicate with servers on that network, you have an intranet. Larger intranets can also be created with commercial Web server software, for example, by refusing access to users on the basis of their Internet address or by protecting a network with passwords. To set up an intranet with your Mac Web server, you will want Web server software that allows you to restrict access with passwords or other means.

An *extranet,* on the other hand, provides private access to Internet servers for communication between a company and a select group of outside organizations. For example, an auto manufacturer may establish an extranet to communicate both with suppliers of auto parts and with independently owned dealerships across the country. There's nothing magic about intranets or extranets. You can establish one either by limiting access to your Internet servers to computers within your organization (for an intranet) or to computers at your organization and selected outside groups (for an extranet).

The World Wide Web. The World Wide Web, or simply the Web, is not equivalent to the Internet, although the words are often used interchangeably. The Web, to be completely technical, is an application built on the Internet. The Web uses the hypertext transfer protocol (HTTP) to request and deliver information from computer to computer. Other Internet applications (and their network protocols) include file transfer via FTP, e-mail via the simple mail transfer protocol (SMTP), newsgroups via the network news transfer protocol (NNTP), and streaming audio and video via the real-time streaming protocol (RTSP).

The Internet, therefore, encompasses much more than just the Web. It is often more accurate to refer to the Mac server you are developing with help from this book as an "Internet server," because I will be discussing other Internet applications in addition to Web services. The term "Web server" technically refers to the software that provides for communication via HTTP and the computer on which that software is running.

However, many Web server packages also provide other services—functionality that blurs the distinction between Web server and Internet server. Because of common usage, I will generally use the term "Web server" to encompass not only Web service, but also these other services. Where a distinction is important, I will refer specifically to the service being provided, as when discussing e-mail servers, FTP servers, or streaming media servers.

Internet Addresses

As I mentioned, the conglomeration of individually managed computer networks that comprise the Internet share one feature: They all communicate via the TCP/IP family of protocols. For our purposes, it suffices to know that computers running TCP/IP

- can communicate,
- are potentially able to recognize each other,
- can decide how to route information to each other, and
- can support other protocols that are used by the Web and other information sharing tools.

IP Address. To communicate with and recognize one another, each TCP/IP-based computer, also called a *host,* has a unique address called an Internet Protocol address, or *IP address*. An IP address looks like a number with a few too many decimal points—*nnn.nnn.nnn.nnn,* where each *nnn* is an integer in the range 0–255. (Certain integers are reserved, notably 0 and 255.) In simple terms and with numerous exceptions, the first integer of the four-integer address defines the network, the second integer the institution, the third the department or division, and the fourth the individual computer.

Since each computer on the Internet must have a unique address, *you cannot arbitrarily assign an address to a machine that is attached to a public network*. Chapter 4 discusses how you can get an IP address.

Domain Names and Name Servers. Since it is simpler for humans to remember words rather than numbers, the numeric IP address is often mapped to a text-based *domain name.* For example, Web server addresses traditionally map to a name of the form *www.company.com,* although that convention is evolving. The name is usually defined in the reverse order to the IP address, that is, of the form *computer.division.institution.domain* or *computer.institution.domain.* While you might be able to maintain on your Web server a short list of local or popular host addresses and corresponding names, there's no way you could maintain the mapping for *all* the hosts on the Internet.

The mapping of integer IP addresses to domain names is called *name resolution,* and a computer (or program) that performs the resolution is a *domain name server*, or simply a *name server.* A name server's primary function is to dynamically maintain tables that map host names to address numbers. On the Internet, mapping is handled transparently through the cooperation of many name servers in the Domain Name System (DNS). Chapter 4 discusses DNS and running a name server of your own.

Web Addresses

Different Internet services use name-based addresses that extend the basic IP address and domain name scheme. As we shall see, most of these addresses can be recognized and handled appropriately by Web browsers. They serve us humans as a guide for recognizing different types of information as it is found on the Internet.

The standard form of address on the Web is known as a *uniform resource locator,* or *URL.* A URL has the following format, which you are probably familiar with, but which we will describe here for completeness:

http://host.name.com:80/folder1/folder2/file.abc?misc-terms

- *http://*—The start of the URL identifies the service being requested. Other schemes you might encounter are *ftp://* or *news:*.
- *host.name.com*—The host name indicates the computer of which the request is being made. The IP address of the server may also be used.
- *:80*—The network port to which the request is being made is comparable to a TV channel. If the service's default port is being used, the port number is often omitted. In this case, the default port for http is 80, and so it would not normally be used.
- */folder1/folder2/file.abc*—The text after the host name and port defines the path from the main server folder (or directory, to use the UNIX terminology) down through the file system hierarchy to a file named *file.abc*.
- *?misc-terms*—The text after the question mark is additional information sent with the request to be processed by *file.abc* as appropriate. Commands to a Web server or the search terms for a database query are sent in this manner.

Several of these service types identify protocols that are Internet applications built on top of the family of TCP/IP protocols, such as HTTP, FTP, e-mail, and telnet. (This notion of layers of protocols on top of other protocols gives rise to the term "protocol stack.") Table 2-4 summarizes the address types you are likely to encounter on the Web.

Clients and Servers

Before we get ahead of ourselves, let's take a step back and define what we mean by the terms "client" and "server." The term "server" has already appeared in the title of the book and in the phrase "Web server," but I haven't exactly defined what that entails. And let's not forget the term "client." You can't have clients without servers, and vice versa.

Client-server computing is a much used and much abused phrase. At the risk of adding to the abuse, let's consider the simpleminded definition used throughout this book. A *client* makes a request of a *server* for a particular resource, which the server dutifully provides—subject to any security and resource constraints. The term "client" refers interchangeably to the software making the request—such as

Table 2-4. Types of Internet Addresses

Address	Description
hart-mac.sdsc.edu	A specific Internet host.
dhart@pauline.sdsc.edu	A user's e-mail address at a specific Internet host.
dhart@sdsc.edu	A user's e-mail address defined uniquely in a subdomain, and the most convenient form of mail address.
http://www.sdsc.edu/	The simplest URL form for accessing a Web page using HTTP. The Web server at *www.sdsc.edu* will serve a default file.
http://www.sdsc.edu:70/	As above, but on a specific port number, in this instance 70. The default port number for HTTP is 80.
ftp://ftp.sdsc.edu/pub/	An FTP archive accessed from a Web browser using a URL.
telnet://info.cern.ch/	A telnet session started from a URL.
mailto:dhart@sdsc.edu	An e-mail address invoked as an HTML hyperlink.
news:comp.sys.mac.system	A newsgroup invoked as an HTML hyperlink.

a Web browser—and to the computer from which the request was made. The same is true for the term "server."

The next question to answer is, what happens when, for example, a Web browser requests access to information from a Web server? If the software or service isn't running—surprise!—nothing happens, and the client software should return an error message. If the service is running, the server accepts incoming requests and performs the appropriate action, such as returning a Web page, transferring a file, or forwarding a message to a mailing list.

The number of possible requests raises some interesting points that I'll elaborate on in Chapter 3. First, your Web server has finite resources—there is a limit on how many requests it can support. You may have encountered this situation in your Web surfing: A popular server may have refused to let you in because of the large number of existing connections. If you are lucky enough to have your server become that popular, most software lets you control the number of simultaneous requests for a given service.

A simple example is a client Web browser requesting information from a server containing HTML-based documents. Figure 2-3 illustrates the basics of client-server interaction in this scenario. What this image doesn't show is types of information the server can deliver. As we shall see, server software can variously

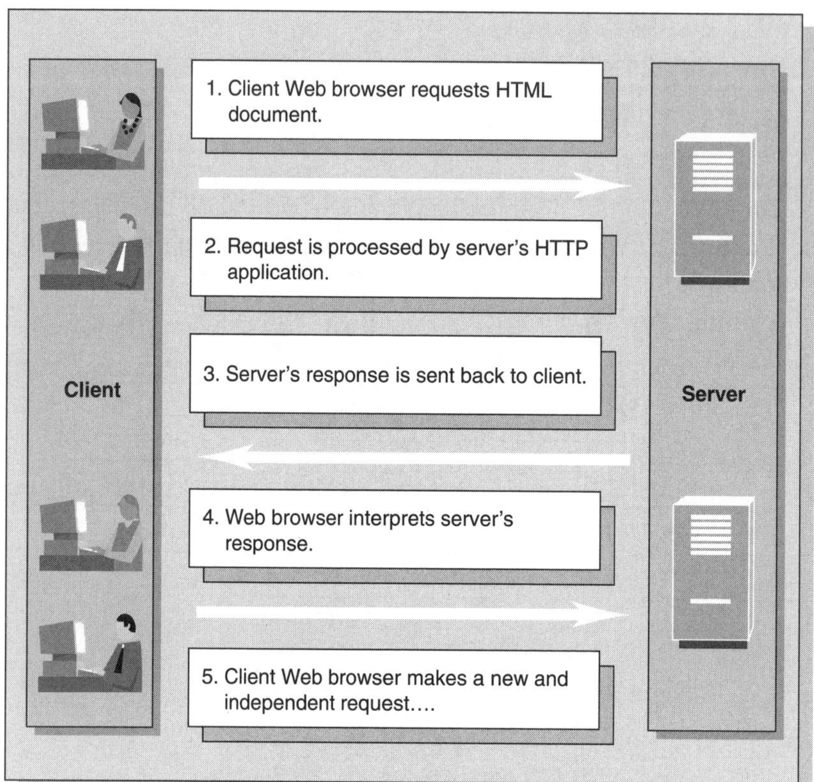

Figure 2-3. Client-Server Architecture Made Simple.

serve text, images, sound, video, and methods (code to perform specific tasks on the client).

"Content"

One last Internet ingredient deserves a quick mention along with this discussion of the Internet, host names and addresses, TCP/IP, servers, and DNS. All these elements combine to enable you and the world to shuffle around heaps of information—so-called Internet "content." How the Internet handles the many types of "content" will be discussed in Chapter 3, for starters. But I felt the need to explain why I'll try to avoid the term "content" as much as possible in this book.

It's a pet peeve of mine that "content" is a euphemism that is used lazily to describe "stuff at a Web site," as if every bit were created equal by virtue of being stored as a zero or one. Before the Web, you rarely heard the word "content" to describe the information in newspapers or even television. Newspapers have stories, photographs, ads, and comics. TV has dramas, sitcoms, news, and commercials. Just because the diverse elements are all produced with paper and ink (in the newspaper) or electrons streaming through a vacuum tube (on television), they do not become equivalent or interchangeable—particularly in the crucial creation phase. Picture a city news desk at your local paper trying to produce a zany network sitcom.

The term "information" is admittedly not much better. Where possible, I will be as specific as possible about the type of information being presented in a given instance. I'll revisit this issue when I bring up the term "authoring" in Chapter 15.

Netiquette

It is *people* who make valuable information available on the Internet. The technology is simply the vehicle that makes it happen; hence the Internet is about people, what they contribute, and how they behave. Like most issues relating to the Internet, Internet etiquette, or "netiquette," for operating an information server has no official policies. Instead, it's just a common-sense way of behaving in this community.

Many sites and Internet service providers (ISPs) have so-called acceptable use policies (AUPs), one of which can be seen at *www.ipservices.att.com/policy.cfm.* Following is a generally useful interpretation for how to behave; parts may be covered by law in various countries. This interpretation is sure to contain shortcomings and omissions, but it does provide the general idea. If we all obey these simple rules, the Internet will continue to be a great place to work and play.

1. Information on a Web server should be considered a form of publication and should be governed by the same rules that govern good publications—no lies, no misleading statements.
2. Do not republish or distribute copyrighted information and software without permission from the creator or creators. It is advisable to have written confirmation.
3. Properly protect information you want accessed only by specific groups of people. Do not lead others into temptation.

4. Do not make available any information that is offensive to members the community. If you feel strongly that the information should be available, include a warning that the information may be offensive to some people.
5. When running a business on the Internet, adhere to the same rules of ethics that apply to brick-and-mortar businesses. Do not defraud your customers, and deliver what you promise.
6. Of course, refrain from illegal activities, such as fraud, threats, and digital trespassing. Many AUPs also define legal but disruptive materials such as spam and offensive matter to be unacceptable uses.
7. Strive to make the information the best it can be—comprehensive but easily navigated and understood. Above all, keep it current.

Internet Growth

As a potential owner, creator, or operator of a Mac Web server, you may find it worthwhile to take a moment to consider what you're getting yourself into. The Web is growing by leaps and bounds, but even so, the digital frontier has rules and conventions that, if you're familiar with them, can make your progress a little easier.

If you think you've got the best idea since e-sliced-bread, join the club. The Web is one of the least exclusive organizations going, and that's both its strength for the Internet community as a whole and its weakness for you as an individual webmaster trying to make your Mac Web server stand out. Consider the following facts and statistics from the past few years.

- *The growth of the Internet is phenomenal.*

  By January 1997, 194 countries had joined the Internet, according to Matrix.Net. About 80 percent of the world's countries have at least one Internet domain.

  There were more than 72,398,092 Internet hosts, according to the Internet Software Consortium's January 2000 Internet Domain Survey, up from 43,230,000 hosts in January 1999 and 213 in August 1981.

  The July 2000 Netcraft Web Server Survey counted 18,169,498 sites, up from 4,062,280 sites in January 1999 and 18,957 hosts in July 1995.

- *The Internet is no longer restricted to universities and other nonprofit institutions but is driven by economic factors and open competition.*

  More than 34 percent of Internet hosts were registered in .com as of March 2000, according to the Internet Domain Survey, compared to the 8.5 percent registered in the .edu domain.

- *The Internet has become as accepted a form of communication as radio and television.*

  In an October 1998 survey by Georgia Tech, 92.6 percent of the respondents reported that they consider access to the Web indispensable, nearly the same percentage as those who feel e-mail is indispensable (96.3 percent).

  The first known Internet message sent by a head of state was written March 2, 1993, by President Bill Clinton.

- *The Internet is an inexpensive, fast, and global form of communication.*

  The round-trip time from Colorado to McMurdo, Antarctica, is 640 milliseconds; the number of hops is 18.

These numbers illustrate the amazing growth of the Internet—perhaps faster than any other invention in history—as well as its rapid, versatile, and commercial nature. The sources of these and more statistics, including a variety of graphical representations, are given in Table 2-5.

The Internet's growth is accelerating as long-distance carriers, local telephone companies, cable TV companies, and other communications companies begin providing Internet services to those who are less computer- and communications-literate. Soon everyone will be able to serve on the Internet.

Table 2-5. Sources of Internet Statistics

Source	Description
www.isc.org/ds	Internet Software Consortium's Internet Domain Survey (formerly conducted by Network Wizards).
www.netcraft.com/Survey	Netcraft Web Server Survey.
www.gvu.gatech.edu/user_surveys	Georgia Tech's Graphics, Visualization, and Usability Center's WWW User Surveys.
www.matrix.net	Matrix.Net provides Internet performance measurement and intelligence services.

CHAPTER 3

GOALS AND PLANNING

Now that you've familiarized yourself with the tools of the trade—Mac OS X and basic Internet technologies—the next step is to plan out your Web server. The capabilities you will need in a Web server depend first on who you expect your customers to be and what they are likely to want. Once you have your customers' needs in mind, you can look at the services available to meet those needs.

This chapter also introduces you to some more basic vocabulary to describe file and information types—the ingredients from which you will whip up your Web site. This chapter is devoted to helping you further distinguish the types of services that exist, which of those you should provide to your intended audience, and the information types associated with those services.

WHO IS MY INTENDED AUDIENCE?

Who is my intended audience, and what do my users want to get from my server? This is the first question you should ask yourself. To use a cooking analogy, think of developing a Web server in the same way you think about preparing a gourmet meal. There is no point going to the butcher, selecting a choice cut of meat, and marinating it for days if your dinner guests are vegetarians. Likewise, there is no point spending months preparing digitized video for your information server audience if 95 percent of your visitors have neither the bandwidth nor the client software needed to play the video.

Describing Your Audience

Let's start by considering what characteristics of your audience are relevant to how you proceed with your future Web server. These characteristics not only help you design and organize your site, but also suggest what types of information and Web services you might want to provide. Here is only a partial list:

- *Demographics.* Your audience's general age, gender, geographic concentration, and education (to name a few characteristics) will guide the design of your site and the way in which information is presented.
- *Profession or avocation.* If your audience comprises a single profession, such as technology workers, lawyers, physicians, or hobbyists, you are likely to provide a different organization or emphasis than for an audience comprised of John or Jane Q. Public
- *Technological sophistication.* The bells and whistles on your Web server must be tempered by an understanding of whether your visitors are primarily novices, amateurs, experts, or technoweenies.
- *Technological access and ownership.* Perhaps your audience primarily owns older computers with smaller monitors over slower network connections, like those you might find in a middle school or elementary school. Or perhaps your audience is connecting via Palm OS digital organizers or digital cell phones. You will have to treat such an audience differently than a corps of technophiles that drools over the latest

hardware with 21-inch monitors over Digital Subscriber Line (DSL) or cable modems.

- *Preferred means of communication.* Some groups have different ideas about the appropriateness of Web sites, e-mail, newsgroups, or instant messaging as the best way to communicate. For example, e-mail remains very popular among a wide audience and can reach people who may not have access to the Web.

Understanding your audience will give you a baseline from which to start determining what you will need for your Web server. We'll discuss a second question that will focus on more specific requirements to meet the expectations of your audience.

Defining Your Audience's Goals

Once you know who your audience is, the next question is to evaluate what the members of that audience will be looking for when they visit your Web server. You can also ask what experience you want to provide for the visitors to your Web server. As long as there are no surprises, the answer to these questions should be roughly the same.

- *Information.* The most common type of Web server is designed to deliver information to visitors seeking answers to their questions. Visitors primarily come to the site with a question in mind and with the expectation that your server has the answer. Your goal as webmaster is to make sure they find that answer as quickly as possible. Your server needs to be well organized, frequently updated, searchable, and will probably use a database.
- *Entertainment.* Some Web servers exist to entertain. Visitors are looking for videos, music, interactive games, puzzles, or other diversions. Your goal as webmaster is to provide the entertainment, so your server will probably need custom interaction, streaming media, images and animations, and dynamic pages.
- *Shopping.* Your visitors are interested in purchasing something you are selling, and you want your visitors to part with their hard-earned money. Your server should provide a well-organized catalog, an easy-

to-use shopping cart, and secure facilities for protecting credit card information.

- *Community.* A growing number of Web servers provide a place for their visitors to ask questions and share experiences with people who have similar experiences or backgrounds. As webmaster, you need to provide them with ways to exchange information, find one another, and leave messages.
- *Portal.* Your visitors are looking for a single starting point that pulls together the information and activities that they use every day. Your Web server must provide custom interaction, dynamic information, and useful tools for your audience.

This is not an exhaustive list, and most servers are not exclusively in just one of these categories, but rather have a combination of these goals. Usually, however, one of these models is the primary organizing principle of a server. This organizing principle dictates some of the services that you will need to provide and suggests where you need to focus your energies as webmaster.

WHAT SERVICES SHOULD I PROVIDE?

After you have sketched out your target audiences and the primary goals they will be trying to achieve when visiting your server, it's time to consider what services you need to provide to meet those goals. We have encountered in passing many of the services that you might want to establish on your server, but we've skipped the formality of defining them. Although I discuss each service separately here, it does not mean that each requires a separate piece of software. As you will see in Chapter 7, your Web server application or server suite will likely provide many of these services.

Web Server

For the sake of completeness, I have to start with a Web server. Technically, you might have a situation in which your information-providing goals could be met without a Web server, but generally, this is the heart of your Internet presence. As a formal definition, a Web server responds to requests sent via the hypertext transfer protocol (HTTP). Web clients—usually Web browsers—try to display or execute the data in files sent by HTTP. Web files are generally platform-independent and can be served to any client with the appropriate software.

File Downloads

The file transfer protocol (FTP), which originated on UNIX systems, is used to transfer files in any format back and forth between any platforms that support FTP, which is most of them. While technically, a Web server can be used to transfer files from server to client and less easily from client to server, an FTP server has some features that make it worth having if your server goals include a substantial number of file downloads. With an FTP service, a Mac can store and distribute compressed data files, Windows documents, or UNIX programs, since the server itself does not need to be able to interpret the file content.

E-Mail and List Servers

If your goal is to reach a worldwide audience, the value of e-mail services should not be underestimated, even with the explosive growth of the Web. Basic e-mail services include the ability to set up accounts so individuals can send and receive e-mail messages. On your server, you may want to provide basic e-mail services, for example, if you are running the main file server for a small organization. However, your ISP will probably provide you with a few e-mail accounts (*webmaster@your-company.com* and *feedback@your-company.com,* for example) that you can use to conduct business with your visitors, so you may not need to provide basic e-mail on your server.

There are, however, two types of services that build on basic e-mail services, which I'll call a list server and an auto-response server. Both of these are usually handled by list server software.

With a *list server,* a user sends an e-mail message to a particular e-mail address. But instead of being associated with an individual, the e-mail address is associated with a list of e-mail addresses for individuals who have subscribed to that list. The list server receives the message addressed to the list name and then broadcasts that message to all of the subscribers. A particular list can be automatic or moderated, whereby a designated person, called the moderator, decides whether a particular message should be broadcast to subscribers.

An *auto-response service* lets a user send an e-mail message to the server, which "reads" the contents of the message and performs some automated and predefined response. This response might include, for example, automatically sending information about a specific product or program. A typical scenario might be that a user sends a message containing only the word "HELP." The auto-response service responds by returning some predefined help information in the text of the message or as an attached file. The popularity of the Web has made auto-response service less common—it's often easier to display this information on or download a file from a Web page—but you might consider whether your audience would benefit.

Search Engines

One server application we have not yet covered becomes more important as the amount of information on your server grows. However good you are at organizing your server, it will still become difficult for some users to find what they are looking for. At that point, you would like to provide them with a way of searching all or part of your server. The software for this purpose is referred to as a *search engine.* Search engines create an index to the static pages on your site and allow visitors to find pages in the index based on words or phrases. More advanced search engines will also allow you to index and search the text of Portable Document Format (PDF) files. (See the section on common information types for more on PDF files.)

Databases

Formally, a database is a collection of information organized into individual records, with each record containing the same data about different items. You or your company will create and maintain databases with a database management system, sometimes referred to as a DBMS. In common usage, the term "database" is often used to describe the database or databases as well as the database management system. For example, you might consider FileMaker Pro to be your database of choice, while at the same time talking about your product catalog database.

In either case, at some point you will probably want to connect your database files and your database software to the Internet. In the early days of the Internet, linking a database with the Web was considered an advanced feature. Today, it's considered essential. Whether or not you think you need to have a database integrated with your Web server initially, you will want to consider how you will add it later on.

E-Commerce

These days, it seems everyone wants to join the e-commerce gold rush. For the sake of our discussion, *e-commerce* means providing basic shopping services through your Web site. As you will see in Chapter 13, e-commerce involves security enhancements to your Web server, specialized database programs, and a somewhat predefined style of interaction between your potential customers. Although you could theoretically build these services from general-purpose database and interaction programs, many software developers now provide tools that have been designed specifically to establish e-commerce services.

Guestbooks, Forums, and Chats

Guestbooks, forums, and chats are different ways to accomplish the same goal: Your Web site visitors are allowed to contribute to the material published on your site. When your regular contributors and visitors reach a critical mass, a self-sustaining online community may form.

Guestbooks allow visitors to chime in with the digital equivalent of "Kilroy was here" and leave comments (favorable or unfavorable) about the information they found on your site. Forums are guestbooks on steroids—not only can visitors leave comments or questions, but other visitors can respond directly to a particular topic. These discussions are archived temporarily or permanently on your server. The most complex community-building service, the chat, permits your Web visitors to carry on discussions in real time.

Web Cams and Streaming Media

While the Web is primarily geared toward the dissemination of text and graphic information, there are a number of ways to provide your Web visitors with live video or continuous-feed audio and video. Web cameras let your site's visitors watch either a live video feed or regularly updated images of activities at your geographic location. Streaming media servers allow visitors to see broadcasts of live or recorded events. Mac OS X has opened up the opportunities for streaming media content from Mac-based servers.

Custom Interaction

Even with all these Web enhancements and extensions, your own situation may demand a different form of interaction with the visitors to your Web site. At this point, you must decide how you want to develop your own Web applications. You can start by selecting from a number of software tools that allow you to construct custom Web applications from common high-level commands without resorting to full-fledged programming. The other alternative is to select one of the popular programming languages used by Web developers and develop your own Web applications from scratch or from existing code fragments shared by other Web developers.

What Human Resources Will I Need?

Because of the fickle and dynamic nature of information on the Web and the techniques for displaying that information, the most important and most expensive resources for serving the Internet are the humans who have to keep your server aimed at a moving target. The cost of the hardware nuts and bolts pales by comparison to the costs of human resources. Setting up and maintaining a good server takes people's time.

How do you measure the time required to maintain a server? That's a difficult question to answer without knowing how complex a server will be. Here are a few observations from my own experience:

- An organization of 10 people serving a minimal amount of information requires 10 hours per week of someone's time to set up and maintain the server in the first year.
- An organization of 20 people with information serving a vital part of their operation requires a *full-time employee* to set up and maintain the server in the first year.

- As the scale of your operation grows, you can expect to add more staff. If your business is your Web server, as with an up-and-coming dot-com firm, you'll need to have even more employees devoted to this task.

Within these guidelines, there are two relatively independent categories of responsibility: technical support and information supply.

Technical Support

Technical support for an Internet server performs such duties as

1. maintaining the server hardware,
2. troubleshooting, installing, and upgrading server software,
3. supporting new MIME types and server tools,
4. guiding the Web site's evolution,
5. monitoring server performance,
6. ensuring server security,
7. interacting with the staff responsible for networking (if this is a separate task), and
8. working with the staff providing information to be served.

In an example from my immediate experience, my employer, the San Diego Supercomputer Center (SDSC), has approximately 300 employees and admittedly a high-end Web presence, particularly on the technological end. In addition to a full-time webmaster, SDSC has evolved a dedicated Server Systems group to ensure a smoothly running Web, FTP, e-mail, search engine, and database setup. This group also provides the staff expertise to ensure that information from SDSC's databases, research projects, and other groups can be served on the Internet and the center's intranet as appropriate.

Information Supply

The other responsibility for your human resources is to develop the information to serve. A large organization cannot depend on a webmaster to provide information as well as keep the server running. *It may be one webmaster who manages the server, but the information supply should come directly from the source, that is, everyone in the organization.*

To continue the SDSC example, the Server Systems group runs close to 100 separate Web servers. There is no way that a small group could develop the content for all of those servers. The External Relations group (the group I'm in) provides updates and new information for the main SDSC Web site and several other sites, while individual research groups develop the information for most of the other Web servers at SDSC.

From these observations and examples, you can try to assess your own needs. Determining what human resources are required is not a simple task, since a successful information server generally has more than one person providing information as an integral part of their job functions. That cost is hard to determine.

These comments do suggest, however, that purchasing Web page editing software for your webmaster will not solve your information supply problem. As your site grows, you should expect to train and equip more and more members of your staff to produce material for your Web site. For a small site, training your existing staff may be enough. As your Web site grows—and grows in importance—you may end up hiring writers, graphic designers, or programmers to fulfill these needs.

(Yes, you can have programmers on the information supply side, separate from the technical support team, to develop the interaction mechanisms or database interfaces that your site uses. Such programming tasks don't affect the server itself, but do affect how your visitors get information at the Web site.)

A Note on E-Mail Aliases

In the same way that you might change or upgrade the computer that serves your Internet information, the webmaster or the server administrator today, through turnover or promotion, may not be the same person next year. Part of your planning process should include establishing *e-mail aliases* to ensure that the mail always gets to the correct person at any point in time.

E-mail aliases allow you to have another person assume webmaster duties without having to scour your Web site for references to the former webmaster's e-mail address. You might establish a "virtual user" named, for example, *webmas-*

ter@your-company.com, or instruct your mail system to direct all mail addressed to *webmaster* to a particular employee.

You may also want to consider whether other mail aliases would be useful to your organization. Many companies have established *info@your-company.com* or *feedback@your-company.com* as generic contact points. Whatever your decision, you should make it a point to have these addresses easily accessible from many areas of your Web site.

What Hardware Will I Need?

Hardware refers to the resources, both computer and network, needed to have your information server operate efficiently. This is a difficult issue to address definitively. Theoretically, any Mac, including a Mac Plus, can run a Web server—in fact there are several Mac Plus servers on the Internet today. (Of course, a Mac Plus can't run Mac OS X.) By comparison, a 600-MHz iMac DV can provide blistering performance, serving tens of thousands of hits per day quite nicely, thank you very much.

Here I can make only a general recommendation on what hardware is required initially: *You should buy as much computer as you can afford for your Web server.* If your budget limits you to resurrecting a mothballed PowerMac 8600, so be it. There's your Web server. (You may not be able to run Mac OS X, however.) If all you can afford is an iMac, that'll work, too. If you can swing for—or can't resist—a dual-processor G4 tower with high-speed RAID disks and 512 megabytes of memory, go for it.

A number of factors affect the hardware your server will require. First, the Web server may also be used for other computing tasks. Many readers, I'm sure, want to use the Mac on their desktops as a Web server even as they continue to use it to surf the Web, read e-mail, and do other work. This is fine—and I do this with this book's Web site—but make sure that you keep realistic expectations of your server's performance.

Second, the demands for information on different servers can vary greatly depending on the popularity of the information. NASA's Mars Pathfinder Web site and dozens of mirror sites, for example, fielded millions of hits during the first days of the 1997 Mars landing. My Web server for this book's Web site gets a few hundred visitors per month, with occasional spikes of several hundred hits a day. Sites like Yahoo! get approximately a bazillion hits every month.

Then again, the number of hits does not necessarily indicate server load, since the amount of information transferred by a single hit can vary dramatically. Further, an interface that permits users to perform a database lookup or a complex calculation will require significant hardware resources.

Apple Computer sells Macintosh systems designed as network servers. You may want to consider these systems for your Web server; however, as shown below, a Web server is not necessarily a large consumer of hardware resources other than network bandwidth. On the other hand, if your Web server doubles as your office file server, your system probably faces a distinctly different workload.

Once your server is established, you should monitor activity closely and try to have the resources—both monetary and personnel—available to respond quickly to the need for a new disk drive, more memory, and so forth. I appreciate that this is a vague recommendation, but Web server growth is difficult to predict. For those of you on limited budgets, let's consider each of the major potential problem areas separately. You can use this information to decide where to focus your dollars.

Processor

As a general rule, processor speed is not an issue for any Mac that will run Mac OS X. Because Mac OS X requires a G3 processor or better, your system has plenty of horsepower for basic and advanced Web serving.

Because most Web servers these days are not "basic" and might include database integration, custom interaction, and dynamic page generation, you should keep an eye on your server's performance as you add new services. Search engine indexing and searching can make heavy demands on the processor, for example. You may want to index your site at off-peak times or eventually consider running some services from a separate machine.

Memory

What is true for processor power is true for memory—other applications on a Web server are more likely to kill you than Web-serving applications. Today's

Macs typically come with a minimum of 64 megabytes of memory, and often with 128 megabytes, which is the minimum required for Mac OS X. Factoring in the memory protection and dynamic memory allocation in Mac OS X, you should not run into too many memory problems.

But here's a good rule of thumb: You can never have too much memory. On a computer dedicated to basic Web serving, memory will not likely be the bottleneck, since a basic Web server does not require a great deal of memory. The key words to note in this statement, though, are "dedicated" and "basic."

If you have other memory-intensive applications running—that is, if the server is also handling e-mail services, e-commerce, and other enhancements—additional memory can improve its performance. Even a basic Web server can benefit from extra memory. If the Web server can cache pages in memory instead of reading the pages from disk for each request, your visitors will see better performance.

Disk Space

Next on the list of hardware requirements is disk space. With today's cheap and roomy hard disks, you'll have to work to fill a 10-gigabyte disk—standard on the iMac DV models—with data from your Web sites. If your computer is not dedicated to Web serving, however, you may want to keep an eye on disk space. Other applications and data files (including databases, search engine indexes, digital video, and digital audio) can run through disk space like a hot knife through butter.

As with memory requirements, you can apply this rule of thumb: *You can never have enough disk space.* Eventually, all available space gets consumed. What varies is the time it takes to consume that space. Here are some basic rules to follow:

- If possible, keep the information you are serving separate from other data. This may call for separate partitions, if not separate disks.
- If possible, spread the information across various disks connected to separate disk controllers so you minimize the load to any one disk.
- If you permit users to upload files to the server or add to database content, as in Web forums, you need to monitor disk space usage more carefully than would otherwise be the case.

- Providing index files to facilitate searching can *double* disk space requirements since the index files (depending on the indexer used) can be as large as or larger than the original files.
- Graphics, sound, and audio files are large even in a compressed state—be prepared with extra disk space.
- Security and reliability may require that you keep multiple copies of information available for each service you are offering.

These rules become particularly important when we look at examples of interacting with the server. If the file system is full, your users might be frustrated by (possibly cryptic) error messages.

For real speed freaks, you can look at your hard disk's performance. The bandwidth of its interface—Ultra 2 SCSI is faster than Ultra ATA, for example—can give you a slight speed boost. A RAID disk system will also do the trick. But if you don't understand the terms in the previous sentence, don't worry. You shouldn't get bogged down here. Unless your server is approaching its processor and memory limits on performance, you'll have to count milliseconds to find the speed boost.

What Information Types Will I Encounter?

When you run a Web server with any or all of the enhancements described in the previous section, you will encounter a wide variety of information types—and the acronyms used to refer to them. Knowing something about these information types is necessary for the server planning process and for the discussions in the rest of this book. Therefore, this topic is discussed in some detail in this section.

File-Name Extensions

Before looking at the various information types, I need to interject a note about naming conventions and file extensions. Although the Mac OS has never depended on the user to identify a file's type, most operating systems—and the Web—still need help from the person creating the file. Traditionally, operating systems and their applications have dedicated a part of the file name for this purpose. The *file extension* is the suffix, usually three or four characters, preceded by a period (now usually called a "dot," as in dot-com), tacked on to the unique part of the file name. In fact, Mac OS X introduces the need for file extensions, although some extensions might be hidden from the average user by the Finder.

Thanks to the Web, however, the file extensions for most common file types have standardized across platforms. To comply with the naming conventions of the Web, you should adopt the following file-naming rules for any files you plan to serve on the Web or share with others:

- Avoid spaces and punctuation—except hyphens, underscores, and the period preceding the extension—in file and folder names. (Folders are equivalent to directories in the UNIX file system.)
- Be aware that Web browsers and most other operating systems *do* distinguish between uppercase and lowercase in file and folder names. The classic Mac OS and Mac OS X do not make such a distinction. (However, note that there is no case distinction in host names; *www.sdsc.edu* is the same as *www.SDSC.EdU*.) As a rule, for Web files, I recommend sticking to lowercase; whatever rule you choose to adopt, be consistent.
- Make a habit of appending the standard Web file extension to the names of any files that may make their way to the Web or to the computer of a non-Mac user.

In the discussion that follows, I will use the shorthand notation "*.xyz* files" to mean "files that have *.xyz* as the file name extension." In discussions of Web technologies, you will often see this shorthand used to describe not only the file name but also the file format that such names indicate. For example, you might see the phrase "*.html* files" also used to mean "text files marked up with HTML tags."

MIME Types

You might think that a file extension would be enough to identify a file's type, but the Internet has an additional layer of redundancy because several file extensions may refer to the same file format. The first Web browsers actually did identify the type of a file based on its file extension; however, the Web powers-that-be soon realized that a file extension of a few characters is helpful only if the person or software receiving a file already knows what the extension denotes.

While file extensions remain necessary, Web servers now recognize the type of information they are receiving based on *MIME types*. Multipurpose Internet Mail Extensions (MIME) is a standardized method of assigning types to documents. It was developed originally for use in e-mail messages, so e-mail programs could recognize embedded documents. The same mechanism has been adopted to assign and detect the format of Web documents.

Current browsers use MIME type information to identify the information being sent. MIME provides a standardized, more extended, and human-readable system of identification independent of the file name and contents. During Web server installation, this system of identification is distributed with most Web servers. Table 3-1 includes some definitions and references for more information on MIME types.

As we configure the various clients and servers described in this book, we will encounter MIME types. The basic idea is that when you, as a client, access information on various servers, your client software runs the appropriate application to interpret that information once it is received. A graphics viewer displays an image file, a video viewer shows a film clip, a molecule viewer displays a molecule, and so on. For example, *image/gif* is a registered MIME type for a Graphics Interchange Format (GIF) image. A GIF file has associated with it an extension of *.gif*. The MIME specification registers the type of file and the file extension that is used by convention. Hence, Web browsers and Web servers can be configured to understand the mapping of a *.gif* file to the GIF MIME type and respond accordingly.

Table 3-1. Additional MIME Type Information

Location	Description
whatis.com	Whatis?com has a brief definition of MIME types and links to other basic information.
www.iana.org	The Internet Assigned Numbers Authority maintains the list of assigned MIME types.
www.isi.edu/in-notes/rfc1521.txt *www.isi.edu/in-notes/rfc1522.txt*	The formal specifications for MIME types.

As a general rule, it is worth noting that Web software has evolved over time to accommodate a larger variety of MIME types. It may not be necessary to download software to handle a MIME type because the standard Web browser or another operating system component can handle it. For example, the QuickTime media layer in Mac OS X handles a wide variety of graphics, audio, and video formats. Table 3-2 lists some of the more common MIME types and their corresponding file extensions.

Common Information Types

The good news is that there are only four basic categories of information: text, graphics, multimedia, and binary. The bad news is that each of these categories includes a variety of formats; the binary category is essentially a "miscellaneous" category. I describe a few information types in greater detail, because you will encounter them as you configure your server and client software.

Table 3-2. Common File Extensions and MIME Specifications

MIME Specification	File Extension
application/msword	*.doc*
application/pdf	*.pdf*
application/postscript	*.ps*
application/rtf	*.rtf*
application/x-shockwave-flash	*.swf*
audio/mpeg	*.mp3*
audio/x-realaudio	*.ra*
image/gif	*.gif*
image/jpeg	*.jpg, .jpeg*
message/rfc822	*.mime*
text/html	*.html*
text/plain	*.text, .txt*
text/xml	*.xml*
video/mpeg	*.mpg, .mpeg*
video/quicktime	*.qt, .mov*

Text

What constitutes a *text file* is somewhat arbitrary. However, for simplicity, let's define a text file as any file containing just those characters in the American Standard Code for Information Interchange (ASCII) character set. Technically, any file that is not an ASCII text file is a *binary file* and produces indecipherable output when you force your Mac to display it as text. However, I have chosen to define separate categories for graphics and multimedia files because they are common on the Web. Table 3-3 contains further references and specifications for text file formats.

Plain text. For the purpose of this book, I'll define *plain text* files to be those files comprising ASCII characters and intended for human consumption. This definition is somewhat arbitrary, since many types of ASCII text files are better interpreted by software.

HyperText Markup Language (HTML). For serving the Internet, the most important special-purpose text files are HTML files. HTML is the so-called language of the Web and the format with which you will most likely become intimately familiar. HTML is used to "tag" standard text; the tags cause a program (in this case, a Web browser) to present that text in a certain way.

HTML was developed by Tim Berners-Lee and the folks at the Conseil Européen pour la Récherche Nucleaire (CERN), now known as the European Laboratory for Particle Physics, and is based on Standard Generalized Markup Language (SGML). SGML has been around for a long time and is used extensively in the publishing industry. Chapter 15 discusses HTML and related Web markup languages—including Cascading Style Sheets (CSS), Dynamic HTML, the Extensible Markup Language (XML), and Extensible HTML (XHTML)—that have emerged to make up for HTML's deficiencies.

Table 3-3. Text File Specifications

Format	Common Extensions	Reference
Plain text	*.txt*	*www.w3.org/Protocols/rfc1341/7_1_Text.html*
HTML	*.html, .htm, .shtml*	*www.w3.org/MarkUp*
XML	*.xml*	*www.w3.org/XML*

Graphics

The major trade-off in comparing graphics formats is size of the image file versus resolution. Table 3-4 summarizes the major graphics formats you will encounter on the Web. (This is far from a complete list of graphics formats.)

GIF. Graphics Interchange Format (GIF) files are the most common graphics on the Web. This format, with the file extension *.gif*, is recognized by all graphical Web browsers. Developed in 1987 by the CompuServe online service, this format has the drawback of supporting only 256 colors, since it was developed for use with 8-bit color displays and may be insufficient to provide the richness needed for some images. Furthermore, since 1995, GIF patent holders have demanded royalties on programs that produce GIF images.

There have been extensions to this standard, notably GIF89A, which includes support for more colors. Most current Web browser versions recognize the enhancements offered by GIF89A, such as GIF animations, the simplest way to add movement to a Web page, and transparent images, in which the image's background appears to be the same as the browser's and the image "floats" on the page. GIF files are best used for simple line drawings and text images with simple shading and fewer colors.

Table 3-4. Web Graphics Formats

Format	Color Depth	Compression	Recommended Uses	Comments
GIF	8-bit (256 colors)	LZW	Simple graphics, logos, clip art	Allows transparent images and animations.
JPEG	24-bit true color	4:1 to 20:1	Photographic art	High compression for small images. Compression is "lossy."
PNG	1- to 8-bit palette; 1- to 16-bit grayscale; 24-, 48-bit	Lossless, 10–30% smaller than GIF	All GIF uses, some TIFF uses	Emerging format. Most recent browsers have built-in support for PNG images.
TIFF	24-bit true color	LZW	High-resolution images	Not Web standard, but useful for cross-platform exchange.

JPEG. The Joint Photographic Expert Group (JPEG) format supports higher resolution and more colors than GIF while generally offering greater compression. Thus, JPEG can create smaller, high-resolution images for faster downloading on Web pages. On the other hand, JPEG uses a "lossy" compression scheme—the quality of an image can be degraded in color or detail when it is compressed. JPEG is best suited for displaying photographic-style images on Web pages.

PNG. Designed to supplant GIF, the Portable Network Graphics (PNG) format is slowly emerging as a Web graphics format, boosted by a recommendation from the World Wide Web Consortium (W3C) and built-in support in recent versions of the major Web browsers. PNG is an extensible, patent-free file format for indexed-color, grayscale, and true-color raster images. PNG is a portable, well-compressed format that does not lose image information as JPEG compression can. As a patent-free replacement for GIF, PNG is designed for online viewing, has a progressive display option, and supports improved color matching across platforms.

TIFF. The Tagged Image File Format (TIFF) was designed by Microsoft and the late Aldus, Inc., and is the format produced by most scanners. This high-quality format is readable by most image-processing applications, such as Adobe Photoshop and Adobe Illustrator, but not within most Web browsers. TIFF is commonly used to exchange high-resolution images across platforms.

Multimedia

Multimedia files include both audio-only, video-only, and audio-video formats. Although many audio and video formats exist, the competition between Apple, Real Networks, and Microsoft is leading to the acceptance of a limited number of core multimedia formats that Mac webmasters and Web users need to concern themselves with. Here I only briefly mention the formats.

Chapter 6 describes the software you'll need to play files in these and other formats, and Table 3-5 points you to resources for each of the major formats.

MPEG. The Moving Pictures Expert Group (MPEG) format is a standard binary-compressed format for audio and video. MPEG files can contain audio, video, or both audio and video, and the popular MP3 music format uses, in fact, MPEG Audio Layer 3 to encode CD-quality music. (The latest versions of Ap-

Table 3-5. Multimedia File Formats

Format	Common Extensions	Reference
MPEG	*.mpeg, .mpg, .mp3*	*www.mpeg.org* *drogo.cselt.stet.it/mpeg*
QuickTime	*.mov, .qt*	*www.apple.com/quicktime*
RealMedia	*.ra, .rm, .ram*	*www.realnetworks.com*
Shockwave, Flash	*.dir, .dcr, .swf*	*www.macromedia.com*
Windows Media	*.avi, .asf*	*www.microsoft.com/windows/windowsmedia*

ple's QuickTime software will play MPEG movies and MP3 files.) The International Standards Organization (ISO) has adopted the QuickTime format as the basis for MPEG-4.

Apple QuickTime. Apple's QuickTime software is another common Web movie format, with free players available for Macintosh and Windows computers. QuickTime files can also encode audio-only files that can be embedded in Web pages.

Microsoft AVI and ASF. Microsoft's Audio Video Interleaved (AVI) format competes with the MPEG and QuickTime formats. Microsoft is moving from AVI toward Advanced Streaming Format (ASF) and the Advanced Authoring Format (AAF). ASF is a format for streaming media distribution, and AAF is a format for exchanging media files among digital production tools and content creation applications. ASF and AAF are succeeding the AVI file format as the new default multimedia file formats for Windows.

RealMedia. RealNetworks is the other major player in the Web multimedia marketplace. Its RealAudio and RealVideo family of formats were designed primarily for "streaming" over the Internet rather than to be downloaded as self-contained files. The popularity and efficiencies of streaming, popularized by RealNetworks, prompted Apple and Microsoft to develop streaming servers and to modify their multimedia formats and players to allow multimedia streaming.

Macromedia Shockwave and Flash. Macromedia has also developed widely used media formats designed for presenting animated graphics on the Web. The free Shockwave and Flash plug-ins are available for Macintosh and Windows platforms. Macromedia's multimedia formats are not in direct competition with the other three formats, and in some cases they can be viewed by Apple, Microsoft, and Real Networks multimedia players.

Other Common Formats

The fourth category of information types you are likely to encounter on the Web—which I have called *binary files*—is essentially a catchall category for any file format that cannot be viewed in a standard Web browser or a major multimedia player. There's no way that I can cover every other information type you may encounter on the Web. Sites that use file types not described here will contain instructions for how to deal with the file type in question—and if they don't, they should.

Here I will discuss a few types of common files that you should be prepared to handle—archive files, compressed files, and PDF files, along with other page definition languages.

Archive Files. Archive file formats bundle an entire folder or directory hierarchy into a single file for distribution. A StuffIt Archive (*.sit*) file is the most common archive format on the Mac OS. On Windows, Zip (*.zip*) and ARC (*.arc*) archive files are common, while UNIX has tape archive (*.tar*) files. A special type of archive file, called a self-extracting archive, is a tiny application that, when executed, expands itself. With a self-extracting archive—*.sea* files on Macintosh and certain *.exe* files on Windows—you do not need a software utility to expand the archive.

Compressed Files. Compressed files are useful for conserving disk space and simplifying distribution, since they take less time to transmit over the Internet. There are various compression algorithms and software to implement them, and Mac OS, UNIX, and Windows each have their compression format of choice. For example, binhex (*.hqx*) and MacBinary (*.bin*) are common Mac OS formats. Windows leans toward ZIP (*.zip*) files, and on UNIX you will see Gzip (*.gz*) and UNIX Compress (*.Z*) formats.

In many cases, you will encounter files that have been both archived and compressed—for example, a binhex-compressed StuffIt Archive (*.sit.hqx*) file on the Macintosh or a Gzipped tape archive (*.tar.gz*) file on UNIX. On Windows, Zip files often combine both archiving and compression. If you are distributing compressed or archived files, your best bet is either to use a format that you know the receiver of the compressed file will have or to offer several formats.

Portable Document Format (PDF). Because of the limited and screen-oriented formatting commands of HTML, documents in which the arrangement and styles for text and images must be retained are often distributed in one of several page definition formats. PDF was developed by Adobe Systems as a compact page-definition format that could also be displayed and navigated easily on screen. PDF files have become the de facto Web standard for distributing documents that must retain their original appearance. The free Adobe Acrobat Reader plug-in and helper application allow you to view and page through longer documents, such as software user manuals, either on- or off-line.

Other Page Definition Languages. The PostScript, Rich Text Format (RTF), and TeX formats use plain text files annotated with printing and display commands. PostScript was developed by Adobe Systems as a device-independent text representation, and it is now recognized by most high-end printers. Although PostScript files comprise only ASCII characters, they generally must be printed to view the contents. Encapsulated PostScript (EPS) is a part of the PostScript language that supports the embedding of images.

Microsoft developed RTF as a document interchange format that could retain common document formatting styles, and RTF has become a standard format for exchanging files between different word processors. However, RTF does not always work well for documents that include complex formatting such as equations and embedded graphics.

TeX and LaTeX, two text formatting languages, were developed by Donald Knuth at Stanford University and have a large following, particularly in the physics, computer science, and mathematics communities. If you interact with UNIX users, you will sooner or later encounter TeX and its derivatives, such as LaTeX. One of the reasons for its lingering popularity is its ability to format complex mathematical equations (and because there are so few WYSIWYG word processors for UNIX). TeX files are processed to produce PostScript files for printing.

A Word on Standards

This discussion of file formats and MIME types should in no way be considered the best or last word on the subject. Web "standards" come and go as software companies introduce new formats that succeed or fail to gain popularity and as older standards are revised to reflect new developments. For example, the Virtual

Reality Modeling Language (VRML), a Web standard for describing 3-D worlds, appears to have peaked and faded, although an XML-based X3D is being pursued; and in the battle over streaming audio and video, no clear leader has arisen.

If your intended audience demands the latest Web technologies, you will have to be aware of new developments and decide whether to support those MIME types. If your audience is satisfied with fewer bells and whistles, you can probably communicate the same information with well-established and stable MIME types.

• • •

You should now have a better idea about the goals of your Web site and the initial level of support—both human and hardware—required for your Internet service. Of course, you will add to and delete from your list of requirements over time, but you will have started on server implementation through some sound planning. Planning lets you balance the level of service that you can provide against the resources that need to be expended to establish and maintain the information service.

CHAPTER 4

NETWORKING

The next step in setting up your Web server is to make sure you have the network connection within your organization, office, or home to provide the desired level of service. If you have yet to get connected to the Internet and are contemplating how best to do this, read on. But even if your computer is already connected to the Internet—that is, you can exchange e-mail and browse the Web—this section will help you consider whether your current connection will suffice for a Web server.

There are four networking requirements for serving the Internet:

- A physical network connection
- An IP (Internet Protocol) address
- A name for your server
- Appropriate networking software

Unless you have Internet access through your place of work, you will need an Internet Service Provider (ISP) to gain access to the Internet. An ISP can provide you with all or none of the essential networking components with various levels of service. But before you make any of these decisions, you need to understand a little bit more about the connection and service options available from an ISP.

Choosing a Connection Method

In most cases, your Web server will benefit most from a faster connection to the Internet. If your server seems slow, you should first check whether your network connection is saturated. (Unless you're serving from a Mac Plus or similarly ancient computer, in which case, it may be time to spend a few bucks on hardware.) The required bandwidth depends on the services you are supporting. Some rules of thumb are:

- Whatever services you provide require a full-time connection—that is, 24 hours a day, 7 days a week. The only exception would be if you know exactly when your customers need to visit your site—or if you *want* to restrict access to certain hours of the day.
- For supporting only e-mail and limited Web and file transfer traffic, you might get by with a connection running across a phone line and a modem at 56.6 kilobits per second. (Face it, congestion on other parts of the Internet beyond your control will limit most connection speeds to less than your modem's peak speed.)
- For high-performance Web access, you need still higher-speed connection to your ISP. Options include Integrated Services Digital Network (ISDN), DSL service, and cable modems, as well as T1, T3, or faster connections.

In simple terms, your physical Internet connection can be characterized in one of two ways: *dial-up* or *dedicated*. The type of connection to the Internet determines the kind of server you can operate. If you want users to have continuous access to your server, a dedicated connection is a must. Since the majority of Web servers operate through dedicated lines, this book concentrates on this type of infrastructure. However, the principles for serving the Internet apply just as well to a dial-up or non-dedicated connection.

Dial-up Connections. As the name suggests, a dial-up connection is active only when you dial into your ISP. A *dial-up connection* is often shared between the Internet and other purposes, usually as a voice line. Typically, such a connection is through a modem and a telephone line attached to a regular telephone exchange. Such nondedicated connections are generally slower and require startup time to establish the connection, for instance, while one modem dials another.

Dedicated Connections. Dedicated connections, on the other hand, are not shared and are "always on," continuously listening for network traffic destined for your Web server and broadcasting information as requested. The wire over which the connection runs may belong to and be maintained by your organization or it may be leased from and maintained by a telephone company or other carrier. Dedicated connections are generally fast in transmitting data and automatic, requiring no human intervention to make the connection.

Dedicated connections include high-end private line services such as frame relay, T1, T3, or faster network links. If you are operating a server connected by Ethernet to the network of a large organization that already has Internet access, that Ethernet network is, in turn, probably connected to the Internet via one of these methods. These options, frankly, are very expensive, and the costs are likely to be prohibitive for all but the larger organizations and enterprises.

ISDN lines, cable modems, and DSL service are lower-cost options for establishing dedicated Internet access for small business or home users. In comparing ISDN, DSL, and cable connectivity, you should be aware that DSL and cable modems typically have very fast "downstream" speeds *into* your computer, but much slower "upstream" speeds *from* your computer to the rest of the Internet—and your audience.

ISDN lines are maintained by the telephone companies, and you pay usage-based fees as you would for long-distance phone calls, albeit at a different rate. ISDN is slowly being supplanted by DSL. However, ISDN has no distance restriction, as does DSL, so remote areas may still need to rely on ISDN service.

DSL service, provided by telephone carriers, offers the advantages over ISDN of being easier to set up, faster, and flat-fee based. The primary limitation of DSL is the requirement that your server, and hence you or your workplace, must be located within a fixed distance (usually three miles) from a carrier's central office. Most telephone carriers are aggressively expanding the reach of DSL.

Cable modems, provided through cable television companies such as Time Warner and Cox Communications, provide transmission speeds approaching that of an Ethernet connection and offer a very cost-effective solution for high-speed Internet connections. A disadvantage of cable modem connections, despite their speed, is that the cable is shared with other cable modem subscribers in your neighborhood. Your server has access only to the unused portion of the bandwidth at any given time.

Table 4-1 summarizes the characteristics of the various types of Internet connections, including peak data rates in kilobits per second (kbps) and megabits per second (Mbps). The information in the table is misleading for various reasons: you never reach peak speeds, compression changes these numbers, and so on. These are valid criticisms. The goal here is to provide perspective, so that you can decide which service or services to investigate further.

A caveat: For each technology, your actual bandwidth also depends on your ISP's connection to the Internet. For example, if you have a cable modem and your ISP is connected to the Internet via a T1 line, you will never see performance greater than 1.5 Mbps to your computer.

DSL and cable modems generally provide the best value for the performance delivered. However, check with your provider regarding possible restrictions on running a Web server. To host a Web server, an ISP may require you to pay slightly higher business rates instead of the basic consumer rates.

Table 4-1. Types and Characteristics of Internet Connections

Connection Type	Peak Speed	Type of Connection	Payment Structure
Dial-up modem	1.2–56.6 kbps	Manual	Usage based
ISDN	56–128 kbps	Automatic	Usage based
DSL	384 kbps (upstream) 1.5–6 Mbps (downstream)	Automatic	Flat fee
Cable modem	2.5 Mbps (upstream) 27 Mbps (downstream)	Manual or Automatic	Flat fee
T1	1.5 Mbps	Automatic	Flat fee
Frame relay	1.5 Mbps	Automatic	Flat fee
T3	45 Mbps	Automatic	Flat fee
FDDI	100 Mbps	Automatic	Flat fee
OC-3	155 Mbps	Automatic	Flat fee

Table 4-2. Further Reading on Internet Connectivity

Location	Topic
www.catv.org	Cable Modem University at CATV CyberLab.
www.cablemodemhelp.com	Cable Modem Help provides answers for cable modem users.
rpcp.mit.edu/~gingold/cable	Cable modem resources on the Web.
www.dslcenter.com	DSL Center, from DNAI, a San Francisco–area ISP.
www.dsldigest.com	DSL Digest, from BizSpace, Inc.
www.sorenson-usa.com/dsl-mac.html	Mac-friendly DSL providers list, from Dale Sorenson.
www.isdnzone.com	The ISDN Zone, from Eicon Technology.
www.isdn4me.com	ISDN information from Cyberus, a Canadian ISP.
www.eff.org/pub/GII_NII/ISDN	ISDN information, including a tutorial.

If you need more upstream bandwidth than a DSL or cable connection provides, a T1 or frame relay connection is the next step up. On the other hand, you may not want to pay the premium price for T1 or frame relay just to run a Web server. At this stage, you may want to investigate server co-location options from a Web hosting service (see the section on Web Hosting in Chapter 7).

Obviously, this is just a gentle introduction to getting connected to the Internet. Table 4-2 provides resources with more detailed information.

IP Addresses and Domain Names

Once your server computer is physically connected to the Internet, it needs a unique IP address so that other computers on the Internet can locate it. (Recall that we discussed the format of an IP address in Chapter 2.) The most likely ways you can get assigned an IP address are from your organization's network manager or from your ISP.

In either case, the result should be an assignment of an IP address or group of addresses, depending on your need with respect to the organization or the ISP service package you sign up for. Table 4-3 provides further information on IP addressing.

Table 4-3. Further Reading on IP Addressing

Location	Description
www.3com.com/nsc/501302.html	"Understanding IP Addressing: Everything You Ever Wanted To Know," by Chuck Semeria at 3Com.
www.isoc.org/internet/standards/ipv6.shtml	IPv6, the next-generation Internet Protocol, changes the IP address format to accommodate more hosts.
netgeo.caida.org	NetGeo from CAIDA maps an IP address to its geographic location.

Static versus Dynamic IP Addresses

I may have skipped a step in saying that your network administrator or ISP would assign you an IP address. In actuality, many ISPs (and large organizations), by default, configure their customers' computers to use *dynamic IP addresses*. In other words, each time the computer boots up, it is assigned a temporary IP address from a pool of available addresses. For the technical minded, the Dynamic Host Configuration Protocol (DHCP) is the networking language that allows your computer to pull its IP address from a DHCP server as it starts up.

As a Web client, having a dynamic IP address presents no problems. Because every request from your computer to any Web, e-mail, or other server includes your current IP address, the results of your requests to other Web and e-mail servers will find their way back to you. On the other hand, a dynamic IP address presents a challenge when your computer operates as a Web server. For a real-world analogy, imagine that your phone company assigned you a new, random phone number every morning when you woke up. How would anyone be able to call you?

There are two solutions to the dynamic IP address problem. The first is to get a *static IP address*, an address that is permanently assigned to your computer. You can request a static IP address from your network administrator; with an ISP, you may have to pay for a higher service level to get a static IP address.

The second option is an example of the old adage "Where there's a Web, there's a way" in action. A number of Web sites have sprung up to provide *static domain names* to users with dynamic IP addresses. The services, ranging in cost from free to around $40 per year, use software on your computer to alias your machine's dynamic address to a permanent domain name. All of these sites, listed in Table 4-4, support Mac customers.

Whether you have a static or dynamic IP address, you still need a full-time Internet connection for your Mac unless you really enjoy annoying Web surfers with "Server is not responding" messages.

Table 4-4. Domain Name Services for Dynamic IP Addresses

Location	Description
www.dyndns.org	Dynamic DNS Network Services is free, but donators can receive additional levels of service.
www.dyndns.com	DynDNS.com service starts at $100 per year.
www.dynip.com	DynIP Internet basic name service is $40 per year.
www.hn.org	HammerNode Internet Services offers free service.
www.tzo.com	TZO.com starts at $25 per year for basic service.

Domain Names

Once you have an IP address, the next step is to determine a host name for your server, so human visitors can remember what it's called. If you get an IP address from your organization's network manager, your host name will already be partly defined. In particular, it will likely end in *your-organization.com.* You need to work out your server's unique name within the organization with your network administrator—for example, *your-server.your-organization.com.*

If you *are* the network manager for your company or organization and you don't already have a domain name, you will need to register one. When you sign up with your ISP, you can also choose and register your own domain name—*bobsleds-r-us.com* or *macrame.org*, for example. There are several places on the Web—a few are shown in Table 4-5—where you can check whether a domain name has already been registered and register your own domain name.

Individuals or smaller organizations, particularly those without dedicated Internet connections, may not want or need to register a full-fledged domain name. Instead, you may just let your ISP dictate your domain name. In this case, your company's URL will be something like *your-company.your-isp.net,* or perhaps something longer. Such URLs can be unwieldy and difficult to remember.

Table 4-5. Checking for Available Domain Names and Alternatives

Location	Description
www.networksolutions.com	Network Solutions, the original keeper of domain name registrations, is now owned by VeriSign.
www.register.com	Register.com is an ICANN-accredited domain name registration site.
www.aaawebnames.com	AAA Web Names is one of many domain name "speculators" who register domain names and then resell them.
www.v3.com	V3 Redirection Services.

There is at least one other alternative to traditional domain name registration. V3 Redirection Services, operating out of the Netherlands, allows you to create a URL for your company of the form *go.to/your-company*. At the time of writing the company was offering this service for free, as long as you agree to display their advertising banner on your site.

Once you've selected a domain name, you also need to assign a host name to your Web server computer. (Again, if you work for a large organization, this name may be chosen for you.) As with e-mail addresses for your webmaster, you may choose to have one name assigned to a particular machine (such as *bob.your-company.com*) and also establish a more general permanent alias (such as *www.your-company.com*) to which all server traffic is directed. You might want to do this if, for example, you expect to move your server to a more powerful computer in the future while keeping your original system on the network. For truly busy systems, you might want to implement a load-balancing system so that requests to *www.your-company.com* are actually redirected to your server farm of two or more computers.

It is traditional practice to provide the alias *www.your-company.com* for your organization's Web site and the alias *ftp.your-company.com* for the organization's FTP site. These names could refer to the same computer or to different computers. The point is, the computer (and hence IP address) can change without requiring the name to change. Therefore, users of your information server who have bookmarked *www.your-company.com* in their Web browsers will not be disappointed when they visit the site in the future, since the URL will remain valid even though you have changed the computer.

To put the host names and aliases into practice, you need to propagate this information to the Internet at large through the DNS. In most cases, you must ask your network administrator or your ISP to add this information to their domain name server. If you are responsible for maintaining your own name server, you must add the alias yourself. (See the section on the DNS at the end of this chapter for more details.)

Virtual Hosts and IP Multihoming

As your Web serving needs grow, it's likely that you will eventually want to run a Web server for more than one host name or domain. For example, although server names of the form *www.your-company.com* have become standard for a company's Web server, major projects or subdivisions in an organization often want their own server. As a more straightforward example, you may just need to provide Web services for two completely different domains—perhaps *your-company.com* and *your-hobby-group.org.*

IP multihoming and virtual hosting are two methods that allow you to use one Web server to serve two apparently different addresses. *IP multihoming,* as the name suggests, assigns more than one IP address to a single machine. Of course, IP multihoming requires multiple IP addresses from your service provider (and hence may involve a fee depending on your level of service) and is permitted by Mac OS X. In fact, Mac OS X introduces support for having more than one physical network interface card on the computer. (For Mac OS 9 and earlier versions, IP multihoming is possible with Open Transport 1.3 or greater.)

Virtual hosting, on the other hand, lets a single Web server host more than one host name on a single IP address. Many sites now use virtual hosts to shorten long and clunky URLs—for example, *www.your-company.com/projects/project-A*—to something like *projectA.your-company.com.* Rather than running a separate Web server program, the main Web server intercepts requests for virtual hosts and translates them into requests for information as in the long form. Virtual hosting is available for Mac Web servers as well.

Setting up IP multihoming or virtual hosting is a two-step process. First, you must configure your domain name server to recognize each IP address or virtual host and direct traffic to your Web server. Again, for most people, you will have to ask your ISP or network administrator, unless you run your own domain name server.

Second, you must configure your Web server to listen for requests to each IP address or virtual host and return the appropriate information in response to requests. WebSTAR, Apache, and Web Server 4D allow you to define rules for accepting requests for virtual hosts, and the Pardeikes Welcome Plug-in *(welcome.pardeike.net)* is a third-party solution for virtual hosting. (At the time of writing, it was not clear if Welcome would be ported to Mac OS X.)

INTERNET SERVICE PROVIDERS (ISPs)

An ISP provides your connection to the Internet as well as the network administration that makes your server accessible. Your ISP maintains a link or links to the rest of the Internet, provides your server's IP address, and maintains your server's domain name in its domain name servers. How much you pay defines the level of service you will get. Which ISP you use and the level of service you purchase should be considered carefully.

To select an ISP, the first step is to get a list of providers in your region. From there, you can examine the services offered by each one. If you are not yet connected to the Internet, evaluating ISP services may seem like you're putting the cart before the horse: How can you look up, on the Internet, details of ISP services when you don't yet have an Internet connection? Some options are to visit a cybercafé, library, or a friend who is connected. Table 4-6 provides the locations of lists of ISPs and additional ISP information.

The discussion in this chapter so far suggests that you should consider a number of factors when evaluating ISPs.

- *The connection speeds and methods available.* An ISP may provide options for dial-up, ISDN, or DSL, all the way up to private line connections such as T1 or T3. You may want to consider not just your first connection, but possible upgrade paths.
- *The levels of service provided.* The basic level of service may target consumers and not be suitable for a server; in fact, some ISPs may place restrictions on running a server with their basic service. Different service levels provide different numbers of static IP addresses, domain name services, e-mail addresses, and technical support, as well as faster connection speeds.

Table 4-6. Selecting an Internet Service Provider

Location	Description
www.thelist.com	Directory of more than 9,600 ISPs (February 2001) in the U.S. and Canada.
home.netscape.com/computing/isp_locator	ISP locator from Netscape.
www.ispc.org	The Internet Service Providers' Consortium.
www.bsdi.com/white-papers/become.php	"Becoming an ISP" by Rob Kolstad of Berkeley Software Design, Inc.

- *The ISP's connection to the Internet.* If an ISP has only a T1 connection to the Internet, then a T3 connection between your server and the ISP is a waste of money. To run a server, you should look for ISPs with at least one or more T3 connections to the Internet.
- *The cost of the service.* This is probably the last factor to consider, and all other factors being equal, you can look at the differences in price.

Network Software

This topic falls under network administration, which this book does not propose to cover in any great detail. The first step is to set up the basic network settings that will allow your computer to communicate with the Internet. Next, you may choose to turn on additional network services provided by Mac OS X. In addition, Mac OS X provides a Setup Assistant to walk you through the steps necessary to get your system up and running, which includes the configuration of basic network services.

Mac OS X includes all the networking software you need to communicate with the Internet. The Darwin kernel of Mac OS X incorporates a new version of Open Transport networking software that inherits many features from its UNIX roots. You'll remember from Chapter 2 that the Internet can be defined as the sum total of all the computers communicating via TCP/IP. The operating system usually runs the TCP/IP protocols directly, while additional application services, such as HTTP, can be thought of as being layered "on top" of TCP/IP.

If you are connecting your server over a dial-up modem connection—which is possible although not recommended—you need additional software to access TCP/IP services. The most common protocol for use on modem lines is the Point-to-Point Protocol (PPP). (Table 4-7 provides pointers to additional information on PPP.) TCP/IP runs on top of PPP. When you connect to an ISP via PPP, you receive a dynamic IP address from a pool of available addresses. Mac OS X allows you to configure your system for PPP dial-up connections through the PPP tab in the Network panel of the System Preferences, shown in Figure 4-1.

Basic Network Settings

For a basic connection, there are really only five things you need to know, and I've summarized them here:

Table 4-7. Further Reading on the PPP Protocol

Location	Description
www.cis.ohio-state.edu/htbin/rfc/rfc1661.html	The official definition of PPP.
www.rockstar.com/ppp.shtml	FreePPP, a popular Mac PPP alternative.

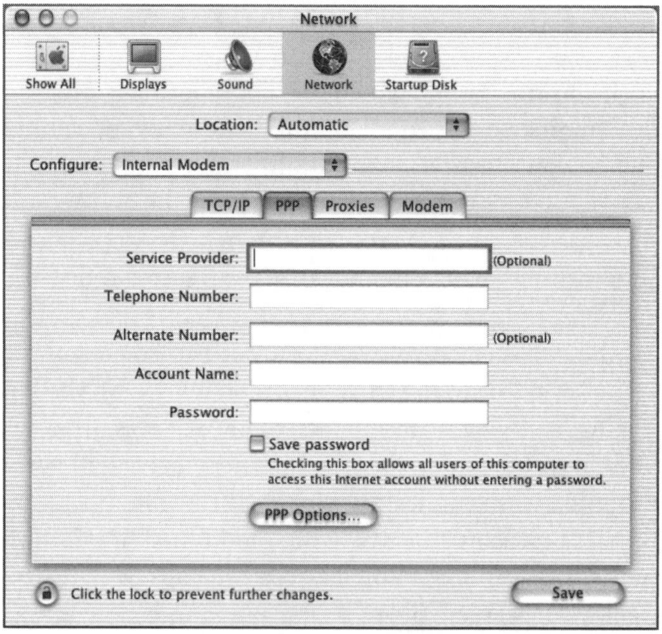

Figure 4-1. Configuring Network Settings for PPP.

- *IP address*. This is the address of the form *nnn.nnn.nnn.nnn* (e.g., 128.59.98.1) assigned in one of the ways described above.
- *Subnet mask*. This number defines how a network segment may be divided further into subnets. The value depends on the size of your network. For smaller networks configured to support 256 hosts (2^8), this is usually set to 255.255.255.0. For larger networks of up to 65,536 (2^{16}) hosts, this is usually set to 255.255.0.0.
- *Default router*. This is where to direct network traffic so that it may be sent correctly. Usually the network administrator designates a computer as a default gateway. This may either be on your organization's network or at the ISP.
- *Name server*. This IP address tells your computer where to start resolving host names to numeric IP addresses. You may want to establish a limited DNS service for local host names and use an ISP's name server for the rest of the Internet.
- *Search domains*. If you provide a partial host name, TCP/IP will look for hosts by concatenating the partial host name with the search domains listed here. For example, at SDSC, the search domain might be *sdsc.edu*, so a request asking for host *rosebud* would automatically be converted to *rosebud.sdsc.edu*.

Many ISPs and organizations use DHCP to establish all these values each time your computer starts up. With DHCP, you may get a new IP address each time. Depending on the level of service you purchase from your ISP—especially if you arrange for a permanent IP address—these same settings may also be configured manually.

To configure Mac OS X manually, you need the information above from your ISP or your network manager. Configuring your Mac network software then involves opening the System Preferences application, selecting the Network panel, and entering the values for your IP address, subnet mask, router IP address, name server IP addresses, and the optional search domains.

Within the System Preferences application, the Network panel, as shown in Figure 4-2, allows you to configure your Mac for one or more Internet connections. You can make changes to these and other network settings only after authenticating yourself with the administrator password. The Lock button on such System Preferences panels allows you to enter the administrator password.

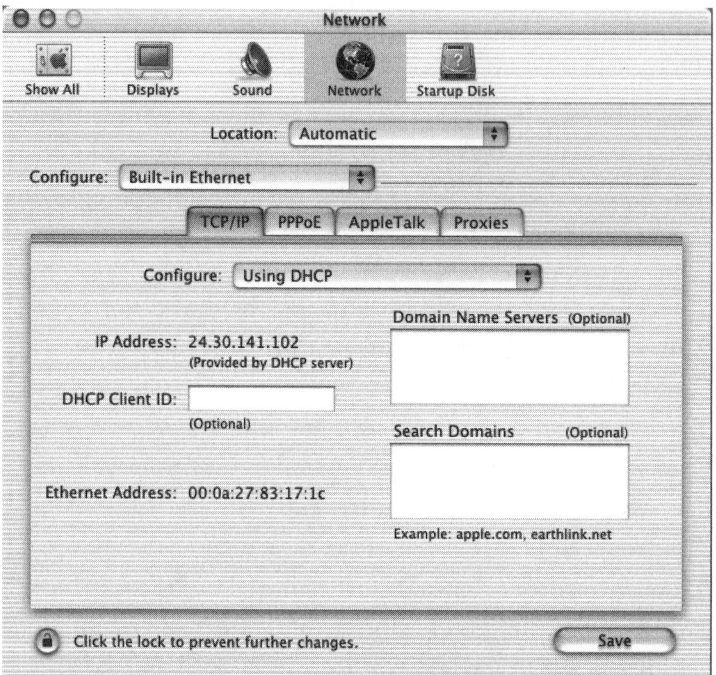

Figure 4-2. Mac OS X Network Settings for TCP/IP.

Network Services

Mac OS X lets you turn on and off your computer's core network applications in the System Preferences. These networking services—provided in addition to basic network connectivity—are controlled under the System Preferences Sharing panel. As a security measure, the basic Mac OS X installation starts with all of these services turned off. As a rule, if you are not using these network services, you should leave them turned off to ensure the maximum level of security.

Web Server. Within the Sharing panel, as shown in Figure 4-3, you can turn Mac OS X's built-in Web server on and off, which is actually a version of the popular Apache Web server. By default, your system's Web documents are kept in the */Library/WebServer/Documents* folder. Individual users can share files placed in their */Users/<username>/Sites* folder. (Chapter 7 has more on Mac OS X's Apache installation.)

FTP Server. Within the Sharing panel, as in Figure 4-3, you also have the option of turning on the built-in FTP server. FTP is the standard Internet protocol for file sharing. (Chapter 8 has more on Mac OS X's FTP server.)

Remote Login. Also in the Sharing panel, you can turn on the Mac OS X telnet server. The telnet server allows you to log in to your computer over the network and access the command-line interface. I recommend strongly that UNIX novices leave this off. Even UNIX experts should leave this off as a security precaution unless they have a definite need for this feature.

Apple File Sharing. Both the Network and Sharing panels hold elements needed to use Apple File Sharing. Under the Network panel, you make AppleTalk active on a particular network connection, while under the Sharing panel, you set the main AppleTalk settings, including your system's name, and turn File Sharing on and off.

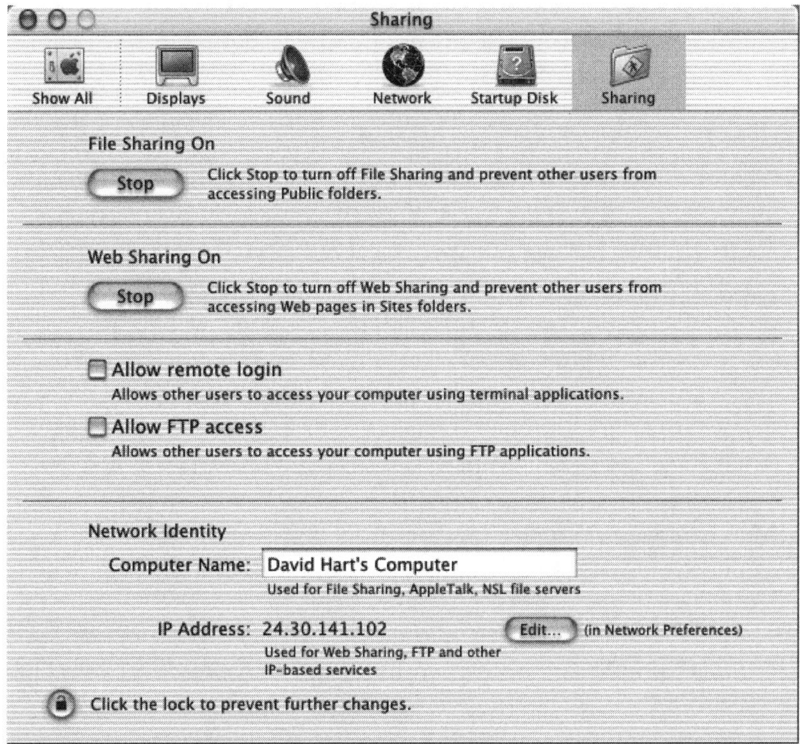

Figure 4-3. Mac OS X Sharing Preferences.

Mac OS X Setup Assistant

When you install Mac OS X, the installation program takes you through a Setup Assistant that helps you configure the vital settings for accessing the Internet and running as a multiuser computer. The Setup Assistant, which can be run only once (during the installation process), walks you through key steps and settings:

- Authenticating yourself as the administrator. Only a person who knows an administrator password can configure most of these settings.
- Setting up the host name, default router, AppleTalk name, IP address, and other basic network settings. You can choose to set these items manually or to set them automatically with your ISP's DHCP server.
- Establishing a NetInfo connection. NetInfo is a network-based database of information for your network that is used for managing the networks within larger organizations. If you are a solo user, you don't need to connect to a NetInfo server.
- Setting date, time, and location. The assistant lets you set your computer's time, date, and time zone.
- Setting automatic login. Although Mac OS X is a multiuser system, you can make it behave as if it were a single-user system and automatically log in at startup as a particular user. This isn't the most secure option—since to get access to your system, a person just has to shut down and restart it—but it can come in handy. If you need to be able to restart your system remotely and continue Web serving, for example, you may choose to have your system login automatically as the less privileged "Web" user.

The Domain Name System (DNS)

While computers prefer to deal with IP addresses that have numeric forms such as 132.249.202.135, humans have a much easier time remembering addresses such as *www.apple.com*. The DNS is the Internet's translator between numeric IP addresses and the text-based names we know and love. A very simplistic analogy is to think of the DNS as a huge table, with the complete list of domain names on the left-hand side and, on the right-hand side, the IP address corresponding to each domain name.

In fact, in the early days of the Internet, just such a table, called the *host table* and maintained by the Stanford Research Institute's Network Information Center, was used to keep track of the name-address mappings. Updates trickled in to Stanford, and every so often, network administrators would download the latest version of the host table to their local domain name servers.

Obviously, the manual host table system could not last long, and in 1984 the current DNS was put into place. The DNS has several key features that have allowed it to support the rapid growth of the Internet since the mid-1980s. First, no single organization is responsible for running it; the database is distributed among all sites that run DNS servers, including your ISP and possibly even you, if you are prepared to set up and maintain your own DNS server. (Because managing a domain name server is an art form unto itself, I do not recommend you try this at home, at least not to start.) Second, the DNS exists on many servers simultaneously, which prevents the entire Internet from crashing to its virtual knees if any one of the DNS servers fails. Table 4-8 has additional information on DNS.

Table 4-8. Domain Name Server Resources

Location	Description
www.isc.org/products/BIND	BIND is an implementation of the DNS protocols.
eeunix.ee.usm.maine.edu/guides/dns/dns.html	Comprehensive and easy to follow tutorial.
www.acmebw.com/askmrdns	Ask Mr. DNS, from Acme Byte and Wire.
www.menandmice.com/dnsplace	The DNS Place, from Men and Mice Software.
www.dns.net/dnsrd	DNS Resource Directory, maintained by András Salamon.
nic.merit.edu/internet/documents/rfc/rfc1034.txt *nic.merit.edu/internet/documents/rfc/rfc1035.txt*	The official DNS description and specification is laid out in RFCs 1034 and 1035.

Domain Name Space

To understand how the DNS works, you have to understand the *domain name space,* or the conceptual organization of domain names. The domain name space is organized hierarchically—that is, much like the file system on your Mac hard drive. In your file system, your hard drive icon points to the top-level folders and files. Inside those folders are more folders and files, and so on. In the DNS, the top-most domain is called the *root,* or sometimes referred to just as "." (the period character). The root is the starting point for the domain name hierarchy.

Below the root are the top-level domains (TLDs)—the suffixes at the end of all domain names. Figure 4-4 presents a graphic representation of the domain name space. The TLDs are classified in the DNS specifications as organizational and geographical, but in practice today there are three categories: restricted TLDs, generic TLDs (further abbreviated as gTLDs), and country code TLDs (or ccTLDs).

Restricted Top-Level Domains

All of the original organizational TLDs were assumed to be U.S. domains (an artifact of the Internet's U.S. lineage), and some organizational TLDs are still restricted to U.S. groups. The Internet's roots in the education, government, and military communities are evident in the four restricted TLDs:

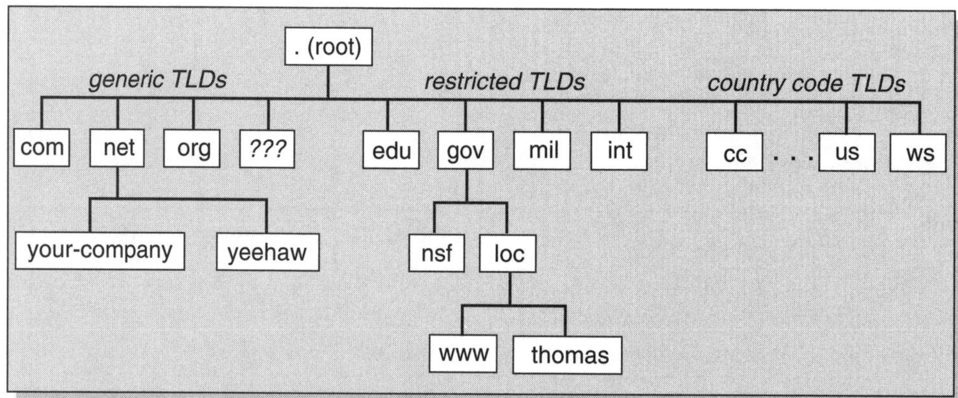

Figure 4-4. The Domain Name Space.

- *edu*—Limited to four-year colleges and universities, primarily in North America—for example, *www.gatech.edu* or *www.ucsd.edu*. Primary and secondary schools, community colleges, and technical and vocational schools in the United States are registered under the *.us* country code (see below). Network Solutions, Inc., administers the *.edu* domain.
- *gov*—Limited to agencies of the U.S. federal government—for example, *www.whitehouse.gov* or *www.uspto.gov*. The *.gov* domain is controlled by the U.S. government's General Services Administration.
- *int*—For use by international organizations, those established by international treaty—for example, *www.nato.int.* The *.int* domain is administered by the IANA.
- *mil*—For use by the U.S. military—for example, *www.army.mil,* which is now hosted on a Mac. The U.S. Department of Defense administers the *.mil* domain.

As the domain name space has evolved over the years, these restricted TLDs have not changed. The *.mil, .gov,* and *.int* domains are still tightly controlled, and *.edu* domains are still four-year colleges and universities and still predominantly North American.

Generic Top-Level Domains

The original DNS specification included three TLDs that had fewer restrictions on who could register a domain name. These are today commonly referred to as the generic top-level domains (gTLDs), and as this book was being written, there were plans in the works for adding to this list:

- *com*—Originally for use by U.S. commercial organizations.
- *net*—Originally designated for use by network providers.
- *org*—Originally for use by miscellaneous organizations, such as charities and other nonprofits that didn't fit in the other top-level domains.

You may have noticed that the word "originally" appears in each of the descriptions. In the same way that the monolithic host table evolved into the current DNS, the Internet has evolved from its military and educational roots to today's backbone of the commercial world. At the same time, the rules for assigning and registering domain names have evolved. The gTLDs have been the focus of the greatest change.

The changes in domain name practices resulted from the Internet's emergence as a commercial force, and its move from government to private control in the mid-1990s. Since 1979, Network Solutions, Inc., had been the sole registration point for the *.com, .org,* and *.net* top-level domains under a contract with the U.S. government to run the Internet Network Information Center (InterNIC), with IANA responsible for most other TLDs. As the network backbone was privatized, the registration of domain names also became a hot topic. The International Internet Ad Hoc Committee (IAHC) was formed in 1996 to settle the domain name issue, and the committee issued its report in February 1997.

The IAHC report recommended the current governance structure for the DNS and resulted in the establishment of a gTLD Memorandum of Understanding (gTLD-MoU). This memorandum of understanding is the international framework in which policies for the administration and enhancement of the Internet's Domain Name System are developed and implemented. Out of the gTLD-MoU has arisen the Internet Corporation for Assigned Numbers and Names (ICANN). (InterNIC still exists under the U.S. Department of Commerce, but only as a Web site that points visitors to the ICANN list of accredited registrars.)

ICANN does not register domain names itself but is responsible for selecting and accrediting domain name registrars, developing equitable dispute resolution for conflicts over rights to domain names, and adding new generic top-level domains to the DNS. This last task has stirred the most controversy.

Today, the domain name space is in flux. Dozens of ICANN-accredited registrars compete for domain name registrations. Just about anyone interested in registering a domain name can request a domain in any of the original gTLDs. However, because ICANN did not drastically alter the pricing structure for domains—competition has kept the cost at less than $100 to register a domain name—domain name speculation has become an unsanctioned result of deregulation. Several companies do business by registering domains at the official price and re-selling them to the highest bidder or acting as brokers for others who have registered potentially lucrative domain names. Competition for addresses has resulted in the near-saturation of the *.com* TLD, and to a lesser extent of the *.net* and *.org* domains.

ICANN's third mission, as indicated by the gTLD-MoU, is to recommend and add new gTLDs to address this saturation. In fact, the IAHC report suggested several additions—*.firm, .store, .web, .arts, .rec, .info,* and *.nom*—that generated a huge amount of controversy at the time.

ICANN announced in mid-2000 a plan for defining new TLDs by the beginning of 2001. The most interesting aspect of the plan may be that ICANN refrained from dictating what the new TLDs would be. Instead, ICANN solicited proposals from companies that wish to sponsor a TLD. (The cost of submitting such a proposal is a $50,000 nonrefundable fee.) In November 2000, ICANN announced the first new gTLDs to be selected. They include *.aero, .biz, .coop, .info, .museum, .name,* and *.pro*. Registration of domains within these new gTLDs should be possible early in 2001.

However, other unofficial solutions to the gTLD shortage have been promoted. Some smaller countries have made arrangements to allow their country code domains to be used as generic domains (see the next section). Other companies are today promoting long domain names—domain names with up to 63 characters. These long domain names are permitted by the DNS specification, but for most of the Internet's history, Network Solutions imposed a 23-character limit on domain names.

Country Code Top-Level Domains

Aside from the *.int* TLD explicitly reserved for organizations established by international treaty, the restricted TLDs and gTLDs started with the presumption that most domains would be in the United States.

The third class of TLDs identifies Internet domains around the world, using two-letter country codes to organize domains along political lines. The list of country codes, and hence the determination of what is and is not a country, is maintained by the ISO. IANA keeps track of the code listing along with the administrative and technical contacts for the country code top-level domains (ccTLDs). The ccTLDs are administered according to rules established by each country's designated network registry.

For example, the country code for the United States is *.us*, which is administered by the Information Sciences Institute at the University of Southern California (which, not coincidentally, is also the home of IANA). The *.us* domain is governed by RFC 1480. (An aside: although RFC actually stands for "Request for Comments," in practice you can translate it as "Internet specification.") Within the *.us* domain, the name structure primarily falls along state divisions, with three possible second-level domain designations:

- *State abbreviation*—Identified by the two-letter postal abbreviation—for example, *.me.us, .ga.us,* or *.pa.us.*
- *fed*—U.S. government agencies can also use the *.fed.us* domain, which is also administered by the General Services Administration.
- *dni*—"Distributed national institutes"—organizations that span state, regional, and other organizational boundaries and have distributed facilities—can register under the *.dni.us* domain.

Within the state-level domains, RFC 1480 defines another level of the hierarchy, with branches that focus on local and state government as well as the educational system. A state-level domain may have further subdomains based on locality names (cities or counties), schools (*.k12* for public and private K–12 schools, *.cc* for community colleges, or *.tec* for technical or vocational schools), libraries (*.lib*), state government (*.state*), or general (*.gen*). So, for example, the city of San Diego has its Web site at *www.ci.san-diego.ca.us* and the San Diego County Office of Education is at *www.sdcoe.k12.ca.us.* However, organizations in these categories may also use the other TLDs, as the California State Assembly does at *www.assembly.ca.gov.*

Outside of the *.us* domain, however, all bets are off. Some countries, such as the United Kingdom (*.uk*) and Australia (*.au*), use second-level domains to identify academic institutions (*.ac.uk* and *.edu.au*), companies (*.co.uk* and *.com.au*), and other entities. But many others have no such second-level organization.

In fact, the domains registered within some country codes have little to do with the originating country. Some smaller countries have made arrangements to allow their ccTLDs to be used as generic domains. The most common examples are *.cc*, *.nu*, and *.ws*, which nominally belong to the Cocos (Keeling) Islands, Niue, and Western Samoa, respectively. Table 4-9 lists some references to further information about the organizational and geographical TLDs.

DNS Architecture

The beauty of the DNS architecture is that it has been designed to handle an Internet with theoretically limitless growth and an evolving domain name space.

And let's not forget the day-to-day pressure: If the DNS were to disappear, the Internet would be broken. Obviously, if the DNS were centralized in any one place or on any one computer, it could not satisfy these requirements. To meet these demands, the DNS is a distributed system, constructed from many computers in many locations. Even if many of the individual computers go down, the DNS keeps right on going.

Table 4-9. DNS Governance

Location	Description
www.nic.gov	The General Services Administration controls registrations in the *.gov* and *.fed.us* TLDs.
www.nic.mil	The U.S. Department of Defense controls the *.mil* domain.
www.iana.org/int-dom/int.htm *www.iana.org/cctld/cctld.htm*	IANA controls the *.int* domain and maintains the list of country codes.
www.iahc.org	The IAHC proposed changes to handling the domain name space.
www.gtld-mou.org	The Generic Top-Level Domains Memorandum of Understanding was the result of the IAHC report.
www.icann.org	ICANN accredits domain name registrars, resolves disputes, and is responsible for new TLDs.
www.networksolutions.com	Network Solutions, Inc., is today an accredited registrar and also the official registrar for the *.edu* domain.
www.long-domain-names-register.com *www.internetdomainregistrars.com*	Long-Domain-Names-Register.com and Internet Domain Registrars are two registrars promoting domain names up to 63 characters long.
www.nic.us	The Information Sciences Institute administers the *.us* domain and delegates authority for state-level domains.
www.isi.edu/in-notes/rfc1480.txt	RFC 1480 defines how the *.us* domain is structured.
www.nic.cc *www.whats.nu* *www.worldsite.ws*	The *.cc, .nu,* and *.ws* country code TLDs are being promoted as generic TLDs.

The basic building block of the DNS is called a *DNS server.* In a nutshell, a DNS server has two parts: a *name server* and a *resolver.* The name server receives client requests for a particular host name and returns the IP address so the client's Web browser or other application can complete its request of the host. That is, the name server returns the IP address assigned to that host, if the server has that information stored away.

If the name server has never heard of the host name or domain in question, however, the client's request is passed to the resolver. The resolver asks for the necessary information from the root DNS server, which in turn refers the request to a server for the correct TLD. At the next DNS server, either the name server returns the information or the resolver asks the name server for the DNS server for the next-level domain. And so it goes, this so-called recursion, until a name server is found that can answer the request.

Table 4-10 includes some references to general information about the DNS architecture.

Guaranteeing a Resolution

The critical element to making the whole operation work, of course, is a guarantee that some name server somewhere will definitely have the answer to any given request. To make this guarantee, the DNS architecture places two requirements on every DNS server.

First, all resolvers have pointers to a domain name server for the root, which ensures that all domain name servers are connected. There are 13 of these root servers, so the DNS doesn't depend on any one machine. The root servers, named *A.root-servers.net* through *M.root-servers.net,* are located at several locations in the United States as well as in Europe and Japan.

Table 4-10. DNS Architecture

Location	Description
ftp://ftp.rs.internic.net/domain/named.root	A list of the DNS root servers.
www.wia.org/pub/rootserv.html	A map of the DNS root servers.
www.dns.net/dnsrd/rr.html	A listing of DNS resource records at the DNS Resource Directory.
www.isc.org/services/public/F-root-server.html	Information on root server F, operated by the Internet Software Consortium.

Second, every registered domain is required to have two domain name servers associated with it, usually a primary server and a secondary server. The primary server handles most requests, but if anything should happen to it, requests are directed to the secondary server. The network administrators for the domain maintain the primary server, while the secondary server checks for changes on the primary server every so often and copies the latest information. (A domain may also have two primary servers, but this requires that administrators maintain the data in each server separately.)

The primary and secondary servers are considered *authoritative* if they have complete information for the domains that they serve. That is, they are guaranteed to have IP address mappings for all the hosts within those domains. (A host, you'll recall, is an individual computer on the network.)

Technically, the slice of the domain name space over which a DNS server has authority is called a *zone*. In many cases, a zone may encompass an entire domain and have information on every host within *your-company.com,* for example. However, a domain such as *college.edu* might be broken down into a number of different subdomains, such as *cs.college.edu, physics.college.edu,* and others. For administrative reasons, the *cs.college.edu* subdomain or other departmental subdomains might be treated as separate zones with their own primary and secondary name servers. When a secondary server updates its information with data from its associated primary server, it is performing a *zone transfer*.

Caching

So far I've described two features that may not appear to be the most efficient way of handling DNS requests. First, every DNS server has to send out requests to provide IP mappings about hosts in any domain over which it doesn't have authority (which would be most of them). Second, all such requests go directly to a root server. You might be asking yourself: Doesn't this put a terrible load on all the DNS servers? Every resolver must be sending out messages almost constantly, the root servers must be swamped, and the name servers for busy hosts such as *www.yahoo.com* must be faced with millions of requests a day, much less the name servers for every other domain on the Internet.

The DNS architects recognized this potential limitation as well. To reduce the number of DNS requests flying around the Internet, local name servers can *cache*, or store temporary copies of, the results of previous requests. Therefore, the name server need only ask the resolver to resolve *www.yahoo.com* once. For later requests, the result is on hand locally. After a start-up period during which the cache is being filled, most common DNS requests are all handled directly by a client's local name server.

Cached information also helps with similar but not identical DNS queries. If a request comes along for *shopping.yahoo.com* and the DNS server has previously resolved *www.yahoo.com,* the cache already knows the name server to query about hosts in the *yahoo.com* domain. However, because the network situation can change with new hosts and updated configurations, cached information can become incorrect over time. Therefore, cached data also has a "time to live," after which it is deleted, or flushed, from the cache. At this point, the name server must consult the authoritative server again.

Resource Records

A name server stores the vital information about the hosts and other pieces of the DNS architecture in a set of resource records, which you can think of as similar to the records stored in a database table. There are nearly three dozen types of resource records defined by various DNS RFCs, but most DNS resource records that you will encounter belong to one of six types.

SOA (Start of Authority). The SOA record identifies a zone for which a name server has authoritative information. An SOA record has several pieces of data in addition to the domain name to which the record applies.

- MNAME: The primary name server for the zone.
- RNAME: The e-mail address of the person responsible for maintaining the data about the zone.
- SERIAL: A unique serial number that identifies the update version for the secondary server. The secondary server checks this value to determine if it has the latest information. The administrator or the DNS software should update this value whenever changes are made to information for which the name server is authoritative.
- REFRESH: The time interval (in seconds) after which the secondary server should check to see if any data on the primary server has changed and hence determine if a zone transfer should be done. A common value is 10 hours, or 36,000 seconds.

- RETRY: If, for some reason, the secondary server can't reach the primary server when it tries to Refresh, the Retry value specifies how long (in seconds) the secondary server should wait before trying to communicate with the primary server again. A common value is two hours, or 7,200 seconds.
- EXPIRE: If the secondary server cannot Refresh and the Retry attempts fail, the Expire time is the period (in seconds) after which the zone information on the secondary server is no longer considered to be authoritative. A common value is one week, or 604,800 seconds.
- MINIMUM: The Minimum field in an SOA record specifies the minimum "time to live" for zone data from this server. Other name servers can cache any data from this server for at least this many seconds, unless a particular resource record overrides this value. A common value is one day, or 86,400 seconds.

A (Address). Address records are the bread and butter of a name server. These are the resource records that map a host name to an IP address.

CNAME (Canonical Name). The name is somewhat counterintuitive, but a CNAME record represents an alias. The CNAME record maps an alias name to a host name for which there is an Address record. For example, the name *www.your-company.com* may have a CNAME record that maps it to a host name such as *blackbox.your-company.com.* Aliases make it easier to move services such as Web servers to other hosts. A CNAME record might also map *ftp.your-company.com* to the same host as *www.your-company.com*, so these services can share hardware but be identified by mnemonic names.

MX (Mail Exchange). An MX record provides the name of a mail server for a particular domain. In addition to the domain name and a mail server for that domain, the record also includes a preference. If a domain has more than one mail exchange record, first priority is given to the mail exchange server with the lowest preference value.

NS (Name Server). An NS record lists the authoritative name servers for a domain or subdomain.

PTR (Pointer). PTR records allow the DNS to use IP addresses to look up domain names. Such a record has a pointer name and its corresponding domain name. This reverse mapping is used, for example, by Web log analysis tools for looking up host names from the IP addresses stored in the log file.

PTR records use a special domain, *.in-addr.arpa,* to keep track of this reverse mapping. A host with an IP address of 132.249.202.135 will be represented as *135.202.249.132.in-addr.arpa.* You'll notice that the IP address components are reversed in the *.in-addr.arpa* domain; from left to right, the components are ordered from most specific to least specific. This allows a DNS server to store PTR records for and perform reverse-mapping on network zones. For example, while *135.202.249.132.in-addr.arpa* reverse-maps to a particular host, a pointer name of *132.in-addr.arpa* reverse-maps to a gateway for all hosts that have *132* as the first component of their IP addresses.

Your Own DNS Server

Table 4-11 lists several of the DNS software options for the Mac OS. The Berkeley Internet Named Domain (BIND) domain name server software, the most common DNS server on the Web, is included with the iTools suite from Tenon Intersystems and with Mac OS X Server from Apple. Both iTools and Mac OS X Server include BIND and a less imposing interface than the standard UNIX command-line interface.

QuickDNS Pro is DNS server software written for the Mac OS. As such, it has a graphical user interface and is generally easier to use than BIND, while delivering comparable performance. Of the other Mac options, MacDNS and NonSequitur have not been updated in several years, and native Mac OS X versions may not be developed. The DNS servers included in the various Vicomsoft products are intended primarily for use on local-area networks.

In my judgment, if you plan to make serious demands of your DNS server, QuickDNS Pro has the edge for ease of use, and it has performance comparable to BIND. QuickDNS Pro also has the bonus of including Men and Mice's DNS Expert software for testing your DNS configuration. BIND has the edge in price (free) and in its wide installation on the Internet. If you're using Mac OS X Server or Tenon's iTools, you have both BIND and the benefit of a friendlier user interface. However, regardless of the DNS software you choose, you should not take the responsibility of running your DNS service lightly because if your DNS server is misconfigured or if it crashes, your Web server is inaccessible.

For most home and small office situations, I recommend that you take advantage of the DNS management from your ISP, generally included as a basic service. At the very least, have your secondary DNS server at another location. For providing DNS caching and DNS service for hosts on a small network, the DNS servers included with the Vicomsoft products listed in Table 4-11 will suffice. And as with every other Internet service, another option is to outsource your DNS needs to a DNS provider (see below).

Table 4-11. Mac OS X DNS Software

Location	Description
www.isc.org/products/BIND	Berkeley Internet Named Domain (BIND), free from the Internet Software Consortium.
www.menandmice.com	DNS Expert, from Men and Mice Software, detects DNS configuration errors.
asu.info.apple.com/swupdates.nsf/artnum/n11264	MacDNS, free software from Apple. Last updated in 1996 for Mac OS 7.5.3.
www.gross.net/sw/nonsequitur	NonSequitur, free DNS software for Classic Mac OS from Stephan Gross.
www.menandmice.com	QuickDNS Pro, from Men and Mice Software, is the leading Mac DNS software.
www.vicomsoft.com	SurfDoubler, SoftRouter, and Internet Gateway from Vicomsoft Technologies have built-in DNS servers for local-area networks.

QuickDNS Pro

QuickDNS Pro from Men and Mice Software of Reykjavik, Iceland, is the leading commercial DNS software for the Mac, and version 3 will be available for Mac OS X. Under the Classic Mac OS, QuickDNS Pro boasts performance comparable to BIND on UNIX systems, so its performance on Mac OS X should remain competitive to BIND.

The advantages of QuickDNS Pro over BIND include QuickDNS Pro's graphical interface and the technical support that accompanies the software. In addition, QuickDNS Pro comes with DNS Expert, a diagnostic tool from Men and Mice. DNS Expert can verify your DNS setup for reliability and correctness and systematically investigate any DNS problem and suggest solutions.

Version 3 of QuickDNS Pro also supports fault tolerance and load balancing for any Mac OS X–based Web server. (These options are available only for WebSTAR in version 2.*x*.) Load balancing lets two or more computers host your site while QuickDNS Pro distributes requests among the available servers. With fault tolerance, QuickDNS Pro removes nonresponding Web servers from the server pool and adds them back to the pool when they become available. Fault tolerance and load balancing are important for sites that must be available 24/7.

Outsourcing DNS Services

If you don't want to run your own DNS server and for some reason your ISP does not provide you with adequate DNS services, there are a number of options for outsourcing this service to a third party. Even if you enjoy the challenge of running your own DNS server, there are a few reasons you might want to look to a third-party provider.

For greater fault tolerance, you might want your secondary server located at another site—not a bad idea in any case. Perhaps you need MX records for a virtual domain on your Web server. You might have more frequent DNS changes than your ISP is able or willing to keep up with. You might want to have a DNS server outside your organization's firewall. If your site is outside of North America, you might benefit from having DNS services closer to the Internet backbones in the United States.

Table 4-12 lists a few DNS service providers, including one free option, the Public DNS Service provided by the Granite Canyon Group. In addition, you can check with the companies that provide DNS service to users with dynamic IP addresses (listed in Table 4-4). Even if you have static IP addresses, they can still provide your DNS service needs.

Table 4-12. DNS Service Providers

Location	Description
soa.granitecanyon.com	The Public DNS Service, a free service from Granite Canyon Group, LLC.
www.easydns.com	Commercial DNS services from easyDNS Technologies, Inc.
www.dnswiz.com	Commercial DNS services from DNS Wizard Corporation.

CHAPTER 5

SYSTEM MAINTENANCE

It's now time to consider the mundane yet important tasks of server maintenance, management, and security. I purposely inserted this chapter just as your head is full of ideas for what you want to serve to whom and how, but before I start to describe how to put your Web server online. This may be the last chance I have to impress upon you the importance of these mundane tasks to ensuring that your Web server is available continuously. Your server is the face your organization presents to the world, and tasks that you might postpone on your personal Macintosh take on a new urgency. If your server goes down, so does your world presence.

This chapter discusses some of the basic steps for making sure your Macintosh server stays clean and healthy. First, we introduce you to basic system maintenance, such as performing regular backups and protecting your system against virus infection. Then we turn to system management for a computer that you want to be "always on" if you are not even in the same city. Finally, we discuss how best to make your Mac OS X server a secure one.

BASIC SYSTEM MAINTENANCE

System maintenance for a Macintosh computer is not a complex undertaking. The most difficult part is *adhering* to a maintenance schedule that you establish. As with your health, the best medicine for a computer system is preventive maintenance—stopping problems before they occur. While you may not fend off everything that might go wrong, recovering from a mishap will be much easier.

Back Up, Back Up, Back Up

My first recommendation should go without saying, but I'll say it anyway. Back up your data on a regular basis—as often as the data on your server changes, which is probably every day. With daily backups of the latest information on your server, you will be able to recover from the worst possible system disasters. Even if the hard drive crashes and the motherboard melts down on your server system, you can recover by restoring your server on a new computer. With daily backups, the worst situation is to lose the changes made in the last 24 hours.

If you are part of a large organization, the systems administration group may already handle this chore for you. A Web hosting company may also provide this service. If you must do this yourself, the leading backup software for the Macintosh is Dantz Development's Retrospect. This highly rated package can back up a network of Macintosh and Windows 98/NT systems. Table 5-1 points you to software and resources for backing up your Macintosh. Many of these applications were not available for the Mac OS X public beta because of the beta's limited support for peripherals. You'll see many of them following the release of Mac OS X final.

You might also consider whether you want to provide another sort of backup—for your electrical power. If you live in an area with frequent power outages or if the availability of your data is of utmost concern, you may want to look into an uninterruptible power supply, which will keep your server running when the lights go out.

A Maintenance Routine

Beyond keeping a regular backup, there are a number of Mac OS X "tune-ups" you should perform on a regular basis throughout the year. Many of these main-

Table 5-1. Macintosh Backup Software and Services

Location	Description
www.backjack.com	BackJack, an online Macintosh backup service from Synectics Business Solutions, Inc.
members.aol.com/realip	Drag'nBack, shareware by Enterprise Software.
www.asdsoft.com	Personal Backup, commercial software from ASD Software.
www.qdea.com	Synchronize! and Synchronize Pro! synchronization, mirroring, and backup software from Qdea.
www.reduxsw.com	Redux, freeware from Redux Software.
www.dantz.com	Retrospect and Retrospect Express, commercial software from Dantz Development Corporation.
www.acts.org/~roland/thanks	SimpleBackup, $5 shareware from Roland Gustafsson.
www.tri-edre.com	Tri-Backup, commercial software from Tri-Edre Software.
www.apcc.com	Uninterruptible power supplies from American Power Conversion.

tenance tasks apply regardless of whether your server is running Mac OS X, older versions of the Mac OS, Windows NT, or UNIX.

The majority of these tasks involve keeping your hard drive performance at its optimum level. The hard drive is the component of any computer with the most delicate mechanical parts while also storing your most valuable assets—the data on your server. Let's look at these tasks according to how often you might consider putting them on your calendar.

Daily. Back up, back up, back up. Did I mention backups?

Monthly. Use a Mac OS X disk utility to check your disk for damaged or missing files. If your file system doesn't see a lot of changes—for example, your server is a dedicated machine, you don't install any new software, and visitors to your site don't cause many new files to be created—you can probably get away with performing this step less often.

You should also make a point of checking for any security updates to Mac OS X and checking for updates to your server applications at least monthly, if not more frequently.

Quarterly. Optimize your hard disk and free up disk space. Your hard drive performance can affect the performance of your Web server, so it pays to take the time to defragment your hard disk every once in a while. If you have database files that see a lot of activity, this will help keep them in shape, too.

Semiannually. Scan for bad blocks. A low-level scan of your hard drive will help you keep ahead of imperfections that can creep into a hard drive that gets ridden hard and put away wet, as might be the case with an active Web server.

Annually. Update your system, driver, and server software. You have to analyze the trade-offs here. If your server is stable and running smoothly, don't run the risk of introducing conflicts with continuous minor updates. On the other hand, you might miss out on performance and stability gains if you never update your software. Of course, you should always be on the lookout for security-related updates and install them as they become available.

For more details on these suggestions, see the December 1997 *MacWorld* article "Timely Mac Tune-ups" by John Rizzo. Although this article is several years old and applies primarily to the Classic Mac OS, most of the advice has stood the test of time. Table 5-2 points you to software utility packages for performing most of these tasks in Mac OS X.

Table 5-2. Macintosh Maintenance Routine

Location	Description
www.alsoft.com	DiskWarrior and other system maintenance tools from Alsoft.
www.symantec.com/nu	Norton Utilities from Symantec.
www.micromat.com	TechTool Pro from Micromat, Inc.
macworld.zdnet.com/1997/12/features/4068.html	"Timely Mac Tune-ups" by John Rizzo, *MacWorld,* December 1997.

Server Management

In addition to maintaining your Macintosh itself, you will want to ensure that your server software is occasionally cleaned up, updated, and generally still working. First, you may want to install remote control software on your server so you can make changes without having to physically take yourself to the server.

Next, you may want to automate the process of making sure the files on your public site match the files you think should be there from your development site. Finally, I'll talk about a few tools that make sure your server software itself is actually running and automatically restart your server if necessary.

Remote Control

There are two ways to manage your server. The first is to sit down in front of its monitor and keyboard and perform the necessary administration and configuration tasks. These tasks range from installing new software and upgrading existing software to changing the settings of the various applications running on your Web server. This tried-and-true method of server administration works well, but it has its limits.

Perhaps your server is not conveniently located in your office, but in a separate machine room. Or perhaps a server in your office building needs attention while you're at home for the evening. Or, in the case of server co-location, your server may be in an entirely different city or state. Because of these common situations, many server applications now provide interfaces for Web-based administration; all configuration options can be changed through a Web form.

But in many cases, particularly in the case of server co-location, you may need to do more than change a few settings. You may want to be virtually sitting in front of your server to install a new software package, restart the server, or perform other low-level tasks. For these situations, you need remote control software. Table 5-3 lists the two options I'm aware of—the widely used Timbuktu Pro from Netopia and the lesser known RIMS Admin from CyberKare Technologies. Figure 5-1 shows a screen shot from the Mac OS X version of Timbuktu Pro.

Table 5-3. Remote Control Software

Location	Description
www.cyberkare.com	RIMS Admin, commercial remote control software from CyberKare Technologies, Inc.
www.timbuktupro.com	Timbuktu Pro from Netopia is the leading remote operation software tools for the Macintosh.

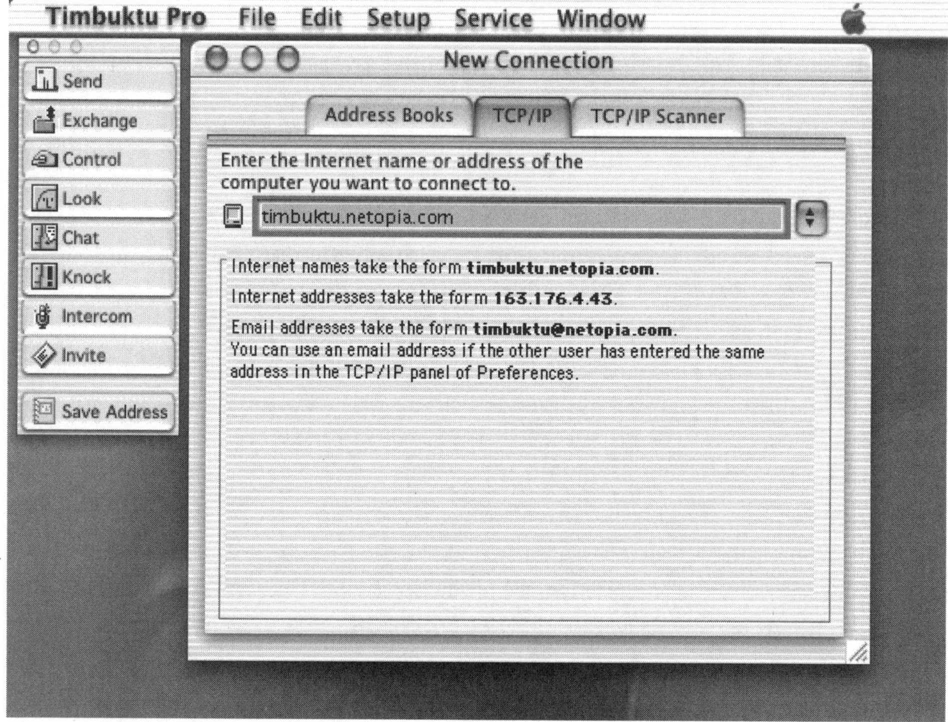

Figure 5-1. Timbuktu Pro for Mac OS X from Netopia.

File Synchronization

If you depend on your server as the lifeblood of your business, you don't want to use it to experiment with untested enhancements. In such cases, you should have a separate machine on which you'll develop and test changes to your site. Once new components are working, you'll want to transfer the latest version to your Web server. It's critical that every new or changed file on your development server gets moved to your production server when you roll out the updates.

What you need is *file synchronization,* a feature often built into programs that must shuttle files between computers, such as remote control and backup software. For example, the Timbuktu Pro remote control software provides this capability, as do Qdea's Synchronize and Synchronize Pro and ASD Software's Personal Backup. Such tools are also useful to anyone who works with different computers at the office and on the road. Check for synchronization features in the remote control software and backup software listed in Tables 5-1 and 5-3.

Mirroring

File synchronization software can also be used to establish mirrors of your Web site. *Mirroring* your site means maintaining a duplicate copy of your site on another server. This could be used within an organization to provide redundancy so that in the event that one system fails, your information would still be available from the other.

You can also think about mirroring to reach a global audience. In a perfect Internet world, global links would be instantaneous; however, in reality, international links are often slow. It is helpful for European users, for example, to be able to get information from a Europe-based server even though the primary server is in the United States. Having a European mirror means European visitors have fast, successful access, rather than frustrating and slow transatlantic downloads. Conversely, if the source of information is in Europe, it is helpful for U.S. users of that information to get it from a mirror site in the United States.

The mirror software works like this. At predetermined times, usually based on how rapidly the information on the server changes, the synchronization software on the primary server connects to each mirror server, compares modification dates for the folder structure and file contents against the server, and distributes any new or updated files and folders. The software optionally also deletes the files on the mirror sites that have been deleted from the server.

Version Control Systems

File synchronization and remote control software work well if only one person—or a very organized and careful small group of people—is responsible for placing files on your Web server. However, for the complex sites with large development teams that have become much more common, it often makes sense to have some software-based assistance to ensure that all the files and all the developers stay in sync.

For the sake of this discussion, I'll call this type of software a *version control system.* There are various forms of version control systems; commercial applications can be quite expensive. On the other hand, there are two open-source, freely available options. The Concurrent Versions System (CVS) is a client-server system most commonly used for programming projects, but nothing prevents it from being used for developing Web sites. The CVS server and various clients should become available for Mac OS X, since the server runs on most UNIX variants and client are available for most platforms.

The second option is Web-based Distributed Authoring and Versioning, or WebDAV. WebDAV is a set of extensions to the HTTP protocol that allows users to collaboratively edit and manage files on remote Web servers. For Mac OS X systems, WebDAV has several advantages. First, there is at least one WebDAV client for Mac OS X, called Goliath, and the latest versions of the popular Adobe GoLive and Macromedia Dreamweaver Web development tools let you interact with WebDAV servers. Second, with the mod_dav module for Apache, any Apache server can be turned into a WebDAV server. In fact, with only a few minor changes, the Apache configuration included with Mac OS X can be turned into a WebDAV server (see Chapter 7). Table 5-4 has links to more information on CVS and WebDAV.

Crash Recovery

If a server crash means that someone in your office—maybe you—has to come in evenings or weekends at a moment's notice to restart the system, you may want to invest in a monitor that watches for system crashes or applications that quit unexpectedly. These software monitors or hardware peripherals use various tricks to make sure your server stays running. There are a number of options available for Mac Web servers; most cost no more than $100. The investment would probably pay for itself the first time you avoid driving across town to restart after a crash. Table 5-5 lists a few of these tools.

Table 5-4. Version Control Systems for Mac OS X

Location	Description
www.webdav.org	WebDAV Resources by Greg Stein.
www.ics.uci.edu/pub/ietf/webdav	IETF WebDAV Working Group.
www.webdav.org/goliath	Goliath WebDAV client by Thomas Bednarz.
www.cvshome.org	Concurrent Versions System home page.

Table 5-5. Crash Recovery Tools

Location	Description
www.vl-brabant.be/mac	AutoBoot and Keep it Up, shareware software monitors from Karl Pottie.
www.sophisticated.com	Kick-off! (USB-attached) and Rebound! (ADB-attached) hardware monitors from Sophisticated Circuits.
www.neuronsys.com	MacCoach, an ADB-attached hardware monitor from Neuron Data Systems.
www.maxum.com/PageSentry	PageSentry by Maxum Development. Uses real HTTP, FTP, SMTP, DNS, and Telnet client services to test the server for crashes.
www.sophisticated.com	PowerKey Pro by Sophisticated Circuits. An "intelligent" power strip with the ability to restart a machine or a crashed application.
www.intellisw.com	Server Sentinel, a shareware software monitor from Intelli Innovations, Inc.
www.sentman.com/whistleblower	Whistle Blower by James Sentman, shareware server monitoring and restart utility for the Macintosh.

Software Monitors. Software monitors are utilities that run on your server or another computer to confirm that the server is still serving. AutoBoot and Keep It Up are two shareware system extensions from Belgium's Karl Pottie. AutoBoot restarts your Mac when the system freezes, and Keep It Up performs a restart when an application quits unexpectedly. Server Sentinel from Intelli Innovations and Whistle Blower from James Sentman (see Figure 5-2) check your servers at specified intervals, and if a server check fails, they can send e-mail or alphanumeric pages, run AppleScripts to open applications, and reset crashed computers. Page Sentry and Page Sentry Pro from Maxum Development use HTTP, FTP, and other high-level protocols to make sure your server is accessible. If the server fails, PageSentry Notifiers can send e-mail or an alphanumeric page or restart your server with PowerKey Pro.

Hardware Monitors. Hardware monitors are small devices that attach to your Mac, along with associated software, that can even perform a hard reboot when your server crashes. MacCoach from Holland's Neuron Data Systems and

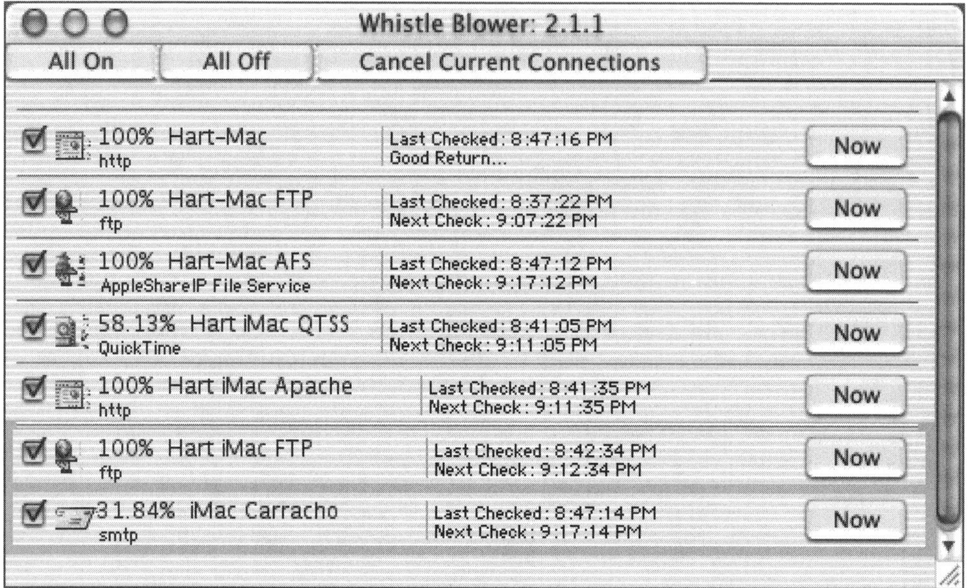

Figure 5-2. The Whistle Blower Server Monitor from James Sentman.

Rebound! from Sophisticated Circuits attach to a Mac's Apple Desktop Bus (ADB) port and will restart a crashed Mac by cycling the power on and off, perform a Finder restart if an application crashes, or generate a crash log to record crashes or scheduled restarts.

The PowerKey Pro hardware monitors from Sophisticated Circuits are a little different. These ADB-attached devices are "intelligent" power strips and surge protectors that let you remotely restart or shut down your server or applications. In addition to the standard crash recovery features, PowerKey Pro will even let you restart your Macintosh by sending it a signal via the ringing of your telephone.

If you're an iMac or G4 owner, you may have noticed one small problem with the hardware monitors listed so far: they all require Macs with ADB ports. ADB ports were standard connections for beige Macintosh systems and are still included in blue-and-white Power Mac G3 towers, but they have been phased out in iMacs and in graphite G4 towers. To address this omission, Sophisticated Circuits has developed a USB-attached hardware monitor called Kick-off! Other USB-attached devices are sure to follow.

Mac OS X Security

Because of its UNIX roots, Mac OS X introduces a few unknowns as far as security goes. I expect that it will be more secure than Windows or UNIX out of the box, but Mac webmasters making the switch to Mac OS X will have to pay close attention to security news and updates for the system.

One of the features of the classic Mac OS that made it secure was that it does not have a command-line interface and does not include much of the high-level Internet software common to UNIX platforms—FTP, sendmail, and other utilities. However, Mac OS X changes all that. Mac OS X has a command-line interface and includes Web serving, FTP file sharing, and telnet connections as part of the basic installation, although by default these services are turned off. Even so, the ability to provide Web, FTP, and other capabilities means a greater risk of security breaches.

General Security Tips

The scope of this book does not allow coverage of Mac OS X Internet security in great detail; however, most security tips apply to any operating system. Here are a few rules of thumb. Following these tips will help you avoid leaving out giant welcome mats to would-be intruders.

- Perhaps the most important piece of advice is to keep your machine locked up. At many large organizations and universities, the most common security risk is computer theft. Make sure your server is in a secured room with access restricted to those employees responsible for its maintenance.
- If their software is configured properly, Internet servers do not have to be susceptible to unwanted intrusions. If you read nothing else, read the security sections of the documentation that accompanies your software.
- With Mac OS X, as with other operating systems, turn off any network services that you do not need or use. Disable anonymous or guest logins unless you need them. If you need to provide anonymous FTP, pay close attention to your configuration. As with your physical well-

being, the best security protection is preventive—don't leave any simple security holes open.

- Share only a small portion of your file system as your FTP archive or Web site, and verify that access privileges are set correctly. Do not, for goodness' sake, give access to the system files. This stricture applies not only to Mac OS X File Sharing, but also to any other security privileges within a server application.
- One of the most often overlooked security measures is your password. Don't give your password out and don't use an obvious password. Obvious passwords include your user name, real name, birthday, or initials; your husband's, wife's, girlfriend's, pet's, or machine's name; your car license plate, make, or model; any common identification number; any of the above backwards; or any word from a dictionary (especially an electronic dictionary). Good passwords are nonsense words or the initials from a common saying. Including numeric characters helps. For example, "Two peas in a pod" becomes a password of "2piap."
- Security risks increase as you add greater functionality and interactivity to your server; you must decide where the risk exceeds the benefits of added features. If you have doubts about any piece of software, don't run it. The creators have done their best to make it secure, but if that's not good enough for the security you need, don't use it.

Apple has taken several precautions to ensure that Mac OS X has the maximum security in place right out of the box. By default, all network services are turned off, and only the administrator can turn them on. Other users cannot turn on the telnet server, for example.

With all the network services turned off, Mac OS X is as secure as it gets. However, once you begin establishing your Web server, you begin to increase the possibility of opening up security problems through the various Internet applications, such as your Web server, mail server, FTP server, and so on. While Apple and third-party developers will have done everything to ensure that these applications are secure, you should regularly check for security updates to the applications you use.

Firewalls

For that extra level of security, you might consider adding a firewall to your server. A firewall, which can be either a software application or a physical device, acts as a gatekeeper for your computer. The firewall intercepts all incoming traffic and adds a layer of protection to active server ports. If you run Dantz Development's Retrospect, for example, you can specify that your computer will only accept incoming traffic on Retrospect's port from a particular IP address—the IP address of your Retrospect server. A firewall will also let you deny requests from particular IP addresses, which can be helpful if you need to block denial-of-service attacks.

You may want to set up a firewall on the network to prevent users from outside your network from accessing the server's administration port in case they are able to guess your administrator password. Firewalls can also log accesses. Then you know if someone's trying to hack in, and, more importantly, if they succeed (for instance, through password guessing). Firewall software can also record requests that are made of inactive ports. However, inactive ports—ports with no software listening for incoming traffic—cannot be used to gain access to your computer.

Firewalls come in both hardware and software form. Hardware firewalls are usually built into network routers or bridges, and many will work with Mac systems. Firewall software can be a less expensive option, but these programs are operating system specific. Table 5-6 lists several Mac software tools that provide firewalls.

Table 5-6. Mac OS X Firewall Software

Location	Description
www.opendoor.com/doorstop	DoorStop Personal and Server, from Open Door Networks.
www.intego.com/netbarrier	NetBarrier, from Intego, Inc.
www.symantec.com	Norton Personal Firewall from Symantec Corp.
www.sustworks.com	IPNetSentry from Sustainable Softworks, Inc.
www.vicomsoft.com	SurfDoubler, Softrouter, and Vicomsoft Internet Gateway from Vicomsoft include firewall capabilities.

Further Information

For further information on general Internet security, you may want to visit the sources listed in Table 5-7. Throughout the rest of the book, I will discuss security aspects of various Web services, rather than trying to have the final word on security here. Look for Web server security issues in Chapter 7 and e-commerce security in Chapter 13.

Table 5-7. Additional Security Information

Location	Description
www.w3.org/Security/Faq	The W3C security FAQ.
www.faqs.org/faqs/computer-security	Frequently asked questions from computer security news groups.
www.cert.org	The CERT Coordination Center at Carnegie Mellon University is the national organization that responds to computer security issues.
web.mit.edu/network/ietf/sa	The Security Area of the Internet Engineering Task Force.

CHAPTER 6

CLIENT SOFTWARE

Knowing how to use the basic Internet software clients—including software for Web browsing, e-mail, and other services—is a prerequisite to setting up your Web server since you will need to download server software and test the functioning of the server. Most information about the Internet, both in books and online, covers client software. This chapter presents a concise summary of installing and using Mac OS X client software and points you to the best sources of additional information.

The chapter begins with a discussion of how to install and configure a couple of the most popular Web browsers and then some FTP and e-mail clients. But wait, there's more! You still need tools and utilities for viewing some graphics and multimedia files. Finally, you may also want to have software for reading newsgroups and participating in Internet chats, either for testing services you provide or for keeping up to date on relevant Web and Internet updates, alerts, and announcements.

I recommend you follow this order of client software installation. A Web browser is the most vital component of your client software toolbox. With it, you can download other software as necessary. As a webmaster, you also need e-mail for communicating with your ISP and members of your Web audience. And an FTP client is usually the easiest tool for maintaining the information on your Web server.

For the sake of simplicity, we'll assume that you already have at least an ISP for connecting to the Internet, browsing the Web, and exchanging e-mail.

WEB BROWSERS

Since you bought this book to learn how to set up an Internet server, chances are that you have some experience with using the Web and other Internet services. If you already have an account with an ISP, you probably also have at least a Web browser installed, but you may want to refer to this section to configure and upgrade your software. For the purposes of this book, a Web browser is client software that can connect to Web servers and receive information in return. Within this simple definition, there are two classes of browser: text-oriented and graphical.

Text-Oriented Browsers. Text-oriented browsers are of interest mainly, but not entirely, from a historical perspective. In the Mac world especially, text-oriented browsers may seem an anachronism since the Mac has never used a text-based interface. For the Mac, WannaBe and Lynx are text-only browsers. Why even consider a text-only browser on a Mac? Speed is one reason people choose text-only browsers. If you don't have to download graphics, Web pages download quickly. Another possible reason: Visually impaired Web surfers can take advantage of Apple's PlainTalk software to read the text downloaded from Web pages. With the continued expansion of the Web to wireless handheld devices, text-focused browsers are once again coming into their own.

Graphical Browsers. Graphical browsers, as the category name implies, support graphics, sound, video, and other applications, and they are the most common Web clients. NCSA Mosaic, developed at the National Center for Supercomputing Applications (NCSA), was the first popular graphical Web browser and was responsible for shifting the Internet revolution into high gear. Netscape Navigator, from Netscape Communications, Inc., evolved out of Mosaic and grew to be the dominant Web browser in a few months. Through plug-ins and programming languages, graphical browsers support not only browsing 2-D graphics, but also running Web-served software on the client. Java-capable browsers can download pieces of code, called applets, from the server and execute them on the client.

In this section, I'll cover how to install and configure two Web browsers—Microsoft Internet Explorer and iCab. At the time this book was being written, Netscape Communicator remains a popular browser on the Mac platform, but it was not available for the Mac OS X public beta or I would have shown how it worked as well. Installing more than one Web browser on your development system is recommended, particularly if you are using high-end Web functions such as JavaScript or Java, since Web pages you develop may not work or look the same in different browsers. You will want to make sure the contents of your Web pages are fully decipherable.

Helper Applications and Plug-ins

As I mentioned in Chapter 3, no Web browser or any single application can be expected to handle every file format and MIME type that you might encounter on the Web. To deal with the variety of file types, Web browsers use helper applications and plug-ins.

A *helper application* is a separate application invoked by a Web browser to handle a particular MIME type. Helper applications extend the functionality of a Web browser since they interpret information that could not be interpreted directly by the browser. A helper application generally appears as a separate window, and beyond the initial loading of the file, there is not necessarily any communication between browser and helper.

Having introduced helper applications, I must also mention *plug-ins*. A plug-in allows a Web browser to handle additional file types, but unlike a helper application, the plug-in is tightly integrated into the Web browser. The file in question will be displayed or otherwise handled within the browser window. While not advanced at this point in time, the opportunity exists for a variety of plug-ins to communicate with each other under the control of the browser.

For both helper applications and plug-ins to work, the browser must be configured with appropriate MIME type mappings—which file extensions indicate a particular MIME type and how to deal with files of this type. If a Web page requires a particular helper application or plug-in to view that page or to view files available for download from that site, the page should also include links to the necessary software. The most widely used helper applications and plug-ins will often configure the browser automatically when you install them.

Choosing a Browser

A Web browser offers the simplest way to download the software for your Web server and to view your own Web documents. In theory, you do not need to view your own documents before serving them, but in practice it's crazy to serve something you have not viewed and tested yourself. Even when using a What You See Is What You Get (WYSIWYG) Web page editor, your first attempts at creating Web pages will generally be What You See Is Not What You Want. Different browsers on different platforms with different preference settings will interpret the HTML generated by the editor in slightly different ways.

Table 6-1 lists most available browsers for the Mac OS, and the Mac OS X installation CD-ROM includes Microsoft Internet Explorer. On the whole, you'll do fine selecting any browser from this list as long as you are aware of its limitations. They are all fine pieces of software. In addition to Internet Explorer, OmniWeb from OmniGroup and iCab by Alexander Clauss and the iCab Company had beta versions available for the Mac OS X public beta.

The BrowserWatch Web site, also listed in Table 6-1, contains statistics that give you some idea about the popularity of different Web browsers. The sample is limited to the browsers used to view the BrowserWatch Web pages. Based on BrowserWatch statistics at the time of writing, Microsoft Internet Explorer was being used by almost 59 percent of BrowserWatch visitors. Netscape Navigator had just more than 28 percent.

At my own Web server, which I've been running for three years, the balance is still tilted toward Internet Explorer, but with a slightly higher ratio of Navigator users. In statistics for the past year (February 2000 through February 2001), Netscape Navigator versions are used by 24 percent of visitors, while Microsoft Internet Explorer versions are used by about 36 percent of visitors. (About 300 other unique user agents, including search engine crawlers, are responsible for the other 40 percent of hits. Most of these are each responsible for fewer than 0.10 percent of the hits.)

Table 6-1. Mac OS Web Browsers

Location	Web Browser
browserwatch.internet.com	BrowserWatch tracks Web browser development and usage statistics.
www.icab.de	iCab, a browser from Alexander Clauss and iCab Company.
www.microsoft.com/mac/ie	Internet Explorer, free software from Microsoft.
lynx.browser.org *www.lirmm.fr/~gutkneco/maclynx*	Lynx and MacLynx, freeware text-only browsers from the Lynx group.
www.mozilla.org	Mozilla open-source browser from the Mozilla Organization.
home.netscape.com/browsers	Netscape Communicator and Navigator, free software from Netscape Communications.
www.omnigroup.com/products/omniweb	OmniWeb, a commercial Mac OS X–native Web browser from OmniGroup. Free to first user at a site; fees for site licenses.
www.opera.com	Opera, a commercial cross-platform browser effort from Opera Software.
mindstory.com/wb2	WannaBe Web Browser, a free text-only browser by David T. Pierson.
developer.webtv.net	WebTV Viewer is free software that lets Web developers see how WebTV will display their sites.

Communicator versus Internet Explorer

I plan to avoid becoming a partisan in the religious browser war by not recommending a particular browser. Both the Microsoft and Netscape browsers work well, but neither is perfect. On the other hand, I've used both and have developed some opinions and will mention a few pros and cons of each.

Of course, there's the option of using an "alternative" browser, such as iCab or Opera. Both have most of the features you'll need for Web surfing, but for casual users, I still have to recommend either Communicator or Internet Explorer. Using iCab or Opera, you may encounter situations in which you have to use Communicator or Internet Explorer because a site takes advantage of features unique to those browsers. You can argue whether the sites should, but the fact remains that some do.

A caveat: I have based the comparisons here on Netscape Communicator 4.7 and 6.0 for Mac OS 9 because Communicator was not available for Mac OS X during the public beta release. Without any further information from Netscape, I made the assumption that a Carbonized version of Communicator—with features equivalent to the Classic Mac OS version—would be made available at least in time for the final release of Mac OS X. At the very least, Communicator will run in Mac OS X's Classic environment.

Security: Advantage Communicator. For certain users, Navigator has a significant advantage over Internet Explorer in security, and at least one feature for which Internet Explorer has no workaround. Unlike the Mac version of Internet Explorer, Navigator will allow you to accept security certificates from corporate or other certificate authorities. Internet Explorer on the Mac OS simply does not accept certificates from certificate authorities that haven't been programmed into it. (Based only on testing the technology preview release for the Classic Mac OS, the Opera browser may offer an alternative to Communicator on this issue.)

Java: Advantage Internet Explorer. Internet Explorer uses Apple's Macintosh Runtime for Java (MRJ), the standard Java implementation for Macintosh systems. Netscape, on the other hand, uses its own Java system—one that is much slower than Apple's MRJ. Netscape 6 may soon offer this capability, too.

Downloads: Advantage Internet Explorer. Both Communicator and Internet Explorer will successfully download files from the Web, so this advantage is more of a preference. Internet Explorer has its Download Manager, a single component responsible for tracking downloads. This is especially useful for downloading multiple files simultaneously or re-downloading a file if the download is interrupted. Communicator opens separate small windows for each download and only allows you to cancel a download; there is no way to restart an interrupted download.

Page Rendering: Advantage Internet Explorer. The latest versions of both browsers have improved the speed with which they display Web pages, but both browsers have idiosyncrasies that may sway your choice. Internet Explorer 5 has had some problems with its rendering engine so that some correct HTML is displayed incorrectly. On the other hand, Internet Explorer 5 for the Mac OS has an advantage in its support for Cascading Style Sheets (CSS). At the time of writing, it was the only browser on *any* platform that fully supported the CSS1 specification.

Memory: Advantage Neither. If you have a limited amount of system memory, both Communicator and Internet Explorer can hog a large amount of system resources. If this is a serious limiting factor for you, you might try using iCab or Opera. This is less of an issue with Mac OS X since memory is allocated dynamically.

Bells and Whistles: Advantage Neither. I realize that one person's bells and whistles are another person's critical features, but let's face it: Both Communicator and Explorer try to be all things to all Web surfers. Both applications do a pretty good job, but you have to wonder if they could do a better job at doing less. The first release of Internet Explorer 5, for example, had errors and problems in displaying basic HTML. On Netscape's part, Communicator 6 will still only use Messenger to handle *mailto:* URLs and has a clumsy interface for configuring helper applications and plug-ins. (You can use alternative e-mail clients with the Netscape Navigator standalone version.)

In a nutshell, I recommend that you choose the browser with the most features that you use regularly. Whichever browser you choose, using the latest version is always a good idea. Granted, many updates add bells and whistles you may not need, but some updates include bug fixes that make the browser more stable or security fixes that close loopholes before hackers exploit them. It pays for you to check occasionally for updates or let the browser check automatically. The browsers from both Netscape and Microsoft have this feature.

Netscape Communicator

Netscape Navigator and its university-developed descendant NCSA Mosaic can legitimately be credited with popularizing the Web revolution. Their simple graphical interfaces for navigating between hyperlinks on the Web helped popularize a tool originally designed for sharing the results of university research. At the time of writing, the long-awaited Netscape Communicator 6 had been released, but only for the Classic Mac OS, not Mac OS X.

To be completely accurate, Netscape Navigator is the browser product from Netscape Communications. As the company's most popular product, it is frequently and incorrectly referred to as simply Netscape. Netscape Communicator is a tightly integrated software suite that includes Navigator for Web browsing, Composer for creating Web pages, and Messenger for reading e-mail and newsgroups. Navigator is also available as a standalone program. Here, I will discuss Communicator, although installation and configuration of the Navigator standalone program is very similar.

As with most Web browsers, the primary Netscape Navigator actions are controlled by a set of buttons at the top of the browser window: Back, Forward, Reload, Search, and so forth. (The Search button can be customized to link to your favorite Internet search engine.)

On Web pages, hyperlinks appear as underlined text by default, and clicking on them downloads a new page. But there are many other ways to navigate the Web these days. There are JavaScript menus, image maps, frames, pull-down menus in forms, and other interfaces to help you move around. Some sites even use Java applets as navigation devices, although applets can have much more powerful applications. As a rule, click on anything that looks as if it might take you where you need to go. The Back button at the top of the window will always take you back.

Once downloaded, uncompressed, and installed (and after restarting if necessary), you start Communicator 6 by double-clicking the program icon. You configure Communicator to suit your needs by selecting the Preferences option from the Edit menu. There are many features that can be configured, some of which change the appearance of Web pages. However, there are several preference sections of relevance to webmasters: security, fonts, and helper applications. We consider each option separately.

Security. Click on the Advanced category in the Preferences dialog. Communicator allows to you choose whether to allow Java, JavaScript, or cookies (see Chapter 12). Netscape also has a Security button in the browser window that opens a more extensive Security window. In this window, you can set other security options as well as verify the security information for an individual page. The defaults are adequate for most sites.

Fonts. It is possible to change the default font for Navigator from the basic 12-point Times. Choose Fonts (under Appearance) in the Preferences dialog. Here you can set your default font and your default fixed-width font. For fixed-width font, you should choose a monospaced font such as Courier or Monaco and probably use a slightly smaller point size. You can also tell Navigator to use or ignore the fonts specified by a Web page.

Helper Applications. Choose Applications in the Preferences dialog. Navigator displays the MIME types it understands and how each is handled. For the most part in Communicator 4.7, the defaults cover all of the basics—and then some. Scroll down and look for a file description of Macintosh BinHex Archive. Double-clicking this entry will open the Edit Type dialog, and you should see that files of this MIME type (which have the *.hqx* extension) are handled by StuffIt Expander, meaning that *.hqx* files will be unstuffed automatically.

Internet Explorer

Internet Explorer from Microsoft has become the leading Web browser due to its inclusion as the default browser for Windows and Mac systems. Internet Explorer 5 for the Mac is a powerful and responsive browser with many nice features, including the ability to change its interface color to match the color of your iMac or Power Macintosh tower. Figure 6-1 shows a screen shot from Internet Explorer 5, which is included with the basic Mac OS X public beta installation. Internet Explorer is installed with the operating system, and an application icon is included in the default Dock.

As Figure 6-1 shows, Internet Explorer has very much the same feel as Netscape Navigator, with a row of buttons across the top of the window providing the key navigation commands. The navigation options within the Web pages themselves should look almost identical in both Navigator and Internet Explorer.

If and when Microsoft develops a new version, it may use an installation process similar to the one it uses on the Classic Mac OS, which is slightly different from most other programs. Once you have downloaded and unstuffed the Internet Explorer *.hqx* or *.bin* file, you open the resulting folder and simply copy the enclosed folder onto your hard drive by dragging and dropping. That's it. When you first run Internet Explorer, it completes the installation automatically.

Internet Explorer also has many customization options, most of which you control by selecting Preferences from the Edit menu. You will find the interface very familiar if you have used Internet Explorer 5 for Mac OS 9. Again, many of the options change the look and feel of Web pages. As with Netscape Communicator, I will describe how to adjust the security, fonts, and helper applications options.

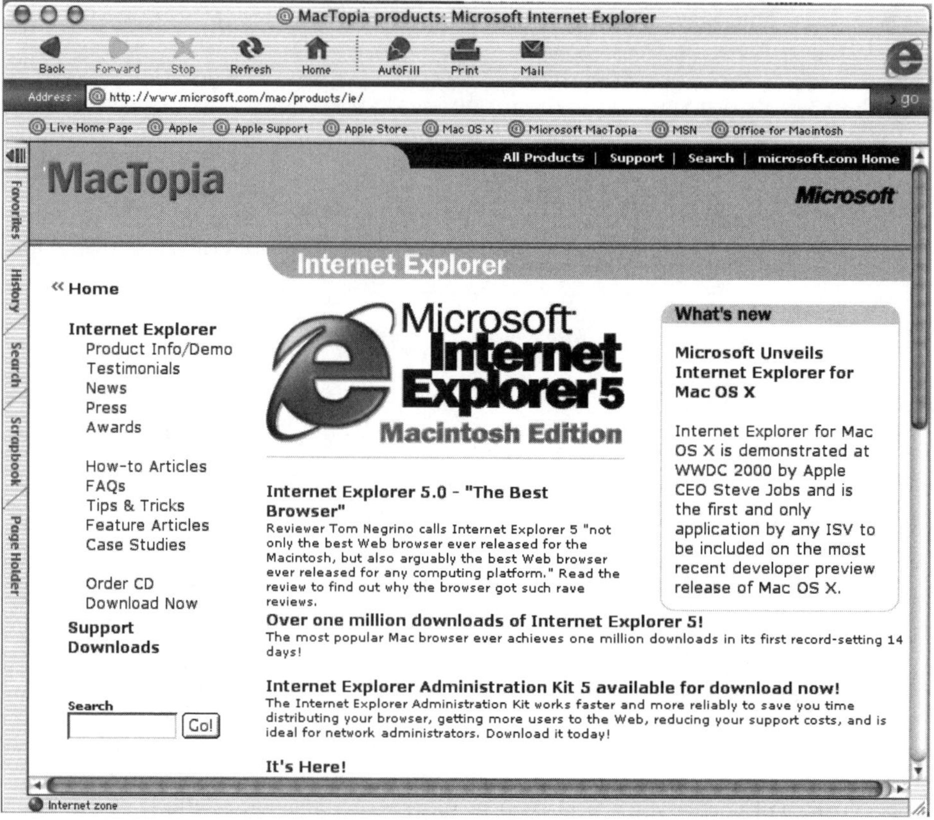

Figure 6-1. Internet Explorer 5. (Screen shot reprinted by permission from Microsoft Corporation.)

Security. Depending on your concern about Internet security, you can set several security options. Under the Web Content set of preferences, you can turn on and off scripting (such as JavaScript). You can turn Java on and off under the Java options. Unless you have a need for stronger than normal security, these are okay to leave on.

Under Security, you control the alerts that appear when you enter or leave secure pages. To minimize the number of these alerts, I recommend turning all of these off, except for the first, "When entering a page that is secure." This way, when you shop on the Web, you should get an alert before or as you enter any page where you are asked for a credit card number or comparable confidential information.

Under Security Zones, you can specify different levels of security for particular sites. For example, you may want to permit Java and scripting on your corporate intranet even if you would rather not have Java and scripting turned on for most Web sites.

Under Cookies, you can also manage—view, delete, or choose to decline—any cookies that Web sites may want to put on your computer. The "Never ask" option is fine for normal security. You can try the "Ask for each cookie" to see how often Web sites try to place cookies on your computer.

Fonts. To change your default font and size from the standard 12-point Times, choose the Language/Fonts option and select the default proportional and monospace fonts. The other font options—sans serif, serif, cursive, and fantasy—are font types defined by the specifications for Cascading Style Sheets (see Chapter 15).

Helper Applications. The Preferences dialog lists options for setting both File Helpers (under Receiving Files) and Protocol Helpers (under Network). For the most part, you can leave Protocol Helpers alone. For less common protocols, the defaults are set to common tools for handling them.

The File Helpers screen works in much the same way as in Communicator, which makes sense since the function is the same. A nice touch, however, is that you can sort this list by Description, Application, Extension, or MIME type by clicking on the headers above the scrolling window. Sorting by Extension makes it *much* easier to see how or whether Internet Explorer will handle a particular file type.

Double-clicking (or selecting and choosing Change...) will allow you to change how a particular MIME type is handled. For the most part, the defaults will work fine. You may want to confirm, however, that file types *BinHex* and *BinHexed StuffIt Archive* are handled as Post-process with Application with StuffIt Expander (see Figure 6-2).

iCab

If you're a rebel who prefers to protest the hegemony of the two major browser options, there are several options available for Mac OS X. During the public beta release, both the iCab and OmniWeb browsers were available for use. For standard Web browsing, these and other alternative browsers offer some advantages. In general, you don't get lots of unnecessary bells and whistles. And as a result, these applications are usually much smaller and consume fewer system resources in operation. On the other hand, since most alternative browsers don't have *all* the features of the Microsoft and Netscape browsers, they may not support a feature or two that you consider essential to your ideal Web browsing experience.

Even though the iCab browser has been available only as a preview release, its core Web browsing has been stable for quite some time. The preview release for Mac OS X, shown in Figure 6-3, is a Carbonized version of the Classic Mac OS version. Installation is straightforward. You download the *.sit* file and uncompress it with StuffIt Expander. The iCab application is inside the resulting folder along with some release notes. You can then move the iCab application into the Applications folder of your Mac OS X system.

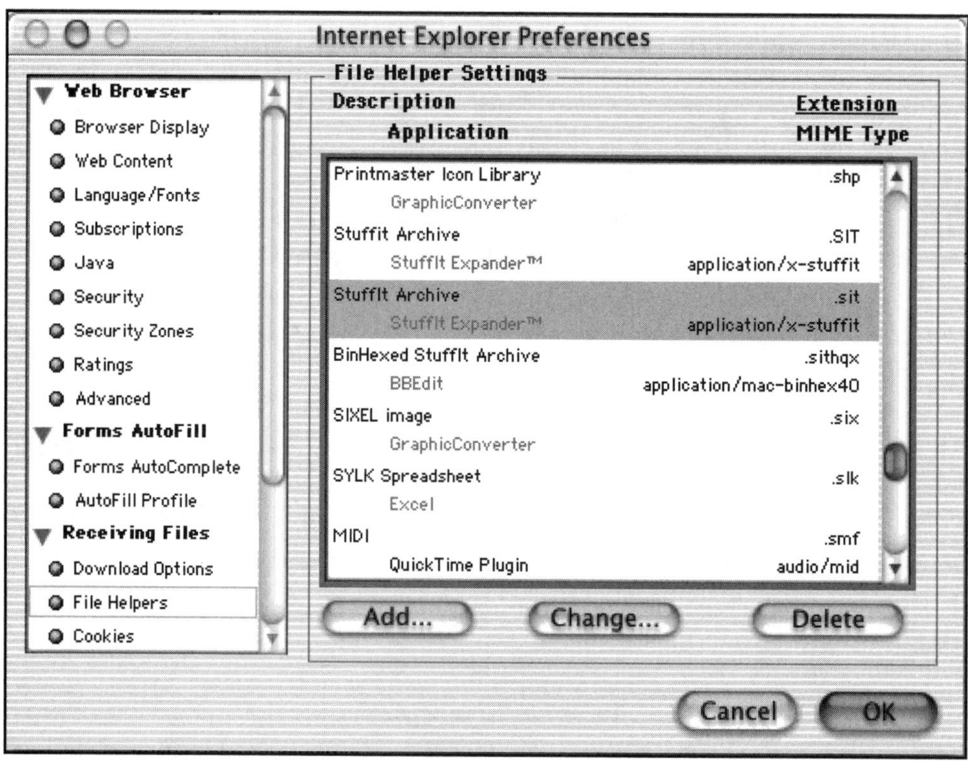

Figure 6-2. Internet Explorer File Helper Preferences.

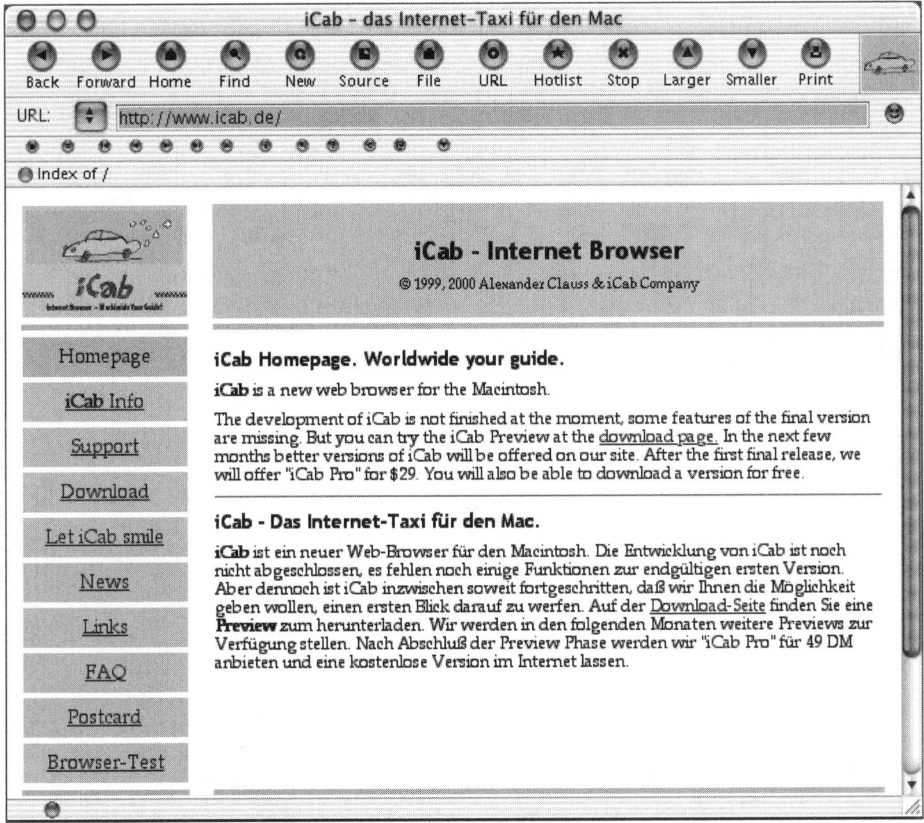

Figure 6-3. Preview Release of iCab for Mac OS X.

As you explore the iCab preferences, you'll find out that you can customize iCab to behave like either Navigator or Internet Explorer in situations those browsers handle differently.

Even though it's a preview, iCab has a comprehensive set of features, including most of those you'll encounter in typical Web browsing. You will find the interface very familiar if you have used Internet Explorer or Netscape Navigator. Again, many of the options change the look and feel of Web pages. As with the previous examples, I will describe how to adjust the security, fonts, and helper applications options. Selecting Preferences from the Edit menu opens the Preferences dialog.

Security. Most security options are set in the Security panel. You can set warnings when entering data in forms, turn JavaScript (InScript) on or off, and decide how to handle cookies, among other settings. There is also a Cookies panel for further fine-tuning of cookie handling, as well as for deleting and viewing the cookies that iCab has stored. It appears that, although iCab can establish SSL connections to Web servers, it does not handle certificates from unrecognized certificate authorities.

Fonts. The Fonts/Language panel allows you to customize the default fonts with which iCab will display Web page text. The same panel lets you choose the default language for sites that offer pages in more than one language.

Helper Applications. Rather than reinventing the wheel, iCab uses the helper applications defined in the Internet panel of the System Preferences. To define the helper application for a new MIME type, enter the information there.

FTP Clients

The file transfer protocol (FTP) provides the simplest way to access files on a remote server. Groups of files can be transferred together, and files can be transferred across slow communication lines typical of modem connections. FTP is also a useful way for users to upload files to your server should that be desirable.

Using FTP requires access to both the server computer providing the file or files and the client computer receiving the files. To get files from FTP servers on which you do not have an account, *anonymous FTP* allows you to log in to the remote machine with a login name of "anonymous" and a password of "guest," your e-mail address, or some other password specified by the FTP server. Anonymous FTP is similar to sharing files on an AppleTalk network and connecting to another Mac as a guest.

In particular, the Macintosh community has one major FTP site—Info-Mac—with collections of Macintosh software and information. A mirror site for the Info-Mac archive is available at *mirrors.apple.com/mirrors.*

Choosing an FTP Client

For downloading files from an FTP archive, you may not actually need software in addition to your Web browser. By pointing to URLs of the form *ftp://ftpsite.com*, you can download and save files from an anonymous FTP archive from just about any browser version.

However, you may need an FTP client if you must exchange files with servers that do not permit anonymous FTP. You may need a secure user name and password (provided by the administrator of the server) to enter such an FTP server. As a webmaster, you may commonly find yourself using FTP to upload new versions of Web pages to your server.

It can also be useful to have a dedicated FTP client if you do a lot of downloads and uploads. An FTP client lets you download or upload more than one file at a time, to name one advantage. In any event, an FTP client is still a useful addition to your toolkit. In these days of distributed computing you will likely need to transfer files between computers on which you have accounts. Table 6-2 lists some Mac OS FTP clients.

Command-Line FTP

Mac OS X does include an FTP client—in fact, two FTP clients—with the basic installation, but you'll have to go to the Terminal window to make use of

Table 6-2. Mac OS FTP Clients

Location	FTP Client
www.interarchy.com	Interarchy, successor to Anarchie shareware for FTP and other Internet services by Stairways Software.
www.fetchsoftworks.com	Fetch, shareware by Jim Matthews and Fetch Softworks.
www.ncftp.com/ncftp	NcFTP, command-line FTP client by Mike Gleason, included with Mac OS X.
www.ozemail.com.au/~pli/netfinder	NetFinder by Peter Li and Vincent Tan, an easy-to-use FTP client with some nice advanced features.
www.vicomsoft.com	Vicomsoft FTP Client, commercial software from Vicomsoft.
www.panic.com	Transmit, commercial software from Panic Software.

them. The two clients are *ftp,* the default UNIX FTP client, and NcFTP by Mike Gleason, which adds numerous enhancements over and above *ftp*. However, for the basics, both *ftp* and NcFTP work essentially the same way. To use either, you first need to open a Terminal window.

- To start the FTP client, at the prompt ("%" here) enter
  ```
  % ftp
  ```
  or
  ```
  % ncftp
  ```
- You will now see the FTP prompt (">" in this example). To connect to an FTP server, use the Open command.
  ```
  > open ftp.yourdomain.com
  ```
  By default Open will use anonymous FTP. To log in with a user name and password, enter
  ```
  > open —u username ftp.somedomain.com
  ```
- To navigate the FTP server, you use the UNIX cd (Change Directory) and ls (List) commands. The ls command is just that:
  ```
  > ls
  ```
  The cd command takes a directory argument. To go down a directory level, use
  ```
  > cd dirname
  ```
  To go up a directory, use
  ```
  > cd ..
  ```
- To download or upload a file, use the Get or Put commands, respectively. These commands move files between the current directories on both the client and FTP server.
  ```
  > get file-to-download.txt
  > put file-to-upload.html
  ```
  You can use UNIX wildcards in the file names to move more than one file at a time. For example, you can upload all files that end in *.html.*
  ```
  > put *.html
  ```
- While still at the FTP prompt, you can use the Open command to connect to another server. To quit the FTP client, enter the Quit command.

Fetch

Fetch was developed by Jim Matthews to let Macs at Dartmouth College talk to host computers and use the Internet. A popular FTP client, Fetch puts a Mac-like interface, reminiscent of the "Open File" dialog box, upon what would otherwise be a series of UNIX commands. Fetch is shareware now being distributed by Fetch Softworks for $25. Figure 6-4 gives a snapshot of the Fetch window.

To install Fetch, go to the Fetch Web page (listed in Table 6-2), then download and uncompress the *.hqx* file. No restart is necessary.

You configure Fetch by selecting the Preferences option from the Customize menu. Under the General tab, you can check the Use Internet Config option to use the Internet preferences you've already set for Mac OS X. This will also add your e-mail address to the default password box.

Under the Download tab, you can set the default folder where you want Fetch to store downloaded files, as well as the editor you want to use for reading text files. Under Upload, you can specify the default formats for uploading files: Text for text files and Raw Data for others are the recommended settings. I also recommend turning off the options for Fetch to add *.hqx, .bin,* and *.txt* extensions automatically to file names—particularly the *.txt* option, which will add *.txt* to the end of any *.html* files you send by FTP, for example.

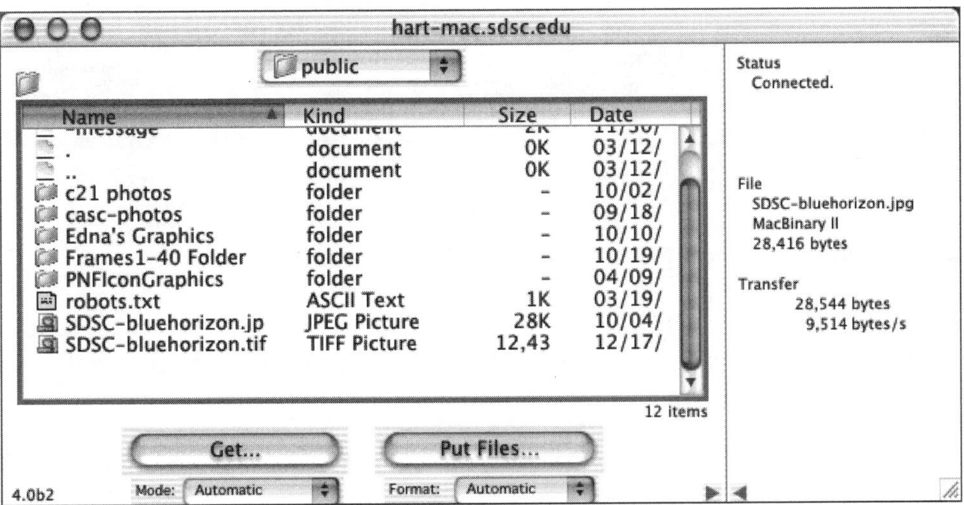

Figure 6-4. Fetch FTP Client by Jim Matthews, Fetch Softworks.

Transmit

Transmit by Panic Software is a shareware FTP client for the Mac OS that has made the transition to Mac OS X. Transmit uses an interface reminiscent of the Mac OS X Finder's Open and Save file dialogs, as shown in Figure 6-5. By default, the window shows both the files on your computer ("your stuff" in the left-hand panel) and the files on the FTP server ("their stuff" in the right-hand panel). You can drag files between the two windows as appropriate. Alternately, you can choose to display only "their stuff" and drag and drop files between the Finder and the Transmit window.

Installing Transmit involves downloading and unstuffing a *.sit* file. You can move the resulting application wherever you like, and the Transmit application is ready to go.

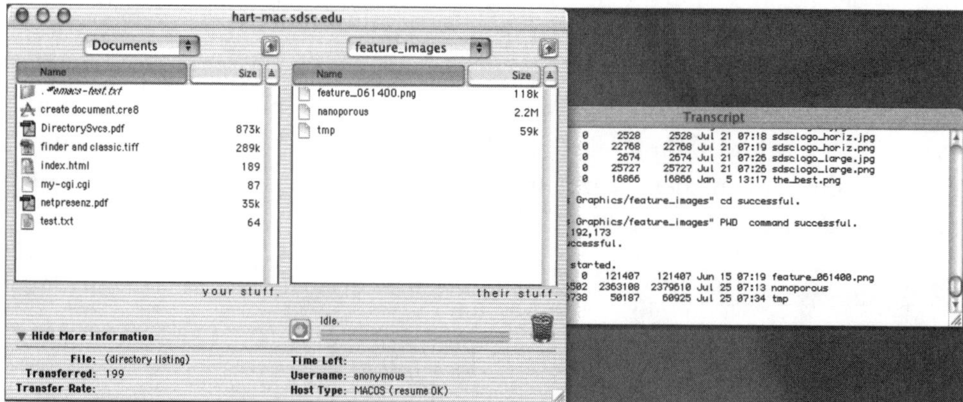

Figure 6-5. Transmit for Mac OS X by Panic Software.

Downloading Example

The basic concept behind FTP is to get a file from a server or send a file to a server, and any FTP client will require similar steps to upload or download a file. A basic interaction with an FTP server proceeds as follows:

1. Start your FTP client.
2. Connect—the Connect command is usually under the File menu—to the remote FTP server, and for guest access, enter a login name of "anonymous" and a password of your full e-mail ad-

dress. (Some FTP servers require you to have an account on the server; if this is the case, enter your user name and password here instead.)

3. Select the files to download (or the directory to upload to) by navigating to the appropriate directory. With Mac FTP clients, the interface should be similar to navigating through your files and folders on your own computer.
4. Make sure the modes—ASCII/text for text files, binary for others—are set correctly for the file(s) to be transferred.
5. Select the file or files to transfer, and click to download or upload the file or files. Most Mac FTP clients let you drag and drop the selected files from the FTP client window to the Mac file system and vice versa.
6. Close the connection.

E-Mail Clients

If you don't already have an e-mail client and at least one e-mail address, you simply must have one to be a webmaster. You need an e-mail account at which to receive e-mail comments from your Web audience, to receive e-mail from your Web server or your server monitor software about activities (or lack thereof) on your server, and to manage and participate in any e-mail lists supported by your list server software.

Table 6-3 lists several e-mail clients available for Mac OS X. Two commonly used Mac OS e-mail clients are Netscape Messenger, part of the Netscape Communicator suite, and Microsoft Outlook, companion software to Microsoft's Internet Explorer. You may already have one of these clients on your system. You also have Mac OS X Mail, the native e-mail client that is included with Mac OS X.

All the clients will allow you to send and receive e-mail and attachments (files sent along with an e-mail message), and all will let you organize your e-mail messages into folders. Those are the basics. Beyond that, each e-mail client has its own set of advanced features.

Table 6-3. Mac OS X E-mail Clients

Location	Description
www.eudora.com	Eudora freeware and commercial software from Qualcomm.
www.eware.fr/dev	Green, a freeware client from eWare.
www.apple.com/macosx	Mail, a free Mac OS X–native e-mail client from Apple included with Mac OS X.
www.barebones.com	MailSmith, a commercial client from Bare Bones Software.
www.cyrusoft.com/mulberry	Mulberry, a shareware IMAP client from Cyrusoft International, Inc.
www.microsoft.com/mac	Outlook Express and Entourage from Microsoft.
www.eidolonsoftware.com	PopOver, a freeware e-mail client from Eidolon Software.
www.ctmdev.com	PowerMail, a commercial POP3 client from CTM Development.
www.cesoft.com	QuickMail Pro, a commercial client from CE Software, Inc.
www.macemail.com	The Macintosh E-mail Resource Page by Omar Shahine and Diane Ross.

Choosing an E-Mail Client

Table 6-3 also refers to a technical feature that may affect your decision, however. There are three standard Internet protocols used by e-mail clients to check for e-mail messages—the Post Office Protocol (POP), the Authenticated Post Office Protocol (APOP), and the Internet Mail Access Protocol (IMAP). The difference affects the interaction with the e-mail server and should, theoretically, be minimal for you as an e-mail reader. However, your e-mail provider may specify that you must use one protocol or the other.

POP has been around the longest and is supported by most e-mail software (except a few IMAP-only clients). With POP, your e-mail client checks with the server for new e-mail messages and downloads any new messages and attachments to your computer, where you read, organize, and respond to them. After a certain amount of time (which you can specify), the server deletes your messages and the only copies are on your computer. The advantage to POP is that, once e-mail is downloaded from the server, it is on your computer and organizing, reading, and otherwise managing e-mail is fast. The disadvantage to POP is that for older messages, your computer has the only copy, which could be disastrous if your hard drive crashes. APOP is the same as POP, except that your password is encrypted before being sent across the network.

IMAP is newer and may not be supported in all clients. With IMAP, your e-mail messages remain on the server. Usually, your client downloads only the message headers (sender, subject, and so forth) and as you open a message to read it, the message body and any attachments are downloaded from the server. In most cases, you organize and store your messages on the mail server, not your own computer. The advantage to IMAP is that the server holds all your e-mail, which could amount to many megabytes of messages over time. The disadvantage is that reading, organizing, and managing your e-mail require many more interactions with the server, which may mean that it takes longer to read and organize your e-mail.

Your e-mail provider can tell you whether POP, APOP, or IMAP is appropriate for your accounts. In selecting an e-mail client, you should first make sure that it supports the e-mail protocol preferred or required by your e-mail provider. Beyond that, you should pick one that has extra features that you use most often. I realize that's not a very definitive recommendation, but in this case, your best bet is to try the various options and select the one that works best for you.

I will tell you that as an e-mail power user who receives up to a hundred messages a day and who has tried Eudora, Messenger, Green, and to a lesser extent Outlook and Mac OS X Mail, I prefer Eudora for its message handling, filtering, and text handling. Your mileage may vary. At the time the book was written, only a few e-mail clients had been released in preview form, so I only describe one option here.

Mac OS X Mail

Apple has included a reasonably sophisticated e-mail client, called Mail, as part of Mac OS X. Mail supports POP and IMAP accounts, and you can configure it to check your e-mail from several accounts. The basic Mail window, as shown in Figure 6-6, has a toolbar with buttons for the most common actions, a section for

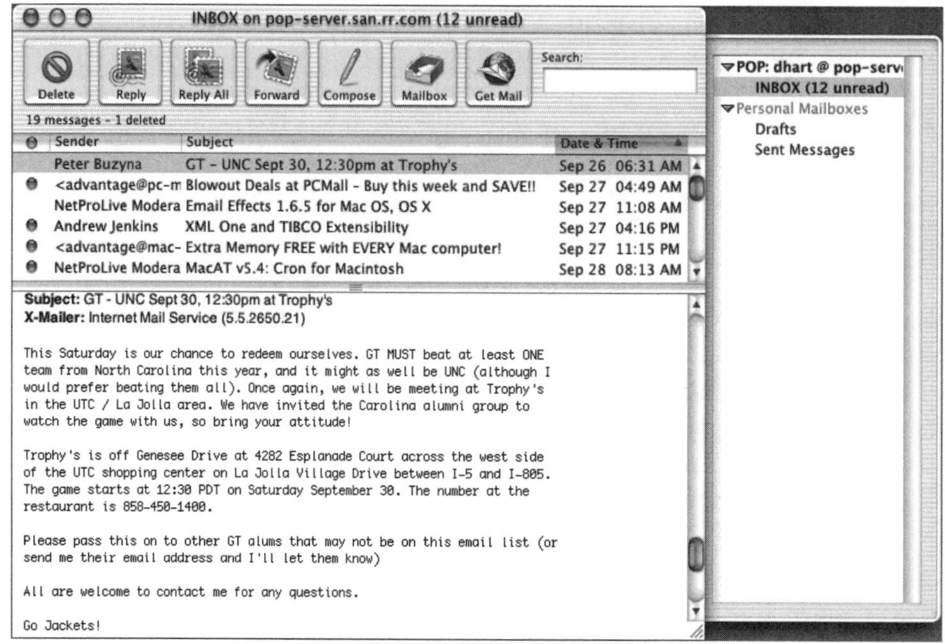

Figure 6-6. Mac OS X Mail from Apple.

viewing the messages in the current mailbox, and a section for reading the current message. There's also a pop-out section that lets you switch among your available mailboxes.

Mail also lets you set up and switch among several signature files, send mail using Mac OS X's Sendmail utility, filter messages, and read HTML-formatted messages. All in all, you will not be sacrificing too many features by using the free Mail client. Readers with extensive amounts of e-mail in another e-mail program (like myself) or who make extensive use of filters to sort the daily deluge of incoming messages may still prefer to use their current client (possibly in the Classic compatibility environment until a Mac OS X version appears). However, with Mail, Apple has set the bar fairly high for developers of other e-mail clients.

Multimedia Players

The Web has evolved to include many different media formats beyond basic text and graphics. Today, a Web site is likely to provide recorded or live audio and video for your viewing pleasure. Some audio and video may be downloaded as possibly large files or streamed across the network in much the same way a television program is broadcast across the airwaves or cable. To be sure you can view the most common formats, you need the appropriate client software.

Because the client software is free, it is probably safest to have all the appropriate players, just in case. If you are going to communicate with your audience with audio and video, you'll eventually have to pick one. Table 6-4 lists the major client players and browser plug-ins for Mac OS X.

Table 6-4. Multimedia Software

Location	Description
www.apple.com/quicktime	QuickTime from Apple.
www.realplayer.com	RealPlayer from Real Networks.
www.microsoft.com	Windows Media Player from Microsoft.
www.macromedia.com	Shockwave and Flash plug-ins from Macromedia.

QuickTime

The QuickTime software built into Mac OS X—and available for Windows systems—lets you view most common formats of digital video and audio, including the MPEG standard, the QuickTime format originated by Apple, and Microsoft's AVI format. Installing the newest version will let you view or hear, according to Apple, more than 200 graphic, video, and audio file formats.

For browsing the Web, you should have the QuickTime plug-in that lets Netscape Communicator or Internet Explorer show QuickTime movies in the browser window. This is a no-brainer—go to the QuickTime Web site and download this software. The QuickTime software for viewing—the QuickTime Player is shown in Figure 6-7—is available for free, but paying the registration fee for QuickTime Pro unlocks the features that allow you to edit, convert, and save multimedia files.

Mac OS X installs QuickTime as part of the basic installation, so the installation details are not repeated here. You may want to check the Apple Web site for more recent versions using the Software Update application. Because this software is tightly integrated with the operating system, you will have to restart after installing or updating QuickTime components.

Figure 6-7. QuickTime Player for Mac OS X.

RealPlayer

Real Networks pioneered streaming media video with their RealAudio software, which has since evolved into video and other formats viewable with the RealPlayer software. RealPlayer plug-ins and helper applications are available for Mac OS, Windows, and UNIX systems, and like the QuickTime software from Apple, the Real Networks software is available in free versions and "plus" versions for which you must pay.

Although QuickTime can be used to serve and view streaming media, you need to have the RealPlayer client installed for viewing the streaming media formats created by the commonly used Real Networks production software.

Other Handy Client Software

There is no end to the software you might one day need on the Web; therefore, at some point, you need to stop downloading and installing client software and get on with establishing your Web server. From my experience, if you have a

Web browser, an FTP client, an e-mail client, and multimedia viewing software, you should be set for the bulk of your client needs.

As you encounter new file formats or interact with new Internet services—they may be new to you or may not even exist as this book is being written—you can download the client software that you need for that format. This section covers a few other common types of client software, including a few you probably already have and almost certainly will need.

Compression Tools

For the Mac OS, Aladdin Systems produces the de facto standard software for compressing and uncompressing files. StuffIt Expander is widely distributed freeware—it is distributed with Netscape Communicator, for example—for uncompressing and unarchiving files. StuffIt Expander uncompresses *.hqx, .bin, .zip,* and other file formats and opens *.sit* and other archive formats.

The shareware DropStuff with Expander Enhancer increases the number of file formats that StuffIt Expander can open. The commercial version, StuffIt Deluxe, will open even more compressed and archived file formats, as well as create compressed and archived files that are accessible by Windows and UNIX users. If you are serving large files for a variety of platforms, StuffIt Deluxe is a must.

OpenUp from Stepwise.com is a new compression entrant that originated on the NeXTStep operating system and that can open more than 40 different compressed and archive file types. Table 6-5 has pointers to StuffIt Expander and other compression utilities for the Mac OS.

Table 6-5. Mac OS X Compression Software

Location	Description
www.mindvision.com	MindExpander freeware from MindVision Software.
www.stepwise.com/Software/OpenUp	OpenUp from Scott Anguish at Stepwise.com.
www.aladdinsys.com	StuffIt Expander freeware, DropStuff, and DropZip shareware, and commercial StuffIt Deluxe from Aladdin Systems.

Portable Document Format (PDF)

Adobe created PDF as a step toward the "paperless office" that may always be 20 years in the future. In the meantime, PDF has become the de facto standard for exchanging graphically designed documents across the Internet and between platforms. Adobe's PostScript language remains popular as the native tongue for documents destined for high-end printers, but PDF files can be easily viewed and searched on screen, as well as printed.

The Quartz engine in Mac OS X adopts the PDF format as its primary display format for text and other 2-D graphics, so PDF files can easily be viewed in Mac OS X's general-purpose file viewer, called Preview, as shown in Figure 6-8.

I should note that PDF files can do much more than retain the formatting of a document. They can also include internal links to various sections and external hyperlinks to the Web. They can include interactive forms and can be used as a cross-platform presentation format. Software documentation is now commonly produced as PDF files instead of printed manuals. You can also install Adobe's Acrobat Reader software or OmniPDF from the Omni Group to view PDF files with more flexibility than the Preview application. Table 6-6 has references to the Acrobat software and to other PDF resources on the Web.

Figure 6-8. Mac OS X Preview Application with PDF Document.

Table 6-6. PDF Software and Resources

Location	Description
www.adobe.com/acrobat	Adobe Acrobat software for creating, editing, and reading PDF documents. Acrobat Reader is free.
www.omnigroup.com/products/omnipdf	OmniPDF, a commercial PDF viewer from Omni Group. Free for the first user at a site.
www.pdfzone.com	The PDF Zone, an independent site of PDF information, user forums, and PDF software.
www.planetpdf.com	Planet PDF, a comprehensive, independent Web site on PDF users and uses.
news:comp.text.pdf	PDF newsgroup.

News Readers

Internet newsgroups were, along with list servers, one of the first ways for individuals with a common interest to exchange information. They are still often referred to as Usenet news groups, since they originated on the Usenet network connecting colleges and universities across the United States. Newsgroups remain a popular way to exchange information; messages are posted to an electronic "bulletin board" for those with similar interests. Today there are thousands of available newsgroups.

Although this book will not discuss how to set up an Internet news server, you may want to consider installing one of the news reader clients listed in Table 6-7 to read and participate in the thousands of online news groups, many of which pertain to the Web and Internet as well as your special interests. Newsgroup participants may be a source of answers that you can't find elsewhere.

The Messenger component of Netscape Communicator and Microsoft's Outlook Express both let you read news groups in addition to e-mail, but many dedicated newsreader applications are also available.

Chat

"Chatting" is a more recent Internet development, most notable, if you watch too many TV tabloids, for men masquerading online as women (or vice versa) and for enabling lecherous older men to seduce impressionable younger women. But

Table 6-7. Mac OS X News Reader Software

Location	Description
www.diiva.com	Diiva, a shareware graphical news reader software.
www.asar.com	Hogwasher, a commercial news reader and e-mail client from Asar Corporation.
home.snafu.de/stk/macsoup	MacSOUP, a shareware news reader by Stefan Kurth.
members.home.net/saulg00d *www.tin.org*	Tin, a text-based newsreader from Tin.org and compiled by Saul Good.
www.newsreaders.com/mac/yanw	Yet Another News Watcher, freeware from Brian Clark.

many legitimate conversations also take place. Celebrities now regularly make appearances in Internet chat rooms, for example. Internet Relay Chat (IRC) provides a way of communicating in real time with people across the Internet.

In some sense, chatting is like participating in a live newsgroup, because many conversations are devoted to particular topics. To chat, you run a client program that connects to a server on one of the IRC networks and ask to join a particular "channel," or conversation. The conversation between you and the other participants is carried on through the server. On average, there are about 20,000 users and 5,000 channels on the large IRC networks. Table 6-8 has resources for more information on IRC and on IRC software for Mac OS X.

Table 6-8. Mac OS X Internet Relay Chat Software

Location	Description
www.BitchX.com *www.chevell.cx/macosx/bitchxpb.html*	BitchX, a freeware IRC client by Colten Edwards.
www.irchelp.org	IRChelp.org, a complete IRC help site by Joseph Lo and a staff of volunteers.
www.ircle.com	IRCle, a shareware client by Onno R. Tijdgat.
www.elsinc.com/chatnet.html	ChatNet, a commercial IRC client by ELS, Inc.
www.virtualmemory.net/~aova/next/ircstep	IRCstep, a freeware IRC client.
www.shadowirc.com	ShadowIRC, an open-source, freeware IRC client by John Bafford.
www.snak.com	Snak, a shareware IRC client by Kent Sorensen.

It is also possible to chat at a Web site that provides chat services through a Web interface. Such capabilities are discussed in Chapter 10.

Graphics and Sound

Graphics and multimedia design and production are some of the strongest areas for Apple and the Macintosh platform, so it comes as no surprise that there are many utilities around for viewing graphics and playing sound files. Table 6-9 summarizes a few locations for downloading some of the many popular graphics viewers and sound players for the Macintosh.

For most common sound and graphics files, the QuickTime software included with Mac OS X should allow you to play or view them, respectively. Table 6-9 also lists two utilities from among the shareware tools available. If QuickTime can't understand a format you've encountered, these programs probably will.

Table 6-9. Graphics and Sound Utilities

Location	Description
www.lemkesoft.de	GraphicConverter shareware from Lemke Software.
www-cs-students.stanford.edu/~franke/SoundApp	SoundApp freeware sound utility by Norman Franke.
mirror.apple.com/mirrors/info-mac	The Info-Mac archive.
download.cnet.com	CNET's Download.com.
www.macdownload.com	ZDNet's Mac Software Library.

GraphicConverter

If you want to view and save images in just about *any* format, you might want to download GraphicConverter. This shareware package by Thorsten Lemke will import about 130 graphic file formats and export about 40 graphic file formats. GraphicConverter also offers batch file conversion, a slide show feature, and some basic image manipulation tools, such as Zoom, Rotate, and Trim. Installation is a snap—download and unstuff the *.hqx* file and double-click the installer.

Sound Player

The first Macs came complete with 8-bit sound; every Macintosh sold today is capable of 16-bit CD-quality stereo sound. Since sound was not an original component of many other systems, sound formats are one of the least standardized information types. Each hardware platform, and sometimes each sound card manufacturer, has a preferred format or formats, and Web browsers typically do not have built-in support for playing sounds.

Some sound types, such as QuickTime audio and MP3 (short for MPEG Audio Layer 3) provide less platform-dependent alternatives for the Web. Common sound formats are listed in Table 6-10. Because of the many sound formats out there, you may need additional software to listen to (or convert) sounds that originated on different platforms.

SoundApp by Norman Franke is a great freeware sound player and converter that can play more than 30 sound formats and convert them to a Macintosh sound file. SoundApp can convert most of these formats to a Macintosh sound and sound suitcase or nearly 10 other formats. SoundApp also supports generic QuickTime conversion, which allows any QuickTime-recognized format to be converted to a QuickTime movie file.

Table 6-10. Common Sound Formats

Name	File Extension	Description
—	*.snd*	Macintosh-produced
HCOM	*none*	Macintosh-produced
QuickTime	*.qt, .mov*	Movie format with audio
IFF/8SVX	*.iff*	Amiga-produced
Amiga	*.mod, .nst*	Another Amiga format
WAVE	*.wav*	Microsoft Windows–produced
μ-law	*.au, .snd*	NeXT- and Sun-produced
AIFF	*.aif, .aiff*	SGI IRIX-produced
RealAudio	*.ra*	Web format by Real Networks
MP3	*.mpeg, .mpg, .mp3*	MPEG Audio Layer 3, highly compressed CD-quality audio

CHAPTER 7

WEB SERVERS

Now we've come to the chapter you've been waiting for, or perhaps been skipping ahead to—installing a Web server on your Macintosh. And in this chapter, we'll discuss not one, but three Web servers. Apache, the most popular Web server software on the Internet, and freeware that's bundled with Mac OS X. The Apache section will also discuss iTools from Tenon Intersystems for configuring and administering an Apache server. WebSTAR is the leading Web server for the Mac OS and will soon be available as a native Mac OS X application. Finally, we'll mention Web Server 4D, the third major Mac OS Web server with a number of interesting features.

In addition, other shareware or freeware Mac OS Web servers have various capabilities and levels of current support. It's not clear how many programs will be revised as native Mac OS X applications that can take advantage of Mac OS X high-end features. You may have to run them as Classic Mac OS applications that will not benefit from the memory protection and preemptive multitasking of Mac OS X.

Choosing a Web Server

Rather than recommending a particular Web server, the goal of this chapter is to help you evaluate which software is right for you. You should keep the following features in mind as you test the Web servers described or mentioned in this chapter.

Cost. Not all servers are free. Whether you buy a server should depend on the support services you need and not necessarily on software quality. Free Web servers, such as Apache, are generally of high quality. Also remember that "cost" does not always equal the price you pay for the Web server. You should also consider the cost of installing and managing the server, the cost of software needed to support services not included in the server software, and other factors.

Performance. You probably want the Web server that delivers the best performance for the money. But you can define performance however you like. For some Web sites, hits per second is the most valid measure. For others, it might be the amount of data that can be moved or the average time between crashes. For e-commerce sites, it might be secure transactions per second.

Administration. For some webmasters, such as those running servers housed at a Web hosting company's facility, it might be vital that a Web server permit Web-based administration. For part-time webmasters at small companies, administrative ease of use might be most attractive. Most servers can be configured to take particular actions based on file type, and if you will be serving up many different types of files, you might consider the server's support for many MIME types, and extensibility to support for new MIME types.

Security Features. This topic is important enough to merit its own section in this chapter. For now, suffice it to say that security can mean both controlling access to all or portions of the data served at your site and protecting private information being exchanged between your customers and your server.

IP Multihoming or Virtual Hosting. In many instances, you may need your Web server software to handle requests for several different Web hosts on the same machine—perhaps a public Web site, a private intranet site, and some project hosts. You may then want your server software to support IP multihoming or virtual hosting. This feature is generally more common in commercial software and may make administration a bit more complex.

Extensibility. You won't want to update your Web server software each time a new Web technology is developed. WebSTAR and compatible servers allow you to add plug-ins—similar to Web browser plug-ins—with new processing capabilities to your server. Apache has modules that perform the same role. Other servers provide other means of extending the basic server functionality.

Additional Services. Some commercial packages, such as WebSTAR and iTools, provide more Internet services besides a basic HTTP server. A search engine, an FTP server, an e-mail server, database publishing, or e-commerce features are some of the extra services that might factor into your decision. Having all these features built into one piece of software from one company may be important from a technical support standpoint if you are a part-time webmaster, for example.

Log Formats. Every event performed by the server is logged to a file. In general, you should look for logging that supports the CERN/NCSA common log format. If the server software supports the common log format for its log files, you can be fairly certain that standard log analysis tools will be able to read and analyze the log files.

Server-Side Includes (SSIs). An SSI is similar to an Include statement in a number of programming languages. For example, rather than manually inserting the date the Web page was last modified into the HTML each time you modify the file, you can simply include a function that returns the modification date based on the file modification date retained by the Mac OS. In any but the most secure environments, SSIs or similar server-interpreted functions help webmasters create easily managed Web sites. You may want to examine the range of functions provided by the server.

If you think this is a large number of considerations, note that it is only a partial list. Table 7-1 provides some links to more information on Web servers, features, and comparisons. Table 7-2 lists some of the available Web servers for Mac OS X and includes those servers that run as native Mac OS X applications. Table 7-3 lists Web server applications that, at the time of writing, either are no longer being developed or supported, or will only run in the Classic environment without the benefit of advanced Mac OS X features.

I should also mention what Tables 7-2 and 7-3 do *not* list, and that is applications that include a Web server, but for which the main function is not Web serving. For example, they do not include database, application, or targeted e-commerce servers that also have built-in Web server capabilities. These programs will be discussed in subsequent chapters. Of course, no matter what dividing line is used, some applications will straddle it. Web Server 4D, for example, can be used either as a standalone Web server or as a CGI application alongside another Web server.

Table 7-1. General Web Server Information

Location	Description
www.webcompare.com	WebServer Compare, a Web server comparison site.
serverwatch.internet.com	ServerWatch Web site and newsletter on Web server developments.
www.w3.org/Protocols	Information on HTTP and emerging Web protocols from the W3 Consortium.

Table 7-2. Mac OS X Web Servers

Location	Description
www.apache.org	Apache, freeware bundled with Mac OS X.
www.tenon.com/products/itools	iTools, from Tenon Intersystems, adds a graphical administration interface and additional services.
www.apple.com/macosx/server	Mac OS X Server, Apple's suite of Internet server and network file server tools.
www.roxen.com	Roxen WebServer, free server from Roxen Internet Software.
www.vqsoft.com	*vq* Server, freeware HTTP server written in Java by Steve Shering and vq Soft.
www.mdg.com	Web Server 4D, commercial Web server with database features from MDG Computer Services.
www.webstar.com	WebSTAR Server Suite, a commercial Web, FTP, mail, and proxy server software from 4D, Inc.
www.zeus.com	Zeus Web Server, commercial software from Zeus Technology Ltd.

Table 7-3. Web Server Software for the Classic Mac OS

Location	Description
www.apple.com/appleshareip	AppleShare IP, Apple's Internet and file server software for Classic Mac OS.
www.ai.mit.edu/projects/iiip/doc/cl-http	Common LISP HyperMedia Server, freeware server written in Common LISP by John C. Mallery.
www.summary.net/soft/easyserve.html	EasyServe, freeware by Jason Linhart.
www.centrinity.com/products/FCIS	First Class Intranet Server Gold, commercial Web, FTP, mail, forum, and chat software by Centrinity, Inc.
www.stairways.com/netpresenz	NetPresenz, Web and FTP server shareware from Stairways Software.
www.tfbbs.com	TeleFinder BBS and Web server distributed by Operator Headgap Systems.
www.tenon.com/products/webten	WebTen, commercial software from Tenon Intersystems, for Classic Mac OS versions of Apache.

SECURING YOUR WEB SERVER

Chapter 5 discussed general security measures, such as careful system administration and firewalls, to protect your Macintosh from unwanted intrusions. Web servers typically have additional security features to be sure that information is seen only by those who are supposed to see it.

There are two sides to the security coin. First, you want to make sure that private information being exchanged between your customers and your server remains private. Second, you may want to restrict access to certain information on your site, such as making sure that personnel information is available only to human resources staff. The first type of security is ensured by encrypting data that is sent over the Internet, the second by controlling access to portions of your site.

Secure Sockets Layer (SSL)

You protect your visitors in two ways, by guaranteeing that you are who you say you are and by guaranteeing that your customers' private information remains private. Achieving these goals requires two elements on your server: a digital certificate from a recognized certificate authority (CA) and Web server software that implements the secure sockets layer (SSL) protocol.

The two parts work hand in hand. Digital certificates are electronic files that uniquely identify people and resources over the Internet. A certificate includes information about its owner and the issuing CA, such as the owner's name, the URL of the Web server using the certificate, the owner's public encryption key, the name of the issuing CA, a serial number, and the dates for which the certificate is valid. See Chapter 13 for more on getting a digital certificate for your site.

The second component you need for e-commerce security is a Web server that supports SSL. The SSL protocol encrypts the data moving between your customers and your server to ensure that private data, such as credit card numbers, remains confidential even if it is intercepted en route. Because of the licensing fees associated with the patent held by RSA Security on the public-key encryption algorithm, U.S. webmasters have not been able to find SSL support in free Web server software, while webmasters outside the United States have had other options. However, the RSA patent expired in September 2000, and since that time, U.S. webmasters have been able to freely use alternatives such as OpenSSL with Apache.

Even though the monetary cost of SSL should come down, SSL still extracts a performance cost. Because of the encryption overhead, SSL transactions take longer than plain vanilla HTTP requests. The Mac Web servers described in this chapter all provide this feature. For more on SSL, you might attempt to wade through the SSL 3.0 specification from Netscape.

Once you have an SSL-capable Web server and a valid certificate, your customers establish a secure connection with your server through a protocol handshake. In short, the client's browser uses your server's public key in the certificate to establish an encrypted session. If the server certificate is valid, the SSL session proceeds. If the server certificate is not valid, the server certificate is rejected and the SSL session is stopped.

The technique that makes the whole process work, for those of you who might be wondering about the "public key" mentioned above, is called *public key cryptography.* Through some mathematical tricks, it turns out that two participants can maintain a secure transaction with a private key and a public key for encrypting and decrypting information. The mathematical tricks ensure that the public key will only decrypt information encrypted by the private key, and vice versa. In addition, it is virtually impossible to discover the private key from the public key. The main external requirement for this to work is that the keys must be handed out by a trusted source; hence, the certificate authorities described above.

Access Control

Most servers provide some way for the webmaster to restrict access to selected files or folders. This capability is useful in creating a corporate intranet, for example. The flexibility and convenience of these access controls can vary from server to server. Table 7-4 lists some of the available tools if you decide you need security measures above and beyond those already provided by your Web server software.

Typical for servers that provide some form of access control, the webmaster can explicitly specify which folders and files are accessible. For example, the webmaster might place restrictions on how CGI scripts can be executed. You might create a set of limited-access pages to share drafts of documents with colleagues at remote locations. Limiting file access increases security but requires more effort to maintain.

Table 7-4. Web Security Tools and Information

Location	Description
www.w3.org/Security	Web security resources from the W3 Consortium.
www.rsasecurity.com	RSA Security, Inc., is the patent holder on the public key encryption system used on the Web.
www.certicom.com	Certicom Security, a competitor of RSA Security.
home.netscape.com/eng/ssl3	The SSL 3.0 specification from Netscape.
www.openssl.org	OpenSSL, an open-source alternative for SSL encryption.
www.purity.com/websentinel	WebSentinel, commercial software to supplement your server's security.
www.cyno.com	WebRADIUS, a shareware WebSTAR plug-in that provides authentication through a MacRADIUS server.

It is also possible to prohibit access by IP address, a range of IP addresses, or domain name. Corporate intranets can easily be constructed with this capability. For example, a webmaster can specify that only IP addresses assigned to the corporate network can access a portion of the site or a virtual domain hosted by the server.

Finally, in addition to the security measures included as part of your Web server software, additional software tools are available to supplement your site security by providing such functionality as password-restricted access on a per-page basis and protection against unauthorized CGI scripts.

APACHE

Apache, the most popular Web server on the Internet, is used by nearly sixty percent of the Web servers on the Internet, according to the February 2001 Netcraft survey (*www.netcraft.com/survey*), and Apple has bundled a version with Mac OS X. (For Mac OS versions prior to Mac OS X, Mac users can use Apache in the commercial WebTen software from Tenon Intersystems.) Mac OS X's UNIX heritage made it possible to include Apache as a replacement for the Personal Web Sharing that added a basic Web server to Mac OS 8 and Mac OS 9.

Apache Web Sharing

Under Mac OS X, Apple has made using Apache for sharing files as easy as flipping on a switch. Web serving is controlled under the Sharing panel of the System Preferences, as shown in Figure 7-1. As with most system-level changes, you must first authenticate yourself to Mac OS X as an administrator of the system. Note the box with the lock on it in the lower left corner of the window in Figure 7-1. To make changes to the Sharing panel, you must click on the lock and enter the administrator password.

To start Apache, click the Start button in the Web Sharing section. That's it. You're running Apache! The files you place in the */Library/WebServer/Documents* folder are accessible to anyone with a Web browser and your server name. Apache is also set up such that any user defined on the system can set up a personal Web page by placing files in the *Sites* folder within their account area. For example, if user dhart places files in the */Users/dhart/Sites* folder, they will be viewable on the Web from *http://your-domain.com/~dhart/*.

There are two changes here from the Mac OS X public beta. First, the Sharing panel no longer tells you what your domain name is (if you have one). If you don't know your domain name, you must use your computer's IP address to view your Web sharing area in a Web browser. To find the domain name for your IP address, if there is one, you can use the Lookup tab of the Network Utility provided with Mac OS X in the */Applications/Utilities* folder.

Second, you no longer have the option of selecting the folder from which Apache serves Web pages. By default, Apache serves the files from */Library/WebServer/Documents*.

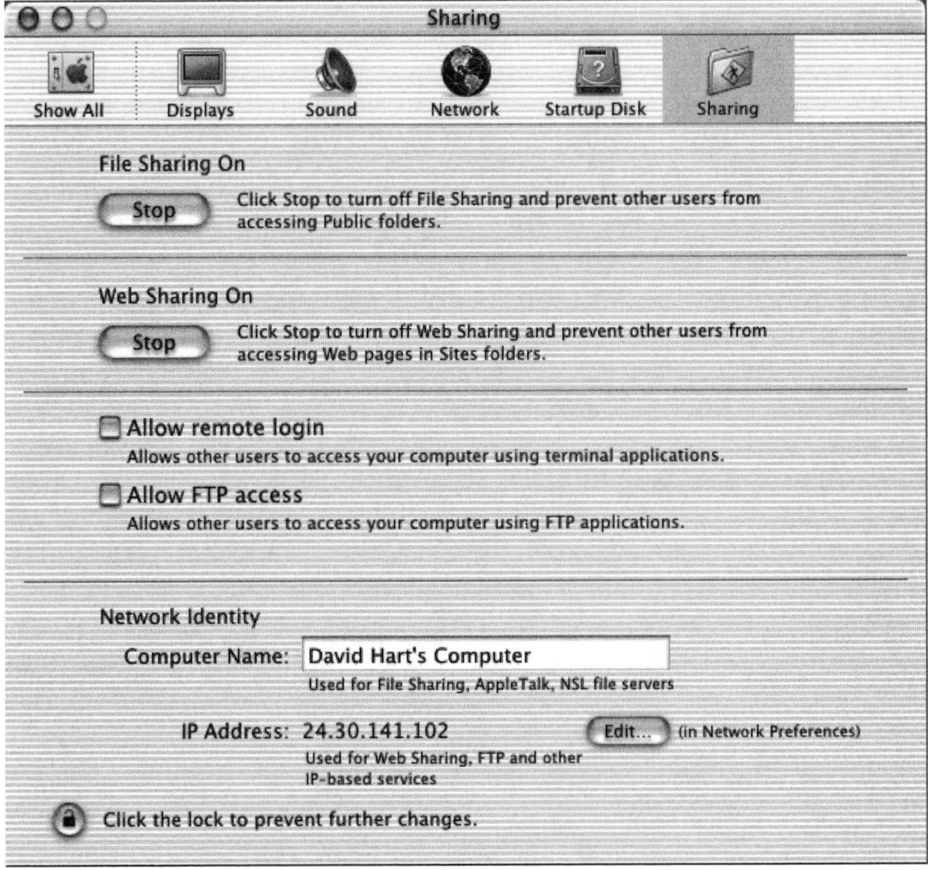

Figure 7-1. Mac OS X File and Web Sharing Services.

The Full Apache

The Sharing panel obviously doesn't let you fine-tune your Apache configuration; however, it is possible to administer Apache on Mac OS X as you would if you were running it on a UNIX system. In other words, you have to edit Apache's configuration file with a text editor to make changes.

The Mac OS X Apache server has four key directories, which are typically found in every Apache server but often under different names. In Mac OS X, two of the default Apache directories are found in the */Library/WebServer* folder, accessible through the Finder. The others are hidden from the Finder and accessible only from the Terminal command line.

- *Documents.* The */Library/WebServer/Documents* folder contains the files you want to be served from your Web site.
- *CGI-Executables.* For security reasons, Apache can keep CGI scripts (see Chapter 11) separate from the rest of the HTML documents. Mac OS X has given a more self-explanatory name to a folder traditionally called *cgi-bin* on UNIX systems. Under the Mac OS X default settings, CGI scripts must be stored in the */Library/WebServer/CGI-Executables* folder to run. The script files must also be set as "executable" from the UNIX command line.
- *Configuration.* The hidden */etc/httpd* directory holds the files that control the Apache settings. The most important is called *httpd.conf,* which is often simply referred to as the config file. This folder also has the file *mime.types,* which lists the MIME types that Apache sends to clients.
- *Logs.* The logs compiled by Apache for accesses and errors are stored in the hidden */var/log/httpd* directory.

As webmaster, you control Apache by modifying the *httpd.conf* file, which is basically a lengthy text file that describes the settings for the Apache application. You can edit this file in any text editor; however, because it is hidden from the Finder, you'll have to copy it back and forth between hidden and Finder-accessible areas of the file system. UNIX experts may prefer to use a command-line tool such as the vi editor.

Apache settings are controlled by more than 150 *directives* (or configuration commands), most of which are referenced in the config file. The config file includes some explanation, but you are encouraged to refer to the Apache documentation or an administration guide to understand the full implications of most of these directives. As a very accelerated introduction, I describe the three major sections of the *httpd.conf* file and the key directives, with examples from the default config file itself.

Section 1: Global Environment. The first section of the configuration file describes settings that affect the general behavior and features of Apache, regardless of the request made of the server. In addition to various time-out settings, this is the section that tells Apache to include various expansion modules. The basic Apache installation has more than 30 such modules, and in the Mac OS X version of Apache, these modules are stored in */usr/libexec/httpd* and handled as dynamic shared objects, which means they can be loaded (or not) each time Apache starts up, based on the LoadModule directives in this section.

In general, the settings in this section will suffice for a basic server. You should read up on the various modules in the Apache documentation before modifying the LoadModule directives.

Section 2: Main Server Configuration. Here is where most of the server settings are controlled. The directives here also provide default values for any virtual hosts (defined in section 3 of the config file). In this section, you'll find some major directives that provide some high-level control of your server, including telling Apache the server's name and the default Documents directory. The ServerName must be a valid domain name, not just something you make up.

```
ServerName dt036n66.san.rr.com
DocumentRoot "/Library/WebServer/Documents"
```

You'll also find directives that set the default port on which Apache listens for HTTP requests, the less privileged account within which Apache runs, and the e-mail address of the server administrator. Mac OS X sets defaults for all of these, except the ServerAdmin directive, which stores the e-mail address for the server administrator. I don't recommend changing the User and Group directives, but you might want to set the ServerAdmin to your e-mail address.

```
Port 80
User www
Group www
ServerAdmin webmaster@your-company.com
```

The config file is also where you can set access restrictions that you want Apache to enforce. By default, Apache is set to allow anyone to view the files in the server's DocumentRoot, but not in any other folder (although you can include aliases to other portions of your hard drive within the Documents folder and Apache will allow visitors to see the files within them. (Apache also has several ways to control access to portions of your Web site.)

The config file lets you specify the logs, stored in the Logs directory, that Apache keeps. An error log records problems encountered by visitors to your server, whether the problems are files not found or CGI scripts that don't work properly. The access log keeps track of successful accesses. This is the file from which your Web server statistics are generated. Apache lets you customize the format of the access log.

The LogFormat is specified with a series of command symbols. The "combined" LogFormat defined above defines a record to have the hostname (%h), client login name if any (%l), remote user if any (%u), date and time (%t), request (%r), status code (%>s), bytes sent (%b), the referring URL (%{Referer}i), and the user agent (%{User-Agent}i). Other fields are available.

```
ErrorLog "/Library/WebServer/Logs/apache_error_log"
LogLevel warn
 LogFormat "%h %l %u %t \"%r\" %>s %b \"%{Referer}i\" \"%{User-
   Agent}i\"" combined
LogFormat "%h %l %u %t \"%r\" %>s %b" common
#CustomLog "/Library/WebServer/Logs/apache_access_log" common
CustomLog "/Library/WebServer/Logs/apache_access_log" combined
```

To allow access to different parts of the server root directory, Apache allows you to define aliases (separate from Mac OS X aliases) to different directories with the Alias directive. To define an alias to a directory from which CGI scripts can be run, you use the ScriptAlias directive. The default Apache config file defines one ScriptAlias: The */Library/WebServer/CGI-Executables* directory is mapped to the traditional */cgi-bin* name. Therefore, a file such as *test.cgi* stored in */Library/WebServer/CGI-Executables* will be accessed through your Web server as *http://your-web-server.com/cgi-bin/test.cgi*. (It is also possible to run CGI scripts from anywhere within your Documents directory, but this default method of segregating executable files is more secure.)

The <IfModule> directive ensures that Apache executes the enclosed directives only if the proper module has been included. The <Directory> block following the ScriptAlias directive below contains the access permissions.

```
<IfModule mod_alias.c>
ScriptAlias /cgi-bin "/Library/WebServer/CGI-Executables"
    <Directory "/Library/WebServer/CGI-Executables">
        AllowOverride None
        Options None
        Order allow,deny
        Allow from all
    </Directory>
</IfModule>
```

The config file also includes directives to instruct Apache how to handle different document types, with the MIME module installed. If you want to use SSIs, or CGI scripts outside of the *CGI-Executables* directory, uncomment the AddHandler lines below. (The "#" at the start of a line indicates a comment.)

```
<IfModule mod_mime.c>
    # To use CGI scripts:
    #AddHandler cgi-script .cgi
    # To use server-side includes HTML files
    #AddType text/html .shtml
    #AddHandler server-parsed .shtml
</IfModule>
```

Section 3: Virtual Hosts. The last section of the Apache configuration file controls the settings for all virtual hosts that you specify in addition to the default server. As described in Chapter 4, virtual hosting allows a single Web server with one IP address to handle requests for several host names. The Web server, Apache in this case, traps the incoming requests and redirects them to the Documents folder for the appropriate virtual host.

Each virtual host can have its own set of preferences, including aliases, log files, and access restrictions, using the same directives available in section 2. In this section, however, the settings for each virtual host are contained within a <VirtualHost> block directive. Any settings not explicitly defined for a virtual host are inherited from the default server settings. The default Apache configuration for Mac OS X does not create any virtual hosts.

In the space of one chapter section, I can hit only the highlights of administering Apache, to which books have been dedicated. If you are interested in taking full advantage of all the features, you can consult the partial list of books and online references in Table 7-5.

WebDAV and Apache

As mentioned in Chapter 5, the Apache installation with Mac OS X can be configured to support WebDAV, the Web-based Distributed Authoring and Versioning protocol. The steps are straightforward. After adding and modifying a few lines in the *httpd.conf* file and entering a few UNIX commands at the Terminal command line, you'll be up and running.

- Stop the Web server in the Sharing panel of the System Preferences using the Stop button. (Leave System Preferences open.)
- Open the *httpd.conf* file. By default, it is located at */etc/httpd/httpd.conf.*
- In section 1 of *httpd.conf,* uncomment the line (remove the leading "#" character from the line) that starts with "#LoadModule dav_module."
- Uncomment the line that starts with "#AddModule mod_dav.c."
- Add two lines of text, one immediately before and one immediately after the line in the *httpd.conf* file that reads "<Directory "/Library/WebServer/Documents">." The three lines, once you've entered them, will look like:

  ```
  DAVLockDB /etc/httpd/davlocks/DAVLockDB
  <Directory "/Library/WebServer/Documents">
  DAV on
  ```
- If you are running virtual hosts on your server and wish to use WebDAV with one or more virtual hosts, you should add the line "DAV on" immediately after the <Directory> directive for each virtual host for which you want to use WebDAV.
- Save and close the *httpd.conf* file. Open the Terminal application and type in the following commands, each followed by a carriage return:

  ```
  mkdir /etc/httpd/davlocks
  chmod 777 /etc/httpd/davlocks
  ```
- Restart Apache by selecting the Start button in the Sharing control panel. (You can close System Preferences, if you like.)

Table 7-5. Apache Information and Resources

Location	Description
www.apache.org	The Apache Software Foundation Web site.
www.oreilly.com/catalog/apache2	*Apache: The Definitive Guide,* 2nd edition, by Ben Laurie and Peter Laurie (O'Reilly, 1999).
apacheunleashed.com	*Apache Server Unleashed,* by Richard Bowen, Ken Coar, et al. (Sam's, 2000).
www.apacheweek.com	*Apache Week,* free online newsletter from Red Hat.
oreilly.apacheweek.com	Apache DevCenter, from the O'Reilly Network.

You can now test your newly configured WebDAV-enabled server with a WebDAV client application such as Goliath or Adobe GoLive 5. You and your collaborators can now lock and download files to work on, then upload and unlock files when you've made changes.

iTools

Technically, iTools from Tenon Intersystems is not a Web server in and of itself. Instead, iTools is a server suite built around the most popular UNIX-based server tools, including the Apache Web server. With iTools, your Apache Web server gets an easier-to-use graphical interface, Web-based remote administration, and access-control management for large collections of users and groups. In addition, the core iTools package includes a virtual-host FTP server, SSL 3.0, the BIND DNS server software, the Squid Web caching server, and the ability to mount Network File System (NFS) disks.

In addition, Tenon has included many other Web server enhancements along with the core iTools package. As separate downloads, Tenon provides WEBmail for browser-based access to e-mail, the ht://Dig search engine, the OpenBase database, Tomcat for Java servlets and Java Server Pages, and the PHP4 hypertext preprocessor for programming custom Web applications. This book will define and describe these additional services in the relevant chapters, while this chapter will focus on the iTools Administration server and SSL 3.0.

Installing iTools

Tenon Intersystems provides a trial download of iTools for Mac OS X from the Tenon Web site. So let's say you want to experiment with iTools for Mac OS X. The first thing you must do before installing iTools is to log in to Mac OS X as "root." It does not suffice to be a user with administrator privileges. Let me repeat: You must login as "root." (This requirement may change in the final releases of Mac OS X and iTools, but it's still a safe way to go.)

Next, you have to be sure your Mac OS X system is configured for the Internet with an IP address, domain name, and so on. Since you've already gotten this far in the book, I'll assume that you're set here. See Chapter 4 for more information. Now, you need to open the System Preferences application and select the Network panel. Click on the Services tab and make sure the Web Server is On and that the Server Name field has the correct host name setting for your machine. You can leave the default Documents folder as is. In other words, turn on Mac OS X's Web file sharing, which starts Apache.

Next, you need to visit the Tenon Web site, register, and download the iTools software. Unstuffing the *.zip* file or untarring the *.tar.gz* file will create an iTools folder on your desktop, inside of which are the *iTools.pkg* package, the file *iTools-installer.sh,* and a Documentation folder. Double-clicking on *iTools.pkg* will start the Mac OS X Installer utility and step you through the process of installing iTools. When the Installer has finished, you should be able to begin using the iTools Administration Server. The installer places an iTools application in the Applications folder, which you can use to change the iTools administration password and check other status information.

iTools Administration Server

The centerpiece of iTools is the iTools Administration Server, which extends Apache in two important ways. First, you get a graphical interface that manages the syntactically demanding Apache configuration file. Second, you can access this interface from any Web browser, which by definition gives you the ability to configure Apache remotely.

If your installation has gone smoothly, you can access the administration server by pointing your browser to the URL *http://yourhost.domain.com/itools_admin.* You'll be prompted to enter the administrator name and password, possibly twice (once to start the administration server and once to access the administration interface), and then you'll see the home page of the iTools Administration Server, as shown in Figure 7-2.

One of the handiest iTools features is the linked Help files. Almost every field name is linked to the relevant passage in the iTools manual. Apache's flexibility means that working with Apache takes some getting used to, so having the manual at the ready helps immensely. Finally, you should note that iTools also gives you the ability to stop or restart the Apache server or administration server

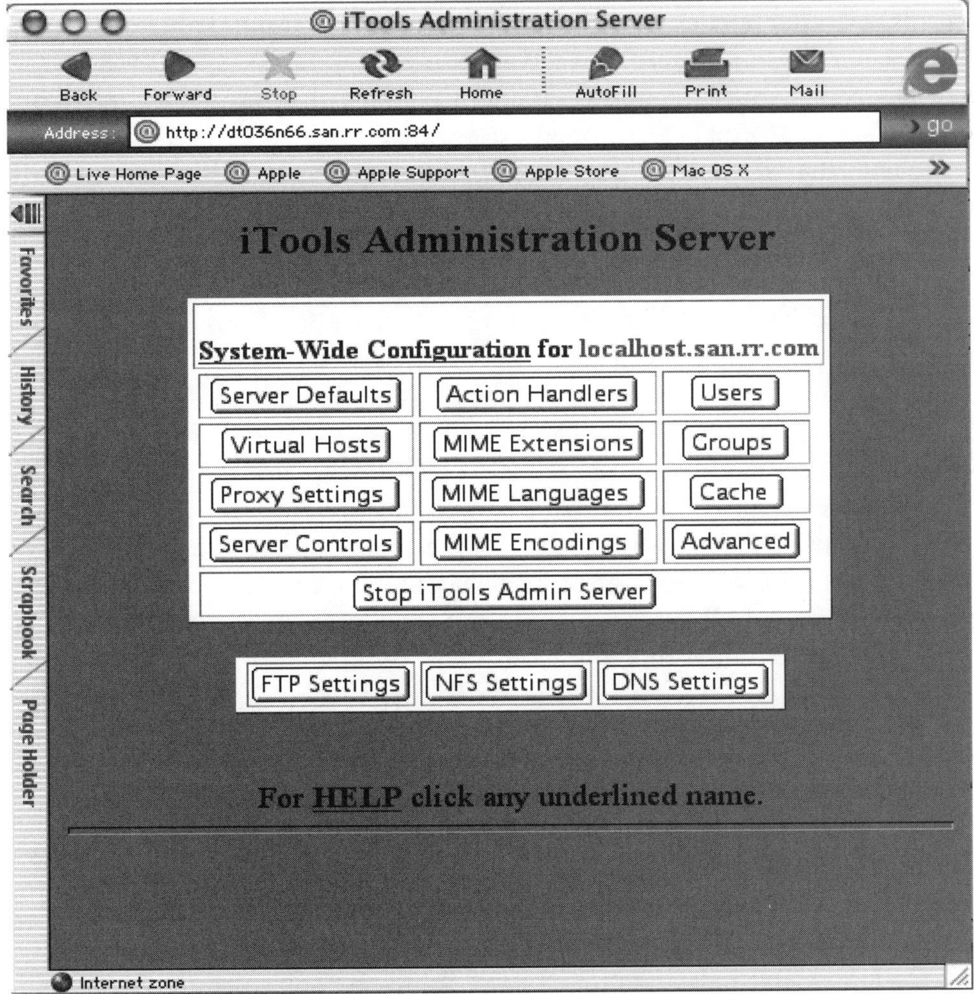

Figure 7-2. iTools Administration Server from Tenon Intersystems.

remotely, as well as to find out information about the current Apache status, with the options found by clicking on the Server Controls button.

If you've read the previous section that describes the Apache config file (*httpd.conf*), you'll see some of the sections reflected in the iTools Administration Server. Section 1 of *httpd.conf* includes some global server settings, which with iTools can be found by selecting the Advanced button. Section 2 of *httpd.conf* includes some settings for the primary or default Web server being handled, and in iTools, you'll find most of these settings by clicking on the Server Defaults button. Finally, section 3 of *httpd.conf* includes settings for virtual hosts, which with iTools you reach by clicking the Virtual Hosts button. Tenon has chosen to define the primary and any secondary Web servers as virtual hosts, as far as Apache is concerned. All the virtual hosts inherit the server defaults, unless you override the settings for a virtual host, as shown in Figure 7-3.

The center iTools buttons control how Apache handles the various MIME types you might be using on your server or making available for download. With the Users and Groups buttons, iTools lets you configure accounts for people who might need to modify the files for one or more of the virtual hosts on your server. Tenon has provided a virtual host FTP service in iTools so that the various content providers have access only to the appropriate section of your system. They may not even know they are sending files to a virtual host.

But wait, there's more! In addition to the administration server, the basic iTools installation adds the Squid Web cache server and the BIND domain name server. As separate downloads, Tenon provides SSL 3.0 (see Chapter 13), WEBmail for browser-based access to e-mail, the ht://Dig search engine (see Chapter 8), the OpenBase database, Tomcat for Java servlets and Java Server Pages (see Chapter 12), and the PHP hypertext preprocessor (see Chapter 12) for programming custom Web applications. Most of these tools are freely available on the Internet and are described in other chapters, but Tenon has done the work of porting them to Mac OS X and creating handy installers that take the guesswork out of putting the pieces together.

MAC OS X SERVER

As you may note as you proceed through this book, many key server applications for the UNIX side of Mac OS X is open source or otherwise freely available. Tenon Intersystems is not the only company that had the idea to provide value-added versions of these tools for Mac webmasters. Apple also built on the free Internet software foundation to deliver Mac OS X Server 2.0. Version 2.0 is a vast departure from the Mac OS X Server operating system that Apple had been selling. Mac OS X Server 1.0 was a distinct operating system. Mac OS X Server 2.0, on the other hand, is a suite of server tools that run on Mac OS X.

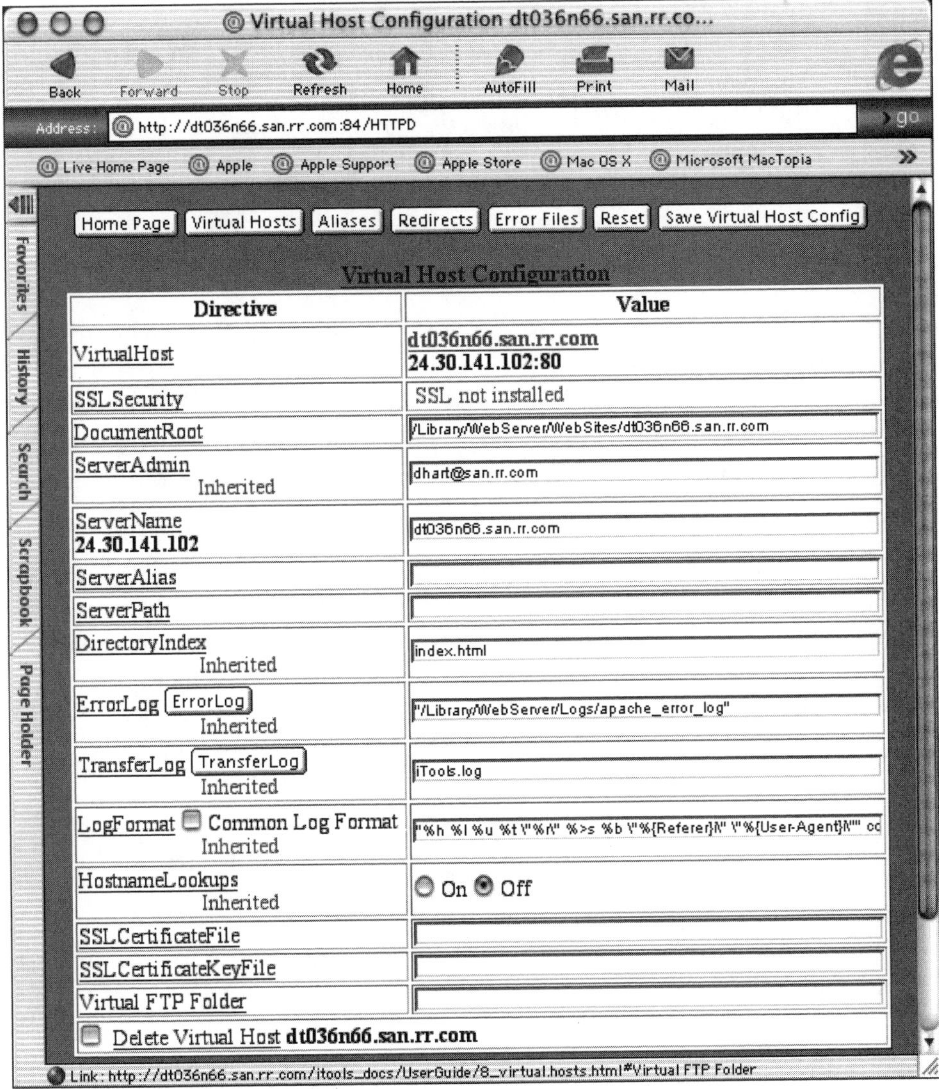

Figure 7-3. iTools Virtual Host Configuration.

Mac OS X Server 2.0 (henceforth, simply Mac OS X Server) performs much the same role for Mac OS X that AppleShare IP performs for the Classic Mac OS. In addition to Internet and Web serving, Mac OS X Server provides file and printing services, and network and directory services.

Internet Services. The collection of services integrated into Mac OS X Server reads like a "Who's Who" of Internet server software. In addition to Apache, Mac OS X Server includes WebDAV, SSL, e-mail servers, Tomcat for Java servlets and Java Server Pages, the MySQL database, PHP and Perl for scripting, WebObjects for Web application development, and QuickTime Streaming Server for streaming digital media. (As this book notes, some of these packages are included in the basic Mac OS X installation but are not accessible to the average user. Mac OS X Server allows less experienced users to enable and configure these packages.)

File and Print Services. Mac OS X Server will allow your system to share files using Apple file services with the AppleTalk Filing Protocol (AFP) over TCP/IP, Windows file sharing, Network File System (NFS) file sharing, and FTP for general Internet file exchange. Print services will allow sharing of network printers over TCP/IP or AppleTalk to Windows or Mac OS computers.

Network and Directory Services. Mac OS X Server provides the tools for IP filtering, a dynamic host configuration protocol (DHCP) server, DNS server, lightweight directory access protocol (LDAP) server, and a service location protocol (SLP) agent. SLP gives IP-based networks some of the capabilities with which Mac users are familiar from AppleTalk networks, with computers and other services located according to scopes (instead of AppleTalk zones). Mac OS X Server also provide a NetBoot server and Macintosh Manager for administering groups of Mac OS computers.

Mac OS X Server was announced only as this book was going into production, so I can't say much more than this. Mac OS X Server was slated to become available a short time after the final release of Mac OS X. The only other tidbit from Apple's early marketing materials is that most (but not all) of the tools in Mac OS X Server will have a graphical user interface.

WebSTAR

The WebSTAR Server Suite from 4D, Inc., with its complete set of features, security, and extensibility via plug-ins—which function much like the plug-ins that add functionality to Web browsers—has been the leading Classic Mac OS Web server and WebSTAR V is now (or will soon be) available for Mac OS X.

WebSTAR V under Mac OS X, according to 4D, will be faster than WebSTAR 4 under Mac OS 9, and plug-ins will have to be Carbonized to work under Mac OS X, which is not surprising. However, 4D has also claimed that WebSTAR V is 50 percent faster than Apache under Mac OS X, which—along with the WebSTAR Server Suite's full complement of server enhancements—should continue to make it a popular Mac Web server option. A minor point to note: WebSTAR 4 will not be ported to Mac OS X, and WebSTAR V will not be ported to Mac OS 9.

Besides being easy to set up and use, WebSTAR includes high-end features including remote administration of essential server functions, Java servlets, dynamic caching, and SSIs. And as its full name—WebSTAR Server Suite—indicates, WebSTAR provides much more than just an Web server. While this book will define and describe these additional services in later chapters, we will list those included with the WebSTAR Server Suite here. Again, these are features of WebSTAR 4, but most should also be available for WebSTAR V.

- E-mail server for IMAP, POP, APOP, and Web-based e-mail
- FTP server
- Proxy server with Web caching
- SSL encryption that supports SSLv3 and integrated HTTP and HTTPS Web servers
- Search engine
- Support for Tomcat's Java Server Pages and Java servlets
- Database integration with the 4D database

If 4D remains true to form, you will be able to download a demonstration copy from the 4D Web site. The WebSTAR 4 demo would run for two hours before quitting. You then must unpack the file, run the installation program, and (possibly) restart your Macintosh. Now you are ready to run a WebSTAR server.

As your first act as a webmaster, you will probably want to change the 4D-provided home page, of course. While you can change the default file, WebSTAR will always serve Web pages starting from the WebSTAR folder. However, you can access other sections of your folder hierarchy by placing aliases to those folders within the WebSTAR folder.

From the bare-bones default setup, you can move on to configure more advanced features and additional WebSTAR services through the application's graphical interface. With WebSTAR's remote administration feature, you can perform all of these configuration tasks from another computer.

I wish I could say more about WebSTAR V in this book, but the realities of publishing schedules mean that I can't wait any longer. WebSTAR 4 continues to be the most popular Web server for the Classic Mac OS, and 4D does have to continue supporting the installed base of WebSTAR 4 users. However, I'm sure that 4D won't want to miss the Mac OS X movement. Be sure to keep an eye on this book's Web site for more information and updates on WebSTAR V.

Web Server 4D

Web Server 4D from MDG Computer Services is hard to categorize. It is another major commercial Web server for the Mac OS (and is also available for Windows systems), but it has integrated database features that make it unique. Built on the 4D database engine from 4D, Inc., Web Server 4D serves data from its internal database, has an extensive repertoire of commands for serving dynamic Web pages, and has advanced server features such as virtual hosting.

MDG Computer Services provides a 300-hour demonstration version of Web Server 4D (and WS4D/CGI) from its Web site. At the time of writing Web Server 4D was not yet available for Mac OS X because 4D, Inc., had not yet made available a Mac OS X version of the 4D database on which Web Server 4D is built. A Carbonized version of Web Server 4D will be the first available for Mac OS X with a feature set essentially the same as the most recent version for the Classic Mac OS.

Because of its integrated database, Web Server 4D sports a search engine built on that database and comes with numerous templates for creating custom

Web site applications such as polls, guestbooks, and phone directories. For additional fees, Web Server 4D has extension modules for e-commerce, e-mail search, and advertising banners. These modules—which make it possible to develop specific types of Web applications without complicated programming—will be available for Mac OS X at the same time Web Server 4D becomes available.

Rather than bundling itself with additional Internet services, Web Server 4D provides the components needed to create custom interaction with dynamic Web pages. While it might not be as extensive as other dedicated custom interaction tools, described in Chapter 12, this feature can come in quite handy. Furthermore, Web Server 4D can be used as a CGI application to extend the functionality of other Web servers. Since one of the more interesting features of Web Server 4D is its built-in Web application language and database, I use Web Server 4D to show an example guestbook application in Chapter 10.

Web Hosting

I wanted to mention one final Web serving option, even though it appears to work counter to my goal of selling this book. While this book shows you that setting up a Mac Web server is not difficult, it will also become clear that this is not a trivial undertaking. There are software updates to watch for, hardware upgrades to buy, regular server administration to conduct, system maintenance to perform, security issues to consider, and new services to evaluate for your system.

All of these tasks take time, many require money, and we haven't even begun to talk about producing the text, graphics, and other information formats that you want to publish on your server. For an individual or small organization, running a Web server may cost more in time and money than you want to spend. (However, if you have the time and inclination, it's a heck of a lot of fun.)

The growth of the Web has created a thriving marketplace for Web hosting, an alternative to the do-it-yourself model of running a Web server. Web hosting companies will run your Web server for you, for as little as $20 per month (and sometimes less). There are three basic levels of Web hosting service that most Web hosting companies offer, and they may subdivide the levels even further.

Table 7-6 includes information for selecting Mac-based Web hosting services. *MacWebserver.com* is a useful directory of such services, which lets you search

Table 7-6. Mac Web Hosting Services

Location	Description
www.macwebserver.com	A place to search from among 200 Mac Web hosting services worldwide.
www.digitalforest.net	Digital Forest offers Web and FileMaker Pro hosting and server co-location.
www.madmacs.net	Mad Macs offers Web hosting starting at $30 per month and server co-location starting at $200 per month.
www.inno-tech.com	Innovative Technologies Group hosts the *MacWebserver.com* site and offers hosting on Mac and Windows NT servers.

for Mac Web hosting companies by location, the Web server software and database software that they support, and other services. I have also listed a few Mac-based hosting services as examples. (These are provided just for reference, not as recommendations.)

Basic Shared Server. With the entry level of service, the Web hosting company provides you disk space on one of its existing servers and uses virtual hosting or IP multihoming to have your domain name serve from that machine. This will give you a basic Web server to handle an average amount of traffic. The Web hosting company will provide e-mail addresses, DNS service, and server maintenance and backup, and you will be able to publish material to your site remotely. In general, you do not get to choose the machine or Web server software, although some companies do offer these choices.

The cost for this service can increase (quite dramatically) if you have Web traffic above a certain number of megabytes or gigabytes per month and if you add extended Web features such as database integration, e-commerce capabilities, or customized interaction through scripts or forms.

Dedicated Server. If you want more control over your server, most Web hosting services will provide you with a computer dedicated to running your Web server. For this service, you do pay a premium fee, but you have more freedom to extend and customize your Web server's capabilities, and you may be able to choose the computer and operating system that the server runs, in addition to the services provided for a basic shared server.

Because the server is owned and operated primarily by the Web hosting company, the software you install may be limited to the server, database, e-commerce, and other software that the hosting company recommends and supports. However, you generally get a higher level of technical support from the hosting company as you customize your site.

Server Co-location. If you really want to own your Web server, but you keep running up against expensive network connections (which can be a large percentage of your Web server budget), you have a third option. Instead of paying for the network to come to your server, you send your server closer to the network. With server co-location, you purchase the Web server computer, purchase and install software, and customize to your heart's content, but the server itself is located at the Web hosting company's facility. In this way, your server is close to a high-speed, dedicated Internet connection, but you can still have an inexpensive dial-up connection from your home or office.

With server co-location, you administer your server remotely (using remote control software or file synchronization software, described in Chapter 5) and decide what software you will run. The hosting service generally provides the Internet connection, DNS configuration, 24/7 monitoring and rebooting, and often an uninterruptible power supply.

Web hosting services can help with many of the nuts-and-bolts tasks that must be done, but this option isn't as much fun or creative as designing and publishing the material on your server. Since this book is concerned about Mac Web servers, there's an obvious question you might be asking yourself: If I choose to use a hosting service, do I lose the chance to use a Mac Web server? Not at all.

Using a Web hosting service doesn't mean you have to forgo serving from a Mac or that you can't benefit from this book. Furthermore, small companies and community-minded groups have sprung up to allow webmasters to outsource individual components of their Web sites, from DNS service and e-mail to community forums and e-commerce enhancements. This book will point out both the do-it-yourself and outsource options as upcoming chapters discuss the various Web server enhancements and extensions.

Log Analysis Tools

Most Web servers, as well as other types of servers, log all requests and accesses to the server as well as any warnings or errors relating to server operation. These log files are both your friends and your enemies. They are your friends, since they let you analyze problems and monitor usage. Usage statistics, for example, may be important for justifying the resources spent in developing the server and for planning expansion. On the other hand, the log files can be your enemies because you cannot ignore them. On heavily loaded servers these log files can grow until they consume all available disk space. For example, a Web server receiving 1 million hits per month can produce approximately 300 MB worth of log files each month.

Not all Web servers use the same log file format by default. Most Web servers can produce a widely recognized format called the *common log format*. A record in the common log format appears as follows:

```
hercules.sdsc.edu - - [12/Mar/1996:18:54:15 -0800]
  "GET /moose/moose.html HTTP/1.0" 200 2238
```

- *hercules.sdsc.edu* is the client requesting the page from the server.
- *[12/Mar/1996:18:54:15 -0800]* is the date and time the request was made. Note that the time zone (U.S. Pacific Standard Time) is eight hours behind Greenwich Mean Time.
- *GET /moose/moose.html HTTP/1.0* is the request made to get the file using version 1.0 of the HTTP protocol where the file is *DocumentRoot/moose/moose.html*.
- *200* is the return status for the request (i.e., normal completion).
- *2238* is the number of bytes transferred.

In addition, many Mac Web servers record data in the WebSTAR log format, which includes additional details. (Unlike UNIX servers, which may maintain separate log files for additional information, most Macintosh servers store this information within the main log file, using extended formats.) WebSTAR log format includes the following entries for every record: date, time, result, status code, host name, agent, referrer, host field, URL, and bytes sent. A record in WebSTAR format looks like this (without the line wrapping):

```
05/29/00  20:42:26  OK  200       204-210-5-229.san.rr.com
Mozilla/4.73 (Macintosh; U; PPC)  http://204.210.5.229/
-  :forms:guestbook:addmain.html  2723
```

- *05/29/00 20:42:26* is the date and local time that the record was added to the log file.

- *OK 200* is the result and status code for the request.
- *204-210-5-229.san.rr.com* is the requestor's host name.
- *Mozilla/4.73 (Macintosh; U; PPC)* is the requestor's browser agent.
- *http://204.210.5.229/* is the referring Web site.
- "-" in this example represents an empty value for the host field token in the log record.
- *:forms:guestbook:addmain.html* is the URL requested from the server.
- *2723* is the number of bytes sent by the server.

Other pieces of information, or "tokens," that a Web server might be able to log—the exact list differs for each server—include user, method, path, search arguments, transfer time, cookie, and language. Many log analysis programs will automatically determine the format from a log record that specifies the format of the tokens in subsequent records.

Choosing Log Analysis Software

When evaluating a log analysis program, there are few general features you should look for and test, in addition to those that you specifically know you will need. Remember that this is only a partial list of features to get you started.

- Graphical versus nongraphical. Graphics are usually easier to interpret with a glance, but not all analysis programs provide this feature.
- Error reports. After basic traffic reports, the most useful information can come from error reports, which tell you the parts of your site that need attention.
- Report selection and customization. Some packages automatically calculate 100 different reports or more. Others have much more limited default reporting. Most can be customized, and you should also consider the effort required to customize reports.
- Virtual domains or subreports. If you run servers from several domains on your server, or even separate projects from the same domain, you'll want to make sure your analysis program will let you create separate reports for each virtual domain or separate section. Some programs limit the number of domains or subreports.

- Online or off-line. Some programs, such as Summary, display their results through a built-in Web server, so they must be viewed from an online computer. Others create reports in text or HTML files that can be viewed off-line.
- Automatic or manual. Some programs can be scheduled to calculate statistics automatically on a regular basis, while others require operator intervention to start an analysis.
- Logs from other servers. Not all analysis programs will analyze FTP or list server log files, so if this feature is something you need, you will want to consider that factor as well.

Table 7-7 lists several programs available for performing regular analyses of your server's Web log files. They all produce the same basic reports, and you might want to compare several to see which combination of available reports, ease of use, graphical reporting, and cost fits your needs.

Using Log Statistics

Monitoring the usage of your Web server is a two-step process. First, you divide the log files into manageable chunks, usually based on a given time period. Typically, once per week or once per month, depending on amount of usage, you will "roll over" your log file—you rename the current log file and create a new one. Next, with the log files in manageable sizes, you summarize the information using a log analysis program. This section also discusses some of the errors and warnings contained in these files and how you should respond to them.

Log analysis programs commonly summarize several categories of information. By keeping an eye on these summaries, you can take action to ensure that your site and your server meet the needs of your audiences.

Number of Unique Visitors. This information is a better measure of your site's popularity than hits, because it tells you how many people are viewing your site, not how many files are moving around. Log analysis programs also identify the domains from which visitors are viewing your site and, from this, you can usually tell which search engine robots have been visiting your site. You might also watch how the number of visitors changes over time. A spike in the number of visits might correspond to an external event or some successful publicity effort.

Visit Analysis. Advanced log analysis tools can also extract information about the length of time and the number of viewed pages for each visit a visitor makes at your site. This can help you identify if your visitors see one page and move on or if they come to your site and spend time looking around.

Page and Graphics Hits. In total, the hit counts describe how busy your server is, but note that one visitor viewing your home page might cause several hits—one for the HTML page itself and one for each graphic on the page. If your log analysis program calculates the number of hits that each page receives, you can also get an idea about which sections of your site are most popular and thus have the information your audience is looking for.

Table 7-7. Programs for Analyzing Web Server Log Files

Location	Description
www.analog.cx *www.sigsoftware.com/analoghelper* *www.reportmagic.com*	Analog freeware provides multiple report options but shows its UNIX roots in its interface. Analog Helper, shareware from Sig Software, adds a graphical interface to Analog. Report Magic, freeware by Wadsack-Allen and Jason Linhart, gives Analog more graphs and reports.
www.maximized.com/products/flashstats	FlashStats, a commercial package from Maximized Software.
www.quest.com/funnel_web	Funnel Web, a commercial package from Quest Software, Inc.
www.opendoor.com/logdoor	LogDoor Real-Time Server Monitor, commercial software from Open Door Networks.
www.flowerfire.com	Sawmill, commercial software by Flowerfire Software.
www.kitchen-sink.com/serverstat	ServerStat, freeware from Kitchen Sink Software.
www.summary.net	Summary and Summary Pro, shareware from Summary.Net.
www.seacloak.com	Traffic Report, commercial software from SeaCloak Software.
www.redpointsoftware.co.uk	WWWStat4Mac, shareware from Redpoint Software.

Bytes Sent and Bandwidth Usage. This is a measure of the work your server does to satisfy the requests from your visitors. If you serve lots of large graphic or media files, you might have a large number of bytes sent and consume a large amount of bandwidth. With this information, you can see if your network connection is being taxed and determine whether you need to upgrade.

Referring Domains. When a visitor reaches a page at your site by clicking on a link at another site, the referring domain name can be recorded in your Web log. By analyzing this information, you can tell which sites are linking to your site and, just as importantly, which sites are *not* pointing to your site but should be. Of course, the leading referrer for your site will probably be your site, as visitors click on links that move them from one page to another.

Browsers Used by Visitors. A Web request also includes the browser, or agent, that each visitor is using. Agent summaries will tell you the most popular browser (and version) used to view your Web pages. This could help you determine whether your audience can view advanced Web technologies or Navigator- or Explorer-specific features.

Errors and Problems. Error summaries might tell you which missing files users are regularly requesting. For example, a referring site that has not been updated might send potential viewers to a defunct portion of your site. Common mistakes might suggest you create a page pointing to the correct new URL or modify your default error page with helpful tips.

Analog

Analog is one of the more popular log analyzers available, primarily because of its extremely attractive price-performance ratio—in other words, it's free. Analog was originally developed by Stephen Turner for UNIX systems, and the software has since been ported to many platforms. Because of Analog's UNIX roots, it was quickly made available for Mac OS X. The primary disadvantage to Analog, if you are more comfortable in the graphical Mac world, is Analog's lack of a graphical interface. It is configured by editing a text file and run from the Terminal command line. On the other hand, Analog is fast, highly configurable, and multilingual.

If you're looking for a power log analyzer at a low cost, Analog is hard to beat. (It's also available for Mac OS 8 and Mac OS 9.) To get started using Analog, you need to download and follow the instructions for installing Analog from the Terminal command line. (These will likely change before the final release of Mac OS X, so I won't go into detail here.) Once Analog is installed, you have to modify the configuration file, *analog.cfg,* that's included with the Analog installation. There are four lines you need to modify to get Analog to work.

If you are using Apache, you need to insert a line to identify the format of your log files. Analog has a command, conveniently called ApacheLogFormat, for this purpose. You need to insert the log format specified in your *httpd.config* file. The LogFile command must point to the log file you want analyzed, and OutFile identifies the file in which Analog will place its results. HostName specifies the host for which you are creating the statistics. (The HostName is used for the file headers, so it can be just about anything you like.) As an example, these lines might look like the following:

```
APACHELOGFORMAT (%h %l %u %t \"%r\" %>s %b \"%{Referer}i\" \"%{User-
     Agent}i\")
LOGFILE /Library/WebServer/Logs/apache_access_log
OUTFILE outfile.html
HOSTNAME dt036n66.san.rr.com
```

Figure 7-4 shows the results of running Analog and displaying the OutFile in your Web browser. Only portions of the Analog results are visible in the figure. The figure also shows that Analog's output is primarily textual, although it does include some simple bars to highlight the magnitude of some values. Other log analyzer software produces more extensive graphical output. Analog also only produces static result files, and you must run Analog—or schedule Analog to run—each time you want to update your statistics.

Summary

Summary by Jason Linhart is shareware, with a commercial Pro version, that generates more than 100 different reports from your Web logs. In addition to the variety of reports, Summary's main strengths are its built-in Web server and remote administration. You configure almost everything in Summary through a Web interface.

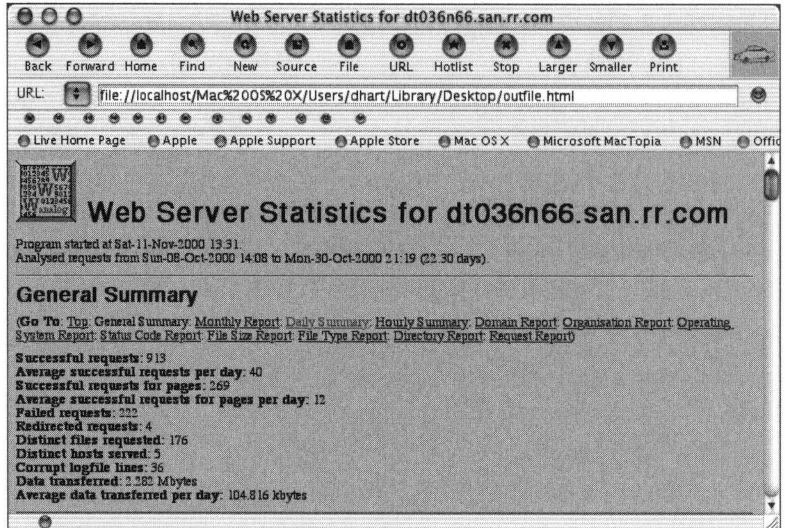

Figure 7-4. Analog Output Statistics.

The only step that must be handled through the Finder—once you've downloaded and uncompressed the Summary software—is to place your Web logs, or aliases to them, into Summary's log folder. After that, you just need to start Summary. (The first release for Mac OS X required you to start Summary from the Terminal command line, but I expect future versions will let you double-click an application icon.)

You can also schedule Summary to recalculate the statistics on a regular basis. Therefore, Summary can provide "live" Web statistics if you place an alias to your Web server's *current* log file in Summary's log folder. If your Web server is busy, it is also possible to run Summary on a different machine and FTP the log files from your main server when needed.

Summary has many other nice features, such as automatically detecting the log format from the log files, making it easy to produce reports for multiple sites from the same log files, sorting reports by column, and password protecting those reports you don't want people to see.

Figure 7-5 shows a portion of Summary's main summary report from a year's worth of log files on my own Web server. You can also see that Summary does provide some graphical elements in the form of bar graphs, but it does not create more general graphics. (Summary Pro lets you export statistics to files that can be read by spreadsheet software, for generating fancier graphics.)

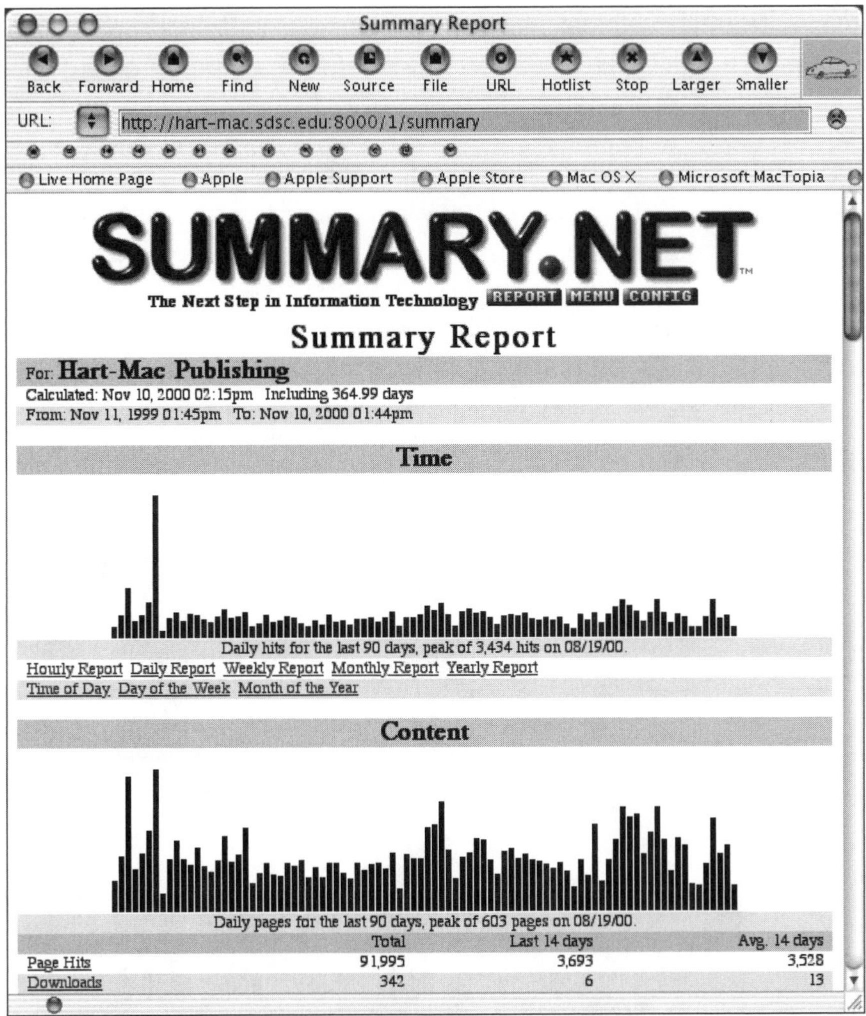

Figure 7-5. Summary Output Statistics.

Funnel Web

Funnel Web from Quest Software, Inc., is one of the top high-end log analysis tools. It claims to be one of the fastest Web log analysis programs, if not the fastest. Funnel Web comes in Standard and Enterprise versions; Funnel Web Standard targets small to medium-sized Web sites with up to 10 virtual domains, while the Enterprise version can analyze an unlimited number of domains.

In addition, Funnel Web is configured through a desktop application with a graphical interface. Funnel Web also shines in the area of graphical output and can produce pie charts, bar charts, line graphs, and other graphics in GIF, JPEG, PNG, and PDF formats. Figure 7-6 shows an example of the graphics that Funnel Web produces (generated by the Web-accessible Funnel Web demo). Funnel Web Standard also features incremental analysis, automated scheduling for report generation, and built-in archiving, compression, and e-mail notification.

Funnel Web Enterprise provides tools for the most demanding Web analyses, including analysis of advertising and streaming media hits. In addition, Funnel Web Enterprise offers real-time analysis of statistics, updating reports and graphs continuously. Finally, Funnel Web's unique "clickstream analysis" provides detailed information on each client's visit, including time spent on site and the path followed.

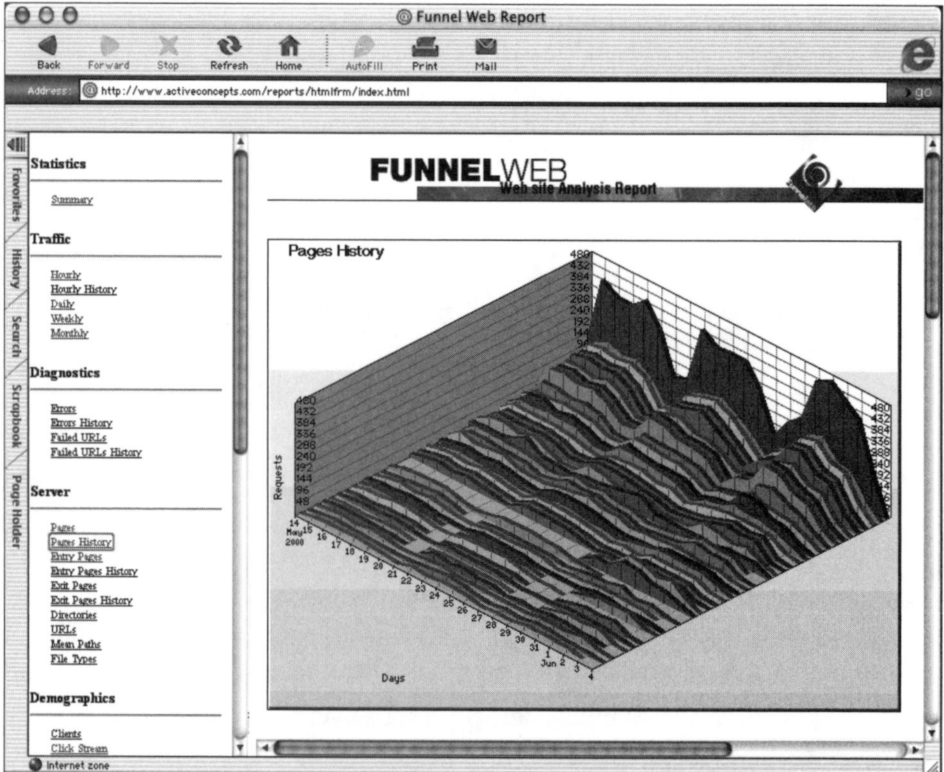

Figure 7-6. Graphical Reporting from Funnel Web by Quest Software, Inc.

CHAPTER 8

FTP, E-Mail, and Search

To establish a full-fledged Internet presence, a Web server is only the starting point. A Web server, after all, only responds to HTTP requests, serving up Web pages, graphics, and other document types to visitors who follow a trail of links within your Web site. If this is all you need—as determined by an analysis of your audience's needs and an assessment of the best ways to meet those needs (see Chapter 3)—then sit back and watch the page hits roll in.

However, you may have other requirements for your server. Perhaps you expect your visitors to download copies of the software you've developed, which you're distributing as compressed files. Perhaps your audience prefers to communicate with your or with one another by e-mail messages or mailing lists. And perhaps, despite your best efforts to make your site's navigation simplicity itself, your visitors could benefit from the ability to search for key words or phrases on your Web pages or in your library of PDF files. If these or similar situations apply to you, then you may be in the market for an FTP server, an e-mail server, a list server, or a search engine. This chapter discusses each of these Internet services in turn.

FTP SERVERS

As you'll recall, the file transfer protocol (FTP) is an Internet standard for moving files between computers. FTP has a few features that make it more convenient than the Web for exchanging files. For example, FTP can transfer entire folders at a time, including all files and subfolders. For moving files to and from a server, FTP and FTP servers have many useful features.

- FTP is the most widely available mechanism for transferring files and is supported on all major platforms. FTP efficiently supports text and binary transfers. (Text files will be transferred successfully in binary mode between your client and the server, albeit at a slower rate. Binary files will *not* be transferred successfully in text mode.) Some FTP servers allow users to resume interrupted file transfers where they left off, and some will uncompress and compress files automatically as they are transferred.
- FTP permits entire directory (folder) structures to be copied, whereas HTTP transfers are generally limited to one file at a time.
- FTP is relatively secure—meaning there are few, if any, ways to use an FTP server to break into a computer—because it has been tested over a long period.
- You can control access to your FTP server by users according to their login IDs and what host or subnet they come from. You can also log who accesses your FTP server and what visitors do.
- You can restrict how many simultaneous users are allowed to access your system, in total or according to each class that you have defined. You can also restrict who can upload files to and delete files from your FTP server.
- You can provide instructions and comments when a user accesses the FTP archive and when visitors access specific directories within the

archive. On some servers, any visitor accessing the archive can be informed of when files were last modified in the archive.

- The server can provide a graceful mechanism for notifying FTP users of an impending shutdown.

You may be more familiar with FTP in its "anonymous" form. Anonymous FTP is analogous to guest file sharing on the Mac; you don't need to use a password to access files. Full-featured FTP servers (and clients) also support password access to files.

Choosing an FTP Server

In addition to the FTP server included with Mac OS X, there are several other options. First, if you are using 4D's WebSTAR, Tenon's iTools, or Apple's Mac OS X Server, you have an FTP server as part of the server suite. The FTP servers included with the Web server suites should suffice for most FTP requirements. Table 8-1 lists standalone FTP servers available for Mac OS X.

Rumpus and Rumpus Pro provide heavy-duty FTP services for the Mac OS and will likely make the move to Mac OS X. Rumpus should also be considered for its ease of use, which will be an advantage over the default FTP server. You should investigate Rumpus for top-of-the-line FTP service—for example, if you expect your FTP server to see dozens or hundreds of simultaneous users.

Table 8-1. Mac OS X FTP Servers

Location	FTP Server
crushftp.terrashare.com	CrushFTP, shareware by Ben Spink written in Java.
www.stairways.com/netpresenz	NetPresenz, FTP and HTTP server shareware by Stairways Software for the Classic Mac OS.
www.ncftpd.com/ncftpd	NcFTPd, a commercial FTP server from NcFTP Software.
www.gravitt.org/osx	wu-ftpd, an enhanced FTP server to replace ftpd, compiled by Brooke Gravitt for Mac OS X.
www.proftpd.net	ProFTPd, the Professional FTP Daemon, freeware from the ProFTPd Project.
www.maxum.com/Rumpus	Rumpus and Rumpus Pro, commercial software by Maxum Development.

Although its registration fee has gone up, NetPresenz is an easy-to-use, time-tested FTP server for the Classic Mac OS. At the time of writing, there were no plans to port NetPresenz to Mac OS X. However, with minimal system requirements, NetPresenz works on older Macs running System 7 or better. The primary limitation of NetPresenz is that it needs Mac OS file sharing to be on, which can slow down network performance on the Classic Mac OS by as much as 15 percent.

Your FTP Archive

The files you serve to users via FTP are called your *FTP archive*. The structure of your FTP archive is the only part of your overall file system that FTP users are allowed to see. (Portions of your archive may be restricted to certain users.) Once you have archived some files and correctly configured the FTP server software, users can access your FTP archive using an FTP client or a Web browser.

FTP also provides a mechanism, beyond e-mail, for users to send you information that you might wish to make generally available on your server. That is, you can create a writable folder in your FTP archive in which FTP users deposit information.

Providing such a guest-writable folder can present a security issue, particularly if you make that folder guest-readable. Although you may specify that your server is for particular information, other Internet residents may decide to "borrow" your server and disk space to exchange files that you do not intend or that may even be illegal. (I speak from experience; it happened to me.) To avoid this awkward situation, you can create two separate folders, one that is guest-writable but *not* guest-readable, and one that is guest-readable but *not* guest-writable. In this way, uploads are not automatically available to the world. On the other hand, you now must manually inspect all uploaded files before moving them to your guest-readable area (or not).

Your FTP archive can be as simple or as complex as you wish to make it. But, as with your Web site, your goal should be to make it as easy as possible for your visitors to find the files they need (unless you're setting up some strange FTP scavenger hunt game). You may want to visit a few of the larger FTP archives, and as you browse through their structure, you should keep in mind a number of points regarding FTP and FTP-accessible software distributions:

- Many information providers go to considerable trouble to ensure that access to information in their FTP archives is straightforward. You should try to do the same.
- The top level of an FTP directory (folder) tree is usually */pub,* but when you log in the directory is usually / (the root directory). Some servers can be configured to automatically start guests at the correct point in the folder hierarchy.
- Because FTP archives do not have the same opportunities as Web pages to provide visual navigation cues, you should provide your visitors with descriptive file names and use "read me" files where needed to explain what your visitors are seeing.

ftpd

An FTP server is built into most flavors of UNIX, and Mac OS X includes the standard UNIX FTP server software, called *ftpd,* for file transfer protocol daemon. You don't have to go to the Terminal to start ftpd, however; the Sharing panel of the System Preferences lets you turn on FTP file sharing by checking a check box, as shown in Figure 8-1. By default, Mac OS X installs with the FTP server off, for security reasons, and it is set to deny access to users attempting to connect via FTP as "root" or "Administrator."

With FTP access turned on, users with accounts on your Mac OS X system can connect via FTP, and by default, they have access to the files in their home directories. Mac OS X, by default, does not permit anonymous FTP access. If you are unhappy with the features of ftpd, the free wu-ftpd or ProFTPd servers provide enhancements to the basic functionality of ftpd.

It is possible to set up anonymous FTP access using ftpd, but it is not for the faint of heart. (As a general security precaution, anonymous FTP is not the preferred means for exchanging files because of the potential for problems.) First, you need to create a user (using the Users panel of the System Preferences) named *ftp* with some arbitrary password. The system will create a directory called */Users/ftp,* with a standard set of folders inside. The remaining steps require issuing UNIX commands as root from the Terminal command line.

Because of the use of root access, the need for an intermediate familiarity with UNIX, the potential for really screwing up your system, and the security problems that could arise if the book has an incorrect command or if you type a command incorrectly, I decided not to include the full details here. For now, I'll say that the manual page for ftpd describes the steps, but they are not complete. I'll post the series of UNIX commands, along with explanations, on this book's Web site. There I can make changes quickly if problems are detected.

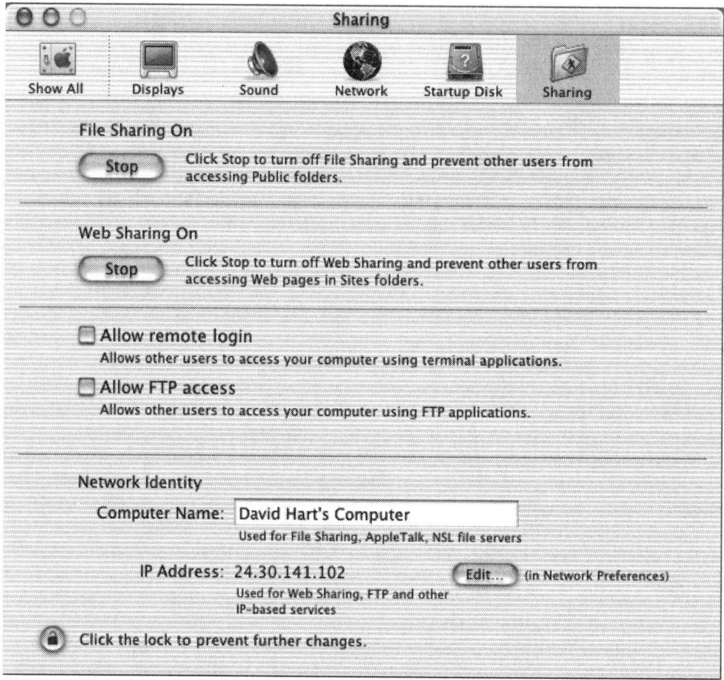

Figure 8-1. FTP File Sharing in Mac OS X.

E-MAIL SERVERS

E-mail services are vital for reaching a wide and diverse audience. Many people have e-mail access but no other Internet connection. Examples are users in developing countries, users at companies that have restricted Web access for employees, and those using free e-mail-only services. Many people prefer to receive information via e-mail because it can be downloaded quickly over slow connections, such as modems and wireless devices, and read at the user's convenience. Furthermore, e-mail has the advantage of being delivered with minimal effort by the user, as opposed to a Web site, which depends on the user making the effort to visit.

E-mail services are the most mature of the Internet services you can provide. Some people believe, therefore, that e-mail is the most secure service. Of course, e-mail security breaches, when they occur, affect more people than the other services. News reports regularly document the widespread losses and expenses of the numerous viruses and worms spread through e-mail attachments. Macintosh users are generally spared the brunt of such plagues, which take advantage of the interaction between various Windows-based applications.

Because of the universal appeal and use of e-mail, Web server suites such as WebSTAR, iTools, and Mac OS X Server already include some e-mail services. For many users, these servers will suffice. Table 8-2 lists a few separately available mail servers for Mac OS X. These standalone servers fall into two basic categories: freeware or heavy-duty commercial software. The next section compares the key features of the various mail server options.

Choosing an E-Mail Server

If you are going to provide an e-mail server, you need to answer one general question: How will you allow your e-mail clients to read their messages? If you

Table 8-2. Mac OS X Mail Servers

Location	Mail Service
www.stalker.com	CommuniGate Pro, commercial software from Stalker Software.
www.eudora.com/products	Qpopper 3 freeware and Qpopper LX 4 commercial software from Qualcomm. EIMS is available for the Classic Mac OS.
www2.opendoor.com/maildoor	MailDoor from Open Door Networks adds multi-domain capability to EIMS 1.*x* for the Classic Mac OS.
www.rockfordsys.com	MailProxy, commercial software by RockFord Systems, does not need a permanent Internet connection.
www.emumail.com	EMU Webmail and EMU Alacer Web mail server additions from EMUmail, Inc.
www.freebsd.org/ports/mail.html	Numerous mail servers and clients for FreeBSD, which will likely work on Mac OS X.
netwinsite.com	DMail Server and various commercial packages for Web access to e-mail, from Netwin Ltd.

plan to operate a mail server only so that you can also run a list server (see the section on list servers in this chapter), then your answer may be not at all. If you are going to provide e-mail accounts for your customers or employees, you have a choice of traditional e-mail accounts, server-based accounts, or Web-based accounts.

You may also need to consider if you are providing e-mail accounts for more than one domain name. Most, but not all, e-mail servers can distinguish between mail destined for different domains hosted on the same server—such as *info@companyA.com* and *info@nonprofitB.org*.

Since you will be operating a mail server, you will need to be familiar with the same e-mail protocols that you encountered when selecting an e-mail client, along with a few others.

POP3 and APOP. The Post Office Protocol, version 3 (POP3), is the traditional protocol for incoming e-mail. With POP3, your e-mail server receives e-mail destined for users that have e-mail accounts with you. The server holds the mail until the user checks for new mail. At that time, the user's client software downloads the new messages and any attachments in their entirety. The server may retain copies of these messages for a limited time, but the user has the ultimate responsibility for keeping track of his or her e-mail. The Authenticated Post Office Protocol (APOP) works in much the same way, except that the user's password is encrypted before being sent across the network.

POP3 and APOP require much less work and disk space on the server, and most e-mail clients support POP3. Another advantage of POP3 and APOP is that users do not need to be connected to the Internet while they read their e-mail; they can connect to their ISP, download any new messages, and disconnect. Some list servers can be configured to use POP3 mail servers.

IMAP. The Internet Mail Access Protocol (IMAP) is another way for users to read their e-mail. With IMAP, however, a user's e-mail messages reside on the server permanently. With an IMAP e-mail client, the user can create folders, organize messages, and otherwise manage mail, and the server keeps the permanent copy and, by implication, must be responsible for keeping a backup copy. IMAP is advantageous for users who travel or who read e-mail from several different clients—perhaps a desktop at home, a laptop at the office or on the road, or even a handheld organizer or digital cell phone.

No matter how the user accesses his or her e-mail account, the server always has the official copy so there are no synchronization issues between devices; of course, each mail-reading device must resynchronize with the server each time it connects. For slow connections, IMAP also permits the message headers to be downloaded first and the (usually larger) message bodies to be downloaded only as needed. The disadvantage to IMAP is that it requires users to be connected to the IMAP server the entire time they are reading e-mail.

Web-Based E-Mail. A third way for users to read e-mail has no distinguishing acronym, but is commonly referred to as Web-mail. With Web-mail, as with IMAP, the server keeps the sole copy of a user's messages. But unlike the case with IMAP, the user can read mail from any Web browser. Web-mail has many of the same advantages of IMAP. Web-mail has the added advantage that a user does not need to carry around a computer to read e-mail. Any computer that has an Internet connection and a Web browser—for example, an airport kiosk or a computer in an Internet café—will allow a user to read and manage their e-mail. Because the server keeps the official copy of e-mail messages in both IMAP and Web-mail, users can often use them interchangeably, from an IMAP client if one is handy, or from a Web client if that is what's available.

SMTP. While POP, IMAP, and Web-mail are three options for receiving mail, you have only one protocol to remember for *sending* mail: the Simple Mail Transfer Protocol (SMTP). An SMTP server takes outgoing messages and delivers them to the appropriate domain. SMTP-based list servers work closely with an SMTP server. Just emerging are standards for extensions to SMTP in the Extended Simple Mail Text Protocol (ESMTP).

Table 8-3 compares the features of the stand-alone Mac OS X e-mail servers (above) along with the e-mail servers included with the major Web server suites (Chapter 7). Note that this is not a complete feature set for these servers. For example, the CommuniGate Pro suite from Stalker Software also includes pager, fax, and print gateways. Other features, not discussed here, that might affect your decision include remote administration, SSL security for password protection, and built-in list server capability.

Free E-Mail Servers

At the time of writing, there were no plans to move the two primary free e-mail servers for the Classic Mac OS to Mac OS X. Because both the Eudora Internet Mail Server (EIMS) and the Stalker Internet Mail Server (SIMS) were free, the

Table 8-3. Mac OS X and Classic Mac OS Mail Server Features

Mail Server	SMTP	POP3	APOP	IMAP	Web-mail	Multi-domain	Spam Filters	List Server
EIMS 1.x freeware	Y	Y				*		
SIMS freeware	Y	Y				Y	Y	
EIMS 3.x commercial	Y	Y	Y	Y		Y	Y	
CommuniGate	Y	Y		Y				Y
CommuniGate Pro	Y	Y	Y	Y	Y	Y	Y	Y
MailProxy	Y	Y						
Mac OS X Server	Y	Y		Y			Y	
WebSTAR Mail	Y	Y	Y	Y	Y	Y	Y	Y
WEBmail and iTools	Y	Y		Y	Y	Y	Y	
First Class Intranet Server	Y	Y		Y			Y	Y

**Multi-domain support for EIMS 1.x is available in MailDoor from Open Door Networks.*

current maintainers are not motivated to move them to an entirely different operating system, which would undoubtedly require a significant amount of effort.

While the final release of the basic Mac OS X will not have basic POP or SMTP servers included, Mac OS X webmasters determined to provide POP3, IMAP, or SMTP services without paying for the privilege should be able to do so by taking advantage of the UNIX-based e-mail server daemons, such as those available for FreeBSD, which provides much of the foundation for Mac OS X.

Of course, the free alternatives may not provide the performance or scalability of commercial alternatives, but what do you want for nothing? In addition, you will have to work with a command-line interface for administration.

CommuniGate Pro

At the other end of the spectrum, the CommuniGate Pro communications gateway from Stalker Software provides a complete range of e-mail services, and then some. CommuniGate Pro bases its e-mail services on Internet standards from the Internet Engineering Task Force and has many additional features for industrial-strength messaging systems. A head-to-head comparison by *Network Computing*

(September 2000) chose CommuniGate Pro over several more costly e-mail server solutions for two hypothetical companies with tens of thousands and hundreds of thousands of e-mail users (*www.networkcomputing.com/1117/1117f1.html*).

In addition to IMAP, POP, and Web e-mail services described in Table 8-3, CommuniGate Pro modules provide gateways to pager, fax, printer, and voice mail services. It also comes with list server capabilities so you don't need to invest in additional software for that function. CommuniGate Pro is administered entirely through a Web interface and its built-in Web server; Figure 8-2 shows the CommuniGate Pro screen for configuring SMTP settings. Remote administration features include configuring the server, the router, and all communication modules; creating and updating user account information; monitoring module activity and system logs; and working with server queues and individual messages in the queues.

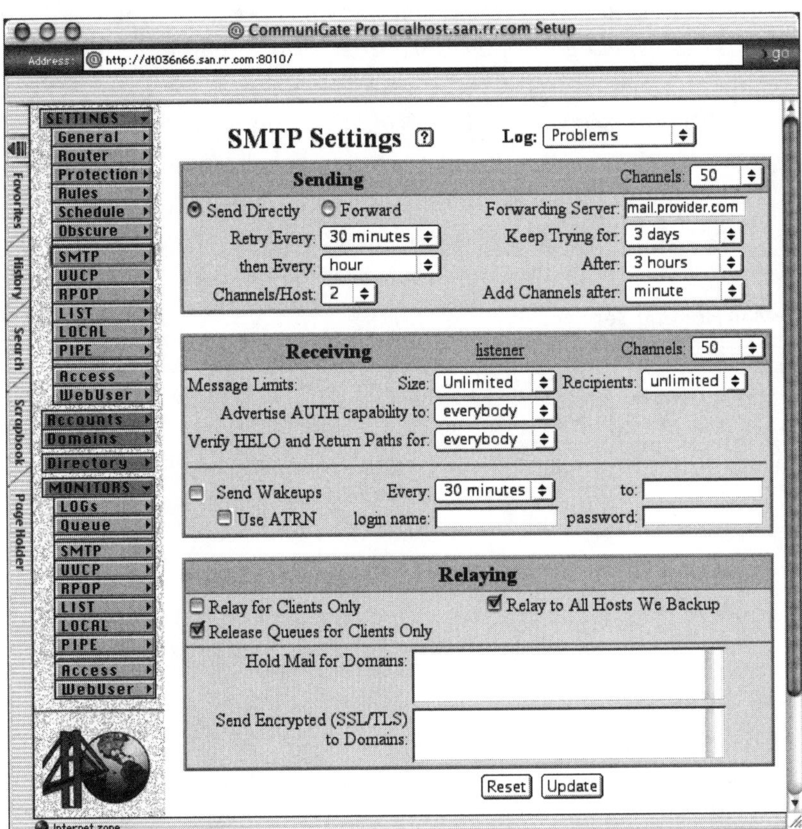

Figure 8-2. SMTP Configuration for CommuniGate Pro from Stalker Software.

Stalker Software offers versions of CommuniGate Pro tailored to small offices with 50 or fewer e-mail users, as well as versions targeting ISPs with up to 30,000 users or, at the high end, an unlimited number of users.

Outsourcing E-Mail

E-mail is one of the more time-consuming services to provide on your server because every account requires its own setup, configuration, and ongoing maintenance. Beyond a handful of accounts, such as those that need to be established to run a list server, it can become more involved than you may intend.

As with many other Internet services, it is possible to outsource your e-mail service. Any number of companies provide free e-mail accounts to individuals, including Apple's own iTools (not to be confused with iTools from Tenon Intersystems). However, I was unable to find a company to host free e-mail service for an entire domain, that is, *all-users@your-domain.com*. On the other hand, there are quite a few companies willing to host your company's e-mail for a fee.

Furthermore, if all you need are a few e-mail accounts—*webmaster@your-domain.com, info@your-domain.com,* and the like—most Web hosting services provide up to five basic e-mail accounts as part of their Web hosting packages. Table 8-4 lists a few companies that will provide e-mail services for your entire organization.

Table 8-4. E-Mail Hosting Services

Location	Description
www.edson.net/services/e-mail.htm	Edson Internet.
www.mail.com	Mail.com.
www.cp.net	Critical Path.

LIST SERVERS

The basic idea behind *list server* software is to distribute incoming messages to all users who choose to subscribe to a particular list. Typically, each list deals with a specific topic. The list server software is used to maintain all of the mailing lists. The major advantage—and potential disadvantage—of a list server is that it requires no action on the subscribers' parts after they subscribe to a given list. After subscribing, they see everything posted to the list—and I mean everything! This may be good if they read with interest most of the material posted to the list. On the other hand, it can be obtrusive since they may have to deal with a large amount of unwanted information. Subscribers have no control—beyond unsubscribing or requesting digests—over what they receive.

List servers and other forms of Internet service cannot be completely disentangled. In particular, list servers work hand in hand with an e-mail server for distributing messages. Furthermore, many mailing lists record all messages to a Web-based archive so users can reference previous discussions. This integration requires software to mark up e-mail messages with HTML so they can be searched as Web documents.

You should also consider whether to provide a Web gateway to your mailing lists. Through such a gateway, a user can subscribe to various mailing lists. Users no longer have to know the names of the lists or the particular syntax for your list server because the Web form ensures the correct syntax for subscribing to the appropriate lists.

As an information provider, typically you establish the list server, assign new lists, and remove old lists as demand dictates. You may also assign a moderator or moderators to each list. It is good netiquette to indicate whether a list is moderated or not to folks when they subscribe. The moderator filters out information that is not appropriate to the list.

Using a List Server

Let's take a minute to understand how a list server operates. The same list server software maintains multiple lists, where each list relates to a specific topic of interest to a community of users. Lists have several common configurations, based on who can post messages to the list. In a standard list, anyone, or more often, any subscriber can send a message to a list and it will be redistributed to all other subscribers. In a moderated list, all potential postings go first to a human moderator who posts only the most relevant to the list. Finally, in an announcement list, subscribers receive messages only from a limited number of sources, such as certain company representatives.

When joining any type of list, subscribers have several rights as members of a list and ways to control how they receive information.

- In most cases, subscribers have the option to subscribe or unsubscribe to the list.
- Subscribers receive all postings to the list. A subscriber can select whether to receive messages either one at a time or lumped together in daily or otherwise collected digests.
- For most lists, subscribers can send a message to the list server and have that message broadcast to all other subscribers.
- Subscribers can also receive information about a list by sending a message with certain keyword commands, for example, a list of responses to frequently asked questions (FAQs) or all postings to the list in the last month.

List Server Commands

Your first contact with a list server or mailing list will most likely be through information in an e-mail message or on the Web. To learn about the commands that can be sent to a list server, you can usually send e-mail to the list server with no subject line and a message whose body contains the single word "help." The Help command will tell you the other commands for setting your preferences at that list server.

However, if you do not know the name of the list you are interested in, the next step is to determine what lists are maintained on that particular server. The list server's Help file should tell you the format for the Index or Lists command that returns details of the available lists—or at least the lists that you can subscribe to.

After obtaining an index of the lists available on the list server, you might again send e-mail to the list server, this time relating to a specific list, with one or more of the sample commands in Table 8-5 as the body of the message. List server commands are usually case-insensitive.

To submit, or "post," messages to a list, you send mail to the desired mailing list at *list-name@list-server.domain.com.* For example, sending a mail message to *talk-list@hart-mac.sdsc.edu* would post your message to the *talk-list* list, assuming it was unmoderated. If it were a moderated list, the message would go to the list moderator, who would decide whether it should be posted.

Table 8-5. List Server Commands

Command	Description
sub talk-list *or* subscribe talk-list	Add yourself to a list called "talk-list."
sub user@place.com talk-list	Add someone else to a list by giving another e-mail address. Requires verification.
unsub talk-list *or* unsubscribe talk-list	Remove yourself from a list called "talk-list."
unsub user@place.com talk-list	Remove someone else from a list. Requires verification.
help talk-list	Find out more about a list called "talk-list."

It is important to remember that you send list server commands to the list server address, not the mailing list address. Sending the message "unsub talk-list" to *talk-list@your-company.com,* for example, is bad form. All subscribers to the *talk-list* list would see your request, but the list server software would not.

Choosing a List Server

Table 8-6 lists some of the list server software available for Mac OS X, along with some prepackaged software for creating Web-accessible mailing list archives. First a disclaimer, and then a word of caution. The disclaimer is that the list server software described here (except for the list server built into CommuniGate Pro) was not available during the beta release of Mac OS X, and so most of my comments are based on the Classic Mac OS versions of the software.

Now the word of caution: Even though mailing lists are the simplest service to use from the client's perspective, the software for managing mailing lists varies and can be quite complicated to configure. If you have come to expect Mac software to be installed and set up effortlessly, some of the available list server packages might surprise you.

As an aside, if all you need are the very basic list server functions—taking an incoming message and sending it to a list of subscribers—some Mac OS e-mail client software can be configured to do this for you. With Eudora Pro, for example, message filters can forward messages automatically or reply with canned responses. If you don't mind a little manual effort to handle requests for subscribing and unsubscribing names from a list, you might get by with the client software you already use.

But let's assume you're looking into list server packages, including the list server capabilities of software you may already have, such as WebSTAR Mail or CommuniGate Pro. Several features could affect your choice.

POP-Based or SMTP-Based. A major distinguishing feature is whether the list server works with a POP3 e-mail server or an SMTP e-mail server. An SMTP-based list server is generally considered a higher-end option because there are fewer delays between messages being received and messages being sent back out again. On the other hand, for an SMTP-based list server, you must control the SMTP server, because the two services work closely together.

Table 8-6. Classic Mac OS and Mac OS X List Servers

Location	List Server
www.dnai.com/~meh/autoshare	AutoShare, freeware for Classic Mac OS by Mikael Hansen. Requires EIMS or SIMS freeware mail servers.
macjordomo.med.cornell.edu	Macjordomo, Classic Mac OS freeware by Michele Fuortes. Works with POP e-mail accounts.
www.fogcity.com	LetterRip Pro, commercial software by Fog City Software. Works with either SMTP or POP mail server.
www.greatcircle.com/majordomo	Majordomo, a popular UNIX freeware list server written in Perl by Brent Chapman and others.
www.mhonarc.org	MHonArc, freeware written in Perl by Earl Hood, for creating Web archives of mailing lists.
www.petidomo.com	Petidomo, a commercial UNIX list server from Cyber-Solutions GmbH.
www.mdg.com	WS4D/E-mail Search, a commercial extension to Web Server 4D from MDG Computer Services, makes Web searchable archives for mailing lists.
www.lsoft.com	LISTSERV and LISTSERV Lite, commercial software from L-Soft International, Inc.
www.liststar.com	ListSTAR, a commercial list server distributed by MCF Software. Works with either SMTP or POP mail server.

A POP-based list server, however, does not require you to control the e-mail server. You just need to be able to ask the e-mail administrator to establish a few e-mail accounts for managing the server and lists, and an account or two for each list that you establish. Some list server software supports both POP-based and SMTP-based list serving.

Ease of Use. If you plan to operate only a handful of lists, you don't want a steep learning curve. If you are managing many lists, however, you will want access to many configuration options and the learning curve may be worth your time. On the other hand, a fully featured list server need not be complicated. I have found LetterRip Pro from FogCity Software to be easy to use and to have a very complete feature set. (At the time of writing, plans to move LetterRip Pro to Mac OS X were uncertain.)

Autoreply. The list server packages differ in their ability to respond to messages with "canned replies" either as text within an e-mail message or as an attached PDF file. Such a feature can be useful, for example, in distributing sales brochures or technical support instructions.

List Options. ListSTAR, a major commercial package now distributed by MCF Software, appeared infinitely customizable for those needing industrial-strength control, but a steep learning curve makes it more difficult to set up. LetterRip Pro has the same level of customizability but is much easier to set up.

Majordomo

Plans for list servers and Mac OS X were hazy at the time this book was being written. There were plans to adapt ListSTAR to Mac OS X, but plans for LetterRip Pro had not been announced. For freeware, Macjordomo's future on Mac OS X depended on an upgrade for the Pascal programming environment in which it had been developed over the years. AutoShare was least likely of all to be seen on Mac OS X because of its integration with EIMS or SIMS.

On the other hand, the UNIX foundation of Mac OS X opened up other avenues and options for webmasters, including Majordomo, a freeware list server written in Perl that uses the UNIX Sendmail utility for delivering messages. However, standard installation of Majordomo does require some familiarity with UNIX commands and the UNIX file structure, as well as the Mac OS X developer tools, to complete. Specifically, even though the bulk of Majordomo is written in Perl, there is one component written in C that must be compiled, so you need a C compiler, and you'll also need the Make utility. Setting up new mailing lists also requires a series of steps from the Terminal command line.

All that being said, it is theoretically possible to get Majordomo up and running under Mac OS X if you are bound and determined to do so. Eventually, a Mac OS X installation package may become available.

Outsourcing Lists

With individual e-mail accounts, there is no shortage of Web sites ready to hand them out free, and while not as common as free e-mail, there are plenty of choices for having someone host your mailing list. All you need is the discussion topic and these companies will provide the server. Table 8-7 lists some companies that offer free hosting of your mailing lists and additional information for mailing list owners.

Generally, to use these services, you must register with the service, then simply fill out a Web form to start the list. In addition, your list gets a Web-accessible archive. The Web access to your list, of course, requires you and your list visitors to view the inevitable banner ads. This service alone may be worth the price of admission.

Table 8-7. Mailing List Services

Location	Description
www.liszt.com	The Liszt directory of mailing lists.
tile.net/lists	Tile.Net, a reference to Internet discussion and information lists.
mail.maclaunch.com/lists	MacLaunch, the Macintosh portal, provides free mailing lists on their server.
www.list-universe.com	List Universe, information for mailing list owners.
www.milomail.com	MiloMail e-mail communities from milo.com, Inc.
www.topica.com	Topica, a directory of lists and free lists.
www.egroups.com	eGroups.com, a free mailing list service.
www.listbot.com	ListBot targets business mailings, but also has free group mailing lists.

SEARCH ENGINES

As your site grows, your audience members will appreciate the ability to search for just the pieces of information they need, rather than having to click through page after page—no matter how well-designed and easy to navigate your site is. A search engine provides your audience with this access. This section introduces software that gathers, indexes, and searches all or parts of the information on your Web server.

This is not, however, a discussion of the various search engines or directories provided by Web sites such as Alta Vista, Lycos, or Google, which help you search through the whole Internet. Those search portals are altogether different creatures, although they share their basic foundations with the search service you want to provide for your site.

A search service, whether it intends to cover the pages of a single Web site, a group of Web sites, or the entire Web, has to perform three tasks: gathering (better known as crawling), indexing, and searching

- *Crawling* means visiting Web pages and all the Web pages referred to from those pages until the entire site has been visited. Tools that perform this task are called crawlers or spiders. This is the same task performed by Web "robots," which, for the purposes of this book, can be defined as the crawlers covering the entire Web for one of the major search services.
- *Indexing* requires creating and maintaining a database, or index, on all the pages that a search services knows about. The index information might come from the HTML <title> tag, the first paragraphs, the <meta> tag, or the entire document.
- *Searching* takes user queries and searches through some database for matches to that query. This database is usually the index created by the crawler, but some search engines directly search every page in a site rather than creating an intermediate index.

Thus, one way to provide search capability on your Web site is to run a crawler that creates an index from the pages on your site and then have a search engine that queries the index. The situation is complicated since gatherers, indexers, and search engines can be mixed and matched and are not always clearly distinct parts of the search software. For example, the gathering and indexing tasks are often tightly integrated.

Choosing a Search Engine

Search capabilities come with some Web server suites—including WebSTAR, iTools, Mac OS X Server, and Web Server 4D, discussed in Chapter 7. Table 8-8 lists separate search tools, including crawlers, indexers, and search servers. Most search tools perform some or all of these functions. When evaluating a search tool, you should consider the following features.

CGI, Plug-in, or Standalone Server. A search tool can operate in one of three modes. A CGI-based tool runs as a separate application called by your Web server. The advantage is that CGI programs can generally run with any Web server software. The disadvantage is the additional overhead of CGI programs; this is not as severe in Mac OS X as in earlier versions of the Mac OS, but it still exists.

A search plug-in runs as an extension to the Web server. The advantage to plug-ins is that they avoid the overhead of a CGI program and therefore are typically faster. The disadvantage to plug-ins is that they will only work with Web

Table 8-8. Mac OS X Search Tools

Location	Search Tools
www.limit-point.com	Blue Crab, a commercial Web crawler, and Boolean Search Server, a standalone server or a WebSTAR plug-in, from Limit Point Software.
www.htdig.org	ht://Dig, a freeware UNIX search engine from the ht://Dig group.
www.maxum.com/phantom	Phantom, a commercial search engine and crawler from Maxum Development.
homepage.mac.com/pauljlucas/software/swish	Swish++, a freeware UNIX search engine from Paul J. Lucas.
www.mill.net/mstark/aboutwarpsearch.html	WarpSearch, shareware by Glen Stewart, works with any CGI-compatible Web server.
www.mdg.com	WS4D/CGI, commercial software from MDG Computer Services, provides local site searching.

servers that support the appropriate plug-in format. On a related note, if you are using Web Server 4D as your Web server, it has an integrated search tool, which has the same advantage of a plug-in and a similar disadvantage—you can only search the server on which Web Server 4D is running.

A standalone search server has its own Web server built-in and runs as a separate application from your Web server. Search requests from clients are directed to the search server. You can run your search server on a separate machine from your main Web server, offloading the time-consuming search requests. Standalone search servers also have other capabilities beyond searching local Web pages.

Local or Remote Site Searching. Local site searching is the bare minimum; any search tool will search the pages on your Web server. Remote site searching, on the other hand, is an advanced feature, more common in standalone servers. Instead of searching only local pages, such search tools can crawl and index any Web site. With this feature, you could use a standalone server to provide search services for Web servers running on different machines, even a portion of an unrelated Web site.

Site Mirroring. Search servers that can perform remote site searching can also be used to maintain a mirror, or duplicate copy, of a Web site. This is generally an extension of the crawler capabilities of the search tool.

Customizable Result Pages. Any search tool should let you customize the look of the query and results pages. This is the advantage of running your own search tool. The free search hosting services (see the section on outsourcing searches in this chapter) earn their keep by displaying their banner ads and limiting the amount of customization for search result pages.

For basic searching, the built-in search capabilities of your Web server software should suffice. To add basic searching to Web servers that don't have search features, you should first consider the CGI-based freeware and shareware options. For high-end search capabilities of standalone search servers, you have Phantom from Maxum Development and Boolean Search Server from Limit Point Software to choose from. (Limit Point's Blue Crab software provides further Web crawler features.) These standalone servers provide your site with all three components of a complete search tool—crawler, indexer, and searcher.

Phantom

Phantom, commercial software from Maxum Development, can function either as a CGI program or as a standalone Web search engine. Phantom is a crawler, indexer, and search engine. Phantom also provides site management capabilities such as server mirroring and archiving, broken link detection, automatic updates, and more. At the time of writing, Maxum had plans for a Mac OS X version of Phantom that will likely maintain the functionality of the Classic Mac OS version. The description here is based on the Classic Mac OS version of Phantom.

Once Phantom has created an index, users can perform searches with simple queries. In fact, Phantom allows you to create indexes and perform searches of any number of Web sites from a single Phantom server. You can therefore use Phantom to provide search capability for other related sites. Pages found by Phantom's crawler are indexed into a relational database engine for searching, including context and location of related pages.

Administered via a Web interface, Phantom allows you to schedule automatic updates and backups of search indexes, indexes keywords (through the HTML <meta> tag that was added to assist search engines), and provides basic Boolean and "begins with" searching options. Phantom's advanced search options include phonetic searches (if you are unsure of a word's spelling), related page, and date searching options. Results are presented in a relevance-ranked order.

You can download a 30-day demo of Phantom from the Maxum Web site. Once you download, unstuff, and install the Phantom software, you are ready to establish a search engine. The Getting Started guide will walk you through the setup; the steps are summarized here.

1. Start the Phantom application. Once started, Phantom is administered entirely through a Web interface, so open *http://your.host.name:8080/Phantom.acgi$admin* with your browser. (If you try to enter the administration page from another computer, however, Phantom prompts you for a user name and password.)
2. Choose New Session from the options at the left of the Web page. A session is roughly equivalent to a Web site to be indexed and searched.

3. Enter the Session name and the root URL to be indexed, and click Create Session. You may want to change some of the other options available, but the defaults will suffice. An important option is the "Disallow crawl on these paths" field. Phantom does not index the URLs you list here; this gives you a way to restrict the depth of the crawl.
4. On the page that Phantom creates, click on Run (to the right of the new session name) to begin indexing. By default, Phantom uses a setting that requires it to wait a minimum of 30 seconds between page downloads. While this is set as a courtesy for indexing sites you don't control, you may want to change Phantom's Preferences: Robot options for indexing your own site. Otherwise, the site-crawling process does proceed at a crawl. For the curious, you can monitor Phantom's progress in the activity log of your Web server.
5. To create search indexes for other sites, select New Session and enter another session name and URL. You can also choose Edit Session and instruct Phantom to re-index a particular site at regular intervals.

Once the Phantom crawler has finished indexing a site, you can use Phantom to search the pages. To link to the Phantom search server from a Web page, create a link to *http://your.host.name:8080/*. (The port number of 8080 is the Phantom default and is changeable.) This will give you the default Phantom search page and will provide you with the option of searching selected sessions from all of those available. To prepare a custom search page for a particular session, see the "Customizing Search and Results Page" in the electronic documentation. Here is a simple example of how to customize a Phantom search page and the corresponding results page:

1. Use your Web browser to view the source from Phantom's default search page. To tell Phantom to search only a particular session, you must find the HTML tag that allows the user to select a session to be searched. This line has the following form:

```
<input type=checkbox name=".Session1" value=1>
```

2. Change this line to <input type=hidden name=".Session1" value=1>. This will tell Phantom which session to search without giving the user a choice. Phantom has other optional parameters that you may or may not want to let the user specify for a search.
3. To tell Phantom to use custom headers and footers when displaying the Results page, add the following line to the HTML for the search form:

```
<input type=hidden name=".CustomHF" value=customHF>
```

4. Load the Phantom administration Web page and click on the session for which you want to define a custom Results page. This loads the Session Details page.
5. Click on Header.
6. Enter the URL for your custom search page. The buttons on the custom results page will now link to this page.
7. Type in the HTML-formatted text to appear at the top of your results page for this session.
8. Click on the Save Changes button.
9. Click on the Footer link and repeat the previous three steps for the custom footer.

Figure 8-3 shows an example of a customized Phantom search page that lets a user search the second session defined by the webmaster after providing search terms and specifying whether to find all or at least one of the search terms and whether to look only in the URL, title, or header of the page.

With this page, Phantom will display at most 25 hits and will use the defaults for the other parameters—including Detailed/Short descriptions, Phonetic/Literal searches, and Begins with/Contains searches.

ht://Dig

The freeware ht://Dig is available for Mac OS X through two routes. Tenon Intersystems provides ht://Dig to iTools customers as an added bonus, or you can download and compile the source yourself. I expect that at some point, a motivated person will make a compiled version available to Mac OS X webmasters.

```
<html>
  <head>
  <title>Your Site: Phantom Search Page</title>
  </head>
  <body>
    <h1>Search This Site</h1>
    <hr>
    <form action="http://your.host.name:8080/Phantom.acgi$search"
      method="post">
    <input type=hidden name=".Session2" value=2>
    <input type=hidden name=".CustomHF" value=customHF>
    Enter some key words to search by:
    <input name=".searchText" size=40>
    <p>Find pages with
      <select name=".andOr">
      <option selected>all <option>any </select> of these words.
    <input type=hidden name=".maxHits" value=25>
    <hr>
    <center>
    Search for key words found only in:
    <input type=checkbox name=".URL" value=URL>URLs
    <input type=checkbox name=".Title" value=Title>Titles
    <input type=checkbox name=".Header" value=Header>Headers
    <hr>
    <input type=submit value="Search">
    </form>
  </body>
</html>
```

Figure 8-3. Phantom Search Page.

The ht://Dig suite has many features that make it an attractive option. It can search many servers, exclude robots, customize search results, use fuzzy searching, search by keywords, index protected servers, and restrict the searchable documents to a portion of a Web site, among others.

The ht://Dig package has separate programs that perform the three tasks of a search engine. The htdig program crawls a site to create a database of the documents that need to be searched. The htmerge program then converts the document database to a searchable index. (Merging was made a separate process for efficiency reasons.) Finally, htsearch performs actual searches on the databases created by htdig and htmerge. As with most search engines, searches are invoked by a CGI program that gets its input through a Web form.

While much of the configuration of ht://Dig must usually be handled at a Terminal command line, the ConfigDig software by James Tillman provides a Web interface for configuring ht://Dig. In addition, the folks at Tenon Intersystems have provided a Web interface for configuring ht://Dig as part of their distribution, as shown in Figure 8-4.

As with Apache, ht://Dig uses a central configuration file, called *htdig.conf,* that is read by htdig, htmerge, and htsearch. The *htdig.conf* file indicates where the search databases are stored, what sites to search, and which files and folders not

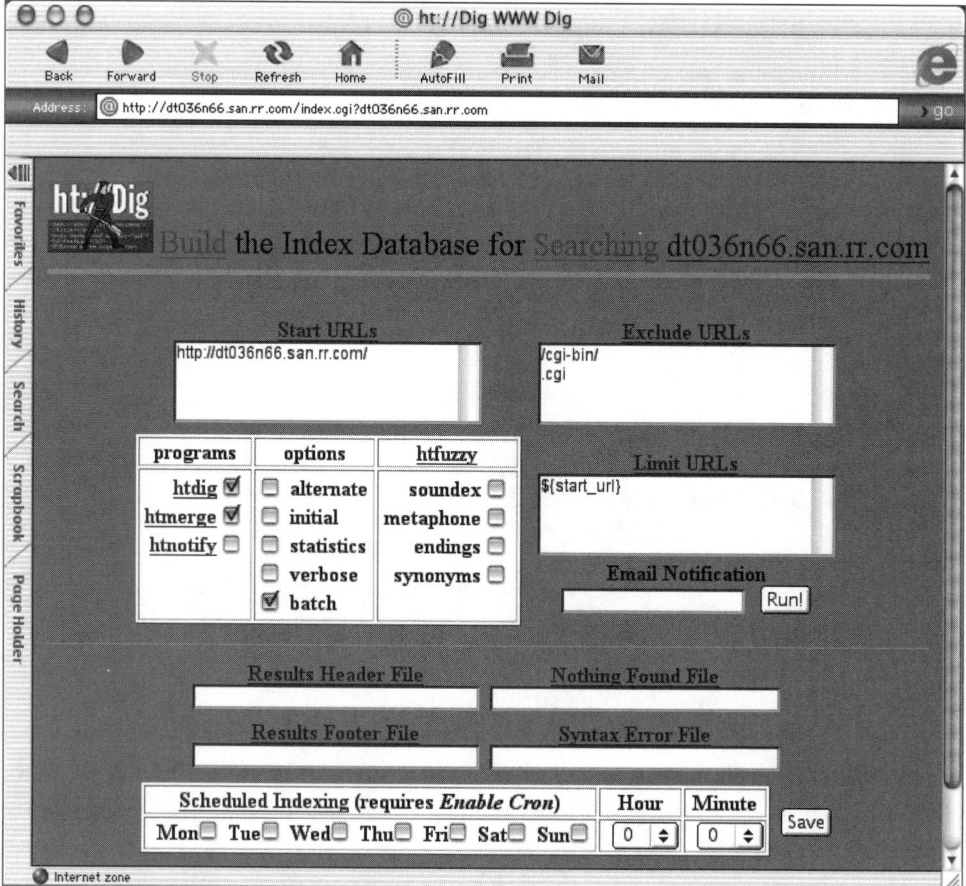

Figure 8-4. Web Interface by Tenon Intersystems to ht://Dig.

to search. It's possible to use ht://Dig to search several sites by creating a different configuration file for each site. While only a few pieces of information in *htdig.conf* are vital to getting ht://Dig to run (and only a small number are configurable through the iTools Web interface), there are many options available for customizing how htdig indexes each file, how and what htmerge stores in the database, and how htsearch returns results to the viewer.

Once you have customized the settings in the *htdig.conf* file, htdig and htmerge can also be run from a Terminal command line. There are various command-line options, but most commonly, you would simply enter the following two commands:

```
htdig -c /path/to/your/site/htdig.conf
htmerge -c /path/to/your/site/htdig.conf
```

When these two commands have completed successfully, Web forms can call the htsearch command to perform Web site searches. The search form and the *htdig.conf* file contain directives that specify how the results of searches will be displayed. Header and footer files can be specified so that the results match the rest of your site, but ht://Dig includes default options that provide all the basics. Figure 8-5 shows an example of the bare minimum ht://Dig search form.

Outsourcing Searches

Outsourcing your search service provides a way to reduce the load on your server by offloading the processing cost and delays of searches from your Web server to the search hosting service. Many of these services provide a free level of service, usually with a limit on the number of pages they will index, as well as commercial service options. For a free service, you will of course be presenting your visitors with a selection of banner ads.

The search services provide various levels of customization, but in general, the services are comparable and not as flexible as running your own search engine. You will probably find that the services are most limited in the options available for customizing the parts of your site (or remote sites) that you want included in the search index. Table 8-9 lists several search services that provide free and commercial search hosting.

```
<html>
  <head>
    <title>Your Site: ht://Dig Search Page</title>
  </head>
  <body>
    <h1>Search This Site</h1>
    <form method="post" action="/cgi-bin/htsearch">
    Match: <select name="method">
      <option value="and">All
      <option value="or">Any
      <option value="boolean">Boolean
      </select>
    Format: <select name="format">
      <option value="builtin-long">Long
      <option value="builtin-short">Short
      </select>
    Sort by: <select name="sort">
      <option value="score">Score
      <option value="time">Time
      <option value="title">Title</select>
    <input type="hidden" name="config" value="htdig">
    <input type="hidden" name="restrict" value="">
    <input type="hidden" name="exclude" value=""><br>
    Search:
      <input type="text" size="30" name="words" value="">
      <input type="submit" value="Search">
    </form>
  </body>
</html>
```

Figure 8-5. Basic ht://Dig Search Page.

Table 8-9. Outsourcing Search Services

Location	Description
www.atomz.com	Atomz.com searching is free to sites with fewer than 500 pages.
www.picosearch.com	PicoSearch hosts free searching for up to 1,500 pages.
www.searchbutton.com	Searchbutton.com offers free searching for non-profit or personal sites up to 1,000 pages.
www.freefind.com	FreeFind.com hosts free site searching with no page limit.

CHAPTER 9

DATABASES AND XML

Even if, in your mind, the information you plan to serve from your Web site will only be a handful of pages to start, inevitably the amount and types of information will evolve over time. Many organizations soon discover that they want to put on the Web the same information that they spend time tracking and keeping records on. Businesses keep records of products, schedules, invoices; universities compile faculty and student directories; and scientists record the sequence of amino acids in proteins, to name just a few examples.

To share this information on the Web, a trivial, brute-force solution would be to create a page in which to display as formatted text a snapshot of all the available information at some point in time. You would probably need to update this page on a regular basis, whenever the information changed. Interested users could scan the text for the information they wanted or use the Find option on their Web browser.

A second solution might be to create a separate Web page for each item you track, along with a list that links to all the individual pages. You could then add new pages, remove outdated ones, or change the information with more flexibility. Web users can then scan the list or search individual pages for the items they are interested in.

DATABASES AND THE WEB

You could take these routes, but you would be reinventing the wheel. In all likelihood, your organization uses computers for keeping these sorts of records and performing the basic functions of adding, updating, deleting, and searching records. The Web is often one of several interfaces, sometimes the primary interface, for interacting with these collections of data.

What Is a Database?

A precise, technical definition of a database is difficult to give. In most respects, a database is nothing more than a computerized record-keeping system. More formally, the term "database" refers to the collection of records being kept, while a database management system (DBMS) refers to the record-keeping system. That general description covers everything from the largest commercial packages for storing millions of complex records in hundreds of indexable files to a few dozen lines of code designed to store a couple hundred items in a plain text file. No matter what form it takes, a database always includes the following common features:

- The data are stored as a set of *records*, each of which stores information about a single item being tracked.
- The database provides ways to add, update, delete, and retrieve records from the database. Retrieval operations generally allow users to search for individual records or sets of records based on the contents of the records.
- The data in the database are *integrated*. Integrated means the records are both unique (nonredundant) and unified (because a single database may consist of many files).

- The data are meant to be *shared*. Shared means that the records are of interest to more than the person or persons doing the adding, updating, and deleting of records in the database.

In any discussion of databases, you will also likely encounter the term *relational database* and its associated relational DBMS, or RDBMS. A relational database can be defined as a database in which all the data are represented as tables. Most large commercial software packages, such as Oracle, are relational database systems. Another common database format is the *flat-file* format, in which database records are stored simply as lines in a single file. The trade-off is search and retrieval power versus complexity. Relational databases typically offer lots of power and flexibility but a steep learning curve. Flat-file databases may not handle as many records or complex searches, but they are usually easier to use.

Table 9-1 lists most of the database applications available for Mac OS X. The tools in this category shares the feature that they can all be used independently of a Web server or Web application server for general database needs. This definition, however, does not mean that they can't have Web capabilities built-in, as do FileMaker Pro and 4th Dimension, or related Web connectivity packages, as do PrimeBase and Panorama. With Mac OS X, Mac webmasters also have access to MySQL, a popular open-source database system, and other databases that originated in the UNIX world.

Why Serve Databases?

The question really isn't "Why should you serve databases on the Web?" but rather "When will you have to and how much effort will it take?" Even if your early plans for your Web server don't call for serving complicated information, before long, if your site and the effort you put into it continue to grow, you will want or need to serve data from a database. The features of databases themselves indicate why this will probably be the case.

- *Sharing.* Your organization is tracking the records in a database because they are meant to be shared, either within the organization on an intranet—for example, departmental budgeting information—or to the entire world through the Web—as with products in a catalog. The Web is the ultimate form of sharing your databases.

Table 9-1. Mac OS X Databases

Location	Description
www.4d.com	4th Dimension by 4D, Inc.
www.filemaker.com	FileMaker Pro from FileMaker, Inc.
www.frontbase.com	FrontBase, a freeware and commercial database server from FrontBase, Inc.
www.helixtech.com	Helix from Helix Technologies.
www.provue.com	Panorama, a fast RAM database engine from ProVUE Development.
instantdb.enhydra.org	InstantDB, an open-source freeware Java relational database from Enhydra.org.
www.hughes.com.au	mSQL (Mini SQL), a freeware database system from Hughes Technologies Pty. Ltd.
www.mysql.com	MySQL, an open-source database from MySQL AB.
www.openbase.com	OpenBase SQL, a commercial database from Open-Base International Ltd.
tabasoft.ancitel.it	QuickBase from Italy's Tabasoft.
www.snap.de	PrimeBase Database Server from SNAP Innovation GmbH.
www.paradigmasoft.com	Valentina, a relational database engine from Paradigma Software.

- *Integration.* The data are organized in such a way that elements can be uniquely and efficiently searched and retrieved. For example, when a customer wants to place a new order, it is also possible to find the previous orders by that customer and track the shipment of the current order. A single Web interface can incorporate all these elements.
- *Easy updates to information.* Because the database includes methods to add, update, delete, and retrieve records, you would like to avoid having to duplicate these capabilities, particularly the retrieval (search) methods, when placing this information on the Web. Database search methods let users find just the information they want, while additions, updates, and deletions ensure they always find the latest information.

- *Organization.* In creating your Web site, as with records in a database, you or your organization probably placed considerable effort into developing logical organization that effectively describes the information. This same logical structure will likely also translate to an effective presentation on the Web.
- *Efficiency.* A database will be more efficient than a basic file lookup.

Databases, like the Web, are client-server applications. The client sends requests to the server to add, delete, update, or retrieve records. Then the server processes these requests; stores, changes, or deletes the necessary data; and returns the results to the client. Placing databases on the Web, therefore, amounts to providing a database-client interface in the form of a Web page.

Database Connection Methods

Serving your databases on the Web requires that you extend the functionality of your Web server application. And in most cases, you provide database methods in the same ways you add other extensions to your server, namely, as CGI scripts, plug-ins, or a database application with its own built-in Web server.

Digging one level deeper, database extensions typically communicate with a DBMS through either native methods or Open Database Connectivity (ODBC) methods. In native methods, the server communicates directly in the native language of the DBMS. These methods work most efficiently but require different software to interact with a different DBMS. With ODBC calls, on the other hand, the server sends database requests from a generic database language and the DBMS translates those commands into its native language. ODBC offers a more general solution and works with databases for which you might not have native methods; however, the price you pay for generality is somewhat slower performance.

Databases can also be served on the Web through Java applets, and Sun Microsystems has created the Java Database Connectivity (JDBC) interface for doing so. As with ODBC, JDBC provides Java programmers with a uniform interface to a wide range of relational databases. As with ODBC, a key concern about JDBC is JDBC's performance and its ability to scale when the number of users grow into thousands accessing a database at the same time. The other drawback to JDBC, of course, is that it is only a programming interface and not a complete database-to-Web solution. If you don't want to write your own code, JDBC is not for you. However, you may want to file this information away for future reference, as more Java-based applets and applications become available from commercial software houses.

In choosing how to connect your database to the Web, then, there are several factors to consider. First, does your organization use one or several DBMS products to maintain the databases you want to serve? If only one database is used across an organization, you will likely get better performance with software that uses native methods. On the other hand, if your organization uses a variety of DBMSs, you may want to look at ODBC-based server additions for the widest applicability.

If you are creating a new database and choosing the DBMS to use with an existing Web server, you have similar choices. The preferred route to maximize performance would be to choose a DBMS for which the plug-in or scripts use native methods. Table 9-2 has pointers to more information on database connection methods. In the next section, we discuss tools for putting your databases on the Web now.

Table 9-2. Database Connection Methods

Location	Description
www.microsoft.com/data/odbc	Microsoft's ODBC page. Microsoft defined the ODBC standard.
www.filemaker.com/support/odbc_primer1.html	ODBC primer from FileMaker, Inc.
java.sun.com/products/jdbc	Sun's JDBC interface for database access.
www.webadvisor.com	A description of JDBC and ODBC, with links to related information.

Choosing Database Services

Now that you have a little background on how databases can interact with the Web, it's time to make the connection. Even more so than selecting your Web server software, selecting your database connectivity tool sets the future development and growth path for your Web site. If you don't think you'll need a database initially, you may still want to investigate potential database solutions early.

The sooner you start using a database, the easier it will be to expand your server's capabilities. If you wait too long, the cost of converting Web pages to a form that can be served from a database could delay or prevent the transition.

Databases are so useful in creating dynamic Web sites that they are integral components of many tools. Table 9-3 lists the tools for Mac OS X. As mentioned above, some database applications (from Table 9-1), such as FileMaker Pro and 4th Dimension, have Web serving built in, although additional Web tools that can communicate with FileMaker Pro and 4th Dimension are listed here. When selecting a database system and a method for serving the data on your site, there are a number of factors to consider.

Table 9-3. Web-Database Connectivity Options

Location	Description
www.xperts.com	FlatFiler from Xperts, Inc., a WebSTAR plug-in for serving tab-delimited text files.
www.blueworld.com/lasso	Lasso Web Data Engine from Blue World Communications puts FileMaker Pro, 4D, MySQL, and ODBC databases on the Web.
www.commongrnd.com	Osmosis Internet Link, from Common Ground Softworks, connects Helix databases to the Web.
www.perl.com/reference/query.cgi?database	Perl scripts for interacting with various DBMSs.
tabasoft.ancitel.it	QuickWeb from Tabasoft puts QuickBase databases on the Web.
www.qilan.com	Quilan, from Common Ground Softworks, links Helix, OpenBase, and FrontBase to the Web.
www.perlguy.net	Simple Perl database, a tutorial and free Perl scripts from Brent Michalski for a simple flat-file database.
www.sentman.com/tabs	Tabs on the Web, shareware from James Sentman for putting tab-delimited text files on the Web.
www.webink.com	WebInk Pro and Webink ODBC from Webink Ltd., provide Web access to its internal database and ODBC databases.
x2o.xperts.com	X_2O from Xperts, Inc., provides Web connectivity for Oracle databases.

Cost. To a greater extent than with other components of your Internet server, you will find a definite difference between the low-cost options and the full-featured commercial options. Chances are, if you aren't already running a DBMS on your network, you will have to pay for the database. The cost of publishing databases once you have the DBMS also varies.

At the lowest cost, if you are comfortable with Perl and customizing and porting your own scripts for the Mac OS (see Chapter 11), then you might use free Perl tools to write your own scripts for accessing most popular databases. Table 9-3 even lists a free set of scripts for creating simple, flat-file text databases. There are also shareware options for serving up data stored in tab-delimited text files, such as those you might export from a spreadsheet.

Open Standards or Custom Tools. You need to decide how you want to develop your site in general. If you want to stay with open standards and free community-maintained tools, you should be prepared to devote the programming and development effort required for creating your database applications from the ground up. If you want to develop applications quickly, you can choose a custom application development and server environment. With this you can produce your site more quickly, but it becomes more difficult to switch tools if you outgrow the capabilities of the tools you selected.

External or Internal Database. You must also consider the features you need from your database. An external database system, independent of the Web server, is often most efficient for applications that must be accessed by employees (or just by you) on your local-area network (LAN). For example, your office LAN may have a FileMaker Pro database for product tracking or contact directories. In this case, you'll probably want to consider your choices for database applications first, and you may want to select a database system that includes Web capabilities. If your organization already uses a database, you'll need to select a Web tool, such as those in Table 9-3, for serving that data on the Web.

On the other hand, you may not need a full-fledged database system, but rather may find it more convenient to develop and serve your site's dynamic pages by storing information in database-style records. Your Web site may be the only place this data is collected and used. In such a situation, you may find your needs met by a Web application environment such as WebSiphon, or the tools described in Chapter 12 with internal-only databases.

ODBC or Native Methods. If you or your organization already have a DBMS or several DBMSs in place (perhaps running on non-Mac platforms), you'll want to choose a Web connectivity product that can serve those databases on the Web. The low-end option is to write your own Perl scripts using free Perl interfaces. If you don't want to write Perl code, you should opt for a connectivity tool that has native methods, if available, for the best Web-database performance. Table 9-3 lists tools with native methods for Oracle, FileMaker Pro, and other databases. However, if you need the generality of ODBC, there are a number of products with that capability.

Extended Web Application Capability. Many of the tools in Table 9-3 provide much more than just a way to connect a database to the Web. Tools such as the Lasso Web Data Engine also include XML capabilities on their extensive feature lists. (See the XML section in this chapter.) WebSiphon also provides a full-featured Web application development environment. While this chapter focuses on tools that can extract and serve data from external databases, Chapter 12 discusses additional tools that use internal databases—accessible only through the Web tool—as a way to customizing your visitors' interaction with your site.

E-Commerce. The core of any e-commerce site—at least sites with more than a handful of items for sale—is a catalog of the products for sale. This catalog is essentially a database of product records, and as such, it is possible to use a general database with Web connectivity to build an e-commerce site from scratch. However, it is neither the only nor the most efficient arrangement if your primary goal is e-commerce. Chapter 13 discusses e-commerce tools, which have databases designed expressly for tracking products from a store's catalog.

XML Support. The Extensible Markup Language (XML) is a Web standard for defining structured documents and document types. XML is rapidly gaining in popularity as the preferred platform-independent means for exchanging structured information—such as that found in databases. You may want to evaluate how well your Web-database solution supports the translation of your databases into XML format. For more on XML, see the second half of this chapter.

Mac OS–Developed Databases

Some of the database applications available for Mac OS X have their origins in the Classic Mac OS world. FileMaker Pro, 4D, and Helix fall into this category, for example. A few other databases were developed to work with the Classic Mac OS, although they also have versions that run on Windows or UNIX platforms. At the time of writing, these applications were not yet available for testing, although FileMaker Pro and 4D should, by the time you read this, have Mac OS X versions available. I expect that these applications will retain the extensive functionality and ease of use that Mac users have come to expect from all of their applications.

In addition, most Mac-developed databases have gone beyond the basics of managing databases. You'll often find graphical interfaces that allow you to create complex database applications with a single package. FileMaker Pro and 4D both have built-in Web servers and languages for creating Web-based database interfaces, so that databases created in those packages can easily be served at your Web site.

UNIX-Developed Databases

The other major category of database applications for Mac OS X includes those that were originally developed for UNIX systems and that can now run on Mac OS X because of its UNIX underpinnings. MySQL, mSQL, and FrontBase fall into this category, to name a few. OpenBase was actually developed for the OpenStep operating system from which Mac OS X is more directly descended.

Appealing advantages of some of these database applications include price—many are freeware—and widespread use on Web servers running on many platforms. In fact, the combination of Apache for Web serving, MySQL for databases, and PHP (see Chapter 12) for creating Web-database applications, is popular for Web development, and it is now available to Mac OS X webmasters.

The disadvantages to UNIX-developed databases are that they often must be installed, configured, and managed from the command line. Until motivated developers of commercial software or advocates of open-source freeware create installer packages for Mac OS X, these systems require greater attention to set up, include a greater chance for error, and may be more work to maintain.

FrontBase is an example of a database originally for UNIX that has used the Mac OS X environment to its fullest, even during the public beta release of Mac OS X. Installing FrontBase consists of double-clicking on the installer package and clicking through a few screens of the Installer application. The

FBManager application, shown in Figure 9-1, lets you manage databases in a graphical environment.

FrontBase has both free and commercial versions. The free version does not permit access to databases from other machines, which means that an application like WebObjects can use FrontBase for databases, but only if both WebObjects and FrontBase run on the same machine. Commercial versions of FrontBase do not have this limitation. The FBWebManager lets you manage databases through a Web interface, but this is most useful only if you purchase a commercial upgrade. The freeware version restricts remote communication with the database, but a local application, such as WebObjects, can be used as the intermediary between FrontBase and the Web.

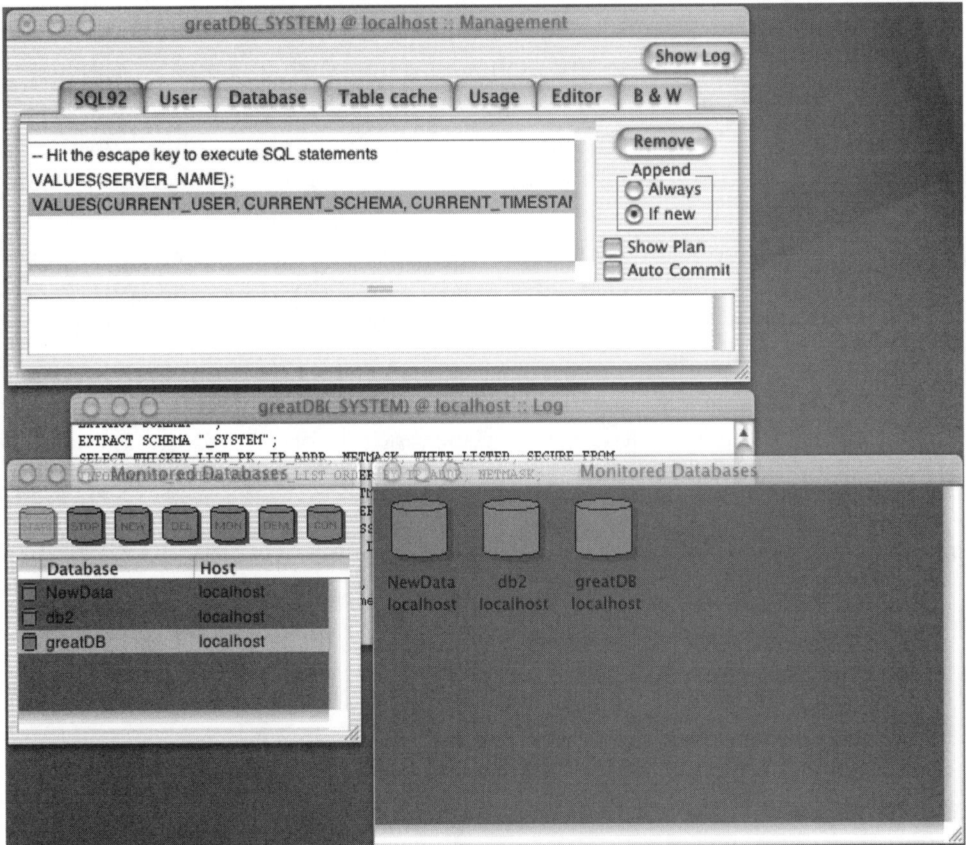

Figure 9-1. FrontBase FBManager.

Lasso Web Data Engine

The Lasso line of Web application development tools from Blue World Communications, Inc., began as a Macintosh program for publishing FileMaker Pro databases on the Web. Over the years, the Lasso Web Data Engine has evolved into a complete Web application environment that includes components for both serving and developing Web applications with a variety of Web server and DBMSs.

During the public beta of Mac OS X, Blue World made available Lasso Lite, a free, but limited, version of the Lasso Web Data Engine software that runs on Mac OS X and Linux with the Apache Web server and allows communication with MySQL and FileMaker Pro. A full release of the Lasso Web Data Engine for Mac OS X and the full range of supported databases is expected.

A significant advantage to using an application such as Lasso to serve databases is the database-independent design that makes it easy to migrate from or interact with virtually any database without changing code. Blue World also boasts of Lasso's performance, security, and extensibility advantages over competing products.

Lasso-based applications are created by inserting Lasso Data Markup Language (LDML) tags into HTML files. The Lasso Web Data Engine processes the LDML tags to dynamically generate the HTML pages to be viewed by Web visitors. Lasso Studio allows Web developers to extend the most popular visual Web authoring tools—Macromedia Dreamweaver and Adobe GoLive—with the ability to develop Lasso LDML-based applications. Users of BBEdit can also get LDML glossaries to speed Lasso development. Both these options make it easier to get Lasso-based applications up and running. And for forward-looking webmasters, the Lasso XML Developer Kit provides tools, templates, and examples to help you get started publishing XML (see the next section) and WML (Wireless Markup Language) data from the Lasso Web Data Engine.

With Lasso Lite, installation involves issuing a command from the Terminal command line. However, once having done so, it's possible to configure Lasso Lite through a Web interface. Future releases of Lasso Lite and the full Lasso Web Data Engine for Mac OS X will almost certainly provide Aqua-based packages and applications for installation and configuration.

Extensible Markup Language (XML)

A chapter on databases might seem at first to be a strange place to insert a discussion on the Extensible Markup Language (XML). However, XML and databases have much in common. XML enters the Web picture as soon as you want to move beyond simply *displaying* information to actually *doing* something with it, such as organizing the data, performing calculations, comparing the data to related information, or conducting other analyses. In many ways, these activities are analogous to the reasons you want to use databases. (This is not to say XML files or database records can't be displayed, but you can do much more with them.)

An explanation of the HTML family tree might help clarify exactly what XML is, so forgive this brief history lesson. The original language of the Web, HTML, is derived from the Standard Generalized Markup Language (SGML), an international standard for defining and describing a document's structure. You use SGML to describe the structure of a document—or types of documents—by defining markup languages such as HTML. The originators of the Web used SGML to define the much simpler HTML to describe the structure of Web pages.

Based on its pedigree, therefore, HTML was designed to describe a document's structure, not its appearance. And because the Web was originally conceived to let physicists share research papers with one another, HTML has six header levels (for levels of sections and subsections) and such orphan tags as <blockquote>, <au> (author), <cite>, and <fn> (footnote)—just the sorts of elements you'd find in a research paper.

As the Web evolved, however, HTML was adopted, expanded, and used ingeniously to describe the *appearance* of Web pages, which it was never designed to do. Today, Dynamic HTML—with its cascading style sheets, font control, and document scripting—is being developed primarily to address HTML's failings for describing appearance. (See Chapter 15 for more on the presentation of Web pages.)

On the other hand, XML returns to the Web's roots as a means for distributing structured data. XML is a subset of SGML for defining custom markup languages. Much like the way external style sheets are linked to HTML documents, an XML document links to a Document Type Definition (DTD) that defines the markup tags used in the document. For example, HTML has now been reformulated as an XML DTD by the XHTML 1.0 specification. (See Chapter 15 for more on XHTML.)

XML and New Possibilities

There are many benefits to explicitly specifying a document's structure. In particular, knowing the structure implies you also know something about what the data in the document mean. You can compare this to defining the fields in a database record; in most cases, you choose the structure of a database record because of what you need to know about the items that you plan to store in the database. As a result, for both databases and XML documents, you can write programs that use structural information to analyze and process the data. In short, XML makes new types of Web applications possible.

- Applications that require the Web client to mediate between two or more differently structured databases. Database structure can be incorporated into an XML DTD, which an application can use to translate from one database to another.
- Applications that attempt to distribute the processing load from the Web server to the Web client. In fact, with an XML document and DTD, a client could send data to an entirely different computer for processing off-line.
- Applications that require the Web client to present different views of the same data to different users. WebTV, Palm Organizers, cell phones, and other nontraditional Web browsers can be programmed to make more intelligent decisions about displaying XML documents. (See the section on WML in Chapter 16.)
- Applications in which intelligent Web agents attempt to tailor information discovery to the needs of individual users. Because XML documents incorporate more meaning into documents, you can write "robots" that can seek out relevant Web-based information and collect it in a consistent format.
- Application-specific browsers designed for a particular DTD. Biologists might have an XML browser for exploring molecular databases, and social scientists might have an XML browser for viewing statistical survey or census data.

For experimenting with XML and XML documents, you need a Web browser that can understand XML. For the Mac, Microsoft's Internet Explorer 5.0 supports XML 1.0. The version 6 browser from Netscape, based on the Mozilla project, should also have the ability to parse XML documents when it becomes available. Table 9-4 lists resources for additional information on XML.

XML Development Tools

With the advent of XML, many Web development tools have begun to add XML capabilities to their feature sets, and there are two dedicated XML editors available for the Mac, so far. High-end Web design tools such as Adobe GoLive and Macromedia Dreamweaver continue to extend their XML support, so you should check whether your Web development tool of choice offers any support

Table 9-4. XML and XHTML Resources

Location	Description
www.developer.com	Developer.com's XML pages include articles, forums, and a directory of XML-specific sites. Any Web development site worth its salt will have a section on XML.
www.everythingxml.com/xml	Everything XML from Intraware.
goxml.com	The GoXML Project is a search engine to index, store, and search XML data. The site includes XML examples and formatted data.
www.w3.org/XML	The XML specification from the W3 Consortium, and a short summary, "XML in 10 Points."
www.xmlinfo.com	XML Info, XML Software, and Schema.Net by James Tauber are good sources of XML information.
www.extensibility.com/xml_resources	XML resources from Extensibility Software, a developer of XML tools for Mac, Windows, and UNIX.
www.xml-zone.com	XML Zone from DevX, the Development Exchange.
xml.com	XML.com, an XML portal from Seybold Publications and Songline Studios, an affiliate of O'Reilly & Associates. They have a free newsletter and a technical introduction to XML.
xml.org	XML.org, an XML industry portal sponsored by companies including IBM and Sun.

for XML. Table 9-5 lists some tools specifically designed to help you create and edit XML DTDs and documents. However, XML development is still primarily the realm of programmers.

In general, developing in XML is a two-stage process. First, you must define the DTD for the document type you plan to serve. Some DTDs are predefined, such as XHTML, and XML resource sites may have DTDs that you can download. Once you have a DTD, you must create document types that are marked up with the tags defined by the DTD.

XML editors ensure that you create only valid XML DTDs, and many tools allow you to visually examine the tree structure of a DTD in progress. The application may provide contextual editing, such that the document type and current set of tags in the document help you determine which tags are allowable at a given point in the document. It may also save an XML document as standard HTML for use with older Web browsers.

As a rule, however, you may want to focus on tools that can automatically create XML DTDs and structured XML documents rather than expecting to do this work all by hand. Hence, you may want to focus on a database environment that can create DTDs based on the structure of your database and can also supports exporting data in XML format. The power of XML lies in the ability to

Table 9-5. XML Development Tools for Mac OS X

Location	Description
www.adobe.com/products/framemaker	Adobe FrameMaker has XML export capability.
www.in-progress.com/emile	Emilé 1.0 by Media Design in•Progress is an XML editor for authoring XML and XHTML documents.
www.blueworld.com/xml	Lasso Web Data Engine from Blue World Communications supports instant XML publishing from FileMaker Pro and other databases.
www.trafficstudio.com/sixpack	SixPack, an open-source XML editor by Geoff Strom of simple/CHAOS.
www.extensibility.com/tibco	XML Authority, XML Instance, and XML Console from TIBCO Software provide graphical environments for editing XML DTDs and documents.
www.alphaworks.ibm.com/tech	XSLeditor and other XML tools from IBM's alphaWorks run on most platforms that support Java.

create and interpret the necessary files automatically from databases, e-commerce catalogs, and publishing software.

Serving XML

Despite the many advantages of moving toward XML for your Web server, webmasters face the well-known Web dilemma: If I code it, will they come? At this point in the XML life cycle, you probably want to assume your visitors won't have the ability to view XML. Of the major browsers, only Microsoft Internet Explorer 5 can display XML. Version 6 of Netscape's browser should also have XML support. But do you want to cut off anyone who doesn't sport the latest browser version?

With server-side XML you aren't constrained by the browser used by your audience. Instead, your XML files are translated into friendly HTML for your Web visitors. For Mac Web servers, you have a few server-side options available to you, listed in Table 9-6.

Interaction. Interaction by Media Design in•Progress provides server-side XML and XHTML as part of its larger goal of making Mac Web sites into dynamic places that adapt to the visitors. To stay on track, I'll gloss over Interaction's many other features (but see Chapter 12). As an XML processor, Interaction can take XML documents and use cascading style sheets to generate standard HTML pages that can be viewed with any standard Web browser.

For serving XML documents, you configure Interaction to work as a preprocessor for your Web server. You define a style sheet to indicate which HTML tag to use as a basis for a custom XML element, and Interaction does its best to make the custom element inherit the presentation of the HTML tag specified in the basis property. With server-side XML, webmasters make a smooth transition from proprietary tags to standard XML.

XPublish. XPublish, also by Media Design in•Progress, lets you develop your site in XML, but serve it as HTML. However, instead of working as a preprocessor, generating HTML on the fly as Interaction does, XPublish generates static HTML files from a Web site created as a collection of XML or XHTML pages. Once you've finished editing your XML or XHTML documents, a Publish command generates the stylized HTML files. With XPublish, you can author in XML or enhance your current documents with XHTML, use XML to manage repeated content such as footers, and design style sheets for a consistent presentation.

Table 9-6. Server-Side XML for Mac OS X

Location	Description
interaction.in-progress.com	Interaction by Media Design in • Progress provides server-side XML and XHTML translation among its features.
interaction.in-progress.com/xpublish	XPublish, another tool by Media Design in • Progress, generates static HTML from XML or XHTML pages.

CHAPTER 10

GUESTBOOKS, FORUMS, AND CHATS

One of the most difficult and time-consuming aspects of running a Web site is ensuring that the information on the site is fresh and relevant. However, you can make this task somewhat easier by putting your site's visitors to work for you. Your visitors can initiate and contribute to discussions of hot topics with the click of a button. Although I hate to introduce an overused word, you can make your site *interactive* through guestbooks, forums, or chats.

Like many Web terms, "guestbook," "forum," and "chat" can mean different forms of interaction at different Web sites. One common denominator is that Web content is provided not by an overworked webmaster or Web development team, but by interested Web users. In addition to providing a dynamic source of informative and often entertaining commentary, having readers contribute to your site helps build a loyal community of regular visitors.

BUILDING A COMMUNITY

Building and expanding a community of regular visitors is the Holy Grail of the Web. Guestbooks, forums, and chats can help build such a community by allowing visitors to contribute their knowledge and experiences, solicit information directly related to their situation, and even vent their frustrations. However, guestbooks, forums, and chats are only one tool for doing so.

Some mysterious combination of a fresh topic, a critical mass of visitors, and a healthy portion of luck is also required to build such a community. I can't help you there. But we can look at the community-building software that's available. For the sake of this chapter, it's useful to distinguish guestbooks, forums, and chats.

Guestbooks

In brief, a *guestbook* is the simplest means of having visitors contribute to your site—a place to post comments about a Web site or a portion of it. Each comment is generally independent of the others. The reader reviews at Amazon.com can be considered a type of guestbook for each selection. Sites that allow you to post comments or feedback to a Web page are also providing guestbooks without calling them such.

As with a guestbook at a historic site or a wedding, visitors leave their name and some comments about the information presented at your site. The comments are usually displayed sequentially with basic information about the commentator—name, e-mail, hometown, and the like—and the posting date.

A guestbook therefore requires only two additional Web pages: a form through which a visitor submits his or her comments and a page for displaying the comments. Guestbook software updates the comment page each time a new comment is added.

Because guestbooks require only the most basic Web tools, it often does not make sense to purchase software solely to add a guestbook to your Web server. Instead, you have three options. First, you can find free scripts for most scripting languages that will let you add a guestbook to your site. Second, most general-purpose tools for custom Web site interaction, such as NetCloak and WebSiphon, can be used to develop a guestbook; many provide a guestbook as a sample application. Chapter 11 includes more information on scripting languages, script sources, and custom interaction software.

Your third option, if you also want to host forums on your site, is to purchase forum software that can also be used to add a guestbook to your site. Most commercial packages provide this flexibility.

Forums

In a *forum,* messages are posted and stored on a Web page and organized by topic. A visitor may initiate a new topic by posting a new question, respond to another visitor's question, or join in an ongoing discussion on a particular topic. A forum might be used for a technical support help desk, for example.

Forums—also called message boards or bulletin boards—add another level of organization and usefulness to information submitted by visitors. Forums organize messages according to topics, usually called "threads." A forum contributor might start a new thread of discussion or add his or her two cents' worth to a thread that has already been established. Threads allow a give-and-take between visitors on a particular topic and usually guarantee that messages in a thread have information relevant to the topic at hand.

Many Web sites have used forums to give readers the ability to post responses and comments to articles—a handy feature and something you just can't do with traditional print or broadcast media. On the plus side, other visitors get to read further details and occasionally entertaining commentary. (On the other hand, other visitors have to read all the gory details and occasionally digressive commentary to find the golden nuggets of information.)

There are a number of software options, ranging from free to very expensive, for hosting forums on your Web server. In addition, as with guestbooks, it is possible to use general-purpose interaction tools to construct your own forum applications from scratch or from sample code.

Chats

A *chat* is the most immediate form of interaction, the Web equivalent of a conference call. A *chat room* is a virtual room in which a chat takes place. Participants in a chat room see each other's comments, questions, and responses in real time. Unlike guestbooks and forums, however, the transcript of a chat is not usually recorded for posterity. Many Web sites use chats to allow site visitors to interact with celebrities and notable figures.

Because chats are "live," they require greater administrative effort while they are taking place, particularly if a webmaster wants to restrict the topics being discussed or the language being used. For example, on a family-oriented site, discussions of a sexual nature may be frowned upon. Or, in some unfortunate cases, a visitor in a chat room may only be interested in "flaming" the other participants with insults or offensive comments. Chat software permits the site administrator to lock out unwelcome participants and sometimes delete past comments.

There are sites that provide almost unlimited chat rooms for all sorts of topics by general Web visitors. Due to the potential administrative overhead, you may not want your site to be open for chats all the time. However, you may find chats useful for a limited number of scheduled events, perhaps with a special guest, or private conferences among a select group of participants who are unable to meet face-to-face.

Selecting Forum and Chat Software

Mac webmasters have a number of options for adding guestbooks, forums, and chats to their servers, often through a single piece of additional software. In choosing a solution, you should think about the full range of services you eventually want to provide. In selecting software there are several other features you may want to consider.

Guestbook, Forum, or Chat. Your first consideration should be what type of interactivity you plan to provide at your site. Guestbooks require the least amount of effort and technological skill. Free scripts are widely available to run a guestbook. Forums require more complex software, which can usually also maintain a guestbook. Chat software is the most complex form of interactivity, and some commercial chat applications, such as Web Crossing and Interaction, can also provide your sites with forums.

In other words, decide first whether you need to host chats on your Web server. If so, your chat software may support forums and guestbooks. If you don't need chats, you have a choice of a wider range of software that supports forums (as well as guestbooks). And if you just want a guestbook, there are many free options for doing so, usually with minimal fuss.

Extensibility. If you think you will ever need to expand your chat or forum capabilities, you want to consider forum software that can expand as your forums grow more popular. If you have to convert from one forum software application to another, you may lose all the messages archived by your older software or have trouble translating messages between formats. While you may have to switch eventually, you should be aware that switching frequently could work against your community-building efforts by erasing the forum history.

Thread Layout and Organization. Because the basics of forums are roughly the same, one of the most important distinguishing features is how they organize and present the threads. Many forum applications display threads as a list of subject lines linked to full messages. However, in Brian Johnson's ConferWeb, for example, each thread is a separate page, with the topic message followed by the responses to the topic. This variation can be handy for scanning, but it makes searching more difficult. Commercial applications will generally provide the most flexibility in how threads and postings are displayed.

Configuration and Ease of Use. Another obvious consideration is how easy the software is to configure and administer. Ceilidh from Lilikoi Software, for example, shows its UNIX roots in the text configuration file that you must edit to install the software. Another factor to consider is how easy the forum pages are to integrate with your existing Web layout and design. This is one of the most significant advantages of maintaining your own forums over outsourcing them through a third-party provider. (See the section on outsourcing forums in this chapter.)

User Registration. You probably don't want just anyone to post to your forums. Forum software can require a user to register before being allowed to post messages in a forum. This can provide the user with the ability to receive e-mail responses to his or her postings and can provide you, the webmaster, with a way to exclude visitors who post inflammatory or unwanted material in a forum.

E-mail Integration. Because of the popularity of e-mail and the similarity between e-mail messages and forum postings, mailing lists and forums naturally complement one another. Forum software differs in the extent to which contributors can receive responses to their postings via e-mail instead of having to revisit the forum to check for follow-up postings. (In fact, mailing lists can be stored for later reading as threaded archives using software such as WS4D/E-mail Search or MHonArc, described in Chapter 8.)

Archiving Flexibility. You may also want to consider the forum software's options for storing forum threads. In particular, you may want the option to delete threads after a customizable amount of time has elapsed. Technical support forums may preserve messages indefinitely, but forums that focus on current events may have threads expire after a week or so.

Search Capabilities and Integration. If you plan to preserve the postings for later reference, you may want to consider whether it's possible to search postings. If each posting is stored on a separate page, it may be possible to use your existing search engine to search through your site's forums. If your software stores postings in a database or in a proprietary format, you may have to rely on the search capabilities of the forum software.

Cost. Finally, cost may play a factor. Forum software ranges from free (ConferWeb, Ceilidh, or WebCrossing) up to thousands of dollars for enterprise versions (Ceilidh or Web Crossing). Depending on the scale of your forum effort, moderately priced commercial software or shareware may offer the best mix of features.

Table 10-1 lists some of the available chat and forum software for Mac OS X. Many of these sites have working demonstrations you can try out, and most have demo software that you can download.

Web Server 4D: Guestbook

Web Server 4D was discussed in Chapter 7 as a Web server application for Mac OS X; however, Web Server 4D also includes an integrated language and database for creating Web applications. Furthermore, MDG Computer Services includes a number of sample applications that are ready to use right from the start, including a guestbook that stores entries in Web Server 4D's internal database. Having worked with Web Server 4D, I have to say the language is definitely unique, but it works quite well once you get the hang of the unusual syntax. Figure 10-1 shows a modified version of the form to add an entry to the guestbook.

The items to note are the references to "[Database]" in the form fields, which tell Web Server 4D where to store the values that will be entered. The numerous "hidden" input items are necessary to Web Server 4D's processing. Tags that appear to be unofficial HTML, such as <DATE_SHORT> and <USER_IP>, are actually instructions for Web Server 4D to insert system variables—in these examples, the date in abbreviated format and the IP address of the Web visitor. To complete the guestbook, Web Server 4D needs a page to query the database for the guestbook entries and a template file to format the entries. I've included the complete set of files for the guestbook application on this book's Web site, with permission of MDG Computer Services.

WebBBS

WebBBS is a shareware bulletin-board system from Darryl C. Burgdorf, written in Perl. I have to admit to being a bit intimidated by WebBBS at first. After you have downloaded and unpacked the software, WebBBS leaves you with a folder of 16 files, most of them pieces of Perl code, including a single documentation

Table 10-1. Forum and Chat Software

Location	Description
www.swconsulting.com/bigboard	Big Board FM by Steve Wilmes Consulting offers a threaded message board system built on top of FileMaker Pro (required).
www.lilikoi.com	Ceilidh by Lilikoi Software provides basic threaded forums and e-mail notification.
www.caup.washington.edu/software/conferweb	ConferWeb by Brian Johnson uses AppleScript to manage forum threads and permit limited e-mail notification of postings.
www.drb-software.com/Dr-B	Dr B's Virtual Message Board and Conferencing Tool manage forums and chats, respectively.
interaction.in-progress.com	Interaction from Media Design in•Progress provides forums, chats, and many other capabilities.
www.robplanet.com/cgi/robboard	RobBoard from RobPlanet is Perl-based forum software that can be run with MacPerl.
www.webcrossing.com	Web Crossing from Web Crossing, Inc., is feature-rich and flexible commercial forum and chat software.
www.awsd.com/scripts/webbbs	WebBBS, shareware from Darryl C. Burgdorf, written in Perl.

```
<html>
<head><title>Main Guestbook Entry Form</title></head>
<body>
<h2>Guestbook Entry Form</h2>
<form action="*ws4d-db-query-Mod1.ws4d" method="post">
<input type="hidden" name="[Database]Name" value="Guestbooks">
<table border="0" columns="2" rows="4" cellpadding="6">
  <tr>
    <td align="right">Name:</td>
    <td><input type="text" name="[Database]Field01-REQ"
      value="" size="20"> (required)</td>
  </tr><tr>
    <td align="right">City, Country:</td>
    <td><input type="text" name="[Database]Field02"
      value="" size="30"></td>
  </tr><tr>
    <td align="right">Email address:</td>
    <td><input type="text" name="[Database]Field03-REQ-EMAIL"
      value="" size="20"> (required)</td>
  </tr><tr>
    <td align="right" valign="top">Comments:</td>
    <td><textarea name="[Database]Text02" rows="5" cols="60"
      wrap="soft"> </textarea></td>
  </tr><tr>
    <td align="right">
<input type="hidden" name="Database" value="Database">
<input type="hidden" name="Success" value="success.html">
<input type="hidden" name="RecordNumber" value="-1">
<input type="hidden" name="Field01" value="Name">
<input type="hidden" name="Field03" value="Email Address">
<input type="hidden" name="[Database]Date1" value="<DATE_SHORT>"
  size=9>
<input type="hidden" name="[Database]Time1" value="<TIME>" size=9>
<input type="hidden" name="[Database]Field04" value="<USER IP>">
<input type="submit" name="Submit" value="Submit">
    </td>
    <td><input type="reset" value="Reset"></td>
  </tr>
</table>
</form>
</body>
</html>
```

Figure 10-1. Adding a Web Server 4D Guestbook Entry.

file. Part of the apparent complexity stems from the software's extensive customizability, but in fact, you can start serving your forums after configuring only a handful of settings.

Here I'll describe how to set up WebBBS for a single forum. It's possible to establish any number of forums, however, by duplicating one file and changing a few settings. This points out a limitation of WebBBS—to create a new forum requires administrative access to your server. It can't be done by a visitor. You may consider this an advantage or disadvantage.

As the first step, you should copy the WebBBS files to your Web server. In the default Apache configuration for Mac OS X, you will have to put them within the *CGI-Executables* directory. In this example, I'll put them in a subdirectory at */Library/WebServer/CGI-Executables/webbbs* to keep them separate from the others.

The two files that require changing are *webbbs_settings.pl* and *webbbs_config.pl*. The settings file contains global settings, while the config file contains settings specific to the forum. In the settings file, you need to complete the line that defines where the WebBBS scripts are stored. For sending e-mail notifications, you need to set the mail program to use. By default, WebBBS is set correctly to use the Mac OS X Sendmail program. Finally, you should also set the name and e-mail address for the WebBBS administrator. The lines below show you how the lines in the settings file should look in this example. You need not change any other line for WebBBS to work.

```
$scripts_dir = "/Library/WebServer/CGI-Executables/webbbs/";
$mailprog = '/usr/sbin/sendmail';
$admin_name = "Administrator";
$maillist_address = "bbs-admin\@your-domain.com";
$notification_address = "bbs-announce\@your-domain.com";
```

In the config file, you need to customize individual forums. You must set the location of the settings file, the directory where WebBBS will store the messages for this forum, and the URL to run the config file. In this example, I created a directory called *forum* in my server's main Documents folder. Given our example so far and the default Apache setup for Mac OS X, the config lines will look like the following:

```
require "/Library/WebServer/CGI-Executables/webbbs/webbbs_settings.pl";
$dir = "/Library/WebServer/Documents/forum";
$cgiurl = "http://your-domain.com/cgi-bin/webbbs/webbbs_config.pl";
```

```
$boardname = "Dave's WebBBS Forum";
$shortboardname = "Dave's Forum";
```

You need to set the permissions on two items to finish installation. First, you need to make the config file executable. Next, you must make the *forum* folder world-writable for WebBBS. In this example, you would enter the following two commands at the Terminal command line:

```
% chmod 755 /Library/WebServer/CGI-Executables/webbbs/webbbs_config.pl
% chmod 777 /Library/WebServer/Documents/forum
```

Figure 10-2 shows the results of setting up this forum and posting a few messages. It's straightforward to create more than one forum by duplicating the config file. The global settings file also has the default values that define the look and feel of the forum pages. If you are running only one forum, you can modify these values in the settings file directly. However, if you are running several forums, you can override the global values by placing updated statements in the config file.

Web Crossing

Web Crossing from Web Crossing, Inc., is Web chat and forum software that runs on just about every operating system, including Mac OS X. The cost of licenses ranges from $695 (for a limit of 5,000 page views per day) to $34,995 for the unlimited enterprise version. Web Crossing is used by such sites as the *Oprah Winfrey Show,* CNN Interactive Community, *The New York Times* forums, c|net's Builder.com, Adobe's user forums, the Library of Congress, and others.

Web Crossing allows you to choose threaded or linear discussions, display HTML in messages or edit format without learning HTML, archive messages automatically, attach files to discussions, track and view messages posted by each user, filter out profanity or other keywords, and receive e-mail notification of new posts. Web Crossing also has a search engine for full-text search of messages, an NNTP server for news-reader access to forums, an SMTP server for e-mail notifications (either of single messages or digests), a chat server with a Java-based chat interface, and a list server. You can also use Web Crossing to provide POP3, IMAP, and Web-based e-mail for users.

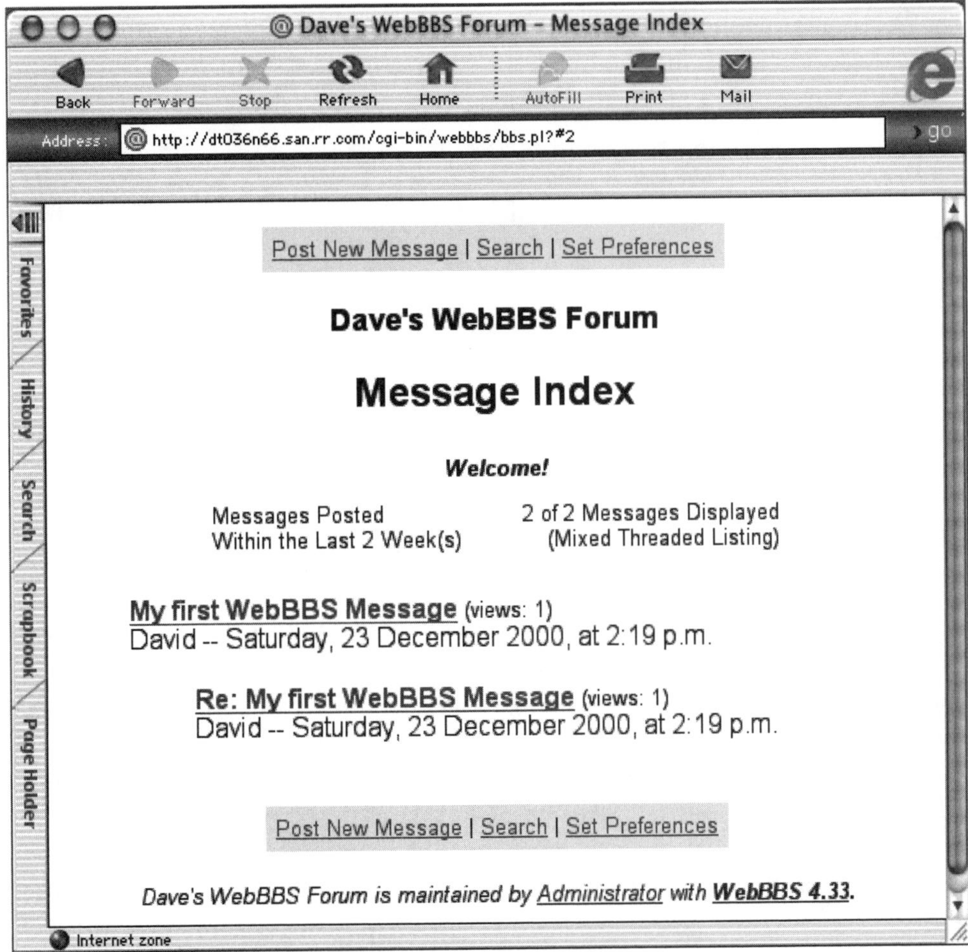

Figure 10-2. A Basic WebBBS Forum.

With all these capabilities, Web Crossing provides extensive customization possibilities. To guarantee that your forums and chat rooms conform to your site's look and feel, Web Crossing also has a language for creating design templates through which your pages and messages are displayed. All in all, for ease of use and installation, features, and starting price, Web Crossing offers a powerful, one-stop shop for your community-building needs. (For free forums with Web Crossing, you can use Web Crossing's World Crossing service. See the section on outsourcing forums in this chapter.)

Web Crossing includes a Setup Wizard, which Web Crossing promises will have your forum setup installed in less than five minutes. I took the challenge, and I was impressed. For an application with so many features, you wouldn't think it could be that easy to install, but I had Web Crossing installed and my first discussion group started in about five minutes (probably less). It's applications like Web Crossing that give applications that require editing of Make files, compiling C modules, manual copying of files into the right places, and setting permissions a bad name.

I unpacked the Web Crossing distribution file and moved the resulting *webx* folder to my Applications area. It doesn't matter where you put the folder. Next, you will have to go to the Terminal command line to start the installation. You need to run three commands. (The "%" is your system prompt.)

```
% cd /Applications/webx
% ./make-install
% ./make-run
```

When you run the Make-install command, you will have to respond to several questions so Web Crossing can complete installation. Your first choice is whether you want to run Web Crossing as its own HTTP server, as a CGI script with images for Apache, or as a CGI script without images for Apache. I went with the second option. The remaining questions are about the Apache configuration on your server—the folders for documents and CGI executables, and so on. Once these questions are answered, the install process completes, and that's when you enter the Make-run command. You complete the initial configuration process, including the selection of your "sysop" password, through your Web browser.

Now you're ready to start your Web community. Although the initial installation and configuration process takes only five minutes, there are so many options and variations possible within Web Crossing that it will take you substantially longer to master them all. You can customize the look and feel of your site and forums, restrict access, manage user accounts, and so on. Figure 10-3 shows the main sysop page for my sample installation of Web Crossing on Mac OS X, with two forums and one chat that I created and the button style that I selected. Most regular users won't have quite so many options, but they can still add discussions, check messages, set their personal preferences, and participate in all parts of the site (at least all those in which they are permitted).

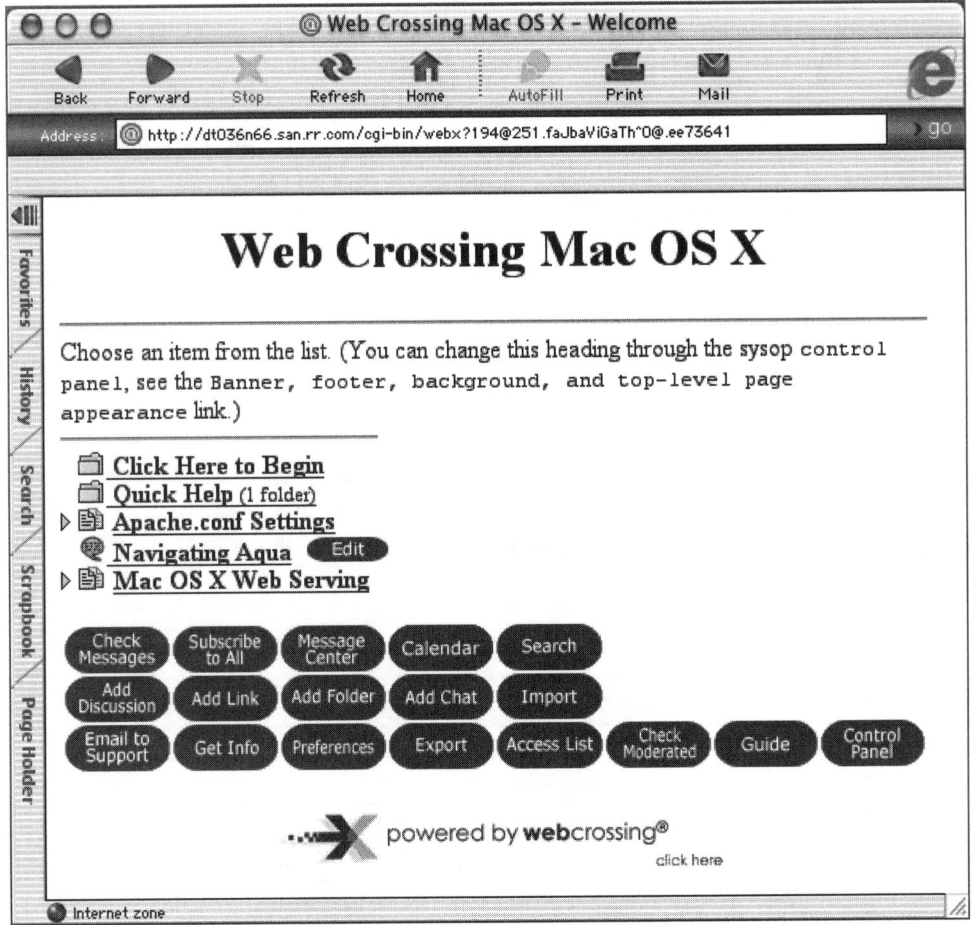

Figure 10-3. The Main Sysop Page for Web Crossing.

OUTSOURCING FORUMS

It should come as no surprise at this point, if you've been following along, that it is possible to use third-party providers to host your site's Web forums on their servers. This is further proof of the well-known Web rule: If there's something you want to do on your Web site, there's a company trying to make a buck doing it for you.

Depending on the traffic on your Web forums, this may make sense because it offloads some of the demanding interactive work to another company's servers. In most cases, such services are provided free; the price you pay is the ad banner plastered at the top of each page of your forum, guestbook, or chat. For a price, these services can provide you with customized, ad-free forums.

Technically, it's not difficult at all. As with most other outsourcing services, you register at the service provider of your choice and fill out a Web form or two, and your forum is created for you. On your own Web site, you just link to the forum page.

In selecting a provider, particularly if you are choosing a free service, your should consider the look and feel of the forum or guestbook. If you can live with where ads are placed and how threads and messages are displayed, then you have a winner. For simplicity, it's probably also easiest to stick with the same provider for many of your Web service needs, so you should evaluate all the services you think you might use. Table 10-2 lists a sampling of guestbook, forum, and chat providers.

Table 10-2. Guestbook, Forum, and Chat Service Providers

Location	Description
www.cluein.com	ClueIN from Inclusion, Inc., hosts forums, mailing lists and other community-building tools.
www.senac.com	Senac Interactive hosts guestbooks, forums, and chats for free or as a paid service.
www.sitegadgets.com	SiteGadgets.com, from The Amusive Network, provides forums, guestbooks, and more than 20 other free Web site additions.
www.worldcrossing.com	World Crossing offers free hosting for forums and chats from Web Crossing, Inc.
www.freecenter.com	FreeCenter.com from Jim Reardon and Amusive Communications lists sources for free guestbooks, forums, and chats.

CHAPTER 11

SCRIPTING AND THE CGI

The standard method of interaction with a Web server involves simple requests from visitors for static information. A visitor reads this information and then navigates to more information on the same or other servers. We've already discussed some packaged ways to add more active types of interaction with databases for dynamically served data and guestbooks and forums for online communities.

However, there is another very powerful aspect of Web technology that you will likely need to support—the ability to customize a visitor's interaction with your Web site by taking input from the client and delivering an appropriate response from the server. With some basic programming skills, you can customize your visitors' interactions with your Web server.

INTERACTING WITH THE WEB

The idea behind customizing the interaction on a Web site is that the same information is not necessarily served to everyone. What the visitor sees or makes happen is exactly what the visitor has requested. For example, you may use your site to collect information from each Web visitor, and all visitors get a simple customized acknowledgment based on their input.

The Web user could provide input to a program that gets executed on the server, and the results of that program would be returned to the Web browser for display. The user could also upload information to the server and see that information immediately made available to a worldwide audience. There are many other ways in which an active server could be used, but the principles are the same.

Providing such interaction through a Web server usually happens through one of two pathways. Each can be thought of as a four-step process. First, the more traditional and more general-purpose method of interaction and processing uses forms and the *Common Gateway Interface* (CGI). Some CGI programs or scripts are developed and distributed as commercial products, but it is possible to write your own scripts.

1. Provide a Web page that collects user input—this is usually through a Web form that might be as simple as a single button or as complex as a tax return.
2. Pass that input through the CGI to an external program for processing.
3. Process the input with a CGI program or CGI script that produces some form of output.
4. Return the results to the user as HTML, graphics, or plain text that can be displayed by the client browser.

Second, an often faster and, in many cases, less programming-intensive method uses software to extend the capabilities of HTML pages with embedded commands. We'll discuss variations on this scheme in Chapter 12.

FORMS

If you have ever written code for a graphical user interface, or any other piece of software for that matter, you will appreciate the simplicity of writing a Web form in HTML. While simple to write, an HTML form is limited in what can be represented, in comparison to an interface generated with a graphical user interface language. Forms incorporate familiar components commonly used to interact with computer software. There are boxes to enter text, pull-down menus, list selections, check boxes, and buttons for taking action.

Most text and visual HTML editors support the construction of forms, providing you with a way to insert the basic building blocks. Even so, you must still know how to assemble the building blocks into a working form.

- A form is delineated by <form> ... </form> tags and associated attributes.
- Within the <form> tags, regular HTML markup tags are used to format and arrange the layout of the form elements and provide labels. HTML does not automatically associate a label with a form element.
- Special tags and associated attributes are used within a form to collect input. Each of these input collection types associates the input with a variable name that will be used for processing on the Web server.
- To process the data or selections, a script of some kind must be associated with the form. A CGI script or program commonly handles complex processing, while simple JavaScript additions can perform basic actions, such as jumping to a particular Web page.
- The contents of a form can be cleared (reset) with a Reset button.
- A form can be submitted to the server for processing with a Submit button, a text box, or a clickable image.

We will encounter some examples of forms and the available input types as we discuss CGI scripts in this chapter; however, you should check out a full HTML guide for all the details. See Appendix B for further references to online HTML resources.

THE COMMON GATEWAY INTERFACE (CGI)

The CGI allows your Web server to execute a program, using as input values passed from client to server. The CGI is a feature of a Web server distinct from Web forms, although forms happen to be the most convenient way of getting information from the Web client to a CGI program using the HTTP protocol. Typically, a CGI program generates some output text and graphics, which are passed back to the client for display.

How does a Web server know that a request is a script or program to be executed and not just some HTML to be served? Typically, the file type *.cgi* provides the distinction. (However, it is possible to use any file-name extension if you configure your server with the appropriate MIME type to handle files with that extension as a script.) Files with this extension are referred to as *CGI scripts* or *CGI programs.* Whether execution of the CGI script on the server is permitted depends on how you configured the Web server. For the Macintosh, there are two common scenarios.

- Some Web servers, including the default Apache configuration with Mac OS X, restrict CGI scripts to a folder named *cgi-bin* in the Web server's main documents folder. (Technically, the default Mac OS X folder for CGI scripts is */Library/WebServer/CGI-Executables,* but it appears to be *cgi-bin* to Web visitors.) This is an optional restriction carried over from UNIX servers for security purposes. The restriction makes it more difficult for hackers to upload and run arbitrary programs on your server.
- Alternatively, most servers can be configured so that any file with an extension of *.cgi* in the folder hierarchy can be executed.

Here is a detailed sequence of events for what happens when a CGI script or program is invoked:

- When you hit the Submit button on a Web form, a text string containing all input to the form is passed to the URL specified by the ACTION attribute of the <form> tag. Specifically, the text string is attached to the URL to form a single string. The text string and URL are separated by a question mark (?).

- The format of this text string depends on the METHOD attribute of the <form> tag. One of two METHOD attributes may be specified, POST or GET.
- The GET method operates like any request for a URL from the server, except the URL has added variables for the script. With the GET method, the server equates the text string with the server variable QUERY_STRING, sets the REQUEST_METHOD variable to GET, and makes both variables available to the CGI.
- The QUERY_STRING defined by the GET method is of limited size—256 characters in most implementations—and is not suitable for large amounts of input. For example, our reader's comment form including name, e-mail address, and comment would easily exceed 256 characters.
- The POST method opens up a separate channel of communication and overcomes the text string size limit by processing the whole input stream as standard input. In using the POST option, the server sets the variable REQUEST_METHOD to POST, sets QUERY_STRING to nothing, and sets the variable CONTENT_LENGTH to the length, in bytes (or characters), of the query string. The variables are made available to the CGI.

When the text string gets to the server, what happens next is a function of your program. For a standard CGI script, the server will run the script and wait for an answer. When the script returns an answer, the server displays the results. Because the waiting can slow down your server, most server software has been extended to handle asynchronous CGI scripts, usually indicated by the extension *.acgi* (although scripts with a *.cgi* extension can also run asynchronously).

With asynchronous CGI scripts, the server can start the script, continue serving without waiting, and display the results when the script ends. FastCGI is another extension CGI, usually indicated by the extension *.fcgi,* that provides for faster CGI interaction with the server. For the purposes of our discussion, asynchronous CGI and FastCGI scripts are just types of CGI scripts. Table 11-1 lists sites for tutorials and further information on CGI programming.

Regardless of whether the POST or GET method is used, the information passed to the CGI script has a well-characterized format. As a Web client user, you will most likely have seen these strings in the Location field of your Web browser. The particulars of the typical formats that you may have seen are described next. What gets passed depends on whether you are using the GET or POST method and whether you are using named parameters (that is, name-value pairs). Code already exists in a variety of programming languages for decoding the various text strings passed to the CGI script, so you don't need to reinvent these. Examples are given for several languages in the next section. Table 11-2 shows the three formats for the text string passed to the CGI program or script.

Table 11-1. Tutorials on CGI Programming

Location	Description
www.comp.it.bton.ac.uk/mas/mas/courses/html/html3.html	A good CGI tutorial by M. A. Smith of the University of Brighton.
www.cgi101.com	CGI101.com, the Web site associated with the book of the same name, by Jacqueline D. Hamilton.
www.fastcgi.com	FastCGI, an extension to CGI that provides faster performance for many servers and scripting languages.
hoohoo.ncsa.uiuc.edu/cgi	The original definition of CGI, from the National Center for Supercomputing Applications.
www.scriptweb.com	A good overview of Macintosh scripting and various scripting languages.
www.awpa.asn.au/cgi	A good introduction to CGI programming and pointers to other places, by Anne Foxworthy.

Table 11-2. CGI Parameter-Passing Formats

Description	Format
Keyword list (escaped) GET method, unnamed parameter	href="/cgi-bin/script_name?John%20Smith"
Keyword list (delimited) GET method, unnamed parameter	href="/cgi-bin/script_name?John+Smith+Jr"
Named parameter list POST method, named parameter	href="/cgi-bin/script_name?first_name=John&last_name=Smith&title=Assistant%20Professor"

Keyword List (Escaped). The "?" separates the script name (the program used to process the input stream) from the variable information. The example from Table 11-2 passes the words "John Smith" to *script_name* on the server for processing. Then *script_name* could, for example, trigger a database lookup for the name "John Smith." Spaces, tabs, carriage returns, and so forth are examples of special characters, and if they are to be taken as literal text, they must be represented correctly. That is, they must be marked to indicate their special meaning. This marking is achieved using the percent sign (%) followed by the two-digit hexadecimal code for each character. For example, "%20" represents a single space.

Keyword List (Delimited). Variables are delimited by the plus character (+), which is the old-style delimiter commonly seen in the Location text box of a Web browser when doing a search for keywords from a search engine.

Named Parameter List. The named parameter list is used by all forms and is by far the most common way of getting information to the server. Again, the question mark separates the CGI script to be executed from the arguments to be passed to that script. The rest are name-value pairs each separated by an ampersand (&). Again, special characters such as white space (space, tab, and carriage return characters) are converted to their hexadecimal equivalents.

Scripting Languages

Today, any Web server of any sophistication requires that you undertake at least some programming tasks, even if it is to modify someone else's script, because programming gives you the most flexible customization and is often the least expensive option for adding just the right functionality. Some Web servers communicate with specific programs through a plug-in or module interface, as with WebSTAR and Apache, but scripts and the CGI provide the most universal form of interaction between a Web server and an external application on your server.

CGI scripts can be written in just about any language with which you are familiar, once you have written (or obtained) the appropriate code to translate the input stream from a Web form. Perl is by far the most common language on the Web used for CGI scripts. It is included with Mac OS X, and many free scripts and commercial programs are available. Mac OS X also includes the AppleScript and Tcl languages, which can be used to write CGI scripts. After an introduction to CGI, this chapter describes and provides examples for Perl, AppleScript, Tcl, and several other languages that are commonly used as CGI scripting languages.

To give you some basis for comparing the syntax and complexity of the various languages, I will provide an example or two for each language. At the very least, however, I will provide the script necessary to process a simple form, contained in a file called *post.html* and shown in Figure 11-1. This file has virtually no formatting, only three fields—Name (a text string), Mailto (an e-mail address), and Comments (a text area)—and a Submit button. Each sample script will accept the form input and display a response page; and in some cases, it will e-mail the contents to the e-mail address provided for confirmation. (Sending e-mail is significantly easier in some languages than in others.)

You can also use other programming languages, such as REALbasic or C++, to extend the capabilities of your Web site. However, these languages often require commercial programming software or compiler as well as a longer start-up time as you learn the language. If you are already developing software with these languages, it may make sense for you to use them to write your CGI programs. For most developers, though, one of the scripting languages included with Mac OS X or available as a free download should suffice in most instances.

Finally, I should mention another scripting-related change since the *Mac OS 8 Web Server Cookbook* was published. Frontier from Userland Software has evolved from a free scripting language to a commercial Web application environment that includes the UserTalk scripting language. A free version of Frontier version 5 is still available, but only for the Classic Mac OS and Windows. For

```
<html>
<head><title>CGI Script POST test</title></head>
<body>
   <form action="/cgi-bin/post-script.cgi" method="POST">
      <p>Name Field: <input type="text" name="Name"></p>
      <p>E-mail Address: <input type="text" name="Mailto"></p>
      <p>Comments: <input type="textarea" name="Comments"></p>
      <p><input type="submit" name="Submit" value="Submit"></p>
   </form>
</body>
</html>
```

Figure 11-1. Example HTML Form: *post.html*.

this reason, I'll mention Frontier in Chapter 12 as a Web application environment for Mac OS X, and not as a standalone scripting language.

AppleScript

AppleScript, created by Apple Computer, controls the actions of Mac OS applications that have AppleScript support and transfers information between applications, computers, or networks. Based on the syntax and structure of spoken language, AppleScript has many of the same elements and components—verbs, nouns, adjectives, and prepositions—that English has. With AppleScript you can customize your Mac OS environment and define commands, as well as write CGI programs for your Web server, which, as far as AppleScript is concerned, is just another scriptable application.

The basic AppleScript software is included with Mac OS X as part of the basic installation. The core AppleScript extension is in */System/Library/Components,* while scripting additions are stored in */System/Library/ScriptingAdditions.* Scripting additions are add-on modules to the AppleScript system that provide special resources or commands to the AppleScript environment, such as those needed to write CGI scripts or parse the input from posting a form. Finally, the Script Editor application (in the */Applications/AppleScript* folder) is used to read, write, and record AppleScript scripts. Table 11-3 lists some sources of information on using AppleScript for CGI scripting.

Table 11-3. AppleScript and the CGI

Location	Description
www.apple.com/applescript	Apple's AppleScript site.
macscripter.net	MacScripter.net for AppleScript news and technical information.
www.osaxen.com	Scripting additions for writing AppleScripts from MacScripter.net.
www.applescriptsourcebook.com	The AppleScript Sourcebook by Bill Cheeseman.
www.infomotions.com/email-cgi	Email.cgi, an AppleScript CGI by Eric Lease Morgan for sending form input via e-mail.
www.latenightsw.com/scripting.html	AppleScript information from Late Night Software, Ltd.

I need to state up front that I *think* the script in Figure 11-2, or something close to it, will work as planned. My problem is that the Mac OS X public beta and the final release—as far as I was able to determine—did not yet have CGI support in AppleScript, so there's no way I could test this. I did test it on Mac OS 9, so it should be close. When AppleScript works for CGI scripts, I'll post a working version on the book's Web site.

The version of AppleScript in the final Mac OS X release should make it easier to write CGI scripts, once you know the appropriate syntax to get your CGI started. The example in Figure 11-2 shows a basic AppleScript that handles a CGI request, parses the arguments from a form that uses the POST method, and echoes the form data back onto the screen.

To try out this script under the Classic Mac OS, you need to install the Parse CGI scripting addition, for the Parse CGI Arguments command, and the Mondo Mail freeware from ACME Technologies (*www.acmetech.com*). Once AppleScript for Mac OS X works for CGI scripts, I assume there will be other ways to send an e-mail message; it may even be built into AppleScript.

Next, copy (or retype) the code into the Script Editor application and save it as a Mac OS X applet. Make sure to select the Stay Open and Never Show Startup Screen options. To write your own scripts, you should replace the sections that echo the incoming arguments, echo the fields and their values, and return the assembled pieces with your own AppleScript commands.

A more realistic CGI script would have sections to process the form data, tell another application (such as an e-mail application) to take some action, and create the necessary HTML pieces to return a complete HTML page. This is more complicated to do with AppleScript, but not impossible. Email.cgi by Eric Lease Morgan (listed in Table 11-3) is a much more complex CGI script written in AppleScript that does just that.

Perl

Perl, which stands for Practical Extraction and Report Language, was written by Larry Wall, and after numerous years, Perl is now in its fifth generation (Perl5). Perl has become one of the most popular languages for writing CGI scripts on Web servers, regardless of operating system, and Perl 5.6 is a standard component of Mac OS X. You'll find the various Perl modules and documentation in */System/Library/Perl.*

```
on handle CGI request path_args ¬
  searching for http_search_args with posted data post_args ¬
  using access method method from address client_address ¬
  from user username using password |password|
  --In your script you have access to the string variables
  -- path_args, http_search_args, post_args, client_address,
  -- username, and password

  try
    set form_fields to ""
    set emessage to ""
    set formData to parse CGI arguments post_args
    repeat with currField in formData
      set form_fields to form_fields & "<p><b>" & ¬
      field of currField & ":</b> " & value of currField & "</p>"
      set emessage to emessage & field of currField & ": " & ¬
        value of currField & return
      if field of currField is "Mailto" then ¬
        set to_mail to value of currField
      if field of currField is "Name" then ¬
        set esubject to "Submission confirmation for " & ¬
          value of currField
    end repeat

    tell application "Mondo Mail.fat"
      send mail emessage subject esubject to ¬
        to_mail from "dhart@san.rr.com" SMTP gateway ¬
        "smtp-server.san.rr.com"
    end tell
    return "<h2>Thank you for your submission!</h2>" & form_fields

  on error WhatsTheError
    return "<h3>Script Error.</h3>" & "Error message: " & ¬
      WhatsTheError
  end try
end handle CGI request
```

Figure 11-2. AppleScript CGI Example.

Because so many Perl scripts have been written over the years, you might find one that performs a task similar to the one you require. Another advantage of Perl is that it's an interpreted programming language, which makes it easier to port and modify scripts as you move them between systems. Finally, Perl is a very good language for string manipulation.

This last point is important, since a text string is what gets passed to the CGI script from the Web form. Table 11-4 has pointers to online sources of Perl references and information on libraries of useful routines for programming CGI scripts in Perl.

Perl: A Minimalist Script

Given the popularity and advantages of Perl, I'm going to give several Perl CGI program examples. For starters let's look at a truly minimalist script. Save the

Table 11-4. Information on Perl and Perl CGI Programming

Location	Description
stein.cshl.org/WWW/CGI	CGI.pm, a Perl5 CGI library, with documentation and examples from Lincoln Stein.
www.perl.com/CPAN-local/ports	Comprehensive Perl Archive Network for many operating systems, including Mac OS X and Classic Mac OS.
www.wdvl.com/Vlib/Providers/Perl.html	Web Developer's Virtual Library section on Perl.
www.perl.com	Perl.com from O'Reilly and Associates, definitive Perl information, software downloads, FAQs, and references.
www.macperl.org	MacPerl, a Classic Mac OS port by Matthias Neeracher.
macperl.sourceforge.net	The SourceForge home of MacPerl.
www.oac.uci.edu/indiv/ehood/perlWWW	PerlWWW, summaries of the Perl libraries for the Web, maintained by Earl Hood.
www.ics.uci.edu/pub/websoft/libwww-perl/archive	libwww-perl mailing list archives, a source for current information on Perl and the Web.
www.perldoc.com	Perldoc.com, a searchable interface to all the Perl documentation.

five-line script below in a file called *printenv.cgi* and place it in the *CGI-Executables* folder. When you invoke the script, it prints out the name and value of the current system environment variables. The first line is the most important: Every Perl script must include such a line to indicate to the system where the Perl interpreter can be found.

```
#!/usr/bin/perl
print "Content-type: text/html\n\n";
while (($key, $val) = each %ENV) {
     print "$key = $val<BR>\n";
}
```

Perl: POST Form Example

A common library used to develop CGI scripts in Perl is the *CGI.pm* library, which is part of the Perl5.6 installation in Mac OS X. The *CGI.pm* library extends the basic Perl language with constructs specifically designed to handle the transfer of information between Web servers and CGI scripts. *CGI.pm* also knows about HTML and provides lots of useful shortcuts for returning formatted HTML code, as shown in Figure 11-3.

Here, the key line is "use CGI qw(:standard);" which tells Perl to use the *CGI.pm* library. The *:standard* specifies which shortcuts you'll be using in your script. "Standard" shortcuts include tags for CGI handling, forms, and HTML. Within the first print statement, you can see references to shortcuts for the http header, the start of an HTML page (with the text string being used as the page <title>), a first-level header (h1), and the end of an HTML page. The *CGI.pm* library makes extracting form field values a snap. The invocations of Param find the value for the specified field name. (In this case, I assigned them to a static variable because the script needed to use them several times.) The second section of the script sends the e-mail message using the Sendmail program included as part of Mac OS X. The Open statement requires somewhat esoteric UNIX knowledge; I copied this version from an older script that I've used successfully before. I just know it works.

One advantage that Mac OS X provides to Mac webmasters is the ability to use Perl scripts written for other UNIX-based systems with little or no modification. Under the Classic Mac OS, scripts that worked with the file system, often required changes and the addition of the *Mac::Files* module. Under Mac OS X, that modification can be avoided.

Perl: An Automated Archive

We'll wrap up our discussion of Perl with one substantial script that addresses the problem of maintaining frequently changing information. In many cases the only hope is to offload the update tasks to client users. This type of fully automated, user-updated resource is sometimes called a *self-sustaining archive*. The disadvantage of such an archive is that you must rely on the users to post useful, accurate, and non-offensive material. However, for certain forms of information for which accuracy and appropriateness are not critical, it works very well.

This example maintains a list of job openings. Employers can use a Web form to post information about a new job, and the job listings are automatically updated. It allows employers to post details of vacant positions via a Web form and the information is added to the job-listing file. I actually use this script and form at *www.npaci.edu/jobs.*

```
#!/usr/bin/perl
use CGI qw(:standard);

$name = param('Name');
$mailto = param('Mailto');
$comments = param('Comments');

print header, start_html("Perl POST Example"),
   h1("Thank you for your submission!"),
   p("Name: ", $name),
   p("E-mail: ", $mailto),
   p("Comments: ", $comments),
   end_html;

open (MAIL, "| /usr/bin/mail -s \"Submission confirmation
   for $name\" $mailto") || die "Can't open mail to $mailto, $! \n";
print MAIL "Name: $name\n",
   "E-mail: $mailto\n",
   "Comments: $comments\n";
close (MAIL);
```

Figure 11-3. Perl CGI Example.

Figure 11-4 gives the annotated HTML Web form used to submit job information. Read it carefully. Note that I've eliminated tables and other elements used to format the page in order to focus on the parts important for this example.

Next, Figure 11-5 gives the annotated Perl script for processing the input to the Web form. For the script to work properly, you must also create an empty job-listing file, *jobs.html,* which contains at least the tags that the script uses to find the different sections. (Any other HTML formatting and headers the script leaves alone.) The file *jobs.html* must have, in this order, the tags <!start shortlist>, <!start listings>, <!end listings>, and <!menu>, each at the start of a line.

Figure 11-6 illustrates the result of posting a position. A brief summary for each available job, including position title, location of position, and date posted, appears in the short list at the top of the Web page. The summary links to a name anchor in the same file. This makes it easier to find details of a specific posting in a long list of available positions.

Tcl

Tcl, pronounced "tickle," stands for Tool Command Language and was developed by John Ousterhout first at the University of California, Berkeley, then at Sun Microsystems, and now at Ajuba Solutions (formerly Scriptics). Tcl and its associated graphical user interface toolkit, Tk, have been ported from UNIX to Windows, Macintosh, and other operating systems, and Tcl is part of the basic Mac OS X installation.

As a scripting language, Tcl is designed to be a shell in which you can execute other programs; it also includes enough programming flexibility to let you build complex scripts by assembling them out of other programs. Like other scripting languages, Tcl is designed to be easy to learn and to develop applications quickly. Some advantages of Tcl over Perl include its extensibility, the ability to embed the Tcl interpreter in other applications, and its graphical user interface component, Tk. Some advantages over AppleScript include its cross-platform portability and its ability to access databases.

Table 11-5 lists Web sites for Tcl information and resources. To use Tcl to write your CGI scripts, you would do well to download and install the *cgi.tcl* support library by Don Libes. By handling the parsing of the input sting and providing shortcuts for common HTML formatting commands, this library makes it easy to write CGI scripts with Tcl.

```
<html>
  <head><title>Post an Open Job Position</title></head>
  <body>
    <form method="POST" action="/cgi-bin/postjob.cgi">
    <h2>Post a Job Opening</h2>
    <p>Type of Position
      <select name="type" size="1">
        <option value="PostDoc">PostDoc
        <option value="Faculty">Faculty
        <option value="Staff">Staff
        <option value="Intern">Intern
        <option value="Other">Other
      </select></p>
    <p>Title of Position
      <input size="50" name="title" type="TEXT"></p>
    <p>Institution
      <input size="50" name="institution" type="TEXT"></p>
    <p>Location
      <input size="50" name="location" type="TEXT"></p>
    <p>Department
      <input size="50" name="dept" type="TEXT"></p>
    <p>URL for more info
      <input size="50" name="site" type="TEXT"></p>
    <p>Start date
      <input size="20" name="start" type="TEXT"></p>
    <p><b>Job Description:</b>
      <textarea name="details" rows="10" cols="60"></textarea> </p>
    <p><b>Contact Information:</b></p>
    <p>Name
      <input size="50" name="contact_name" type="TEXT"></p>
    <p>E-mail Address
      <input size="50" name="contact_email" type="TEXT"></p>
    <p>Phone
      <input size="50" name="contact_phone" type="TEXT"></p>
    <h4>Caution: Please carefully check the information you have
provided before submitting the form, as all submissions will be
posted automatically to the job lists.</h4>
    <p><input type="SUBMIT" value="Submit Position">
      <input type="RESET" value="Clear Form"></p>
    </form>
  </body>
</html>
```

Figure 11-4. Post Job Form.

```
#!/usr/bin/perl
use CGI qw(:all);

$oldfilename = "jobs.html";
$newfilename = "$oldfilename.tmp";
$date =  `/bin/date +%D`;
chop $date;
$anchor = time;

open (OLDFILE, "$oldfilename") || die "Can't open job file
   $oldfilename: $!\n";
open (NEWFILE, ">$newfilename") || die "Can't open job file
   $newfilename: $!\n";

while ($line=<OLDFILE>)
{
# If the "<!start shortlist>" string is found, make a new entry
# immediately following it in the new file. Thus, the script puts
# the newest entries first when scrolling through the file.
  if ($line =~ /^<!start shortlist>/) {
    print NEWFILE $line;
    print NEWFILE "<LI>", a({-href=>"\#$anchor"}, param('type'),
       param('title'),
    param('institution'), "[$date]"), "</LI>\n";
    next;
}

# If the "<!end listings>" string is found, write summary information.
  if ($line =~ /^<!end listings>/) {
    print NEWFILE $line;
    print NEWFILE "<P><SMALL>Last posting: ", $date, "<br>\n";
    print NEWFILE "Problems?  Send mail to the webmaster.<br>\n";
    while ( !($line =~  /^<!menu>/)) {
       $line=<OLDFILE>;
    }
    print NEWFILE $line;
    next;
  }

# If the "<!start listings>" string is found, enter the full job
# description, with formatting based on input from the Web form.
  if ($line =~ /^<!start listings>/) {
```

Figure 11-5. Job Posting Perl Script.

```
    print NEWFILE $line;
    print NEWFILE hr, h4("<A NAME=\"$anchor\"></A>", param('type'));
    if (param('title') ne '') {
      print NEWFILE h3(param('title')), "\n"; }
    if (param('institution') ne '') {
      print NEWFILE h3(param('institution'));    }
    if (param('location') ne '') {
      print NEWFILE "<B>Location: </B>", param('location'), br; }
    if (param('dept') ne '') {
      print NEWFILE "<B>Department: </B>", param('dept'), br; }
    if (param('site') ne '') {
      print NEWFILE "<B>URL: </B>", a({-href=>param('site')},
        param('site')), br; }
    if (param('start') ne '') {
      print NEWFILE "<B>Start Date: </B>", param('start'), br; }
    if (param('details') ne '') {
      print NEWFILE "<B>Description: </B>", param('details'), br;}
    if (param('contact_name') ne '') {
      print NEWFILE "<B>Person to contact: </B>",
        param('contact_name'), br;        }
    if (param('contact_email') ne '') {
      print NEWFILE "<B>Email address: </B>",
        param('contact_email'), br;       }
    if (param('contact_phone') ne '') {
      print NEWFILE "<B>Phone number: </B>", param('contact_phone'),
        br;}
    print NEWFILE "<B>Job Posted: </B> $date<br>\n";
    print NEWFILE "<B>Job ID Number: </B> $anchor<br>\n";
    next;
    }
    print NEWFILE $line;
}
close OLDFILE;
close NEWFILE;

# Copy the NewFile back into the OldFile.
open (OLDFILE, ">$oldfilename") || die "Can't open job file
    $oldfilename: $!\n";
open (NEWFILE, "$newfilename") || die "Can't open job file
    $newfilename: $!\n";
while ($line=<NEWFILE>) {
    print OLDFILE $line; }
```

Figure 11-5. Job Posting Perl Script (continued).

```
close OLDFILE;
close NEWFILE;

# Print a message.
print header, start_html("Job Posting Results"),
   h2("Job Posting Results"), hr,
   p, "Your job was successfully posted to our ",
   a({-href=>"$oldfilename"}, "job list"), ". ",
   "For further assistance, send mail to the Job List Editor. ",
   "If you would like a job removed from the listings, please
   include the ", b("Job ID Number."),
   end_html;
```

Figure 11-5. Job Posting Perl Script (continued).

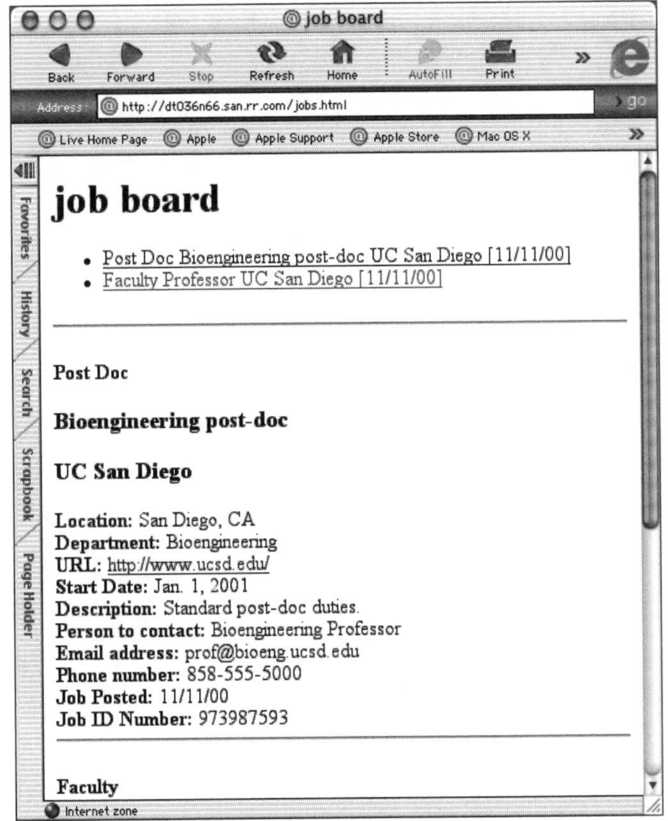

Figure 11-6. Result of Posting a Job with Postjob.cgi Perl Script.

Table 11-5. Tcl Information and Resources

Location	Description
dev.ajubasolutions.com	Tcl Developer Xchange, maintained by Ajuba Solutions.
expect.nist.gov/cgi.tcl	Information on *cgi.tcl,* the CGI support library for Tcl programmers, by Don Libes.
expect.nist.gov/doc/cgi.pdf	"Writing CGI Scripts in Tcl," by Don Libes. Proceedings of the Fourth Annual Tcl/Tk Workshop 96, Monterey, CA, July 10–13, 1996.
www.nyx.net/~tpoindex/tcl.html	Fcgi.tcl and other Tcl software from Tom Poindexter.
www.zveno.com/zm.cgi/in-tclxml	TclXML for manipulating and processing XML documents, by Steve Ball of Zveno Pty Ltd.
pitch.nist.gov/cgi-bin/cgi.tcl/examples.cgi	Downloadable example CGI scripts written in Tcl. by Don Libes.

Installing cgi.tcl

If you follow the steps below, you should be able to run CGI scripts written in Tcl. I had to wing it when getting Tcl and the *cgi.tcl* module to work with Mac OS X, so pay attention: This will make your life a lot easier. For starters, you should be logged in as "root" so you can execute commands from the Terminal command line and not worry about file permissions. Once logged in, you should do the following steps. (This has been checked with Mac OS X final version, so the details should be correct.)

1. Download the *cgi.tcl.tar.gz* file from Don Libes's site in Table 11-5. I'll assume you download it to the Desktop. You can probably let the final release version of StuffIt Expander expand the file. (At the time of writing, the earliest versions of StuffIt Expander had some problems with *.tar.gz* files.)
2. If StuffIt Expander returns any errors, open a Terminal window and enter the following commands, which will put a folder called *cgi.tcl-1.3* on your Desktop. (% is the system prompt.)

```
% cd Library/Desktop
% tar -zxvf cgi.tcl.tar.gz
```

3. Open a Finder window and navigate to */System/Library/Tcl/8.3/*.
4. Put the *cgi.tcl-1.3* folder inside */System/Library/Tcl/8.3/*.
5. According to Libes's INSTALL file, you should be able to run the Make Install command from the Terminal command line; however, my Mac OS X did not have the Make utility. Instead, return to your Terminal window and enter the following commands, which I extracted from Libes's *install.mac* file.

```
% cd /System/Library/Tcl/8.3/cgi.tcl-1.3
% tclsh8.3
% pkg_mkIndex cgi.tcl
```

Tcl POST Form Example

A basic script to process the *post.html* example form would look like that shown in Figure 11-7. Again, Tcl scripts begin with a line that locates the Tcl interpreter, and the "package require cgi" line includes the shortcuts from the *cgi.tcl* module. The key line for accepting and parsing the CGI input is the statement "cgi_input."

As with the Perl version, a Tcl script starts with a line that locates the Tcl executable. The "package" line includes the *cgi.tcl* library for CGI processing, and the "cgi_eval" block surrounds the main component of the CGI script. The "cgi_input" line processes the CGI input (obviously enough), and the "cgi_import" statements extract the values associated with the named fields and assign them to Tcl variables. The "cgi_body" block encloses the results returned to the Web browser, and the "cgi_mail" statements send the message to the Mailto address.

Tcl: A Universal Mailer Script

As a more complex example that includes some error checking, I've included in Figure 11-8, with permission from Don Libes, a script that will mail the contents of any form to the designated recipient. Such a script is handy for all sorts of uses. It's not something you would use in an extremely complex Web application, but it will get you up and running quickly since it requires no additional programming at all.

```
#!/usr/bin/tclsh8.3
package require cgi
cgi_eval {

  cgi_title "Tcl POST Example"
  cgi_input
  cgi_body {
    cgi_mail_start [cgi_import Mailto]
    cgi_mail_add "Subject: Submission confirmed for [cgi_import
Name]"
    cgi_mail_add

    h2 "Thanks for your submission!"
    foreach item [cgi_import_list] {
      p "$item: [cgi_import $item]"
      cgi_mail_add "$item: [cgi_import $item]"
    }
    cgi_mail_end
  }
}
```

Figure 11-7. Tcl Form Posting Example.

In many ways this script is very similar to my first Tcl example. You'll notice primarily the addition of several Catch statements, which are calls to the Tcl error handler. For example, the "[catch cgi_input errormsg]" line returns a true (non-empty) value if Tcl catches an error in receiving the *cgi_input.* The error handler returns an error message, with the script displays in the Web browser to let the visitor know something went wrong. This script and several dozen others are provided with the *cgi.tcl* download.

REBOL

I have to say that REBOL is cool. It's a free, networking-based messaging language from REBOL Technologies, designed with common Internet protocols in mind. It's somewhat surprising that this is the only such language, given the prevalence of the Internet. To see what this marketing-speak translates into for CGI scripts, here's the REBOL needed to e-mail someone a Web page:

```
send dhart@maccentral.com  read http://hart-mac.sdsc.edu/Handbook/
```

```
#!/usr/bin/tclsh8.3
# Universal Mailer Backend
# Author: Don Libes, NIST

# To use, make your form look something like this:
#  <form action="/cgi-bin/ unimail.cgi" method=post>
#  <input type=hidden name=mailto value="YOUR EMAIL ADDRESS HERE">
#  ... rest of your form ...
#  </form>

package require cgi
cgi_eval {
   cgi_title "Universal mail backend"
   cgi_body {
   if {[catch cgi_input errormsg]} {
       h2 "Form Error"
       p "An error was detected in the form.  Please send the
       following diagnostics to the form author."
       cgi_preformatted {puts $errormsg}
       return
   }
   if {[catch {cgi_import mailto}]} {
       h2 "Error: No mailto variable in form."
       return
   }
   if {![info exists env(HTTP_REFERER)]} {
       set env(HTTP_REFERER) "unknown"
   }
   cgi_mail_start $mailto
   cgi_mail_add "Subject: submission from web form:
$env(HTTP_REFERER)"
   cgi_mail_add
   catch {cgi_mail_add "Remote addr: $env(REMOTE_ADDR)"}
   catch {cgi_mail_add "Remote host: $env(REMOTE_HOST)"}

   foreach item [cgi_import_list] {
       cgi_mail_add "$item: [cgi_import $item]"
   }
   cgi_mail_end
   h2 "Thanks for your submission."
   }
}
```

Figure 11-8. Tcl Universal Mailer Script by Don Libes.

In fact, the REBOL examples include an entire Web server written in 39 lines of code. And REBOL is truly cross-platform; the same REBOL code should work on any platform without changes. However, a disadvantage of REBOL, aside from having to write its name in all capital letters, is that if REBOL fails to catch on, you may be stuck with scripts that can't be updated or might become obsolete in the future.

REBOL/Core is the free component of the software being offered by REBOL Technologies. REBOL/View is a free extension, at least at the time of writing, that includes a graphical compositing system for creating interfaces. REBOL/Command is the commercial product that allows access to external libraries, operating system commands, and databases. Table 11-6 includes pointers to REBOL information and examples.

Installing REBOL

It takes a few steps and a visit to the Terminal window to install REBOL, but the steps are straightforward. You should also be logged in as "root" to be sure you have the necessary file permissions.

1. Download the REBOL distribution for Mac OS X from the REBOL Technologies site listed in Table 11-6. As with most *.tar.gz* files, be sure to use the final release of StuffIt Expander.
2. In the Finder, you need to create a home folder for REBOL. For this example, let's say you create a folder called *Rebol* in the */System/Library* folder.

Table 11-6. REBOL Information and Examples

Location	Description
www.rebol.com	REBOL by REBOL Technologies, a multi-platform network-enabled language.
www.rebol.com/library/library.html	REBOL script library from REBOL Technologies.
www.rebol.org	REBOL.org, a third-party resource of REBOL information and examples.
www.rebol.org/archive.html	REBOL.org's Open Script Library.

3. Open a Terminal window. If you don't want to use StuffIt Expander, you need to unpack the *.tar.gz* file by entering the command

```
tar zxvf core024.tar.gz
```

4. In the Finder, copy the files from the uncompressed folder into the */System/Library/Rebol* folder you created. (For the UNIX adept, you can also do this from the Terminal if you prefer.)
5. Back in the Terminal window, enter the following commands—the first changes the directory, the second runs the REBOL interpreter. Respond to the REBOL program with the appropriate network configuration information. It will ask for your system's SMTP (mail) server, for example, and other settings. When completed, REBOL will have created two files, *rebol.r* and *user.r,* in the */System/Library/Rebol* folder.

```
cd /System/Library/Rebol
rebol
```

6. Wherever you plan to run REBOL scripts, REBOL needs the *rebol.r* and *user.r* files to be in that folder. In this case, you'll need to copy (using the Finder or the Terminal) *rebol.r* and *user.r* into */Library/WebServer/CGI-Executables.*

Another heads-up for using REBOL: Unlike most Mac applications, which are pretty flexible, REBOL cares (because the UNIX-like part of Mac OS X cares) what the end-of-line characters are in your REBOL scripts. If you are getting unexplained errors in your scripts, you might try viewing them in the Terminal (using the More command) or editing them in the vi editor. If they look incorrect, try retyping all the end-of-line return characters. In one case, I introduced incorrect end-of-line characters when copying and pasting out of a Microsoft Internet Explorer window.

REBOL POST Script Example

The REBOL script to handle our simple form-posting example is straightforward, but a little longer than the Tcl or Perl versions. However, while Tcl and Perl require additional libraries and modules to handle CGI processing, all the functions provided by those libraries are built into the REBOL core and the script in Figure 11-9.

```
#!/System/Library/Rebol/rebol --cgi
REBOL [
    Title: "REBOL Form Post"
]

input-cgi: func [/stdin] [
    either system/options/cgi/request-method = "POST" [
        length: make decimal! system/options/cgi/content-length
        stdin: make string! length
        read-io system/ports/input stdin length
        return stdin
    ][
        system/options/cgi/query-string
    ]
]

cgi: make object! decode-cgi input-cgi
mailto: make email! cgi/Mailto

header: make system/standard/email [
    FROM: dhart@san.rr.com
    subject: join "Submission confirmation for " cgi/Name
]
message: join "" [
    "Name: " cgi/Name
    "^/E-mail: " cgi/Mailto
    "^/Comments: " cgi/Comments
]

send/header mailto message header

print [ "Content-Type: text/html^/"  ;-- Required Page Header
    <html><body><h2>"Thank you for your submission!"</h2>
    "Name:"  <B> cgi/Name </B><P>
    "Email:" <B> cgi/Mailto </B><P>
    "Comments:" <B> cgi/Comments </B><P>
    </body><html>
]
```

Figure 11-9. REBOL Form Post Example.

As with Perl and Tcl, the first line locates the REBOL interpreter. The subsequent REBOL block is also required, to provide information about the script.

I've only provided a bare minimum of information. Let's step through each of the remaining pieces.

1. The *input-cgi* function is required so the script can handle forms that use the POST method as well as those that use GET. The CGI arguments for a GET are stored in "system/options/cgi/query-string," but a POST requires reading a certain number of bytes ("content-length") from the standard input. In either case, *input-cgi* returns a string containing the escaped keyword list.
2. The next significant line is the line beginning "cgi: make object!" This line does a lot. It calls the *input-cgi* function, calls the REBOL operation *decode-cgi* to parse the escaped keyword string, and then makes an object containing keyword-value pairs. The values are all strings.
3. The next three sections create the e-mail message. The "make email!" command converts the Mailto string to a variable of type email (a standard REBOL variable type). The next block creates a custom e-mail header; you can set any e-mail header in this block, not just the ones shown here. Finally, the next block creates the e-mail message. The "join" statement is REBOL's way of concatenating objects.
4. The "send/header" statement sends the e-mail, using the custom header and message defined by the script.
5. The final print statement displays the results to the Web browser.

The REBOL Technologies and REBOL.org script libraries, listed in Table 11-6, contain additional examples of scripts for CGI, Web, FTP, and e-mail tasks.

Python

Python is another popular scripting language that is freely available for many platforms. It was developed and named after Monty Python's Flying Circus by Guido van Rossum starting in 1990 at CWI in Amsterdam, and continuing today at CNRI in Virginia. Python can be extended by the addition of new modules implemented in a compiled language such as C or C++. Such extension modules can define new functions and variables as well as new object types.

Proponents emphasize that Python is an elegant language, an object-oriented programming language for those who appreciate programming, data structure design, and readable (and maintainable) code. Table 11-7 lists further information and resources on Python. Of particular note, the *cgi.py* Python module provides the shortcuts needed for quick and easy CGI programming.

Installing Python for Mac OS X

The exact steps for installing Python for Mac OS X depend on the actual distribution you use. Jack Jansen's MacPython page, listed in Table 11-7, should point you to current Mac OS X distributions. You should be logged in as "root" and follow the instructions provided. When completed, the Python interpreter should reside at */usr/bin/python* and the Python libraries and modules should be within */usr/lib/python2.0* (assuming you're using a distribution of Python 2.0).

Once it is installed, you can run the Python interpreter from a Terminal command line by entering the command "python." This installation also means that your Python CGI scripts should begin with the following line:

```
#!/usr/bin/python
```

Table 11-7. Python Information and Resources

Location	Description
www.python.org	Python.org, the official home page of the Python Software Activity.
www.cwi.nl/~jack/macpython.html	MacPython page by Jack Jansen.
www.oreillynet.com/python	Python DevCenter from the O'Reilly Network.
www.python.org/topics/web	Web programming guide from Python.org.
www.python.org/doc/lib/module-cgi.html	Documentation for *cgi.py,* the Python module for supporting CGI scripts.
starship.python.net	Starship Python, a Python community site hosted by BeOpen.com.
www.vex.net/parnassus	The Vaults of Parnassus, Python resources.
www.devshed.com/Server_Side/Python/CGI	"Writing CGI Programs in Python," by Preston Landers at the Developer Shed.

Python POST Script Example

The Python script to handle our form-posting example should look familiar to you. The key line is the assignment statement "form=cgi.FieldStorage()," which parses the CGI arguments and places them in a list called "form." This script, shown in Figure 11-10, also creates a string object called "email" to hold the e-mail message as it is being assembled. The first three "email.write" statements create the message headers, the "for" loop prints the form contents, and the next two statements send the e-mail message.

```
#!/usr/bin/python

import cgi,StringIO,string,smtplib  # Standard modules

form=cgi.FieldStorage()

mailserver="your-smtp.server.com"
mail_from="your-web@server.com"

# Create email headers and message
email=StringIO.StringIO()
email.write('Subject: Submission confirmation for %s\n' %
    form["Name"].value)
email.write('To: %s\n' % form["Mailto"].value)
email.write('From: %s\n\n' % mail_from)
for fieldname in form.keys():
    email.write('%s: ' % fieldname)
    email.write('%s\n' % form[fieldname].value)
# Send email
mail=smtplib.SMTP(mailserver)
mail.sendmail(mail_from,[form["Mailto"].value],email.getvalue())

# Display confirmation screen
print "Content-type: text/html\n"
print "<html><head>\n"
print "<title>Python CGI Post Example</title></head>\n"
print "<body>\n"
print "<h2>Thank you for your submission!</h2>\n"
for fieldname in form.keys():
    print "<p><b>", fieldname, ":</b> ", form[fieldname].value, "</p>"
print "</body></html>\n";
```

Figure 11-10. Python Form Post Example.

The HTML display portion of the script is fairly self-explanatory. If you are unfamiliar with Python, I should note that indentation is significant in Python. Within the first "for" loop, for example, the two statements are inside the loop body, but the next unindented line is outside the loop body.

Server-Side JavaScript

If learning a new scripting language is not your cup of tea, you might want to consider another option, the last we'll discuss in this chapter, for scripting your Web server. JavaScript, the language you are likely to have used in delivering dynamic Web pages to your Web visitors, can also be used to write scripts that your server executes.

In other words, you've probably used JavaScript in developing Web pages. However, that JavaScript code is only run on client computers. When a visitor downloads the Web page that contains JavaScript, the visitor's own Web browser takes it upon itself to run the JavaScript instructions as it's reading the HTML file. (Chapter 12 has more about such client-side JavaScript for your Web pages.) With *server-side JavaScript,* on the other hand, you write JavaScript programs that do not get downloaded to client computers; instead, as with CGI scripts, the server carries out the JavaScript instructions.

Even though you're probably used to thinking of JavaScript as somewhat less than a complete programming language—one that works only on Web browsers and Web pages—JavaScript is a fully featured object-oriented programming language. This particular language just happens to be built into every Web browser. Because it's built into the client browsers, though, you still need to worry about how your server will learn to understand JavaScript.

As with REBOL and Python, you have to use software that provides a JavaScript interpreter for your server. As yet, there are no free interpreters for server-side JavaScript, but you can get server-side JavaScript through two commercial options—the Lasso Web Data Engine from Blue World Technologies (Chapter 9) and Web Crossing from Web Crossing, Inc. (Chapter 10).

CHAPTER 12

BEYOND SCRIPTING

Rarely does a Web server these days deliver only basic HTML files. Most servers of any sophistication have at least a CGI script or two, and many incorporate databases for presenting regularly updated information. We've also discussed tools for adding guestbooks, forums, and chats to a Mac OS X server. More and more, however, organizations and companies think of Web servers as more than just information delivery services. Today, Web servers are expected to be application delivery services, in which visitors are provided the same level of interactivity that they've come to expect from applications on their desktop.

E-commerce is one such Web application, for which specialized tools have been developed and which is described in Chapter 13. This chapter describes some of the more general tools that Web developers have at their disposal to tie together Web pages, standalone CGI scripts, and complex interaction between Web servers, Web browsers, and the human clients.

Web Application Development

In many ways, developing full-fledged Web applications is like developing traditional desktop applications. As a developer, you must consider interface design, selection of programming languages, and the flow of control as users interact with the application. In the case of the Web, you also have the more difficult decision of determining how tied you want to be to a particular Web technology.

You may choose to stick with the more general-purpose options, such as CGI scripts in Perl. The disadvantage is that you may have to develop much of your application from scratch and concern yourself with many low-level details. The advantage is that you can be reasonably sure that Perl, and the CGI will be around for a long time. At the other extreme, you can adopt a tool that provides a comprehensive Web-based application environment. The advantage is that you can create complex applications quickly by programming in languages that look more like HTML and less like Perl. The disadvantage is that you have to worry about the longevity and portability of your solution, in the event that some piece of the technology changes.

In other words, the trade-off is development and maintenance time versus application longevity and portability. It's a tough call to make.

Overcoming Stateless Interaction

Now for a slightly more technical discussion. The major issue that you must confront in most Web applications is the notion of *state*. Under normal circumstances, a Web server receives a request from clients and processes those requests by returning HTML documents to the client browsers. The server does not "remember" which client requested which piece of information, so when a client makes a second request, the server does not recognize that client as having made the previous request. This works fine for requesting most Web pages in which the client simply displays the served information.

On the other hand, consider what this stateless behavior means when, for example, you are querying a database through a Web server. You pass the query to the server and results are returned. No problem here, but what if you want to use those results in a subsequent query? With stateless interactions, all the necessary information must be passed *back* to the server for the second query, since the server retains no results from the first query. This is inefficient in terms of the network bandwidth required, the load on the server, and the management of the information sent back and forth with each incremental request.

It would be better to have the server store the results of the query. Then if a second query is needed, it would ideally be performed on the data already stored on the server. So how do you associate a set of query results with a particular client for subsequent access? Or to ask the more general question: How do you associate a Web visitor's previous server interaction with the same visitor's subsequent interaction?

There are various tricks for making this association. All use the same basic idea—provide each client with a unique identifier so that it can be identified repeatedly by the server. Thus, every Web application has to account for the following interactions with a visitor:

1. The Web visitor takes some action on a Web page. This might be uploading a file, filling out a form, or clicking on a link.
2. Processing begins on the server to create the requested results, perhaps in the form of a file on the server or a record in the database. These results contain an identifier, created by the processing, which is the key to accessing your results on the server.
3. The identifier is returned to the Web visitor, perhaps as information stored in a browser cookie or as a user name, an order number, or some other alphanumeric string displayed by the browser.
4. Later, by accessing the same Web server with your Web browser, you can follow a link to the previously stored results, which remain on the server for a designated period of time. With a browser cookie, the server may automatically present you with your the results from your earlier visit.

Using a text-based identifier that the Web visitor must remember is not as secure as using a browser cookie; however, using an encrypted transaction can limit the potential for other parties learning the identifier.

Now that we've introduced the issues of stateless interaction, this chapter describes the basic approaches to creating an interactive server. The sophistication of the interaction between client and server, including how it handles the stateless nature of the Web, depends primarily on the capabilities of the program processing the input from the Web visitor.

Cookies

Cookies were developed by Netscape Communications specifically to overcome the Web's stateless nature and provide a powerful way to develop Web applications. Shopping applications, for example, can store information about currently selected items, pay services can store your registration information and free you from retyping a user ID the next time you visit, and sites can store client preferences on the client. This last use of cookies is what allows repeat visitors to customize the appearance or behavior of a site.

When a server returns a Web page to a client, the server may also send a small amount of data, the so-called cookie, which the client will store. When the client makes a future request of that same server, the client sends the current value of the cookie from the client back to the server.

You can look at the cookies stored on your Macintosh. If you use Internet Explorer, choose the Preferences option from the Edit menu. From the left side of the dialog, select the Cookies option under Receiving Files. This will display the cookies that Internet Explorer has stored. You can also view the contents of each cookie or delete those you don't like the looks of.

Obviously, letting Web servers write information to your computer presents some security and privacy issues. As far as security goes, cookies are constrained both in what they can store and in which servers can read them. A browser will not give up cookie data to any server except the one that set the cookie; if your browser tossed its cookies to every site you visited, this would be a security risk and would make cookies worthless.

As for what they can store, according to Netscape, cookies are limited to

- A total of 300 cookies in the cookie file.
- 4 kilobytes per cookie, for the sum of both the cookie's name and its value.
- 20 cookies per server or domain. Completely specified hosts and domains are treated as separate entities and have a 20-cookie limitation for each, not combined. (That is, you can have only 20 cookies for *yahoo.com,* but you can have another 20 cookies each for *my.yahoo.com, shopping.yahoo.com,* and so on.)

Even though security should not be a major concern, privacy might be. Unless you provide additional information, a Web site's cookie can only indicate that you, or more specifically your browser, visited that site (or pages on that site) and when. When you make choices or enter data into forms or dialog boxes, the site might also store that in the cookie, since this information distinguishes you from other visitors. Even though the information is being stored on *your computer*, you might have qualms about your privacy, so as a general rule, you should not provide information—or, as the host of a Web server, ask for information—that could compromise your or your Web visitors' privacy.

A Web server has three methods of sending these cookies to a client and later retrieving them: CGI scripts, Java applets, and JavaScript in an HTML page. JavaScript is the most common method, and the JavaScript section of this chapter describes how to bake your own cookies. Table 12-1 has general information on cookies, as well as writing and reading cookies with CGI scripts.

Table 12-1. Information on Cookies

Location	Description
home.netscape.com/newsref/std/cookie_spec.html	Netscape's specification for persistent client-state HTTP cookies.
www.ietf.org/rfc/rfc2109.txt	The RFC 2109 cookie specification from the IETF.
www.cookiecentral.com	Cookie Central, including CGI cookie demos.
privacy.net/cookies	Basic cookie information and discussion of privacy issues from Privacy.Net.

JAVASCRIPT

JavaScript is often an important component of Web applications. Used effectively, JavaScript can make your Web applications more efficient, by offloading some processing tasks to the client's computer. For example, you can manage cookies with JavaScript (on the client) instead of with CGI scripts (on the server). You can also handle some aspects of the interface manipulation with JavaScript (as a component of Dynamic HTML) or ensure that visitors enter correctly formatted values into forms or enter required fields at all. Such verification potentially saves a lot of exchanges with the server to detect and correct errors. On a busy server, your visitors will appreciate it.

Developed originally by Netscape Communications, JavaScript was originally called LiveScript and was designed as an object-oriented language that would let Web pages take advantage of capabilities built into the Navigator browser that exceeded the "official" features provided by basic HTML. LiveScript was renamed JavaScript about the time that the Java programming language appeared on the scene by virtue of Netscape's licensing the "Java" name from Sun.

JavaScript code is embedded in HTML documents and is interpreted by the viewer's Web browser. Most modern graphical Web browsers include support for at least some form of JavaScript. The ECMA international standards organization has developed a standardized form of JavaScript, with the not-so-catchy name of ECMAScript, but the final ECMA-262 specification has not yet been fully adopted by all browsers. Table 12-2 contains pointers to further information on JavaScript.

Table 12-2. Sources of Additional Information on JavaScript

Location	Description
www.webreference.com/js	Doc JavaScript by Tomer Shiran and Yehuda Shiran at WebReference.com.
www.ecma.ch	The ECMA-262 specification defines a standard form of JavaScript called ECMAScript.
javascriptgate.com	JavaScript Gate, by Yehuda Shiran.
javascript.internet.com	The JavaScript Source from internet.com.
www.javascript.com	JavaScript.com, "the definitive JavaScript resource" with scripts and tutorials.
www.javascripts.com	JavaScripts.com, example scripts and tutorials, from EarthWeb, Inc.
developer.netscape.com/docs/manuals/javascript.html	Netscape's introduction to JavaScript basics.
www.webcoder.com	WebCoder.com, "your source for JavaScript and Dynamic HTML on the Web."

Now let's look at what may be the most basic JavaScript example, a script that tells the Web browser to pop up an alert window. Note the following features in Figure 12-1:

- We defined a function—*helloworld()*—that calls a built-in JavaScript function called *alert(),* which takes a single text string argument—in this case, "Hello, world!"—and pops up an alert window with the text string and a Dismiss button.
- The Onclick attribute of the <input> tag defines what happens when a button (specified with the Type attribute) is pressed. In this case it invokes the *helloworld()* function.

```
<html>
<head>
<script language="javascript">
<!--  For non-supporting browsers
  function helloworld() {
          alert("Hello, world!")
                        }
// end hiding contents from old browsers  -->
</script>
</head>
<body>
<form>
<input type="button" value="Press me!"
     onclick="helloworld()">
</form>
</body>
</html>
```

Figure 12-1. JavaScript "Hello, World!" Example.

JavaScript Cookies

This chapter has already discussed why you might want to use Web browser cookies (and why you should use them carefully). Here I'll provide the basic JavaScript framework for managing cookies. At minimum, you need two pieces: first, a function to write or update a cookie, and second, a function to get information from a cookie. In addition to the JavaScript resources provided in Table 12-2, Table 12-3 lists some further sources of JavaScript code for cookies.

As an example of creating and using a cookie with JavaScript, I've borrowed with permission the example from Marc Matteo, which records and displays how many times a user visits the Web page that creates the cookie. To try this out, save the code in Figure 12-2 as an *.html* file and view it in your browser.

This example also gives you a feel for some longer JavaScript functions. In particular, note the references to *document.cookie,* which contains the value of the cookie that the client sent along with the request for this page. It uses string methods such as *substring, indexOf,* and *lastIndexOf* to determine the content of the cookie.

Table 12-3. JavaScript Cookies

Location	Description
javascript.internet.com/cookies	Cookie examples from the JavaScript Source.
www.cookiecentral.com/demomain.htm	Cookie Central's JavaScript demos.
www.ozemail.com.au/~dcrombie/cookie.html	Duncan Crombie's JavaScript Cookies page.
www.lectroid.net/projects/javascript/cookies	Marc Matteo's Cookies with JavaScript page.

```
<html>
<head>
<title>A Cookie Counter</title>
<!-- Basic JavaScript cookie code. By Marc Matteo, -->
<script>
cookie_name = "Counter_Cookie";
// Updates the Counter_Cookie.
// Called as the client leaves the page.

function doCookie() {
  if(document.cookie) {
     index = document.cookie.indexOf(cookie_name);
  } else {
     index = -1;
}
```

Figure 12-2. JavaScript Cookie Example by Marc Matteo.

```
    if (index == -1) {
       document.cookie=cookie_name+"=1; expires=Tuesday,
          01-Apr-1999 08:00:00 GMT";
    } else {
       countbegin = (document.cookie.indexOf("=", index) + 1);
       countend = document.cookie.indexOf(";", index);
       if (countend == -1) {
          countend = document.cookie.length;
       }
       count = eval(document.cookie.substring(countbegin,
          count end)) + 1;
       document.cookie=cookie_name+"="+count+"; expires=Tuesday,
          01-Apr-1999 08:00:00 GMT";
    }
}

// Gets the count that the client sent when requesting this document.
// Returns string for the number of times client has visited.

function gettimes() {
    if(document.cookie) {
       index = document.cookie.indexOf(cookie_name);

       if (index != -1) {
          countbegin = (document.cookie.indexOf("=", index) + 1);
          countend = document.cookie.indexOf(";", index);
          if (countend == -1) {
             countend = document.cookie.length;
          }
          count = document.cookie.substring(countbegin, countend);
          if (count == 1) {
             return (count+" time");
          } else {
             return (count+" times");
          }
       }
    }
    return ("0 times");
}
</script>
</head>
```

Figure 12-2. JavaScript Cookie Example by Marc Matteo (continued).

```
<body onUnload="doCookie()">
<!-- When page is loaded, client browser increments Cookie_Counter. --
>
<h3>Here is the counter:</h3>
<script>
    document.write("<b>You have been to my site "+gettimes()+" be-
fore.</b>");
</script>
<p>If you reload this page, the counter above will update. The count
is kept in a cookie being stored in your browser.</p>
</body>
</html>
```

Figure 12-2. JavaScript Cookie Example by Marc Matteo (continued).

Form Validation

Another handy use of JavaScript is to validate the information being entered into a form by your Web visitors. For example, you might check that all required fields are filled in before sending the data to your server; you might check that a particular field has an appropriate format, as with an e-mail address; or you might want to offer a second chance to review the entered values.

It is possible, and certainly appropriate, to have the CGI script on your Web server confirm the values being entered in the form. However, it's much faster for your visitors and less taxing for your server if your visitor's Web browser can check for valid input without the wait associated with going to and from the server.

The example in Figure 12-3 performs the basic validation step of checking that required text fields have been filled in. The function CheckREQ, which is called when the Submit button is pressed, looks for any text field whose name begins "REQ" and confirms that a value has been provided. Note that the function stops at the first required field found to be missing a value. It does not examine the entire form before notifying the visitor of an error. Further examples of form validation scripts can be found at the JavaScript resources in Table 12-2.

```
<html>
<head>
<script language="JavaScript">
<!-- Begin
function CheckREQ(which) {
  var pass=true;
  if (document.images) {
     for (i=0;i<which.length;i++) {
        var tempobj=which.elements[i];
        if (tempobj.name.substring(0,3)=="REQ") {
           if ((tempobj.type=="text"||tempobj.type=="textarea")&&
           tempobj.value=='') {
              pass=false;
              break;
           }
        }
     }
  }
  if (!pass) {
     shortFieldName=tempobj.name.substring(3,30).toUpperCase();
     alert("Please make sure the "+shortFieldName+" field was properly
        completed.");
     return false;
  }
  else
     return true;
}
//  End --></script>
</head>
<body>
<center>
<form method="get" action="your.cgi" onSubmit="return CheckREQ(this)">
<p>Name: <input type="text" name="REQname"><br>
   E-mail: <input type="text" name="REQemail"><br>
   Comments: <textarea name="REQcomments"></textarea><br>
<input type=submit value="Submit">
</form>
</center>
</body>
</html>
```

Figure 12-3. Basic Form Validation with JavaScript.

Reusing JavaScript

You may have noticed that in each of the previous examples, the JavaScript code was included within the HTML file. Most of you probably realized that this would make it difficult to maintain and reuse JavaScript code. There would be a lot of cutting and pasting every time you added a new form to be verified or a new page that created a cookie.

To avoid these issues, it is possible to link a file containing JavaScript code to an HTML page. In this way, you can write your JavaScript functions and import them into any HTML file. (There's not much you can do about the JavaScript function calls that are embedded within the tags of an HTML file.)

For example, with our form verification example, you could create a file called *form-verification.js* and with the JavaScript code shown in Figure 12-4. This file may also have other JavaScript functions that you want to use in your pages.

```
function CheckREQ(which) {
  var pass=true;
  if (document.images) {
    for (i=0;i<which.length;i++) {
      var tempobj=which.elements[i];
      if (tempobj.name.substring(0,3)=="REQ") {
        if ((tempobj.type=="text"||tempobj.type=="textarea")&&
        tempobj.value=='') {
          pass=false;
          break;
        }
      }
    }
  }
  if (!pass) {
    shortFieldName=tempobj.name.substring(3,30).toUpperCase();
    alert("Please make sure the "+shortFieldName+" field was
    properly completed.");
    return false;
  }
  else
    return true;
}
```

Figure 12-4. Reusable JavaScript Function Example.

Then, you would modify the HTML file to read as follows. The line beginning "<script language...." tells the browser to load the JavaScript source code in *form-verification.js* before processing the rest of HTML. The trade-off, of course, is that this adds another server request to every page that includes this JavaScript code.

```
<html>
<head>
<script language="JavaScript" src="form-verification.js">
</script>
</head>
<body>
… rest of form here …
</body>
</html>
```

SERVER-SIDE INCLUDES (SSIs)

Simply stated, the main use of *server-side includes* (SSIs) is any situation in which you want the same information to appear on many Web pages. This information might be generated by you, the webmaster, or by the server software itself to reflect the current state of the server. SSIs are especially useful when that same information is going to change frequently. Thus, SSIs save you the labor of editing each page to make the changes.

There are negative aspects to using SSIs—notably, performance and security. Performance is an issue since you are not just sending some HTML to a client. Instead, the server must read through each file on the fly or actually execute commands on the server and create a new HTML result for the client each time the page is requested. Security can be an issue since, with some SSIs, the client has access to some server commands.

While the principle is the same, invoking SSIs differs from one Web server to another, and some servers, such as Web Server 4D, have extended SSIs with server-specific commands. The description given here is for the Apache installation that comes with Mac OS X. To use SSIs, you need to understand the syntax employed by your Web server, since most server software has its own idiosyncratic way of handling them. Table 12-4 has pointers to online tutorials for learning about SSIs.

Table 12-4. Information on Server-Side Includes (SSIs)

Location	Description
www.internetter.com/ssi/index.shtml	Tutorial for SSIs that work with most servers.
www.useforesite.com/tut_ssi.shtml	SSI tutorial from UseForeSight.com.
www.newbreedsoftware.com/ssis	General SSI information by Bill Kendrick (with source code specific to UNIX machines).

Using SSIs in Apache

To use SSIs with the Apache Web server requires only a few lines in the *httpd.conf* file. In fact, the lines are already in the file; you just have to remove the "#" characters that have turned them into comments. The relevant lines, located in Section 2 of *httpd.conf* are

```
AddType text/html .shtml
AddHandler server-parsed .shtml
Options Includes
```

In Section 2, these lines will allow SSIs in the main Apache server and any virtual hosts. All files that end in *.shtml* will be parsed by Apache to look for SSI commands. The *.shtml* extension is commonly used to indicate a file that uses SSIs, but you can just as easily use *.ssi, .bob,* or any other extension. You can even use *.html* so that every *.html* file will be parsed for SSIs, but this procedure incurs extra processing that could become noticeable on busy servers.

Because some SSIs instruct Apache to execute commands or CGI scripts on the server, you may choose, for security reasons, to replace the Options Includes line with Options IncludesNoExec, which allows all SSIs except those that execute commands or programs on the server.

The Include Command

The most common SSI is the Include command. If you are familiar with the use of #include statements used in programming languages, the idea is the same. If you have information that you want to show on many Web pages, such as headers, footers, or menu options, you can keep that information in a separate file and use the Include command to insert that information, HTML tags and all, into each file in which it should appear.

Using SSIs in this way makes site maintenance much easier. To have a change propagate throughout your site, you only have to make the change to that one included file, and every page that includes it will be automatically updated when the Web server finds the SSI command. An Apache SSI Include command looks like this:

```
<!--#include virtual="another-file"-->
```

Therefore, to begin experimenting with SSIs, you simply create an HTML file that contains this line. The *another-file* can be any URL relative to the current document. It cannot contain an absolute URL (that is, one starting *http://*), but it can be a relative URL that points to a CGI script. You can have an Include command execute a CGI script even if you've set the IncludesNoExec option. The logic is that such a CGI script could be executed by typing in its URL so visitors aren't getting access to anything they couldn't by other means. (As an aside, the "virtual" in this command can be replaced by "file," but "file" has limitations that "virtual" does not, so it's almost always better to use "virtual.")

```
<html>
<head><title>An Example of a Server-Side Include</title></head>
<body>
<!-- Include a menu bar -->
<!--#include virtual="/includes/menubar.shtml"-->
<h1>This is the rest of the document.</h1>
</body>
</html>
```

An important point to note is what happens when a client views the source for a Web page that uses an SSI. What you see is the page *after* the additional file has been included. There is no indication to the client (other than perhaps the *.shtml* extension) that the contents came from two separate files.

System and Server Information

Notice that we said earlier that the "main use" of SSIs is for including the same information on multiple Web pages. There are other uses; another common use is to display server or system information on the fly. The SSI commands in this category include Config, Fsize, Flastmod, and Echo.

Config. The Config command describes how to format the results of other SSI commands, including an error message if anything goes wrong. The three configurable attributes are Errmsg, Sizefmt, and Timefmt. Apache will use default values if you do not set them explicitly with Config commands.

```
<!--#config errmsg="Oops!"-->
<!--#config sizefmt="bytes"-->
<!--#config timefmt="%A %B %d"-->
```

The Errmsg is displayed if an SSI command can't be completed. The Sizefmt tells how to format file size information, either as Bytes or Abbrev for kilobytes. Finally, Timefmt is, conveniently, the time format. You can find the conversion codes available by opening a Terminal window and entering this command:

```
man strftime
```

Fsize. The Fsize command reports the size of a file, using the measurement specified by Sizefmt. This SSI looks much like the Include command.

```
<!--#fsize virtual="this-file.html"-->
<!--#fsize virtual-="/another/file.html"-->
```

Flastmod. The Flastmod command reports the last modification time of a file, using the time format specified by Timefmt. This SSI has a familiar syntax.

```
<!--#flastmod virtual="this-file.html"-->
<!--#flastmod virtual-="/another/file.html"-->
```

Echo. The Echo command reports the value of various system and server variables. Table 12-5 lists the variables that can be echoed as part of an SSI command. Your server software may allow more variables to be displayed with the Echo command. For all such variables the syntax is as follows:

```
<!--#echo var="VARIABLE"-->
```

Table 12-5. Variables Associated with the ECHO Command

Variable	Description
DATE_GMT	Current Greenwich Mean Time.
DATE_LOCAL	The current date and time in the local time zone.
DOCUMENT_NAME	The current file name.
DOCUMENT_URI	The virtual path to the file.
HTTP_REFERER	The link used to get to this page.
HTTP_USER_AGENT	The browser and operating system used to view the page.
LAST_MODIFIED	The date the current file was last modified.
REMOTE_ADDR	The client's IP address.
SERVER_NAME	The name of the server.
SERVER_PORT	The port to which the request was made.
SERVER_SOFTWARE	The Web server software on the server.

Executing Commands

The final SSI command, Exec, causes a CGI script or a UNIX command to execute on the server, then inserts the results into the current file. In general, this is the most risky SSI to use, because it potentially allows visitors to run commands or programs on your server to which they would otherwise not have access. The Exec command can take one of two forms.

```
<!--#exec cgi="/path/to/cgi.script"-->
<!--#exec cmd="cd /usr/bin; ls -l"-->
```

The Exec CGI variant causes the referenced file to be run as if it were a CGI script, even if the Web server would not normally recognize it as such. However, the directory has to be set up to permit the running of CGI scripts within it. The Exec Cmd variant allows you to run any UNIX command as if you were running it from the command line. Obviously, both of these should be used with great care.

In fact, you will probably want to disable this SSI command. If you turn SSIs on as described above, the Options Includes line permits the Exec SSI to be used. As mentioned above, it is still possible to insert the results of a CGI with an

SSI command. Simply use the Include command to refer to a legal CGI script. You can disable Exec SSIs by changing the Options line to read:

```
Options IncludesNoExec
```

Web Application Tools

While SSIs provide the ability to insert dynamic information such as date and time stamps or repetitive information such as menu options on your Web pages, they have a limited vocabulary. Furthermore, while most SSI commands are supported by most server software, some commands and variables are server dependent. If you write pages that depend heavily on SSIs and then upgrade your server application to a different program, you may have a difficult time translating or removing invalid SSI commands throughout your site.

If you like the idea of dynamic pages but don't think that SSIs have enough power to support your needs, you might want to consider some of the various Web server extensions that support even more processing power within your HTML files. These tools extend the basic HTML tags with tool-specific or programmatic tags that essentially integrate the best of both HTML markup and program scripting. These tools often also simplify database integration with your Web application. You could accomplish much of the same with the CGI and the scripting languages described in Chapter 11, but these Web application tools provide faster development time while avoiding the performance overhead incurred by starting up CGI scripts.

You may have heard of Microsoft's Active Server Pages or may have seen the *.asp* files used to serve such pages. ASP is essentially Microsoft's own Web application development tool. It's available only for Microsoft's Internet Information Server. (Instant ASP from Halcyon Software provides a way to use ASP pages on a non-Microsoft server, however.) But there are plenty of comparable products available for Mac OS X, as well as the Classic Mac OS and UNIX Web servers. "Active server pages" is a nice description of the general concept we're discussing, but I'll avoid the term so as not to confuse the general concept with Microsoft's product.

With Mac OS X, the Mac webmaster community will begin to have access to some of the popular Web application development tools and HTML preprocessors available to UNIX Web servers, as well as those that have been developed for the Classic Mac OS. Table 12-6 lists some of these Web application tools.

Table 12-6. Web Application Development Tools

Location	Description
frontier.userland.com	Frontier and Manila from Userland Software.
www.aestiva.com	HTML/OS from Aestiva LLC runs on many platforms, including Mac OS X.
www.halcyonsoft.com	Instant ASP from Halcyon Software lets developers use pages developed for Microsoft's ASP on non-Microsoft servers.
interaction.in-progress.com	Interaction by Media Design in•Progress supports server-side XML, visitor tracking, membership management, access restrictions, personalization, and chat rooms.
www.blueworld.com	Lasso Web Data Engine from Blue World Communications, Inc.
www.pageplanetsoftware.com	MGI from Page Planet Software.
www.maxum.com/NetCloak	NetCloak commercial software from Maxum Development adds 30 new commands.
www.vampiresoft.com	OpenScript and OpenWorld WebSTAR plug-ins from Vampire Software allow embedded scripting languages in HTML files.
www.php.net	PHP from the PHP Group, an open-source hypertext preprocessor.
www.snap.de	PrimeBase Application Server from SNAP Innovation GmbH works with PrimeBase and ODBC databases.
www.roxen.com	Roxen Platform, enterprise-level environment and version-control system from Roxen Internet Software.
www.smithmicro.com	Typhoon, Web scripting language, and WebCatalog, an e-commerce solution, from Smith Micro.
www.mdg.com	Web Server 4D from MDG Computer Services extends SSIs to create basic Web applications.
www.apple.com/webobjects	WebObjects from Apple Computer.
www.purity.com	WebSiphon from Purity Software.

PHP

If you enjoy the sheer self-absorption of recursive acronyms, PHP today stands for PHP: Hypertext Preprocessor. As with the other Web application tools described in this section, PHP allows you to embed scripting commands within HTML pages. The PHP preprocessor then carries out those commands before returning a completed HTML page to the Web visitor.

PHP was originally developed by Rasmus Lerdorf as a set of Personal Home Page tools, such as a guestbook, a page counter, and other utilities, that Lerdorf used on his own home page—hence the name. Today, PHP is a collective effort of many programmers and used by hundreds of thousands of sites. Because of this collective effort, there are also many sites that provide tutorials and example PHP code for handling various common tasks.

One of PHP's strong suits is its support for accessing many different databases, including Informix, Ingres, Oracle, MySQL, and many others. PHP also has support for talking to other Internet services such as e-mail, Web, and general networking. You can also open raw network sockets and interact using other protocols.

Installing PHP with Apache

PHP is easy to install because it gets installed when you install the final release of Mac OS X. PHP is also available from Tenon Intersystems to purchasers of iTools and from Apple with Mac OS X Server. For iTools purchasers, installation amounts to double-clicking on the PHP package and following the instructions in the installer utility. Nothing else is required; the package modifies the necessary configuration files and restarts Apache.

To use the version of PHP included with Mac OS X, you have to make only a few changes to the Apache configuration file, *httpd.conf*. (However, in the very first releases of Mac OS X, the default PHP files were broken. I expect Apple will update them at some point, but if you can't wait, I'll try to provide a pointer to a working version from this book's Web site.)

- In the section that loads modules, add this line:
  ```
  LoadModule php4_module  /usr/libexec/httpd/libphp4.so
  ```
- In the section that adds module source, add this line:
  ```
  AddModule mod_php4.c
  ```

- At the end of section 2, you need to add the statements that tell Apache how to recognize PHP files. These lines will process any file ending in *.php* with the PHP preprocessor. You can choose any extension you like, but *.php* is the norm.

```
AddType application/x-httpd-php .php
AddType application/x-httpd-php-source .phps
```

PHP Form Processing

In a PHP file, PHP instructions are enclosed in the characters <?php ... ?> to distinguish them from standard HTML. The PHP file in Figure 12-5 handles the sample form from Chapter 11. (As a reminder, the form had three fields—Name, Mailto, and Comments—and we wanted to respond by echoing the field values and sending an e-mail confirmation.) The PHP instructions should be straightforward to understand.

```
<html>
<head><title>PHP Form Post</title></head>

<body>
<h2>Thank you for your submission!</h2>

<p>Name: <b><?php echo $Name ?></b></p>
<p>E-mail: <b><?php echo $Mailto ?></b></p>
<p>Comments: <b><?php echo $Comments ?></b></p>

<?php
$Subject = "Submission confirmation for $Name";
$Message = "Thank you for your submission!\n";
$Message .= "Name: $Name\n";
$Message .= "E-mail: $Mailto\n";
$Message .= "Comments: $Comments\n";
mail("$Mailto", "$Subject", "$Message", "From: dhart@san.rr.com");
?>

</body>
</html>
```

Figure 12-5. PHP Form Posting Example.

To use this file, first, save this code as *post.php*, for example. Next, modify the sample form HTML file. All you have to do is change the <form> tag line to read

```
<form action="post.php" method="POST">
```

That's it. You have your first working PHP script. When you click on the Submit button, PHP will echo the form variables and send an e-mail message to the submitter.

HTML/OS

HTML/OS from Aestiva LLC is an example of an integrated tool for developing and serving Web-based applications. As the name implies, it's possible to think of HTML/OS as a Web-based operating system. With HTML/OS installed on your Web server, you can develop your Web site from any computer with a Web browser using Aestiva's Web-based desktop, shown in Figure 12-6. HTML/OS provides a file manager, editing tools, a built-in database manager, and control panels for developing and maintaining your site. HTML/OS lets you avoid the need to develop CGI scripts, write Perl code, define SQL queries, install plug-ins, or even use telnet or FTP to maintain your site.

As with other tools, HTML/OS lets you develop dynamic Web pages and Web applications by inserting special scripting instructions within otherwise standard HTML pages. In Aestiva's terms, these scripting instructions, enclosed within <<...>>, are called "overlays" and the tags within them "Otags." Because these tags are defined by HTML/OS and because HTML/OS runs on many operating systems, HTML/OS applications can be ported to any HTML/OS site without change.

Another advantage of HTML/OS is that Aestiva provides several options for installing the software. If you have an FTP server running on your system, Aestiva can install it for you. If you prefer, you can install it yourself by downloading and running a CGI script. Aestiva also provides free technical support for making sure you get everything running.

I installed HTML/OS myself, using the downloaded CGI script. After unzipping the compressed file, I placed it in the *CGI-Executables* folder of my Web server and ran the CGI program by accessing the appropriate URL in my browser. I had some moments of frustration due to some file permission prob-

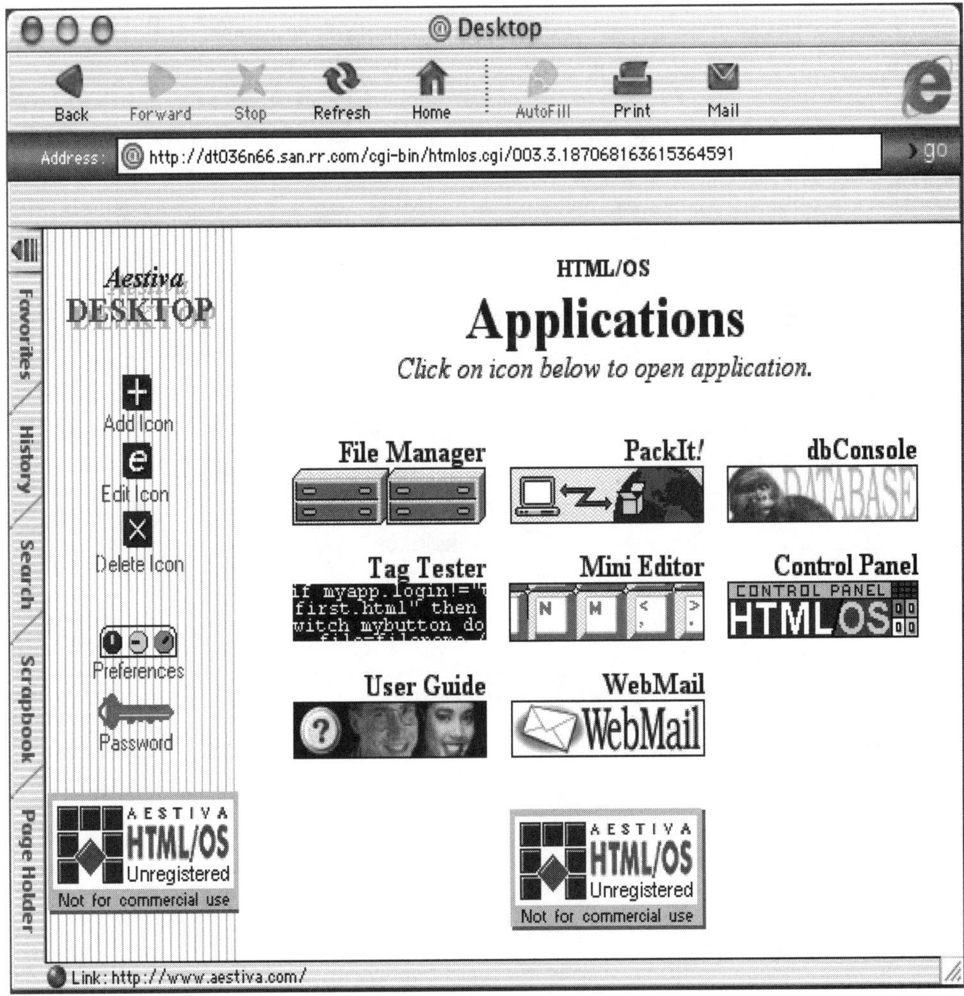

Figure 12-6. Desktop of the HTML/OS Environment from Aestiva LLC.

lems, but the Aestiva online technical support helped identify the problem. A few UNIX Chown and Chmod commands later, the installer worked without a hitch. The installer ends by displaying instructions for how to access the Aestiva desktop.

From that point, you can use the Aestiva desktop to manage your site and create Web applications. It's also possible to create your Web files outside of HTML/OS—for example, if you prefer to use a graphical Web page editor such as Adobe GoLive or Macromedia Dreamweaver—and upload them to the server.

To give you a feel for the coding difficulty of Aestiva's Otags, I present yet another variation on the form e-mail example. With HTML/OS, form processing requires you to place an overlay at the end of your HTML page that is executed when the user clicks on the submit button. In the overlay, which appears at the end of the HTML page after the </html> tag, you describe how HTML/OS should handle the submitted data, as shown in Figure 12-7.

There are several points to note. First, I ran into some troubles that resulted from the field names I had been using in the example form, which cleared up when I modified the names as in Figure 12-7. Second, to get the mail message to display correctly, I had to precede it by two line feeds (LF). Finally, the file *display.html* handles the presentation of the confirmation screen to the user. It also demonstrates how HTML/OS variable names continue to exist and hold values between pages. The code for *display.html* looks like this:

```
<html>
<head><title>Thanks!</title></head>
<body>
 <h2>Thanks for your submission!</h2>
    <p>Name:  <<aName>> </p>
    <p>E-mail:  <<anEmail>> </p>
    <p>Comments:<br> <<Comments>> </p>
</body>
</html>
```

Frontier

Initially just a scripting language for the Macintosh, created by Dave Winer and Doug Baron, Userland Software's Frontier has evolved into a full-fledged Web content management system and application development tool. Frontier builds an object-oriented Web site framework around an object database, an integrated scripting language (UserTalk) with a large set of verbs, a multithreaded run-time environment, and a Web-based site management tool called Manila.

Frontier implements Web site management by storing all the pages of the site internally in a database and publishing the actual HTML for your site. The database stores not only text, but also objects of various types including tables,

```
<html>
<head><title>HTML/OS Form Test</title></head>
<body>
<form method=post action=processtheform>
    <p>Name: <input type=text name="aName" size=20></p>
    <p>E-mail: <input type=text name="anEmail" size=20></p>
    <p>Comments: <input type=text name="Comments" size=20><br>
    <input type=submit value="Submit"></p>
</form>
</body>
</html>

<<OVERLAY processtheform
  mymessage =    LF+LF+
    "--- Name: "+aName+LF+
    "--- E-mail: "+anEmail+LF+
    "--- Comments: "+Comments+LF+LF

  MAIL mymessage to ADDRESS=anEmail
    SUBJECT="Submission confirmation for "+aName /MAIL
  GOTO "display.html"
>>
```

Figure 12-7. HTML/OS Overlay Example.

images, menus, constants, and other page elements. Frontier stores the data to be published in its database and then creates the HTML pages by using object database information such as link data, macro expansions, page templates, or graphics. You publish your Web site via FTP with a single command.

For writing Web applications, the key component of Frontier is its scripting language, UserTalk. UserTalk has more than 600 built-in system management verbs for retrieving system status information and folder contents, operating on files, starting applications, and sending information between scriptable applications. However, Frontier does allow you to use other scripting languages instead of UserTalk.

One disadvantage to Frontier is its somewhat steep learning curve. Because Frontier is not only a scripting language, but also a Web site management tool, Web server maintainers must learn new concepts about using the object database as well as the scripting language.

The Frontier system is being made available as a commercial product for Mac OS X. The final freeware distribution of Frontier, Frontier 5, is still available but only for the Classic Mac OS and Windows.

It's difficult to present a standalone script for Frontier to handle the sample form from Chapter 11. In Frontier, the script and the sample form both have to be included in the main object database, and explaining that relationship requires a greater familiarity with Frontier than I can present here. However, the Frontier site presents instructions for a very similar example in "How to Handle Forms" at *frontier.userland.com/stories/storyReader$81.*

WebObjects

With Mac OS X, those Mac webmasters who had not already moved to Mac OS X Server will also have the opportunity to use another of the applications that Apple inherited in its acquisition of NeXTStep: WebObjects. Conveniently, Apple has also recently reduced the price of WebObjects from $50,000 to $699, bringing it into the range of most Web sites. WebObjects for Mac OS X will be available shortly after the final release of Mac OS X and will be included with the Mac OS X Server suite.

WebObjects combines a development environment that you can use to create Web applications in Java, Objective-C, or WebScript and an application server to integrate the application with your Web server. As examples of what WebObjects can do, Apple's own iTools, iCards, and iReview sites are all WebObjects applications.

For developing applications, WebObjects includes a Project Builder to manage the editing, compiling, and debugging of projects, an Enterprise Objects Modeler that provides a graphical interface for building database queries, a WebObjects Builder for developing Web interfaces, and an Interface Builder for developing interfaces to Java applets. WebObjects includes native methods for accessing Oracle, Sybase, Informix, ODBC, and LDAP data sources within your applications.

And for those organizations taking advantage of XML, WebObjects uses the industry-standard IBM XML parser, which makes it easy to build WebObjects applications that operate smoothly with other XML-based applications.

JAVA

The main disadvantage to Web applications is the performance demands they place on your Web server. Except for some JavaScript validation or browser manipulation, every action by a visitor requires a reaction by the server. The next logical step is to download more of the processing to client computers. However, most programs are very platform-specific—they work only within the operating system in which they were created. What you need for Web applications is a language that allows the server to run arbitrary programs on any client. The most common of these Web programming languages is the Java platform, developed by Sun Microsystems and supported by a number of major computer companies, including Apple.

With Java technology, Web sites can embed small programs, called *applets*, that perform complex functions ranging from graphic menus to image processing and spreadsheets. Most current Web browsers, including Netscape Communicator and Microsoft Internet Explorer, support Java technology. The basic idea is that the browser downloads a piece of code from a server and runs it locally on the client computer.

For these reasons, the Java platform is compelling for any software developer. However, the trademarked Java goal of "Write once, run anywhere" has never completely been achieved. The Java platform's rapid rise to fame came at the expense of product maturity, and bugs and nonuniform behavior across platforms have become expected. Some vendors have tried to include operating system–specific extensions to the Java platform, further diluting the platform-independent objective.

And make no mistake, the Java language is a programming language and requires programming skills to use it effectively. It is much more complex than using HTML and about as complex as C++. Moreover, like C++, the Java language is an object-oriented language and not a procedural language like C or Fortran. If you are not familiar with the techniques of object-oriented programming, there will be an additional learning curve.

The Mac OS has often straggled behind other Java platforms. Not helping the matter have been the competing Java implementations from Apple (used by Microsoft's Internet Explorer) and Netscape's own Java interpreter (used by Communicator). With Mac OS X, Apple has implemented Sun's Java 2 specification. With a Java 2 implementation, the Mac OS X Java run-time environment should be back in the Java race. Apple is also working on a Java interface for QuickTime.

Another issue to consider when deciding whether to use Java technology is performance. At the start of the Java movement, many Web sites used Java applets to handle relatively small interface elements, including some bells and whistles that could be handled just as well with JavaScript or, better yet, avoided altogether. It turns out that Java applets can be slow, both due to download times and due to the speed of the Java interpreter. As a rule, Java technology is better suited for more significant applications rather than as a substitute for standard Web interface components.

It is beyond the scope of this book to teach you the principles of object-oriented programming. However, to understand what Java technology has to offer, I will touch on some of the basics. Additional sources of information on the capabilities and shortcomings of the Java platform can be found in Table 12-7.

The Java Environment

There are two sides to the Java coin—running Java applets and applications and writing Java programs. To view Java applets from the Web in your browser or to run software written in Java, you need the Mac OS X Runtime for Java (MRJ). This software comes on the Mac OS X CD-ROM and is part of the basic installation. The MRJ includes system extensions and the code libraries needed to run Java programs and view Java applets on your Mac.

Table 12-7. Additional Information on Java

Location	Description
java.sun.com	Source for Java Technology from Sun Microsystems.
java.sun.com/cgi-bin/java-ports.cgi	Java platform ports, from Sun Microsystems.
www.apple.com/java	Apple's Mac OS Runtime for Java site.
developer.apple.com/java	Apple's Java information for developers.
www.ibiblio.org/javafaq/javatutorial.html	"Brewing Java: A Tutorial" by Elliotte Rusty Harold.
www.jars.com	Jars.com, Java review source from EarthWeb, Inc.
www.wdvl.com/Authoring/Java	"Learning to Write Java" from the Web Developer's Virtual Library.

On the other hand, to develop applications in the Java language you need a full-fledged programming environment. Because of the Java platform's popularity, third-party ports of the Java Development Kit (JDK) are available for almost any operating system, including Mac OS X.

The first thing to understand is that there are two types of Java source code, one written to be run as an application and one written to run as an applet. We have met the term "applet" at other points in this book. Recall that an applet is Java code that runs from within a Web browser. An application runs as a standalone program on your Mac. The main difference between an applet and an application is the libraries you use as part of your code.

Either way, the source code is compiled, which produces an output file called *program.class*. The file *program.class* is in machine-independent *byte code* and will run on any computer for which a Java interpreter, such as the MRJ, is available. If your source code produces an applet, then that applet can be referenced within an HTML file and passed to a Web browser, which will use the client computer's Java run-time environment to run the applet.

You should now have some sense of the various Java components and should be ready to consider some of the major features of Java. We will move on to a couple of simple examples of writing, compiling, and using Java, both from an application and an applet standpoint.

Java Technology Features

The major features of Java technology should show you why there is considerable excitement about the Java platform. Other languages have some of these features, but only Java has them all. This section is heavy on technical terms but should give you some idea of the power of Java. In a nutshell, Java retains the best features of previous languages while discarding those features affecting portability, security, and ease of programming. Moreover, it is designed specifically for use via the Internet.

Network Ready. Java was designed with the network in mind. In addition to standalone applications, self-contained applets are easily transferred from the server using the HTTP protocol and can subsequently be executed on Java-ready browsers.

Assuming a Web browser is Java-ready and can interpret an applet, how it handles the applet is browser and configuration dependent. Most browsers will not permit the applet, when read as part of a remote URL, to read or write to the client disk, since this poses a security risk. Browsers that access the applet as part of a Web page that is a local file often behave differently. And browsers have the ability to enable and disable features of Java.

Hardware Independent. As indicated in the previous section, hardware independence is a great feature of the Java platform. When you compile a piece of Java code, you are not compiling it into machine-specific code, but rather into byte code. This is possible because Java is statically typed, which is a fancy way of saying that you declare all objects (numbers, variables, arrays, etc.) in the Java language to have an explicit data type (for example, character or integer) that has a specific storage requirement. For example, an integer is 32 bits and a long integer is 64 bits. When running an applet, it is the byte code that is passed from the server to the client; thus, the client must be running a Java interpreter to use the Java code.

GUI Independent. Only a single graphical user interface (GUI) need be developed for Java applets and applications—a major accomplishment because up to 90 percent of the coding effort can be expended on interface development. That interface can be displayed and used on all Macs, UNIX platforms, and Windows systems, since all these platforms support Java-ready browsers. In the future, more computing is likely to be done through Java-ready browsers. At the time of writing, idiosyncrasies do exist in interface look and feel, depending on the operating system and browser type and version, but these are slowly disappearing with every new JDK and browser release.

Extensive Class Libraries, Language Support, and Documentation. The Java platform is enabling the use of the Internet, and, conversely, the Internet is enabling the use of Java. Java is evolving with the Internet, rather than predating it. For example, extensive Java-shared class libraries and applet libraries are being developed and shared. The documentation covering these developments is available worldwide, since it is written in HTML and available on the Web.

Standards Compliant. The hardware-neutral and portable language platform of Java is known as the Java Virtual Machine. The Java Virtual Machine is based primarily on the POSIX interface specification, an industry-standard definition of a portable system interface.

Support for Threads. For the purposes of this discussion, threads can be thought of as lightweight processes. A *process* is the element to which the operating system allocates resources (e.g., processor time and memory). A process has a certain overhead that must be incurred when it is started. The overhead in starting a thread is less than that of starting a process; hence the term "lightweight." Java supports threads, and the results can be seen in applications that can simultaneously download multiple animation sequences while scrolling and displaying graphics.

Java supports multithreading at the language level with the addition of sophisticated synchronization primitives to manage concurrent and dependent threads of execution. The language library provides the Thread class, and the run-time system provides monitor and condition lock primitives, again necessary to synchronize multiple dependent threads of execution. At the library level, Java system libraries have been written to be thread safe. That is, the functionality provided by the libraries is available without conflict to multiple concurrent threads of execution.

Object-Oriented. *Classes* and *inheritance* are of proven value in shortening the software development cycle, since, if done properly, these object-oriented features make it easier to reuse code. The downside is that you need to put more thought into the initial design so that you will have bits of code that you can reuse. Those "bits" come in the form of classes. Classes have *attributes,* that is, variables with static or dynamic values, and *methods,* code that performs some function. Classes, with their associated attributes and methods, are inherited, modified, and reused for a variety of purposes. An *object* is an instance of a class.

Encapsulation hides complex programming in objects that have a simple calling interface and, hence, can be used in a straightforward manner. *Polymorphism* implies that the same message is sent to different objects. This results in behavior that is dependent on the nature of the object receiving the message. *Strong typing* helps make Java portable. Other than the primitive data types, everything in Java is an object. Even the primitive data types can be encapsulated inside library-supplied objects, if required. There are only three groups of primitive data types, namely, numeric types, Boolean types, and arrays.

Security. Several features help define the security of the Java platform. Memory layout is determined at run time and is not defined by the code itself. Without knowledge of how the application maps to memory, interfering with the application is made more difficult. Furthermore, networked byte code is treated differently than local byte code by memory partitioning. Finally, there is user-level control over what byte code is run and from what machines.

JavaBeans

If you plan to make extensive use of Java applets on your Internet server, you no doubt would like to reuse as much of your Java code as possible. While the Java platform's object-oriented features provide some degree of reuse, you will still have to modify or customize your Java classes whenever you write a new applet.

JavaBeans, an extension of the Java environment, offers a way to create customizable software "building blocks" that are written once and can then run anywhere—in different applets or on different computer platforms. In more technical terms, JavaBeans is a *component model* or component architecture, which defines a set of interfaces for creating interoperable software components. By combining the components in new ways, developers can build new software applications much more quickly. JavaBeans, therefore, allows Java programmers to create the "blocks" out of which to build a wide array of applets.

Individual JavaBeans components, or Beans, have different functions, of course, but all Beans share several distinguishing characteristics, according to Sun's JavaBeans documentation:

- Introspection enables a builder tool to analyze automatically how a Bean works.
- Customization lets a developer use a builder tool to customize the appearance and behavior of a Bean.
- Events allow Beans to communicate and connect together.
- Properties let developers customize and program with Beans.
- Persistence enables developers to customize Beans in a builder tool and then retrieve those Beans, with customized features intact, for future use.

Properties, events, methods, and persistence are standard features of a component model, and JavaBeans add introspection and customization to make the programming task easier. In particular, these characteristics mean that Beans can be manipulated visually in a builder tool to construct new applets or applications from the Beans you create—all without writing any code. A JavaBeans-enabled builder tool maintains Beans in a palette or toolbox. To develop with these building blocks, you select a Bean from the palette, drop it into a form, customize its appearance and behavior, and compose it and other Beans into an applet that meets your requirements. (If you really want to write code, though, you can use text-based tools to manipulate Beans through programming interfaces.)

JavaBeans is a standard part of the JDK; therefore, any JDK 1.1–compliant browser or tool supports JavaBeans. Table 12-8 provides some links to further JavaBeans information.

Table 12-8. JavaBeans Information

Location	Description
java.sun.com/beans	Sun Microsystem's JavaBeans site.
java.sun.com/docs/books/tutorial/javabeans	Sun's JavaBeans tutorial.
jars.developer.com/listing-JavaBeans.html	The JavaBeans listings from EarthWeb's JARS Java resource.

Java Servlets and JavaServer Pages

The Java platform also provides the tools that parallel both CGI scripts and the Web application tools such as PHP or HTML/OS, described earlier. If you have already chosen Java technology as your development tool of choice, it is possible to apply that knowledge to developing Web applications with your server.

Java Servlets. *Java servlets* are to Web servers what Java applets are to Web browsers. Servlets are another option, analogous to CGI scripts, for extending the power of your Web server. For example, a servlet, instead of a CGI script, might take data in an HTML order-entry form and apply the business logic used to update a company's order database, perhaps using the JDBC interface.

Because servlets run on the server and not on the client (as applets do), they are freed from some of the tight security restrictions that limit them in browsers. In addition, since you always know where a servlet will run (on your server), servlets avoid the headaches that result from applets that look and feel different on different client platforms despite Java's cross-platform intentions. Other features of servlets make them advantageous for non-Web applications: They can run as standalone applications, can be written to listen to non-HTTP requests, and can be chained together with one servlet calling another.

As a taste of servlets, Figure 12-8 shows the code for a "Hello, World!" servlet.

JavaServer Pages. *JavaServer Pages (JSP)* is an extension of Java servlet technology that allows an HTML preprocessor to read programmatic instructions within your HTML pages. JSP technology embeds XML-like tags and scripts written in the Java programming language from which the page content is generated. Additionally, the JSP logic can access server-based resources (such as JavaBeans components or Java servlets).

In JSP technology, *actions* create and access programming language objects and affect the result. The JSP specification defines six standard actions and supports the development of reusable modules called *custom actions*. A custom action is invoked by using a custom tag in a JSP page. A *tag library* is a collection of custom tags. Custom actions can be developed to process forms, access databases, handle e-mail, or control the flow of a Web application.

```
import java.io.*;
import javax.servlet.*;
import javax.servlet.http.*;

public class HelloWorld extends HttpServlet {

    public void doGet(HttpServletRequest request,
                      HttpServletResponse response)
    throws IOException, ServletException
    {
        response.setContentType("text/html");
        PrintWriter out = response.getWriter();
        out.println("<html>");
        out.println("<body>");
        out.println("<head>");
        out.println("<title>Hello, World!</title>");
        out.println("</head>");
        out.println("<body>");
        out.println("<h1>Hello, World!</h1>");
        out.println("</body>");
        out.println("</html>");
    }
}
```

Figure 12-8. "Hello, World!" Java Servlet.

There are pros and cons to using Java servlets and JSP. The pros include access to the rich features of the Java platform, including JavaBeans, and the ability to use a single language for applications, applets, servlets, and other tasks. However, the cons are the exact same features. The need to use the Java programming language can be more complex than scripting languages or HTML preprocessors, and the rich features of the Java platform sometimes make simple tasks more complex than they perhaps ought to be. You might have gathered as much from the "Hello, World!" servlet.

Many Web servers already support Java servlets and JSP. Tomcat is software that adds Java servlet and JSP capabilities to Apache, and a Tomcat implementation for Mac OS X is available as part of the iTools from Tenon Intersystems and Mac OS X Server from Apple. To help you get a feel for JSP, numerous examples are included with the Tomcat distribution, which you can download from the Apache Foundation Web site. This brief discussion only touches on the highlights of Java servlets and JavaServer Pages. Table 12-9 provides links to additional information to get you started writing servlets.

Table 12-9. JSP and Java Servlet Information

Location	Description
www.builder.com/Programming/JSP	"Intro to JavaServer Pages" by John Zukowski at Builder.com.
java.sun.com/products/servlet	Sun's Java servlet site.
java.sun.com/products/jsp	Sun's JavaServer Pages site.
www.servlets.com	*Java Servlet Programming* by Jason Hunter (O'Reilly, 1998).
www.coreservlets.com	*Core Servlets and JavaServer Pages* by Marty Hall (Sun Microsystems Press/Prentice Hall PTR, 2000).
jakarta.apache.org	Tomcat by the Jakarta Project of the Apache Software Foundation, Java servlet and JavaServer Pages implementation.

CHAPTER 13

E-COMMERCE

E-commerce has the potential to be the great retail equalizer. Theoretically, anyone with a Web server and a garage full of products—or "widgets," to use the technical term for a hypothetical product—can compete with the likes of Wal-Mart. Reality, however, is another story. If you plan to get into e-commerce and sell more than a handful of products or software downloads, be prepared. Running an electronic store will take almost as much effort as, if not more than, it takes to run a real business. That being said, the necessary components of e-commerce are the same regardless of how extensive a presence you intend to establish.

CHOOSING E-COMMERCE SERVICES

Depending on whom you ask, you might get a different breakdown of e-commerce services, so for the sake of discussion, we'll choose one categorization and run with it. To get started in e-commerce, you need to consider security, storefronts and order tracking, payment methods, and marketing.

But even that basic list assumes the first step, that of establishing your initial Web presence. As you've read so far in this book, this involves rounding up a network connection, a domain name, a computer for running your server, and your Web server software. If you have already developed a site, you may decide that your current investment in Web servers predetermines your e-commerce choices. Alternately, switching Web servers to take another route to e-commerce may be an additional cost or development effort to factor into your plans. If you haven't yet established a Web server, you should factor your e-commerce goals into your evaluation of the options ahead of you, as described in Chapter 3.

Security. For a basic Web site, you want visitors to see all the information you make available, and your Web server software should make sure that they don't see any information you don't want them to see. For e-commerce, you have several other security considerations. So that your customers know that you are who you say you are, you have to register your site with a recognized *certificate authority* (CA). And for getting money in exchange for your products, you need to ensure that your customers can provide payment information securely. You might want to provide this service on your site or contract it out to a payment-processing service.

Storefront. Next, you need to let your customers shop for your products. If you sell only a single piece of shareware or a handful of items, a simple Web form may suffice. However, as your product options become more complex, your storefront interface becomes more complex, and you may want to look into software that helps manage the store. This component also incorporates your business product catalog and your store's shopping cart interface.

Payment. Once your customers have filled their virtual shopping carts, you need to transact some business—their money for your goods. In addition to ensuring that credit card or e-cash transactions happen smoothly and securely, you must also establish a *merchant account* so that the purchases can be authorized. Again, depending on the scale of your e-commerce activities, you may want to contract this part out. Hand in hand with accepting payment for orders, you should provide a way for customers to track their orders in process.

Marketing. Before you can get customers, they must be able to find you. However, in this list it's the last step, because you need to establish your Web store before you can recruit customers. While this may be the least technical step, the success of your store relies just as heavily on how well you market your site. This step is not unique to a Web business.

That's a quick peek into the world of e-commerce. Now we'll address each of these components in turn. Appendix B directs you to some general Web developer sites, which all have introductions to e-commerce.

E-Commerce Security

Chapter 7 discussed the basic components needed to protect your Web site's visitors—digital certificates and the secure sockets layer (SSL)—and how they work together to encrypt the data flowing between your customers and your Web server using public key encryption.

As a quick refresher, digital certificates are electronic files that uniquely identify the certificate's owner and associated Web server, along with additional information about the CA that issued the certificate. Certificates typically are valid for one year, and therefore must be renewed each year. For your e-commerce site, especially if you plan to collect money yourself through credit cards or other electronic payments, you need to have a digital certificate from a widely recognized CA, such as those listed in Table 13-1.

The second component you need for e-commerce security is a Web server that supports SSL. The major Mac Web servers—WebSTAR from 4D, Apache with iTools from Tenon Intersystems or Mac OS X Server from Apple, and Web Server 4D from MDG Computer Services—all provide this feature. Once you have an SSL-capable Web server and a valid certificate, your customers establish a secure connection with your server through a protocol handshake. In short, the client's browser uses your server's public key in the certificate to establish an encrypted session. If the server certificate is valid, the SSL session proceeds. If the server certificate is not valid, the SSL session is stopped.

That's your quick introduction to the security of e-commerce. In practical terms, this does mean a financial investment in your site if you want to carry out the full e-commerce cycle on your Mac Web server. This chapter's section on outsourcing e-commerce talks about alternatives for Web sites if the costs of renewing your certificate annually or purchasing an SSL-capable server are not justified by the amount of income you're expecting.

Table 13-1. Certificate Authorities

Location	Certificate Authorities.
www.entrust.net	Entrust.
www.thawte.com	Thawte Digital Certificate Services.
www.verisign.com	VeriSign.

SSL for Your Server

It is possible to extend the capabilities of Apache to support SSL transactions on Mac OS X using free software, but it is not for the faint of heart. In fact, the installation instructions begin with a quotation from Ben Laurie, author of Apache-SSL: "The world does not really need Apache-SSL easier to install." Because of that advice and because I freely admit to not being an expert in such matters (and because I don't want to set myself up as an unofficial supporter for anyone who has problems with their installation), I am going to gloss over the manual installation process.

If you wanted to do this from scratch, first you'd need the Mac OS X development tools, because you'll have to compile software along the way. Second, you'll need to download the open-source library OpenSSL. By itself, OpenSSL doesn't do much; it's a library of routines that other software needs to run. Therefore, and finally, you'll also need *mod_ssl* by Ralf S. Engelschall and others. It is an Apache module, based on the older Apache-SSL, that links the Apache Web server with the OpenSSL library.

To summarize the installation process, take OpenSSL, *mod_ssl,* and extensive knowledge about the other Apache modules you've installed, mix well with the Mac OS X developer tools, and bake. The entire installation process, aside from possibly unpacking the various *.tar.gz* files with StuffIt Expander, takes place at the Terminal command line and involves mucking with directories in parts of Mac OS X where non-UNIX users are not recommended to tread. Table 13-2 includes references to information on SSL software for those interested in pursuing this path.

Fortunately, however, Apple saw fit to include OpenSSL and *mod_ssl* in the Mac OS X final release. Unfortunately, it's still not a straightforward process to get an SSL-capable server running. I don't recommend it to novice or even intermediate webmasters. As alternatives, you could pay someone who has done it before to get SSL running with your server, or you could invest in one of the commercial server suites that provide SSL security. WebSTAR from 4D, Inc., which uses its own SSL libraries, and iTools from Tenon Intersystems and Mac OS X Server from Apple, which both use OpenSSL, make it much easier to establish SSL services. As a further advantage of the commercial products, consider that they also provide technical support.

Table 13-2. Free and Open-Source SSL Software and Information

Location	Description
www.modssl.org	mod_ssl, a freeware Apache interface to OpenSSL by Ralf S. Engelschall.
www.openssl.org	OpenSSL Project, an open-source effort.
www.netscape.com/eng/ssl3	Secure Sockets Layer specification from Netscape.

Storefronts and Shopping Carts

An e-commerce storefront is your site's window display, store layout, retail sales staff, and merchandising, all rolled into one. Whether it's simple or complex, your site's storefront is your first and only chance to make a good impression on your customers. A storefront can be simple or complex.

At the simple end, you may want to sell only a handful of items, such as the latest shareware releases from your software company. At this level, you may not need the full-blown storefront software mentioned here. A basic Web form might suffice, allowing your customers to indicate the quantity and other applicable information about their purchase. You may or may not choose to integrate this form with the payment and shipping information.

As a rule, though, you want to put as few clicks as possible between your customer's decision to buy and the option to pay. Therefore, it may pay, literally, to combine the order form and payment information on the same page. On the other hand, as the number of items for sale grows, you must weigh the usability and complexity of a single page against requiring a customer to navigate more than one page.

At the complex end of the scale, let's say your goal is to be the next Amazon.com, except not for books. Maybe you're going to corner the Web market on trivets—thousands upon thousands of decorative, yet functional, kitchen trivets. You need to let your customers browse the many trivet options, selecting the one or ones that best match their personality and kitchen decor.

Now you need a serious storefront interface to your online catalog, which is, in fact, a database. A customer's shopping cart is a temporary database record containing the customer's order. Theoretically, therefore, you could develop your own storefront and shopping cart using your favorite Web-database tools. In reality, it probably pays to invest in software that's been developed and tested as a storefront. Since your goal is to make money, you will want to get your e-commerce site online quickly.

There are several e-commerce storefront and shopping cart alternatives available for Mac Web servers, listed in Table 13-3. Each of them can be used with any Mac Web server, but some require that your server have additional software.

Ch-Ching! by Imacination Software lets you build an Internet storefront, complete with credit card processing. Ch-Ching! requires the Lasso Web Data Engine (see Chapter 9) and includes templates for FileMaker Pro; however, it is possible to use any other database with which Lasso is compatible.

Table 13-3. Storefront Software for Mac OS X

Location	Description
www.imacination.com	Ch-Ching! by Imacination Software requires the Lasso Web Data Engine from Blue World Communications.
www.pageplanetsoftware.com	MGI Deluxe from Page Planet Software includes e-commerce storefront features.
pims.executron.com	PIMS, Executron's Professional Inventory Management System, has extensive features but a high price.
www.webclerk.com	WebClerk by James Technologies, an all-in-one e-commerce application. At the time of writing, the single-site version was being given away free.
www.smithmicro.com/isd	WebCatalog from Smith Micro Software is a full-featured but high-priced option.
www.mdg.com	WS 4D/eCommerce by MDG Computer Services.

Executron's Professional Inventory Management System (PIMS) and its associated Internet Commerce Module have extensive capabilities for e-commerce, but this software also has the highest cost and the steepest learning curve.

WebCatalog from Smith Micro Software (which purchased Pacific Coast Software) allows you to develop e-commerce storefronts and provide order processing. WebCatalog runs as a CGI and uses its own internal database for storing your product lines (although it also provides support for accessing ODBC databases). An interesting feature is that storefronts created by WebCatalog are automatically viewable by customers on wireless devices. WebCatalog is, however, one of the more expensive options.

WS4D/eCommerce, a storefront package combined with Web Server 4D, lets you create and maintain storefronts using extensions of the server's integrated database functionality. If you're using Web Server 4D, you can purchase a registration key to unlock the e-commerce features. WS4D/eCommerce can run as a standalone server or as a CGI extension to another Web server.

Those are the e-commerce storefront tools that I'm aware of. If all you need is an e-commerce tool, you may want to consider one of the more specific options listed in Table 13-3. In addition to the software designed specifically for e-commerce, there are also more general tools that include features for building storefronts. These tools have the advantage of being useful for many types of Web interaction tasks, but they require more programming effort for each task.

MGI Deluxe by Page Planet Software, for example, includes features that let you use its internal database for e-commerce functions. You could also count many of the general database tools (see Chapter 9) and Web application environments (see Chapter 12) in this category; with those, you could build your own storefront from scratch.

Payment Processing

Once you have filled out your virtual storefront with products for sale, the next step is to collect money in exchange for those products—the capability that distinguishes e-commerce from giving stuff away free. The options for payment processing, most commonly through credit card payments, include real-time or manual transactions. In addition to credit cards, there have been attempts to popularize electronic cash, but so far these haven't really caught on. I should add that some of the storefront development tools listed in the previous section also include payment-processing features. Table 13-4 has links to additional payment-processing software and other resources mentioned in this section.

However, your first decision regarding payment processing actually happens much earlier in the planning process. Your decision whether or not to provide SSL transactions with your Web server affects how you collect credit card information. If you choose not to provide secure transactions, you can theoretically still collect credit card information on your server, but the privacy concerns of your potential customers may limit your income. In this case, you'll need to work with a payment-processing service that provides a secure server. On the other hand, if you're already providing a secure Web server, it is possible to handle the payment processing through your site. To do so, you need three more items.

First, you need to set up a *merchant account,* a special bank account that allows you to accept credit card payments. Second, you may need software to send credit card information to a transaction bureau for processing. Some storefront software, including Ch-Ching!, WebCatalog, and PIMS, already has payment-processing software built-in. Third, you need to select a transaction bureau that transfers money from your customers' credit cards to your merchant account.

In many cases, you get all of these elements from the same provider, and in fact, you may even want to proceed in the reverse order. Your transaction bureau may have its own software and arrangements with a preferred merchant account provider. For example, OuterNet is a transaction bureau with its own ONcommerce software and a preferred merchant bank associate. The software you choose may also have arrangements with transaction bureaus or merchant account providers for lower rates.

The main technical distinction is whether your credit card purchases are authorized in real time or as a separate, off-line task. Real-time authorization can protect you from giving away your products on credit cards that later fail in the

Table 13-4. Payment-Processing Software and Resources

Location	Description
www.cybercash.com	Payment software and services from CyberCash, Inc.
www.wmotion.com/cc_auth_info.html	oAzium cc Authorize, by Waves In Motion, a FileMaker plug-in for authorizing credit card payments.
www.authorize.net	AuthorizeNet payment processing bureau.

authorization step. On the other hand, off-line authorization is quite reliable, can cost much less, and can provide an additional level of security by keeping the data exchange with the transaction bureau off the Internet.

OUTSOURCING E-COMMERCE

In some sense, you always have to outsource some component of your e-commerce activities. For example, the payment-processing step requires you to conduct business through a transaction bureau and a merchant bank. Of course, it's possible, for a price, to work with third parties to outsource every step of the e-commerce process, including secure servers and storefronts. Generally, commerce service providers have packages for just about any situation, and many will customize the packages to your needs. Table 13-5 lists a few of these commerce service providers.

In outsourcing e-commerce services, it may help you to think in terms of three possible packages: order processing; secure server plus order processing; and storefront, secure server, and order processing. In most cases, you will not choose to outsource your storefront but will handle the secure server and order processing in-house. Similarly, you wouldn't outsource the secure server but provide the storefront and payment processing in-house.

Order Processing. You provide the storefront and collect customer payment information on your secure server. You may have off-line authorization software. You work with a transaction bureau to authorize payments and transfer money into your merchant account. Transaction bureaus, such as iTransact.com or The Processing Network, do not require any additional software on your server but handle payment processing in real time.

Secure Server and Order Processing. You provide the storefront and shopping cart software. The shopping cart software links to the e-commerce provider's secure server to collect confidential credit card information and authorize and process payments. The Processing Network, iTransact.com, Digital River, Kagi, and others provide complete payment processing through their own secure servers. Kagi may be unique in that the company makes it possible to collect payments without a merchant account. Instead, Kagi collects payments through its own merchant account and sends its clients checks for the payments collected.

Storefront, Secure Server, and Order Processing. You provide only the products being sold. The commerce service provider provides the storefront software, secure servers, and payment processing. You customize your storefront, usually through a Web interface. You may host the nonshopping portion of your Web site and link to your storefront, or a full-service provider may even provide the DNS services to host your domain name and Web home page. Digital River, IBM's Home Page Creator, and other companies provide complete e-commerce services.

Table 13-5. Outsourcing E-Commerce

Location	Description
www.ibm.com/hpc	Home Page Creator by IBM.
www.kagi.com	Kagi's e-commerce services don't require you to have a merchant account.
www.digitalriver.com	Digital River can provide all or selected e-commerce levels of service.
www.itransact.com	iTransact.com, a real-time transaction bureau.
www.processing.net	The Processing Network, a real-time transaction bureau.

Site Promotion

Once you've gone to the trouble of setting up a Web server, whether you plan to open your own e-business or just serve up information to an adoring public, you need to remember that modesty is not a virtue. And unless you're selling a better mousetrap, the world is not going to beat a path to your Web site as soon as you put your server online. You need to advertise.

I use the term "advertise" very loosely. Sure, you can pay for newspaper, magazine, television, Web, and radio ads, but you may quickly deplete your budget. If you don't have much of a budget, you might not be able to afford much better placement than the classified ads in the paper or a late-night public access cable station. But, hey, if that's your target audience, more power to you.

For the rest of you, money need not be an object in promoting your site. The Web has plenty of inexpensive opportunities to get your site noticed. They're called search engines and indexes. AltaVista and Lycos are two of the major search engines. Visitors to these sites enter keywords, and the search engine digs through the millions of sites it knows about for pages with those keywords. Yahoo! is the best example of an index. An index organizes a selected set of Web sites according to topic categories. The organization is done by hand; therefore, what the indexes lack in volume, they make up for in quality. Many search engines now provide indexes and vice versa.

Preparing Your Site

Before jumping right to Yahoo!, AltaVista, or another major search engine and adding your URL, you should take a moment to prepare your site.

First and foremost, make sure your site is working properly. No matter how successful you are at attracting visitors to your Web site, your efforts will be for naught if once they get there, they find an unusable, unavailable, or unprepared site.

Second, be ready to adjust your site for the search engines. Even though you've made your site ready for visitors, it may not be tuned to return the best rankings from the search engines. You may have to consider the keywords your target audience will most likely be searching for and adjust your page title, <meta> tags, and first paragraph to showcase those keywords.

Site Promotion Services

You can find plenty of Web sites that promise to make the promotion process a piece of cake. As a rule, tread carefully among Web promotion services, and take many of their claims with a grain of salt. It is possible to automate many of the repetitive tasks of entering your URL, keywords, and other basic information for the thousands of search engines and indexes out there. However, no one can guarantee that your site will place top in the rankings for most, if not all, search engines. Furthermore, don't base your choice of search services solely on the number of search engines they promise to submit your site to. Can you name a thousand search engines, or even two dozen?

This book doesn't have space to discuss the wide range of search services available, but Table 13-6 lists a few such services. However, I would like to point out one such site. SelfPromotion.com, created and maintained by Robert Woodhead, is served up on a Mac. In addition to its Mac use, the site serves up an amazingly detailed, comprehensive, and well-documented set of articles on the ins and outs of site promotion. And he gives great advice, but makes no promises that he can't keep. For example, the site is invaluable for the in-depth tips for being listed in Yahoo! The site also tells you up front that the best way to get into Yahoo! and other primary search engines and indexes is to do it yourself.

SelfPromotion.com is a "shareservice"—it's free to use, but paying the registration fee gets you a year's subscription and access to additional promotion tools that help you track and evaluate the progress of your promotion efforts. At the very least, you should visit the payment page and check out the recommended registration fees for Steve Case of AOL, Bill Gates, and Larry Ellison.

Table 13-6. Web Site Promotion Resources

Location	Description
www.selfpromotion.com	SelfPromotion.com, a "shareservice" created by Robert Woodhead.
www.selfpromotion.com/yahootips.t	How to get listed in Yahoo!—tips from Robert Woodhead.
www.mcpromotions.com	MC Promotions, a Merle's World Production, has free tips for promoting your online presence.
www.goto.com	GoTo.com uses a pay-for-ranking scheme.
www.realnames.com	RealNames Corporation, a pay service for attaching your business to keywords or key phrases.

Do-It-Yourself Promotion

If you don't want to pay for a promotion service, you can do pretty well on your own. All it takes is a little time and effort registering your site with the appropriate Web search engines. Even though you may not be able to register your site with 15,000 search engines as some promotion sites promise—a dubious achievement at best—you can get substantial coverage by submitting your server to the major search engines and indexes.

Search Engines. First, consider submitting your site to the major search engines, AltaVista, Lycos, Google, Go, Excite, HotBot, MSN Search, and Netscape Search. Most people use these search engines for their searches. Because search engines generate their keywords from the information on your site, their submission forms are often fairly simple. They generally accept your URL and possibly some contact information and send their robots to your site. Submitting to search engines is usually the strong suit of Web promotion services. However, the major search engines can take months to add new listings.

As you submit your site with each search engine, be sure to note any tips for how to make your site rank highly on searches. Ignore this free advice to your detriment. Table 13-7 lists some of the major sites you should target for do-it-yourself site promotion.

Indexes. As the most important place to have your site listed on the Internet, Yahoo! should also be one of your primary targets. A properly crafted submission to Yahoo! will increase your chances of getting in as well as getting hits. Writing your site description for Yahoo! may be the most important step you will take during site promotion, and description will help your postings to other indexes as well. At this point, submitting your site to the Open Directory and Snap indexes may make sense. Listings in these major indexes are sufficiently valuable that hand-done, optimized submissions are worth the time.

Table 13-7. Leading Web Search Sites and Promotion Targets

Location	Description
www.macinstein.com	Macinstein, the Mac-only search engine.
www.yahoo.com	Yahoo!, by Yahoo! Inc.
www.nbci.com	NBCi.com from NBC.
www.dmoz.org	Open Directory Project by Netscape, used by several major search engines.
www.altavista.com	AltaVista, by AltaVista Company.
www.lycos.com	Lycos, by Lycos, Inc.
www.google.com	Google, from Google, Inc.
www.excite.com	Excite, from At Home Corporation.
www.hotbot.com	HotBot, from Wired Digital, Inc.
search.msn.com	MSN Search, from Microsoft Corporation.
search.netscape.com	Netscape Search, from Netscape Communications.

Topical Indexes and Search Engines. Your next targets should be search engines and directories that target the same audience as your Web server. For example, if you have a Macintosh-related site, you should probably register with a Mac-only search site such as Macinstein. For any product you're selling, there are almost certainly search engines or link pages that you'll want to register with. For example, let's say you own a vineyard and want to sell your wine online. You can start with a search for wine on Yahoo! or AltaVista—or because you already have an interest in wine, you might have bookmarked a set of wine-related sites, such as Wine Spectator, which has a Wine Search section. There are certainly others.

Paying for Rankings. Although listings in the search engines and indexes are free, you don't have much control. Even if you follow all the tips for scoring high rankings, you're not always guaranteed to get the ones you want. A few services, such as GoTo.com and RealNames, provide various methods to generate targeted traffic at your Web site.

For example, you can register the name of your business, brand, or motto with RealNames, and when a visitor to AltaVista or another search engine enters your keyword or key phrase, your Web site will be listed above all the other ranked listings. On the other hand, GoTo.com works much like other search engines, except that your site's ranking is calculated based on how much you pay to have your site listed when a Goto.com visitor types in a particular keyword.

Newsgroups and Mailing Lists. Just as you can enter your URL at a search engine, you can post a message to newsgroups or mailing lists related to the subject matter at your site. However, if you are selling products, you should check that it's appropriate to post commercial messages to a given newsgroup, or else you could do yourself more harm than good.

A slightly more formal method, but not much more difficult, is to write a short press release and submit it to sites that run news items about your product category. For example, you might try *MacCentral* for Macintosh-related sites, or *Wine Spectator* for wine-related sites. Keep it short, keep it professional, and the worst that can happen is that a site doesn't publish your press release.

On the other hand, your news might reach readers all around the world—all for the cost of a few hours online. I'm sure that if you're creative you can discover many other free promotion opportunities. I leave that to you as an exercise.

Web Advertising

There are two sides to the advertising question: purchasing ad space from other sites on which you want to promote your site, and selling ad space on your site to let others promote their sites. In most ways, purchasing ad space on the Web is no different from the print or broadcast world. You determine where you want your ad to go and buy space from the publication or time from the broadcaster.

In the non-Internet world, measuring the impact of such advertising is a tricky subject. You can count how many times your ad is printed (in how many copies of a magazine or newspaper) or broadcast (on what television or radio time slots). On the Web, you can get similar information—how many Web surfers have viewed your ad. In addition, you have the ability to count "click-throughs"—the number of times someone clicks on your ad to visit your site. But again, whether this translates to purchases or return visits or greater visibility remains almost as difficult to assess as in the print and broadcast world.

If you have a large advertising budget, there are plenty of people willing to help you spend that money among a diverse selection of media. DoubleClick, for example, is one of the major Internet advertising sites that provides ads to some of the most visited sites on the Web.

However, the Web has other options for low-budget or no-budget advertising operations if you run your own Web site. The main venues for such promotions are *banner advertising networks,* some of which are listed in Table 13-8. What you do is submit your ad into a pool of advertisements that get selected when visitors view the ad network's host sites. In a free banner advertising network, such as LinkHut.com or LinkExchange, by joining you agree to show other sites' banners on your site, and in exchange, your banners appear on other sites.

The technical details for joining a banner ad network are minor. You sign up, you add some HTML code to your pages, and your site has banner ads. Here are some factors to consider when shopping around for a banner ad network.

Standard Ad Sizes. To keep ad graphics interchangeable as far as the space they consume on a Web page is concerned, Web ads must be designed in standard sizes.

Table 13-8. Web Advertising Resources

Location	Description
bannertips.com	Banner Tips from Pinnacle WebWorks.
www.doubleclick.net	DoubleClick, Inc., commercial advertising/publishing options for large sites.
adnetwork.bcentral.com	LinkExchange Banner Network from Microsoft's bCentral.
www.linkhut.com	LinkHut.com.
www.webreference.com/promotion/banners	More banner ad networks from internet.com's WebReference.
home.pennyweb.com	PennyWeb banner advertising network.

- Full banner—468 by 60 pixels
- Half banner—234 by 60 pixels
- Button 1—120 by 90 pixels
- Button 2—120 by 60 pixels
- Square button—125 by 125 pixels
- Micro button—88 by 31 pixels

For simplicity, most free banner ad networks stick to the full banner ads. As an advertiser, you might encounter the other sizes when purchasing ad space through a commercial service. (The micro button is more common in exchanging reciprocal links with other sites. And you thought designing a Web page to be viewed within the confines of an 800 by 600 pixel screen was constraining.)

Targeting. Most banner ad networks provide some level of targeting—the ability to select the types of ads that will appear on your site and the category of sites on which your ad will appear. For example, if you have a sports memorabilia site, you might want to have ads for sports and hobbies, but maybe not cosmetics or computer hardware.

Ratios and Credits. Be forewarned that, on free banner ad networks, you get what you pay for. As a nonpaying participant, you must show more banners than you get back in exposures. For example, if the ad network's ratio is 2:1, two ads must be viewed on your site for you to get one credit to have your ad displayed elsewhere. A ratio of 3:2 is a slightly better deal. In many cases, you also get a "signing bonus" of a thousand or more *credits*. More credits means more people will get to see your ad before your Web site has to become self-sustaining.

Impressions and Click-Throughs. The mathematically astute reader may have calculated a problem. With a 2:1 ratio and only nonpaying member sites, the ad-displaying sites will consume credits faster than they generate them. You've just discovered how these banner ad networks are able to operate for free. Many sites pay to have their ads displayed by the member sites (while not being required to display any themselves). Paying to advertise through free banner ad networks is often much less expensive than paying to place your ad on a major Web publication, but it's difficult to say where your ad will turn up.

You may have the option of paying for impressions or click-throughs. Impressions are the number of times that your ad is displayed on an ad network member's site. For example, you may pay $50 for 5,000 impressions (or $0.01 per impression), with volume discounts for larger purchases. Click-throughs, however, count the number of times that some Web surfer clicks on your ad to visit your site. Because click-throughs mean guaranteed traffic at your site, a click-through is more expensive than an impression. You may pay $75 for 250 click-throughs (or $0.30 per click-through).

Payments. Banner advertising can also be a source of income for your Web site, particularly if you are willing to display banner ads without placing your own ads in the banner pool. Some banner ad networks, such as PennyWeb, provide payments to host sites for every click-through that their sites generate. These payments may be up to $0.25 per click-through.

CHAPTER 14

LIVE AND STREAMING MEDIA

The Web has started to converge with the traditional broadcast media, both radio and television. As faster Internet connections become more commonplace, more and more people use the Internet to listen to the radio or watch live broadcasts of television programs and other special events. With your Mac OS X Web server, you too can add live media to your site.

LIVE AND RECORDED MEDIA

The techniques and technologies for producing television-quality programs is beyond the scope of this book. In addition, broadcasting a program over the Web, or *webcasting,* to a large, Internet-wide audience requires a much more substantial server and networking setup than a single server regardless of platform.

But webcasting of small-scale live and recorded events requires three specific components.

- You'll need a camera for capturing video and a microphone for capturing audio. The quality of the camera and microphone depends on the quality you need from your live or recorded event.
- You need to be able to connect the camera and microphone to your server. Some less expensive cameras can be plugged into a USB port. Many digital video cameras have FireWire connections. For high-end solutions you may require a video-digitizing card.
- You'll need software to link the captured video or audio to the Web, either through your existing Web server or through a separate media server.

There are two major mechanisms for putting live media on your site that fall within these intentionally broad guidelines: Web cams and streaming multimedia. At the low-cost end of the spectrum, you can add a Web cam to your existing Web server for less than $100. At the high-cost end of the spectrum, a streaming multimedia production and server environment can cost as much as you're willing to pay.

Note that this chapter is not going to consider the creation of movie files that a Web visitor downloads and views on the client computer. In this case, the techniques are no different that putting an image, a text file, or another document on a Web site for download.

Lights, Web Cam, Action

It's easier to describe a Web cam (short for "Web camera") than to define what one is. It doesn't suffice to say it's a digital camera, because that term could describe not only a Web cam but also a digital still camera or a digital video camera. To further muddy the waters, Web cams can capture both still photos and video. In fact, there is no product category called "Web cameras" at any online store. To be completely technical, the term "Web cam" more accurately defines a *use* of a particular kind of digital camera to display images on a Web site, but to keep things simple, and because this *is* a Web handbook, I'll call them Web cams.

Choosing a Web Cam

A typical Web cam has the following characteristics that distinguish it from a digital still camera and a digital video camera.

- Although a Web cam can capture still images and video, it has no memory or recording device for storing the images or video.
- A Web cam is tethered to a computer from which it is software-controlled and from which it is powered, instead of being self-contained.
- A Web cam generally costs much less than digital still or video cameras, primarily because of the previous two characteristics.

Web cams today are most commonly designed to plug into a USB port, although new—and more expensive—FireWire cameras are now available. (Owners of older Macs may still be able to locate digital cameras that plug into a Mac serial port.) The cost ranges from $50 to $100, and with rebates, you can find them for less. In general, the factors to consider are

- *Image resolution.* The highest resolution for these cameras is typically 640 by 480 pixels, although 320 by 240 should suffice for Web use.
- *Video frame rate.* This is relevant only if you plan to capture video with the camera. Thirty frames per second is the speed of movie film. Less expensive cameras may support only 15 frames per second.
- *Connection type.* Most cameras these days have USB connections. Higher-speed FireWire connections are available on some cameras. FireWire's performance will matter only when capturing video. For still images, there's no real advantage to FireWire.
- *Cost.* As you might expect, a camera with higher resolution, a faster video frame rate, and a FireWire connection will cost more than a USB camera with 320 by 240 resolution and a slower frame rate.

Even at the high end, you won't be filming the next blockbuster Hollywood film with any of these cameras; their resolution is typically lower, and they have fewer of the bells and whistles that mark a professional-caliber camera. However, they work nicely for capturing photos and live film clips for viewing on the Web. Virtually any such camera will come with the basic software you need for snapping photos—of the items you're planning to auction on eBay, for example—and often the software for using the camera as an Internet video phone. Table 14-1 lists a few companies that manufacture Mac-compatible Web cams.

Table 14-1. Mac-Compatible Web Cameras

Location	Description
www.ariston.com	iSee USB digital cameras from Ariston Technologies.
www.irez.com	iREZ video products by PAR Technologies, Inc.
www.logitech.com	QuickCam family from Logitech.
www.supercaminc.com	FireCam and WonderEye cameras from Supercam Data, Inc.
www.zoomtel.com	ZoomCAM by Zoom Telephonics, Inc.
www.philips.com	Vesta PC cameras from Philips Consumer Electronics.
www.kensington.com	VideoCAM from the Kensington Technology Group.

Web Cam Software

Despite the name given to them here, Web cameras don't usually come with Web cam software, but that can be taken care of quite easily. In principle, Web cam software is simply a variation on the image capture software that is included with the camera. You'll want to consider the following features when looking at Web cam software.

- *Image triggers.* The camera may be triggered to capture a new picture at a customizable time interval or in response to motion or sound.
- *Captioning and image filtering.* You will probably want to place captions, such as the time, date, company logo, or other identifying information, on each captured image. Some software provides additional image filtering.

- *Integration with remote Web servers.* If you don't want to run the Web cam on your Web server computer, you need a way, such as through FTP, to place captured images on the Web server. Some Web cam software, on the other hand, has a Web server built-in to run on a separate computer.
- *Time-lapse animations.* Some Web cam software will also create time-lapse movies from the captured images. You can often configure a separate interval for capturing frames for animation as well as specify the length of such animations.
- *Streaming video.* With high-end Web cam software, you can use your Web cam to stream audio or video to Web clients. Streaming video will also put pressure on your network connection, however.

Table 14-2 shows software packages that will turn your digital camera into a Web cam. Oculus and CoolCam are shareware at the inexpensive end of the spectrum, with the emphasis on still images, but both have many handy features. CoolCam has a live motion preview and more natural caption editing, but Oculus has the ability to capture time-lapse movies. At the high end of the spectrum, SiteCam from NuSpectra Multimedia is a commercial package with a wide range of still-image features plus a built-in Web server and audio and video streaming to clients through a Java applet.

Table 14-2. Mac OS Web Cam Software

Location	Description
www.intlweb.com	Oculus, shareware from Poubelle Software and International Web, Inc., can create time-lapse animations.
www.evological.com	CoolCam, shareware by Evological Software, permits easy WYSIWYG caption editing and a live motion preview.
www.nuspectra.com	SiteCam, commercial software from NuSpectra Multimedia, has a full range of features, a built-in Web server, and streaming audio and video. SiteZAP includes a robotic camera and Web-control software.
hsoftware.8k.com	WebVideo, shareware from Hsoftware, with a minimal set of features.
www.stripcam.org	StripCam, Web cam freeware by David van Brink, with a minimal set of features.

At the time of writing, these Web cam software options had not yet been made available for Mac OS X, mostly due to the incomplete support for peripheral devices in the public beta. These tools will likely be available soon after the final release.

Site Cam

At the high end of Mac OS Web cam software, the commercial option is the $149 SiteCam from NuSpectra Multimedia. The highly rated SiteCam originated as MacWebCam several years ago and has evolved into a full-featured Web cam environment. The SiteCam software includes its own Web server software, so you can serve your Web cam from a computer and free your main server from Web cam traffic.

SiteCam's built-in Web server is tuned to serve streaming video to your viewers' browsers, without third-party viewing software and regardless of intervening firewalls. SiteCam automatically selects the best streaming format for the viewer's browser and streams images to fit the available bandwidth. Live streaming video requires a static IP address and a high-speed connection, but SiteCam can also be used with low-speed connections to serve still images. With SiteCam, you can also archive images and create time-lapse movies.

SiteCam allows you to have several documents open at once so you can capture images at several sizes, image qualities, and formats. Anti-hijacking support in SiteCam keeps your live streaming video from being stolen by other Web sites, and standard log files help you track the visits to your Web cam.

If you're not happy with a Web cam that can display images of only a single location, capturing the movement of people or objects as they pass in front of the viewfinder, NuSpectra's SiteZAP can take your Web cam to the next level. SiteZAP combines the capabilities of the SiteCam software with a robotic camera that your Web visitors can control from their browsers. Web visitors can zoom, pan, and tilt the camera through a Java applet or a Flash interface. There's even an optional enclosure if the camera is to be mounted outdoors.

Oculus

Oculus from International Web is shareware with a comprehensive set of features for handling still images and creating time-lapse animations. It does not, however, include a built-in Web server, so you'll need to have a Web server to use Oculus. Oculus does not need to run on the same machine as your server, however; it can send the captured images by FTP to the appropriate place on another machine.

Oculus also comes with a handy Setup Assistant that walks you through the configuration settings and even creates a basic Web page for viewing your Web cam images. (You'll have to edit this page to match the look of your site, but it gets you started.)

For my test setup on Mac OS 9, I used the Oculus Setup Assistant to create a basic Web page using the default settings. Running the Web cam on the same machine as my Web server, I then placed the page, named *webcamtest.html,* in my main Web server folder. Next, I chose the Settings: Photo menu item to tell Oculus where to store the captured images on my server. This is also where you can tell Oculus how to FTP the images to your server. (Note: Until you pay the shareware registration fee, Oculus does not save these FTP or file settings, so you must reset them each time you start Oculus.)

You may have to adjust the details of the Web cam page so that it finds the camera image and is set to refresh properly. I wish I could be a little more specific here, but much of this depends on your Web server configuration. Suffice it to say that it's not too complicated. If you've managed to get a Web server running, you can handle Oculus.

STREAMING MULTIMEDIA

Thanks to the growing convergence of the Web and broadcast media, you can now serve up the experience of television and radio for truly devoted webophiles. The Web offers a unique opportunity for small-scale broadcasters—just about anyone with a video camera and a streaming server—to reach a potentially worldwide audience. (However, for the life of me, I don't see many advantages to listening to local radio or cable TV if you already own equipment that accomplishes the same task without sucking away precious bandwidth.)

For those budding broadcasters among you, *streaming multimedia* describes the delivery of continuous video or audio across the Internet. The continuous feed of streaming multimedia differs from the still images typically captured by Web cams. And unlike downloadable movie files, which require a Web visitor to move a file from the server to the client computer for viewing, no more than a few seconds of a streaming video resides on the client computer at any given time. Once the client plays the video, it is discarded. (The server may also discard the video once it has been streamed, unless the server is recording the event.) Also, with a live stream, new viewers pick up the stream in progress rather than starting at the beginning.

Streaming is a handy way to distribute media files to clients because of the rapid response. The audio or video begins playing almost immediately without requiring a lengthy download. However, live streaming is not a minimalist option. You'll need at least two computers, an encoder and a server, perhaps in addition to your actual Web server, along with a camera and a substantial enough network connection to handle all the viewers.

Live Streaming Setup

Getting set up for live streaming is a chore unto itself and probably worthy of a book unto itself. I poked around, but quickly learned that I was in an entirely different ballpark from Mac Web servers. I'll give you the condensed version and a few pointers to send you on your way. Setting up for live media streaming requires you to assemble several components, sketched out in Figure 14-1.

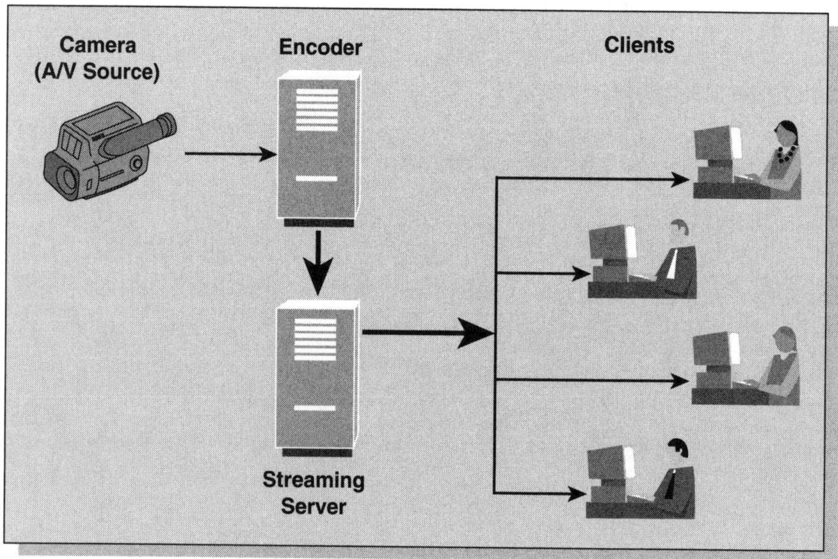

Figure 14-1. Live Streaming Video Hardware Setup.

- You'll need a video camera, preferably with a built-in microphone. If you have a separate camera and microphone, you're entering the realm of mixing boards.
- The camera must be connected to an encoding station, which is a separate computer and a means to convert the camera signal to digital video if your camera doesn't produce a digital signal. Because of the computational demands, this conversion, or encoding, is often handled in a hardware peripheral or expansion card.
- You'll need a connection from your encoding computer to your streaming computer—the faster the better. You'll use your encoding software to create a Session Description Protocol (SDP) file that will reside on the streaming server.
- On the streaming computer, you'll need streaming server software. The streaming server will serve the SDP file, which you can think of as the nozzle of the media stream.

The most direct solution is to use a digital Web camera and NuSpectra's SiteCam to take care of the whole kit and kaboodle. No encoding is necessary and SiteCam is the streaming server software. You will have to determine for yourself if the quality of the video and audio is sufficient for your broadcasts. A more recent all-in-one software solution that permits you to use higher-end video and audio equipment is Live Channel from Channel Storm.

Moving toward the high end, however, you can spend thousands of dollars to produce professional-quality broadcasts. Table 14-3 lists some pieces, including the Sorenson Broadcaster encoding software, and some streaming media Web sites where you can learn more. RealNetworks produces the most common streaming media format and the software to produce and serve it; however, at the time of writing only the production software is available for the Mac OS. My advice: If you're not proficient in video production, you should consult someone with more experience than me.

Choosing Streaming Server Software

Now we're back on the familiar ground of servers. A streaming server distributes streaming media across the Internet. Like a Web server, a streaming server still

Table 14-3. Streaming Media Production Resources

Location	Description
streamingmediaworld.com	Streaming Media World provides a wide range of tutorials, reviews, references, and other information.
www.realnetworks.com	RealProducer Plus, from from RealNetworks, Inc., lets you create RealMedia content.
www.sorenson.com	Sorenson Broadcaster, from Sorenson Media, Inc., is a live audio and video broadcasting tool for QuickTime.
www.dragoontech.com	Dragoon Technologies sells several complete Mac-based streaming servers, including hardware and software.
www.channelstorm.com	Live Channel from Channel Storm, a software-based live media production and streaming server combination.
www.media100.com	Media 100, Inc., a leading developer of solutions for producing videos.
www.terran.com	Media Cleaner Pro from Terran Interactive, highly regarded video compression software.
www.icanstream.com	iCanStream.com, a site with information on producing videos for streaming.

handles requests from clients. However, unlike a Web server, a new request directs the current stream at the client viewer.

For a forced analogy that I feel compelled to include, imagine that the streaming server is a garden hose and the water coming out is the video. If no one is watching the video, the water is just splashing on the lawn. When clients send requests to view the stream, the hose is pointed at them. (For the sake of argument, pretend the hose can point in hundreds of directions at the same time.) But instead of having a bucket to catch the water, the client has a paper cup with a hole cut in the bottom. The cup stops the water just long enough for the client to look at it before it drains away to the lawn.

Back in the much drier world of Internet media streaming, there are several factors to consider when you're streaming media across the Internet.

HTTP versus RTSP. There are actually two types of streaming—HTTP streaming and Real-Time Streaming Protocol (RTSP) streaming. With HTTP streaming, you download an entire movie to your hard disk, but you can view the file during download. HTTP streaming does not require special server software, but the video viewing may have jumps or pauses, depending on network traffic. HTTP streaming works best for short movies that you intend to play over and over again.

RTSP, on the other hand, is what you normally think of in terms of streaming, as in the garden hose analogy above. It's a "just in time" streaming technology that keeps your computer in constant touch with the server running the movie. Digital data is transferred and displayed and discarded. A cache of data—three to ten seconds of the data stream—is stored to compensate for occasional network "burps" that might otherwise compromise quality. RTSP streaming is ideal for full-length movies and live events.

Network Bandwidth. In most cases, network connections at 56 kbps (kilobits per second) or higher suffice for standard Web serving to a limited audience. Streaming media, on the other hand, will quickly consume all your available network bandwidth. To calculate how much bandwidth you need, multiply the maximum number of users you expect by the bit rate of the files they will view. Fifteen clients viewing 100-kbps files would saturate a 1,500-kpbs connection—a full T1 link. One thousand clients viewing a 22-kbps stream would take up a 22-Mbps (megabits per second) connection, which could be carried on 100-Mbps Ethernet LAN or externally on a fractional T3. Plan on even more bandwidth consumed if some viewers are watching at faster bit rates. These calculations do not include other network use.

Proxy. If your server has a slow Internet connection that is easily saturated by streams to your clients or it is located several hops from your external connection to the Internet, a proxy server may help alleviate some network congestion. To have an impact, the proxy server should be connected to the Internet at a faster speed than your streaming server or at a point on the network where streams from this server will cause less congestion for the rest of the organization. Aside from those requirements, a proxy server is just a relay station between your streaming server and your clients. Clients won't notice a difference, but your internal network could benefit.

Firewalls. Firewalls—belonging either to your organization or to your clients' ISPs—can cause problems for streaming media. Because of access restrictions on certain ports, clients may have difficulty making connections to your stream. If you are experiencing firewall problems, you should first make sure that you have the latest updates for your streaming server, and your clients may need to update their client software. There's not much you can do about firewalls, except be prepared to field questions about viewing streaming media through them.

All that having been said, there aren't many options for streaming server software on Mac OS X. At the time of writing, one of the most popular streaming media formats, from RealNetworks, does not have a RealServer version that runs on the Mac OS. Table 14-4 has pointers to streaming server and proxy software for Mac OS X.

Table 14-4. Streaming Server and Proxy Software

Location	Description
www.evological.com	CoolStream, a shareware QuickTime Streaming server application (for Mac OS 9 at time of writing).
www.apple.com/quicktime/servers	QuickTime Streaming Server, free software from Apple.
www.realnetworks.com	RealServer from RealNetworks was not available for Mac OS X at the time of writing but is available for several UNIX variants.
www.nuspectra.com	SiteProxy from NuSpectra Multimedia provides a proxy server for SiteCam and other Web cam streaming.

SiteProxy

SiteProxy from NuSpectra Multimedia is an Apache module for streaming live Web cam video from any Web cam application that supports server-push streaming to concurrent Internet viewers. The number of viewers who can watch a Web cam simultaneously is often limited by the network bandwidth at the camera location. With SiteProxy, a single video stream from the Web cam connection is sent to the SiteProxy host, from which it can be webcast through a fast network connection, perhaps co-located at an ISP. This solution will appeal to you if your number of simultaneous viewers hovers above 10 most of the time or if you experience poor performance at your server location due to bandwidth constraints. Initially, SiteProxy was made available for Apache on the Linux operating system only, but versions for Mac OS X and other operating systems are likely to follow.

QuickTime Streaming Server

QuickTime Streaming Server can serve over 2,000 high-quality broadcast streams to QuickTime users. Through the Darwin project, QuickTime Streaming Server is also available for Linux, Solaris, FreeBSD, and Windows NT/2000. A preview of QuickTime Streaming Server 3, with Web-based administration, was made available for the Mac OS X public beta, and it will be included with Apple's Mac OS X Server suite.

QuickTime streaming is very processor intensive. Therefore, the server computer should be dedicated as much as possible to streaming. The recommended configuration is at least a 400-MHz Macintosh Server G3 with 1 GB of memory, 9 GB of free disk space across three disk drives, a 4-port Ethernet card, and Mac OS X.

The installation of QuickTime Streaming Server for Mac OS X is straightforward. Download the compressed *.tar.gz* file, unpack it using StuffIt Expander, and double-click on the resulting package. The Installer utility will step you through some screens of information and then install the software. It will set up your system so that the streaming server starts when your computer boots up.

To configure the QuickTime Streaming Server settings or check the status, you can open your browser and go to *http://localhost:1220/,* which is the only location at which you can change the Administrator password. The status page is shown in Figure 14-2. Alternately, you can configure any setting except the Administrator password remotely at *http://your.host.name:1220/*.

In addition to serving live video, you can stream prerecorded QuickTime movies. To do so, you first need to set up the movie as a streaming movie and then put the movie in the configured Movie Folder, which by default is */Library/QuickTimeStreaming/Movies.* A sample movie is included with the streaming server installation.

A normal QuickTime movie, such as a movie you create with iMovie, is usually not quite ready to be served via a streaming server. You need to save it in a special format that includes "hints" for the streaming server, and you will need a special tool for this. In particular, QuickTime Pro software—the $30 upgrade from the free QuickTime download—lets you save movies in this format:

1. Open the movie in QuickTime Player.
2. Select Export from the File menu.

3. In the Save dialog box, give your movie a name, and select the Movie to QuickTime Movie option from the Export pull-down list.
4. Click on the Options button.
5. In the Movie Settings dialog box, turn on the check box for the Prepare for Internet Streaming option, and select Hinted Streaming from the pull-down list.
6. Click Okay, then Save to export your streaming movie.
7. Place the movie in the QuickTime Streaming Server Movie Folder.

To view your movie through your streaming server, you need to point your visitors to the URL *rtsp://your.domain.nam/yourmovie.mov,* which they should open with their QuickTime Player. (Tell users to select Open URL from the File menu.)

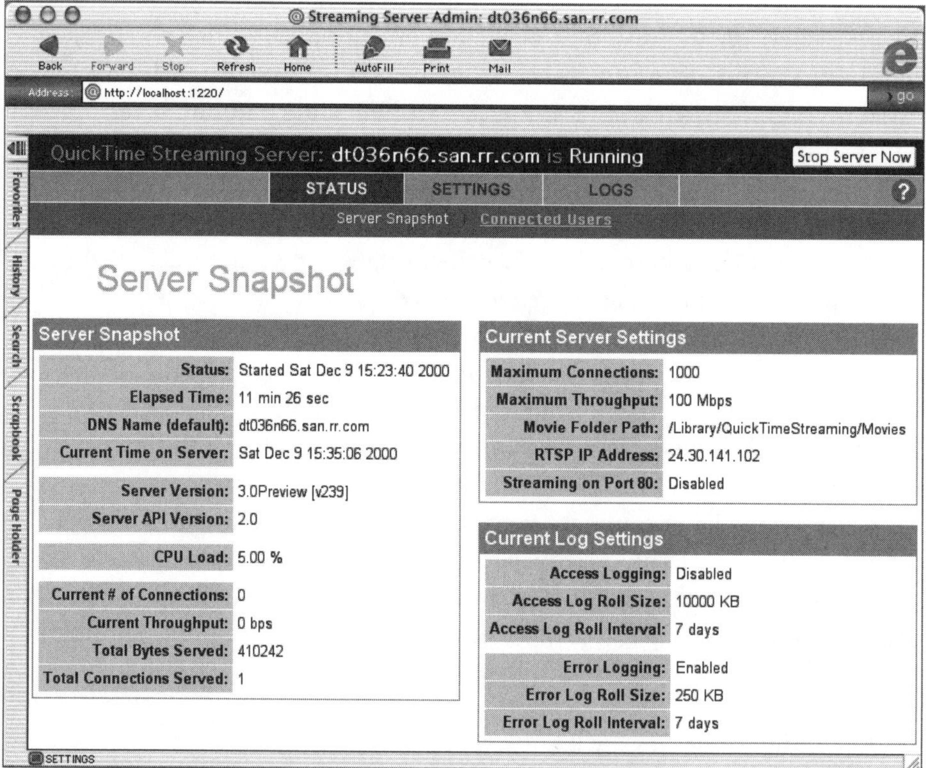

Figure 14-2. QuickTime Streaming Server Configuration.

Voilà! You're serving streaming media. Note that a streaming QuickTime movie will be larger than your original, so you should be prepared with a little extra disk space if you plan on storing significant numbers of movies.

Synchronized Multimedia Integration Language

The Synchronized Multimedia Integration Language, or SMIL (pronounced "smile") is a markup language similar to HTML that solves the problems of coordinating the display of multimedia on Web sites. (SMIL is actually a subset of XML.) SMIL is designed to be easy to learn and deploy on Web sites. By using a single timeline for all of the media on a page, you can properly synchronize the display of the components.

In large part, SMIL has been propagated by RealNetworks, so you might think that SMIL is specific to that company's products. In reality, SMIL is a standard from the W3 Consortium and can be used to synchronize media elements for any SMIL-aware player—including the QuickTime 4.1 Player and the latest versions of Windows Media Player. Therefore, you can use SMIL to synchronize QuickTime movies and audio, MPEG files, RealMedia, and just about any media format. However, if you mix QuickTime movies and RealMedia clips into one SMIL session, there's no telling what will happen since the players can't play all of the pieces.

As with HTML and XML, SMIL sessions are defined by tags. The two most important to the synchronization are the <par> and <seq> tags, for parallel and sequential, respectively. The <par> tag encloses elements that you want to play at the same time—for example, a still image and an audio voice-over—and the <seq> tag encloses elements that you want to occur in sequence, such as several video clips. SMIL allows you to incorporate HTML elements, links, text, and still images, as well as movies and audio files. In addition, SMIL lets you format your presentations for display with cascading style sheets.

While this book is neither the time nor place to delve into the details of coding SMIL, the example in Figure 14-3 should give you the gist of it. If you're familiar with HTML, much of this should look familiar. If you aren't, don't let this scare you off. In brief, the layout of the presentation is defined in the <layout> tag and the body of the presentation in the <body> tag. In this example, the presentation consists of two QuickTime movies played sequentially (within the <seq> tag).

```
<smil>
  <head>
    <layout>
      <region id="region1"
              background-color="black"
              left="0" top="0"
              width="192" height="160" />
    </layout>
  </head>
  <body>
    <seq>
      <video src="movie1.mov" alt="The Intro"
           region="region1" />
      <video src="movie2.mov" alt="The Second Movie"
           region="region1"/>
    </seq>
  </body>
</smil>
```

Figure 14-3. SMIL Example.

Now that the three major media players support SMIL, it is likely that the use of SMIL will become more widespread. However, SMIL still lacks support from a significant number of authoring tools on the Mac OS. The one notable exception is the commercial GRiNS authoring tool from Oratrix. Table 14-5 contains pointers to more information on SMIL.

Outsourcing Streaming Multimedia

Given the cost of producing and delivering streaming multimedia, combined with the fact that viewers can quickly consume all available bandwidth from your server, it may make sense to look into the services provided by third-party content distributors if you want to extend streaming media beyond your organization's internal Ethernet. Eight viewers of a 200-kpbs stream would saturate your dedicated T1 link to the outside world, and a national event that can reach only eight viewers may not accomplish your goals. Even if you can reach a thousand viewers, but each must view a low-end 22-kbps stream across your fractional T3, this may not be the professional image you want to project.

Third-party content distributors can provide a streaming infrastructure that extends way beyond the Macintosh on your desktop. However, don't expect these services to come cheap. Table 14-6 directs you to a few of these service providers.

Table 14-5. SMIL Resources

Location	Description
www.w3.org/AudioVideo	SMIL information from the W3 Consortium.
hotwired.lycos.com/webmonkey/98/23/index1a.html	"SMIL: Multimedia Markup," by Shvatz for Webmonkey.
www.justsmil.com	JustSMIL, SMIL resources from internet.com's Streaming Media World.
www.oratrix.com/GRiNS	GRiNS for SMIL, by Oratrix, is a commercial SMIL authoring tool.
www.cwi.nl/SMIL	The CWI SMIL Page from the National Research Institute for Mathematics and Computer Science in the Netherlands.

Table 14-6. Internet Content Distributors

Location	Description
www.clearway.com	FireSite content delivery from Clearway Technologies.
www.akamai.com	FreeFlow Streaming from Akamai Technologies, Inc.
www.speedera.com	Speedera Streaming from Speedera Networks, Inc.
www.digisle.com	Footprint Streaming Services from Digital Island.

CHAPTER 15

Development and Design

If you have gone to the trouble of establishing a Web server, you need to create information to serve. The creation of information is just as important to the success of your Web server—if not more so—as the Web server software and all the other enhancements you've taken great pains to install.

The presentation of your information has a strong influence on how that information is perceived, navigated, and absorbed by the audience. Presentation affects the impact whether it is for a school project by ten-year-olds or a Fortune 500 company advertising its products.

This chapter is devoted to the basics of creating, editing, and publishing a Web site. Even though this is a hefty chapter, chock full of information, it only scratches the surface. Consider this chapter and Appendix B, "Web Reference Guides," to be an introduction to the world of Web development tools and resources.

"AUTHORING" AND PUBLISHING

To begin our discussion of creating Web documents, I want to draw your attention to the distinct phases of preparing these documents. By default, the first step in the production of Web "content" has become termed the "authoring" process.

On the one hand, "authoring" is a useful term because "writing," "designing," and "coding" individually do not cover all the aspects of Web page creation. On the other hand, lumping the writing, designing, and coding tasks into a single term suggests that Web sites can be or should be created by one person in one step. Maybe a few highly paid souls out there who are equally adept at writing, graphic design, and programming can whip up a Web site by themselves, but *should* they?

Only for the Web have these multiple tasks become so intertwined in common parlance. In print media and publications, writers, photographers, artists, designers, and editors all work together to "author" the end product. In television and film, writers, directors, camerapersons, set designers, newscasters, actors, and others combine to produce the evening news or a Hollywood film. As the Web has matured, professional Web design firms have also come to the realization that Web production is not a one-person or one-skill job. Professionally created Web sites are the handiwork of a team of writers, designers, programmers, and other contributors.

The point here is that the term "authoring" is all well and good as long as you remember that producing Web pages comprises several steps:

- Deciding on the information content. For smaller sites, this can be an easy step. For sites encompassing a large enterprise, this can be a highly charged political and strategic decision involving many arms of the organization.
- Determining which portions of the information should be expressed as text, as graphic elements, or as interactive Web elements (scripts, forms, etc.). This step commonly involves studies of Web site visitors and their expectations of the site.
- Writing the text. Even writing style, format, and length need to be adjusted to meet the needs of the Web.

- Designing or creating the graphic elements, including audio and video. As with writing, this skill often goes far beyond static images to animations and other moving elements.
- Coding the HTML, scripts, and other elements for the Web. This step includes organization of the underlying file structure or working with the content management tools selected by the organization.
- Designing and testing a page that combines the text, graphics, and interactive elements. This step includes debugging the code and interactive elements and editing the text and graphics.

And this might just be for a fraction of a Web site. Add to this list the whole matter of creating an entire Web site, which adds the issues of organizing information, mapping the site for effective navigation, and specifying site-wide standards for design and text, among other issues.

I will go out on a limb and say with 99 percent certainty that neither you nor any single person within your organization is an expert at all of these aspects of Web page and site creation. Major Web sites require a team effort.

At the same time, there is still room on the Web for individuals to make their mark. Web technology is making writers, designers, editors, and programmers out of all of us. Before the arrival of the PC, and hence of widespread word processing, the various steps in document production were more distinct—you wrote something on paper, and if you were lucky, a secretary or office assistant performed the editorial role by controlling the look and feel of the document. Graphic design was limited to a very few publications and the domain of graphic designers. Word processors have turned all of us into editors as well as writers. The Web has added "designer" and "programmer" to our résumés.

In creating for the Internet, what you write may immediately be made available to a potentially huge audience. While Web tools open up a new medium for your creative efforts, the technical underpinnings make it essential that you do a good job, right from the start.

For example, good books have good content and are well organized. (I hope this book is one of them.) Good Web servers are exactly the same. It is the implication of "organization" that has changed. Books are a sequential medium with a well-established form, and usually a single theme—the plot of a novel, the explanation of words in a dictionary, the steps in setting up an information server, and so on. The Web is less structured and can present multiple themes;

that is, the same Web page can be used to make many different points. Global hypertext has taken us away from the sequential organization with which we are familiar and has plunged us into the world of random access.

Books are also a very static medium. If you exclude pop-up books for kids, about all you can do to interact with a book is turn the pages. Web publishing brings the full world of interactive multimedia to bear. Creating content specifically for the Web is a different experience from traditional writing. Good writing skills are still critical but are now accompanied by skills in using different media to get the message across. There is no end in sight for the electronic creating-editing-publishing continuum that the Web is making possible.

I'm getting ahead of myself. Before you can change the world, first you must understand the basics.

Web Page Languages

The Web would not have proliferated if it were not easy to edit and publish this new medium. Web publication is not restricted to the computer savvy—anyone who wants to spend a few minutes can add commands to a text file to create a Web page.

Over the years since the birth of the Web, however, the original markup language of the Web—the HyperText Markup Language (HTML)—has evolved into a family of more specialized and more general tools for the exchange of information.

Hypertext and Text Markup

Hypertext is not a new concept. Ted Nelson first coined the phrase back in 1965. It is beyond the scope of this book to delve into the history of hypertext, but if you are interested, have a look at the references in Table 15-1. One of the first commercial uses of hypertext was in the HyperCard products developed initially for the Macintosh computer. Many innovative HyperCard programs—called *hypercard stacks*—have been built; however, it is the global HyperCard stack—the Web—that has really popularized the use of hypertext.

Table 15-1. Background Information on Hypertext

Location	Description
www.w3.org/Markup	The W3 Consortium page on HTML.
www.isg.sfu.ca/~duchier/misc/vbush	"As We May Think," an article by Vannevar Bush (*The Atlantic Monthly,* July 1945), in which the hypertext concept was first suggested.
www.picosof.com/850	Home page of Xanadu, the company resulting from Ted Nelson's ideas.

Creating hypertext requires *marking up* your text information—inserting additional text that has nothing to do with the information content but causes a particular appearance or behavior when read by a Web browser. For example, the Web browser may display a region of text in boldface, provide a link to another home page, or display an image.

Text markup, like hypertext, is not a new idea. It has been used in text processing for many years. You take your basic text, insert (or embed) a set of commands that describe how to format that text, pass that file to a program, and have that program either display or print the formatted text based on the embedded commands. Before the advent of personal computers and word processing, document formatting was commonly handled by marking up text for programs such as Digital Standard Runoff, nroff, troff, TeX, and LaTeX, which have enjoyed some popularity on UNIX platforms over the years. None have become a standard, partly because they were overtaken by word processing programs on personal computers that are simpler to use, although LaTeX remains popular among scientists because of its powerful formatting for mathematical formulas and special characters.

HTML

HTML is a subset of yet another markup language, called the Standard Generalized Markup Language (SGML), which was, until recently, used mainly by the publishing industry. SGML is a well-developed language for describing the most complex documents. As a subset of SGML purposefully designed to simplify the markup task, HTML does not have all the formatting features required for more complex documents. However, each new release of HTML has included more features described in SGML.

Using HTML, you can produce simple Web documents in a few minutes if you understand and remember a few markup commands, or *tags*. If you invest more time, you can produce more sophisticated Web documents with the advanced capabilities of HTML. Even if you use an HTML editor, it is useful to have some knowledge of HTML. While the editors hide the details, the current sophistication of HTML editors means that some manual "tweaking" of the HTML code will probably take place at some point in the development process.

HTML tags tell the Web browser or other software reading the Web document, "Hey, wake up and format me." HTML tags are distinguished from regular text by being contained in angle brackets as follows: <tag_a>. Most tags also have terminators that are introduced by a slash: </tag_a>. For example, the <b> and </b> tags turn on and off a boldface version of the current font.

```
<b>This text will appear in boldface.</b> This will appear in the
standard font.
```

Some tags—such as the <br> tag that forces an end-of-line break—have not had terminators up through HTML 4.0 since they don't enclose anything. However, in XHTML 1.0, the successor to HTML 4.0, tags such as <br> are written <br/> to indicate termination.

The structure of an HTML document is straightforward. A basic page includes four tags and their terminators, properly arranged. First, the entire document is enclosed by <html> ... </html> tags. Next, the <head> ... </head> tags delimit the header of the document, which is not displayed. The header annotates the document for you, the Web client, and for anyone displaying the HTML source code of your document.

Within the header, the <title> ... </title> tags define what appears in the title bar of most Web browsers and what appears in your browser's bookmarks. The header also contains additional information used by the browser to display the document, as well as information about the document that is used by search engines indexing the page.

Finally, the <body> ... </body> tags delimit the main content of the document. The example in Figure 15-1 illustrates the bare minimum markup for an HTML document.

```
<html>
  <head>
    <title>This text appears in the bookmark.</title>
  </head>
  <body>
    This is the body of the document.
    ...
  </body>
</html>
```

Figure 15-1. Basic HTML Document Structure.

If you add no other tags to the body of your document, something sensible will usually result when the page is viewed with a Web browser. Even without any HTML tags at all, provided the file has an *.html* or *.htm* file extension, the contents of that file will likely appear in the browser. You will certainly want a little more control over the look and layout of your document, however.

A key point to make here is that, in its conception and ancestry, HTML is a language to describe the *structure* of documents, not the look and feel. If you explore the older specifications for HTML, you will encounter such obsolete tags as <au> (author), <cite> (citation), and <fn> (footnote) that were included in the original specification because it was believed that the primary use of the Web would be to format and share scientific publications. As the Web grew in popularity, the various tags and the assumed display of those tags by Netscape Navigator and Microsoft Internet Explorer were commandeered to describe the *design* of a document.

Today, HTML has come full circle. Under the guidance of the W3 Consortium, the current HTML recommendation is XHTML 1.0, an XML-defined version of HTML that returns to HTML's roots as a structure definition language. The display function of HTML has been "spun off" into a separate language for cascading style sheets.

With the quantity of HTML information available on the Web and in dozens of books, it doesn't make much sense to repeat it here. A number of excellent Web sites provide extensive details about HTML and other Web development techniques and technologies. Appendix B, "Web Reference Guides," points you to some of the more popular and extensive resources available. I'll talk about software tools for creating HTML files later in the chapter.

Cascading Style Sheets (CSS)

With the recommendation for the HTML 4.0 specification, the W3 Consortium included support for cascading style sheets (CSS). Cascading style sheets parallel the use of style sheets or paragraph styles in word processors like Microsoft Word and desktop publishing programs like QuarkXPress.

The primary advantage of CSS is that it makes it possible to separate the look and feel of information (the style) from the structure information (the HTML tags). As a result, the HTML code for documents that use CSS will typically have fewer HTML tags because many of the directives that define how a section should look appear in the CSS file, not the HTML file.

Also, with CSS, a designer can specify the look of a site's pages once—for example, headlines will be in an 18-point sans serif font, and paragraphs will have chartreuse, 11-point text and a 1-pica indent—and all pages that link to that style sheet are guaranteed to have the same presentation. CSS is gradually becoming more widely used. Both Netscape Navigator 4.0 and Microsoft Internet Explorer 4.0 introduced some support for CSS, although each browser supported only parts of the CSS specification, and not all of the same parts. Furthermore, even if both Navigator and Internet Explorer support a CSS feature, you can't be sure that they both support it the same way.

Microsoft Internet Explorer 5.0 for the Macintosh was the first browser to completely support the full CSS1 specification. At the time of writing it was still the *only* browser on any platform to do so. The CSS2 specification was formally accepted by the W3 Consortium in May 1998, and the browsers have not yet fully implemented the more extensive specification. However, the general idea behind CSS is straightforward.

1. To link an external style sheet to an HTML document (this is the most common use of style sheets), include the <link> tag in the <head> section of your HTML file.

   ```
   <link rel="StyleSheet" href="style.css" type="text/css">
   ```

2. Create the text file *style.css* in your favorite text editor or style sheet editor. The very simple style sheet in Figure 15-2 redefines the HTML tags <body>, <p>, and <a> and the six header tags.

```
/* The page will have black text on a white background. */
body { background: #ffffff; color: #000000; }

/* Headers will be dark blue in a sans serif font. */
h1, h2, h3, h4, h5, h6 {
        font-family: Verdana, Arial, Helvetica, sans-serif;
        font-weight: bold;
        background: transparent;
        color: #111199; }

/* Normal paragraph will have the first line indented
   one pica and be justified. */
p    { text-indent: 1pc;
        text-align: justify; }

/* Links will be dark blue, active links red,
   visited links gray. */
a:link    { color: #000099; }
a:active  { color: #FF0000; }
a:visited { color: #666666; }
```

Figure 15-2. Example Style Sheet.

3. Code your HTML document without the extra attributes and font tags normally used to manipulate the design of these elements. Figure 15-3 is a bare-bones HTML file that uses this style sheet.
4. Place the HTML file and the file *style.css* in the same folder, and view the HTML file with your Web browser. Remove the *.css* file to see how the HTML would display in a browser that does not support style sheets. (Some browsers will return an error message if the CSS file is missing.)

This example is only the tip of the CSS iceberg. CSS can also be used for precise positioning of text and other elements. For designers of Web pages, this promises to be one of the most appreciated features of style sheets. CSS creation and editing is also being incorporated in most Web production tools, including Adobe GoLive and Macromedia Dreamweaver. Table 15-2 points to some CSS references and editors for Mac OS X. Appendix B lists further resources and tutorials on CSS.

```
<html>
  <head>
  <title>CSS Example</title>
    <link rel="STYLESHEET" href="style.css" type="text/css">
  </head>

  <body>
    <h1>Header level 1</h1>
    <h3>Header level 3</h3>

    <p>Style sheets let you use the same styles
    in many documents.</p>

    <p>Updating the style sheet automatically updates
    the look of all the pages using that style sheet.</p>

    <hr>
    <a HREF="http://www.w3c.org/Style/css">See the W3C CSS
    page for more information.</a>

    <h6>&copy; 2001 David Hart.</h6>
  </body>
</html>
```

Figure 15-3. HTML File Using an External Style Sheet.

Table 15-2. CSS Resources and Software

Location	Description
www.w3.org/Style	CSS specification and information from the W3 Consortium.
www.webreview2.com/style	Browser Compatibility Charts from Web-Review.com for CSS1 and CSS2.
www.htmlhelp.com/reference/css	CSS information from John Pozadzides and Liam Quinn.
www.westciv.com/style_master	Style Master and Style Master Pro, CSS editors from Western Civilization.
interaction.in-progress.com/cascade	Cascade, a CSS editor by Media Design in•Progress.

Dynamic HTML (DHTML)

While cascading style sheets have been standardized, the Web page description language known as Dynamic HTML (DHTML) remains a much greater point of contention. (Dynamic HTML is not to be confused with "dynamically generated HTML" that is produced by CGI scripts or database queries.)

According to the W3 Consortium, "'Dynamic HTML' is a term used by some vendors to describe the combination of HTML, style sheets and scripts that allows documents to be animated." In DHTML, JavaScript code is used to react to the mouse movements of the client user and act upon the elements of an HTML document. For the most part, therefore, DHTML affects the look and feel of a Web site; DHTML is HTML with a makeover.

As yet there is no standard DHTML—defined at least in part as DHTML that works the same in both Navigator and Internet Explorer—because neither browser provides support for precisely the same flavor(s) of HTML, CSS, and JavaScript. Both Netscape and Microsoft claim to offer the best implementation based on the most open standards. Table 15-3 has some links to DHTML information.

In fact, the issues over a DHTML standard are more subtle and technical. The reason that Navigator and Internet Explorer don't handle HTML, CSS, and JavaScript exactly the same way lies in the way each "perceives" a Web document. In other words, each browser has a different document object model—an internal representation of a document and how to act upon it.

So the W3 Consortium is wrestling with a standard Document Object Model (DOM), which is "a platform- and language-neutral interface that will allow programs and scripts to access and update dynamically the content, structure and style of documents. The document can be further processed and the results of that processing can be incorporated back into the presented page." The DOM defines how a language such as JavaScript can manipulate the page when carrying out its instructions.

Despite supporting the specifications for HTML, CSS, and some form of JavaScript, the technical differences between Netscape's and Microsoft's DOMs become a major stumbling block when it comes to formulating a DHTML standard. These differences currently manifest themselves in the "tricks" required to write JavaScript that runs the same on both browsers and most likely mean that one of the browsers will have to make substantial internal changes to support the final DHTML standard.

Also caught up in the DHTML fray is the ability to include custom fonts with Web pages. Both Netscape and Microsoft have (of course) latched onto completely different standards. Table 15-3 points out a few DHTML resources, and Appendix B lists others.

Table 15-3. Dynamic HTML Information

Location	Description
www.w3.org/DOM	The W3 Consortium's page on the Document Object Model recommendation.
www.dhtmlzone.com	Macromedia's Dynamic HTML Zone.
www.insideDHTML.com	*Inside Dynamic HTML* by Scott Isaacs.

XHTML

While browser support for the W3 Consortium's DOM recommendations has yet to make the life of Web programmers easier, other aspects of the Web continue to move at a frantic pace. In particular, the Extensible Markup Language (XML) has emerged as a powerful new tool in the management, organization, and analysis of information. As described in Chapter 9, XML returns to the Web's roots as a means for distributing structured data.

XML is a markup language for defining custom markup languages. In much the same way that CSS files are linked to HTML documents, an XML-structured document links to a Document Type Definition (DTD) that defines the markup tags in the document. Even though XML is not compatible with current HTML documents, you do not need to rewrite all of your existing HTML files to take advantage of XML.

HTML has been reformulated as an XML DTD known as XHTML 1.0, which is the W3 Consortium's recommendation for the latest version of HTML, succeeding HTML 4.01. The purpose of XHTML is to provide many of the benefits of XML to Web developers, without requiring them to throw out all of their working HTML pages. Note that XHTML 1.0 does not enhance or broaden the capabilities of HTML but redefines it in XML terms.

XHTML 1.0 has four "flavors," and the flavor for a document is specified in a line in the <head> of the document. Each variant has its own DTD, which lays out the HTML rules succinctly and definitively and which makes it possible to validate the document with automated tools.

- *XHTML Transitional.* Most Web pages for the general public will use this flavor of HTML 4. This flavor takes advantage of XHTML features including style sheets but permits small adjustments to the markup for older browsers that can't understand style sheets.
- *XHTML Strict.* XHTML Strict allows only the cleanest structural mark-up, free of any layout-related tags. Such pages must use CSS language to achieve design and layout effects.
- *XHTML Frameset.* Web pages that partition the browser window into two or more HTML frames will use this flavor.
- *XHTML Basic.* This is not really a flavor of XHTML but a subset, which is permitted by the language's modular design. XHTML Basic is a fairly minimal subset that is targeted at mobile applications.

XHTML brings the rigor of XML to Web pages and is a key step to delivering Web pages to an increasing range of browser platforms, including cell phones, televisions, cars, wallet-sized wireless communicators, kiosks, and desktops.

You can prepare for XML by making sure that your HTML documents conform to the XHTML specification. In practical terms, this means that you should refrain from "sloppy" HTML. The W3 Consortium recommendation lists ten differences between HTML 4.0 and XHTML 1.0. Glossing over some of the more technical ones (such as SGML exclusions), you're left with about six.

1. XHTML documents must be well formed—all opening tags must either have closing tags or be written in a special form, and all the elements must be properly nested.
2. Tag and attribute names must be in lowercase letters. XHTML and XML are case-sensitive, unlike HTML.
3. For nonempty tags, end tags are required. For example, a paragraph must begin with <p> and end with </p>.
4. Attribute values must always be quoted. For example, in <table rows="3"> the quotation marks are required.

5. Attribute-value pairs must be written in full, even where minimization was permitted in HTML. For example, the "checked" attribute for check box options in forms must now be written as checked="checked".
6. Empty elements, such as <hr>, either must have an end tag or the start tag must end with />, for instance, <hr/> or <hr></hr>.

Most HTML authoring tools allow you to produce almost (but not quite) well-formed HTML, which will be readable as XHTML. As XML becomes more widely adopted—and implemented in Web browsers—authoring tools are being revised to produce well-formed HTML. Therefore, XHTML means no substantial work on the part of Web developers since most Web pages are the products of visual editors or programs that can check syntax. Tidy for Mac OS is freeware that validates Web pages for XHTML correctness.

On the other hand, XHTML makes life much easier for browser developers, who no longer have to accommodate all the variations and inconsistencies that the earliest generations of browsers permitted. If an XHTML page does not conform to the correct syntax, the browser doesn't have to bend over backward to deal with it.

The XHTML 1.0 recommendation describes the differences in greater detail and offers some suggestions to ensure backward compatibility with older HTML browsers. Table 15-4 directs you to some more information on XHTML.

Table 15-4. XHTML Resources

Location	Description
www.w3.org/MarkUp	The W3 Consortium's Markup home page.
www.geocities.com/SiliconValley/1057/tidy.html	Tidy for Mac OS, freeware ported to the Mac OS by Terry Teague, checks HTML pages for XHTML compliance.
www.w3.org/TR/xhtml1	XHTML 1.0 specification from the W3 Consortium.

SITE ORGANIZATION

Even in the random access, nonlinear world of hypertext, visitors need a place to start. This is a physical idea in a virtual world, since the moment you link your page to the Web, there is no beginning or end, no top or bottom. What's there is a complex pattern of cross-links, hence the name "Web." To orient yourself and your visitors in this virtual maze, every Web site needs a starting point. A *home page* is the starting point for a Web site, which is often viewed as the top of an information hierarchy.

For example, an organization might have a home page, which is a general, top-level entry point for getting information on that organization. Likewise, an individual in the organization may have a home page, which is the top-level page for getting information on that individual. The individual's page exists somewhere in the company's hierarchy, where it is no longer the home page as far as the organization is concerned. Hence, what constitutes a home page in this case depends on how you view the information—from the perspective of someone interested in the company or someone interested in the individual.

Knowing that you need a home page is also the starting point in developing a Web site. To get past that point, you need to focus on the content you wish to serve and the organization of that content. An ad hoc approach now will cost you dearly in the future. It takes a great deal of time to reorganize a large amount of poorly organized information, and downtime could disrupt the services you are providing.

As you develop your site, you need to consider how to map your virtual information world—organized by content—onto the physical world of disks, files, databases, and the Macintosh file system. Your goals should include the following:

- Making it easy to find a specific program or piece of information when you need to modify or reference it.
- Maximizing maintainability, which in turn implies easing the burden of moving information to new file systems and disks, minimizing the number of copies of redundant information, backing up files for emergency recovery, and providing a suitable growth path as the amount of information increases.

- Maximizing access efficiency, which might suggest a file system organization, but may also recommend using a database or database tools to store and access various types of information.
- Making it straightforward to navigate your complete information hierarchy should that be desirable for indexing or other purposes.

Folder Hierarchy

How you organize your information will be based on the types of information you support, the complexity of that information, and the format in which you store that information. However, it is worth describing one possible scenario since it highlights the issues to consider.

Let's assume you are going to be maintaining a list server and a Web server, and within your Web server, you plan to have forums and a database for your organization's staff directory. The traffic on your list server is going to be archived to the Web. One possible folder hierarchy you might employ is shown in Figure 15-4.

Note that Macintosh folders are equivalent to UNIX and Windows directories, and common Web usage refers to the information layout as a *directory hierarchy*. We will use the terms somewhat interchangeably. In general, I will use the term "folders" when discussing information layout from the Macintosh perspective and "directories" when discussing it from the Web perspective.

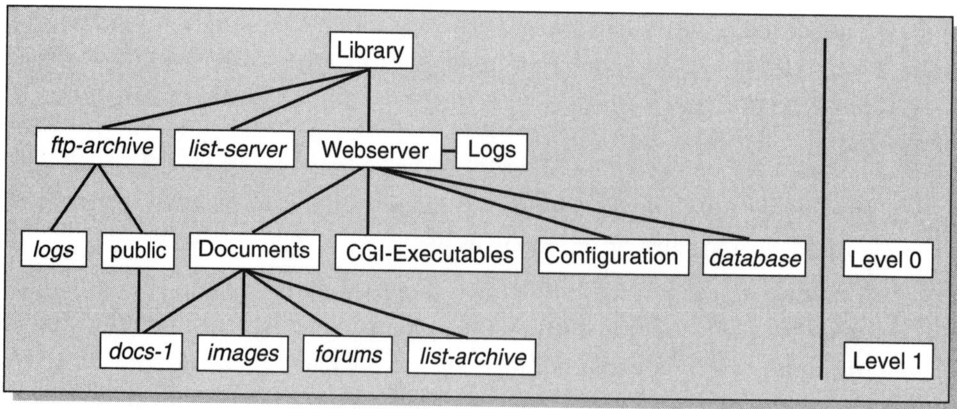

Figure 15-4. Example Folder Hierarchy for a Web Server.

The directory names shown in roman type are actual folder names defined by Mac OS X or the application software—they may or may not have the same names as in the figure—whereas italicized names may be folders or aliases to actual folders. An *alias* is a placeholder that allows an actual folder to appear to exist in two places in the folder hierarchy.

In Figure 15-4, the */Library/WebServer/Documents* folder is, for example, the default Mac OS X location for the information being served by your Web server. You should also note how few of these elements have predefined names. When setting up your folder structure, you may want to emulate these conventions so that others can more easily navigate and maintain your site. Folders linked into multiple parts of the hierarchy, such as *docs-1*, exist as a physical folder in one hierarchy and as an alias in the others.

This example server is arranged with information at different levels based on how general it is. The standard practice is to organize your information from most general to most specific. Within the */Library/WebServer* folder are subfolders for CGI scripts, along with files used by the database program (in this case) but not served directly. Within the */Library/WebServer/Documents* folder are usually the HTML file for the site's home page, a set of top-level Web pages, and any associated information used by those pages or any pages lower in the hierarchy, such as the data for this site's forums or mailing list archives.

Images of icons used by many pages should be placed in the *images* folder so they can be referenced by all documents lower in the tree by way of a relative path name. The relative path name maintains the virtual relationship even when the physical relationship changes. Following these guidelines will allow you to move the whole document tree without having to change references to other Web pages or images.

Note that the WebServer and *list-server* folders would most likely share the subfolder called *list-archive* in this example hierarchy. In Mac OS X, you would include your list archive within the *list-server* folder and place an alias in your Web documents, or vice versa. This organization makes it easy and logical for both your Web server and list server software to access the same folder; you don't have to remember that the archive files are in some other part of the file system.

Organizing Files by Service

It should be obvious that the rule of thumb used in the preceding example is to organize the types and locations of information on your server by service type. As another example, if you are running an e-mail server, an FTP server, and a Web server, you would probably organize your files into three groups.

E-mail Services

- Incoming mail for each user receiving e-mail
- E-mail messages converted to HTML for Web access
- Log files

FTP Services

- Generic FTP folders—public, incoming, outgoing, and so on
- Text, images, and compressed *.tar* files organized by subject areas
- Log files

Web Services

- HTML documents
- Images
- Multimedia files
- Configuration and administrative files
- Log files
- CGI scripts and other programs executed or downloaded through the information server

Such an organization is not mandatory, merely a way to think about the information types you will be faced with and how they might be arranged. On UNIX systems, for example, most service types map to a fairly standardized directory structure that has evolved over time. On the Macintosh server, the default location may vary. Each software package will create some specially named folders and configuration files, but most data folders and their relative placement on your hard drive are up to you as the server administrator.

The preceding simple classification is complicated by various subcategories of information. For example, you can think of subcategories of images associated with Web documents rather than grouping them as a single category. One subcategory is images used by many documents, for example, horizontal bars, arrows, and other basic icons seen in HTML documents. Another subcategory is images used in a specific group of Web documents, for example, a logo for a particular product. Finally, there are those images that will likely appear on only a single Web page. Organizing these subcategories of images should aim to minimize redundancy and make it easy to reference these images (if needed) as you add new pages.

Either Mac OS X or the software you are installing may impose constraints on how you organize your information. The Mac OS, for example, dictates where it wants the system Extensions and Preferences folders to be stored. These constraints can sometimes be overridden, but doing so may not be advisable. As a rule, do not change the default (that is, the recommended) folder and file layout of software you are installing unless there is a compelling reason to do so. Making changes can lead to a more significant installation and maintenance effort. If you have to make a technical support phone call, the supporter won't be familiar with your nonstandard installation, for example.

File Naming

Once you've imposed some level of organizational logic to your folders and files, you should give some thought to how you plan to name files as they're added to your site. Consistent file naming is an important aspect of information layout for three reasons:

1. It helps you recognize the information content of files.
2. It helps other people recognize the contents of your files.
3. It helps applications recognize the correct files upon which to act and, subsequently, how to act on them.

For Macintosh Web servers, reasons 2 and 3 also probably imply a change in your file naming habits. First, you should limit your use of punctuation marks and spaces in your file names, particularly if you intend for them to be shared across platforms. Second, you must use appropriate file extensions for files you intend to serve. Mac OS files include information about which applications can act upon them, and they indicate some of this information to you in icons. However, users on other platforms may not be provided with such visual cues, and most other operating systems and most Web browsers will not know how to act on a file that is missing the proper file extension.

This brings us back to MIME types, which were introduced in Chapter 3. Recall that a MIME type is a specification of particular types of files that are universally recognized by programmers and, hence, applications. Thus, *image/gif* is a registered MIME type for a graphical image in GIF format. This GIF file has associated with it an extension of *.gif*. The MIME specification registers the type of file and the file extension that is used by convention. Hence, Web browsers and Web servers understand the mapping of a file with an extension of *.gif* to the GIF MIME type and respond accordingly.

WEB DEVELOPMENT TOOLS

Now we've come to the fun part. Finally, you can start to think about developing actual Web pages. (I bet you thought we'd never get here.) Let's assume you have some information that you want to serve on your site. Let's also assume that you've used a software application to create or store that information on your computer. With the prevalence of the Web, it's almost a given that the software you're using has some features designed to get your work onto the Web or at least into Web-ready form.

You have to decide how much money you want or need to invest in additional tools to help you produce your Web site. Good tools exist for creating and publishing material for Web sites; if necessary, however, your HTML pages can be created and edited using the most basic text editor.

Development tools can be divided into site development, HTML editors, image editors, file converters, and site maintenance categories. The first category includes tools that help perform a wide range of development tasks, from page creating and editing to site management and maintenance. The tools in the next three categories generally focus on one task, either editing HTML pages, creating images, or converting files to HTML form. Finally, the last category recognizes that Web development is an ongoing process, and that keeping your site in order is as important as creating it in the first place.

Site Development Tools

As the Web has evolved, so have the challenges faced by Web developers. The initial challenge was simply to create individual HTML pages with correct HTML tags. Next, designers were faced with designing HTML pages that incorporated images as well as carefully formatted text. The challenges then quickly piled on—incorporating JavaScript for dynamic pages; integrating CGI scripts for working with forms, databases, and other enhancements; and managing large numbers of files.

As the challenges mounted, professional-level tools expanded their capabilities and grew from basic HTML editors to complete site development and management tools. These site development tools generally handle all aspects of the Web development challenge except for image creation and editing. Table 15-5 lists most of the high-end Web development tools. From my experience, if you spend time creating Web sites with more than a handful of pages, these tools quickly pay for themselves in the time saved and headaches avoided.

Table 15-5. Site Development Tools

Location	Description
www.macromedia.com/software/dreamweaver	Dreamweaver by Macromedia, Inc., has many advanced features, including work group collaboration.
www.softpress.com/freeway	Freeway by SoftPress Systems Limited brings a familiar desktop publishing environment to Web publishing.
manila.userland.com	Frontier, by UserLand Software, Inc., includes a Web content management system and the Manila group Web publishing tool.
www.adobe.com/products/golive	GoLive by Adobe Systems, Inc., has many advanced features, such as work group collaboration.
www.blueboxsw.com	Simple Site, shareware by Blue Box Software and Consulting, provides site management capabilities.
home.earthlink.net/~thomasareed/shareware/siteranger	SiteRanger by Thomas Reed, is a shareware tool that focuses on Web site management.

Of the tools listed, Adobe GoLive and Macromedia Dreamweaver are the leaders in this area. Both products have feature-equivalent versions for the Mac OS and Windows platforms. I have to admit being partial to GoLive because I've been using it since it was GoLive CyberStudio.

SoftPress System's Freeway comes at the problem from a different angle altogether and focuses on making the Web design process as familiar as the print design process for graphic designers. UserLand's Manila tool allows work groups to develop sites using a Web-based publishing and editing system, although working with the underlying Frontier system requires adopting a new mindset. Finally, Thomas Reed's SiteRanger and Blue Box's Simple Site slice out some of the site management features familiar to users of GoLive or Dreamweaver and make them available to developers who use other HTML editing tools.

Site Maintenance Utilities

The most noticeable error on any Web page is not necessarily a page with incorrect information, but a link within your site that returns an "Error: Page not found" message or a similar response. Most visitors will take such an error message as a sure sign that a site is not being maintained. To avoid this problem, you could plan to visit every link in your Web site regularly to make sure you haven't broken any links in the latest round of updates, but this could rapidly consume huge amounts of time if you're serving hundreds of pages.

A better solution is probably to take advantage of software tools that automatically check a Web site for broken links or missing pages. Most major Web site development tools, including Adobe GoLive and Macromedia Dreamweaver, let you verify that links within your pages point to valid locations. You can then fix bad links or add appropriate pages. Some search engines, such as Maxum Development's Phantom, will also report back any broken links as they crawl and index your Web site. If you choose not to use a site development application, there are software and online utilities to help you avoid broken links. A few of these are listed in Table 15-6.

HTML Editors and Optimizers

Perhaps your primary job responsibility is to maintain the Web server, but on occasion you need to make a few quick Web page fixes or create basic Web

Table 15-6. Site Maintenance Utilities

Location	Description
pauillac.inria.fr/~fpottier/brother.html.en	Big Brother, a freeware link validator by François Pottier.
www.matsumoto.co.jp	JChecker, a shareware link checker and HTML validator from Matsumoto and Company, Ltd. (Japan).
www.netmechanic.com	Net Mechanic, Inc., an online Web site maintenance and monitoring service.
vse-online.com/link-tester	VSE Link Tester by Voget Selbach Enterprises GmbH tests your site for bad links and malfunctioning features.
websitegarage.netscape.com	Web Site Garage by Netscape Communications is an online Web site tune-up service.

pages. Or perhaps you just want to create a simple page to show off your family vacation photos. In such situations, you don't really need all the features of the high-end professional tools. There are many textual and visual HTML editors with features that make it easy to create and edit basic Web pages.

The question to ask yourself is, "Does the HTML editor support the advanced features that I wish to use?" In fact, if you are comfortable writing HTML and don't have many occasions to edit Web pages, basic HTML can be relatively easy to edit with a standard text editor or word processor. However, text-based editors are available to make the editing process more pleasant. And visual, What You See Is What You Get (WYSIWYG) HTML editors simplify the creation and debugging of complex documents by presenting you with a final view of the Web page as you work.

When deciding whether to use an HTML editor, it helps to keep the following factors in mind:

- An HTML editor will shorten the development cycle.
- Documents produced using an HTML editor nearly always look better than those written directly in HTML, simply because most people do not remember all the syntax necessary to produce a high-quality document.

- The evolution of HTML is occurring faster than the editing software. Thus, some features in HTML may not be available to users of older tools.
- With visual editors, you can avoid the two-step process of coding and viewing.
- The code produced by WYSIWYG editors may be difficult to maintain and edit by hand. However, the code produced is getting better. On the other hand, the basic functionality of modern Web sites may demand complex combinations of HTML, JavaScript, Perl, and tool-specific tags.

In choosing an HTML editor, cost will undoubtedly play a major role. At the low end, you can learn HTML yourself and use SimpleText to edit the HTML code and view it in your browser. Cost: $0. Another low-cost option is to upgrade your word processor to a version that can produce HTML-formatted versions of your documents. This way, you can place images and format text and view the results in a Web browser.

HTML Text Editors

If cost is a major factor in your decision and you don't blush at the sight of naked HTML, you might consider investing in a low-cost, text-based editor. The primary advantage of these editors is a combination of closely controlling the HTML source without the tedium of typing the HTML tags. Among the text-based editors listed in Table 15-7, BBEdit is one of the few commercial editors and gets rave reviews from its users. Most of the other editors are shareware.

Visual Page Editors

Originally the only way to create Web pages was to buckle down and learn the necessary HTML. Today, many programs can create Web-ready HTML files with a visual interface in much the same way that word processors virtually eliminated text formatting languages and editors.

Visual Web page creators give you more precise control over the look of your pages while requiring very little HTML coding. Even here, though, features can vary widely. At the very least, the editors support text formatting, tables, and placement of GIF and JPEG images. More advanced features include support

Table 15-7. Text-Based HTML Editors

Location	HTML Editors
alpha.olm.net	Alpha, shareware by Pete Keleher.
www.barebones.com	BBEdit (commercial) and BBEdit Lite (freeware) from Bare Bones Software.
www.pinehillproducts.com/creativepage	Creative Page, shareware by Pine Hill Products.
www.htmlcreator.net	HTML Creator, shareware by Aram Kudurshian.
www.optima-system.com/pagespinner	PageSpinner, shareware from Optima Systems.
www.darkeagle.com	Wallaby, shareware by Dark Eagle Software.
www.miracleinc.com	World Wide Web Weaver and HTML Web Weaver Lite from Miracle Software, Inc.

for frames, pixel-level control of layout, and varying preview capabilities. At the highest end, the site development tools mentioned above include advanced visual page editors as part of their capabilities.

I probably don't have to sell you very hard on the merits of visual Web page editors. The question becomes which visual editor to choose. Since the previous version of this book was written, the selection of visual editors has changed dramatically. Most early tools have been phased out for the Mac, including Adobe PageMill, Symantec Visual Page, NetObjects Fusion, FileMaker (formerly Claris) Home Page, and SoftQuad's HoTMetaL Pro. It remains to be seen whether the release of Mac OS X results in the revival of any of these tools. The remaining low-cost visual editors are Microsoft FrontPage 1.0 and Netscape Composer. Neither has been substantially updated in several years, although they are still available for Macs running Mac OS 9 and earlier versions.

HTML Optimizers

If you use a visual Web page editor, you might have noticed that the HTML source code the application produces may not be ideal. Certainly, if you had the time you could go through every page and clean it up, but that would be so time-consuming that it defeats the purpose of using a visual editor and you won't get much further than wishing for more streamlined HTML source. Even if you use a text-based HTML editor, your HTML source might not be optimal. You probably add unnecessary white-space characters (spaces, tabs, carriage returns) and comments to make the code easier to maintain.

But every such character or less-than-ideal HTML construct adds to the time your Web visitors must wait for a page to download. And in the cutthroat world of the Web, a second here and a second there can add up. Enter the HTML optimizers, listed in Table 15-8.

These handy utilities take your automatically generated or carefully hand-formatted HTML source code and strip out anything unnecessary. The resulting HTML source code may not be easy to read, but it will be as small as it can get. Even a basic 5-kB HTML file might be crunched to three-quarters of its original size—those white-space characters add up.

The benefits grow with the size of your HTML documents. A 60-kB HTML document, which will take at least two seconds to download over a 33.6-kbps dial-up connection, might have its download time cut in half. Although the use of cable modems and DSL is growing, a second saved in download time might be another customer or repeat visitor earned.

File Conversion

One of the most direct ways to create information for your Web site is to convert files that may already exist in a variety of formats, such as word processing documents or spreadsheets, into HTML files. Most software applications these

Table 15-8. HTML Optimizing Utilities

Location	Description
spidernet.nl/~ton_brand/optimizer.htm	HTML Optimizer, shareware by Ton Brand.
www.maczsoftware.com/optimahtml.shtml	OptimaHTML, shareware by MacZ Software.
www.insidersoftware.com	SpaceAgent, a commercial HTML optimizer by Insider Software, Inc.
vse-online.com/web-site-turbo	VSE Web Site Turbo, a commercial HTML optimizer from Voget Selbach Enterprises GmbH.
www.blueline-studios.com	WebsiteCompressor, a commercial HTML optimizer by Blue Line Studios.

days provide a Save as HTML command if there is the slightest chance that a document created in the program might find itself on the Web.

In addition, *filters* are programs that translate one file format to another format—or for our discussion here, a non-Web format to a Web-deliverable format. There are a large number of filters available via the Internet. The trick is to not download those filters that you think you might need, but to wait until you need a filter and then download it. This way you get the most recent version when you need it. Table 15-9 provides a list of the more common HTML filters.

Filters are characterized by whether they filter word-processed documents, computer code, e-mail files, graphics, or other types of textual information. Again, you may not need these filters if you're using an application that can save documents in HTML format. Also worth mentioning is Terry Morse's Myrmidon, a virtual printer that "prints" to HTML and so can produce an HTML file from any application that can print.

Web Image Editors

Even though visual Web editors and site development tools help you place images on your Web pages, very few of them help you create and edit the images. Unless you plan to stock your Web pages entirely with clip art, you will need some sort of image editor to create your images. An image editor might range from a low-end graphics or photo retouching program—one was probably in-

Table 15-9. Common HTML Filters

Location	Information Type/Filter
www.logictran.com	RTF to HTML, shareware by Chris Hector.
www.extensis.com/beyondpress	BeyondPress, commercial software from Extensis for converting QuarkXPress documents.
www.msystems.com/websucker	Websucker, freeware for PageMaker from Multimedia Systems Consulting.
www.maczsoftware.com	HTML Converter, shareware from MacZ Software, converts special characters in a file to their corresponding HTML character codes.
www.terrymorse.com	Myrmidon, commercial software by Terry Morse that "prints" to HTML files from any application.

cluded in your Mac's software bundle—to professional graphics tools such as Adobe Photoshop.

As with desktop publishing, Web image creation remains a strong suit of the Mac. The tools that made Macs the platform of choice for professional designers have all been upgraded to provide varying degrees of support for the Web. The Web adds a new dimension to image creation, however, because it introduces the possibility of animating your graphics. No longer do the images have to sit still on a printed page; they can move across the page, disappear and reappear again, or spin in three dimensions.

I'll discuss this area only briefly, since again it digresses from this book's primary subject of establishing and running a Web server.

Still Image Editors

For the Web, you need an image editor that is capable of producing images in the formats recognized by Web browsers, which were discussed back in Chapter 3: GIF and JPEG for the basics, and PNG for more advanced Web uses. With the prevalence of the Web, virtually any graphics program worth its salt can produce at least GIF and JPEG graphics, and most graphics programs targeting Web designers can now create PNG images.

Table 15-10 lists some of the tools available from Adobe, including Photoshop and Illustrator, Macromedia, and a few other developers. Most of these products are available in professional and lower-cost standard or limited edition versions. I don't make any claims that this is a comprehensive or balanced selection. See Appendix A for resources that will point you to more complete lists of graphics programs.

Animation Editors

A unique feature of the Web, especially in comparison to print media, is the ability to display animated graphics. Animation can be used effectively to highlight important features of a page, attract attention to advertising, or add flexible navigation techniques to a Web site. If you're not careful, though, animation can easily be overused or abused. Blinking icons or gratuitous animation can distract or annoy a Web visitor.

In selecting the appropriate animation format, there are some general rules you can follow. If you're producing a full-color photographic or video anima-

Table 15-10. Still Image Editors

Location	Description
www.deneba.com	Canvas Professional and Standard Editions from Deneba Systems, Inc.
www.corel.com	CorelDRAW and free CorelDRAW Limited Edition from Corel Corporation.
www.macromedia.com	Fireworks and FreeHand from Macromedia, Inc.
www.graphicconverter.net	GraphicConverter from Lemke Software, shareware for converting images between dozens of formats.
www.adobe.com	Illustrator, Photoshop, Photoshop Limited Edition, and other image tools from Adobe Systems, Inc.

tion, you'll probably need to go with QuickTime or another video format. If you want to animate some line drawings, illustrations, or graphical Web page components, the Flash format may be the best way to go. If you want to guarantee almost universal viewing (as you might with banner advertising), at the sacrifice of some flexibility, you may want to use GIF animations.

In addition, there are other formats competing to be the next Flash. Typically, these formats are promoted by a software developer, which provides a free plug-in for viewing as well as a commercial tool for developing animations in that format. As a rule, you'll want to use these carefully. Unless you are intentionally creating a site with experimental features or have a site for which visitors are willing to work to see your graphics, such as Victoria's Secret, most Web visitors won't take the time to download a new plug-in. At the very least, you should prepare a fallback version of the site with a more widely used animation format.

GIF Animations. The original and still a commonly used animation format is animated GIF. From the perspective of a Web designer, an animated GIF image behaves just like a still GIF graphic. From the perspective of a Web client, an animated GIF image displays a series of still images in sequence. Depending on the speed at which the series displays, the animation can appear as a slide show or as a continuous, repeating animation.

The advantage of GIF animations is that virtually every graphical Web browser can display GIF animations without any additional software. Animated GIF images are also easy to create, and the software to create them is usually free or inexpensive. A few animated GIF utilities are listed in Table 15-11; many high-end animation packages will also export animated GIF images. The disadvantages of GIF animations include files that quickly balloon in size and choppy playback at different connection speeds. Finally, you can't add sound or interactivity to animated GIF images; they are playback-only.

Table 15-11. Animated GIF Utilities

Location	Description
vse-online.com/animation-maker	VSE Animation Maker, shareware from Voget Selbach Enterprises GmbH.
www.peda.com/ggg	Gif•gIf•giF, shareware from Pedagoguery Software Inc.
www.boxtopsoft.com	GIFmation, shareware from BoxTop Software, Inc.
www.totallyhip.com	WebPainter, a commercial tool from Totally Hip Software.
www.recosoft.com	WebShocker, a commercial tool from RecoSoft Corporation.

Flash. The Flash animation format, developed by Macromedia, has caught on as a widely used format with several available creating tools, including Macromedia Flash itself and Adobe LiveMotion. Flash has a number of advantages that add to its appeal. It permits streaming, so you don't have a long wait for the graphics to start; it is vector-based, so the file sizes are compact. The format produces high-quality animations with sound and interactivity, and the latest browsers support Flash without a plug-in.

However, as a disadvantage, all but the newest browsers require a plug-in to view Flash animations. In addition, the vector-based imagery limits the type of graphics you can use. It doesn't work well with photographs, for example.

QuickTime, Shockwave, and DHTML. GIF animations and Flash are the two main formats for creating animated illustrations, but animated effects can also be created with QuickTime, Shockwave, and DHTML. If you need to work with animating photographic-quality images, you are approaching the realm of video and should consider a video format such as QuickTime. Macromedia's Shockwave predates Flash and supports many of the same features, but Shockwave is not a Web-native format. Originally targeted at designing interactive CD-ROMs, its ancestry limits Shockwave's flexibility on the Web. For example, you can't incorporate Shockwave animation as part of a Web page, as you can with Flash. Finally, DHTML lets the browser do the animating. Using JavaScript, you can animate the text and graphics of a Web page. One advantage here is that the components of the Web page can be indexed and searched by standard search engines.

Table 15-12 lists some high-end software for creating Web animations. In most cases, these tools can export many different formats and can help you choose which format is the best to use for a particular situation.

Table 15-12. Web Animation Software

Location	Description
www.macromedia.com	Flash from Macromedia, the original tool for developing Flash animations.
www.adobe.com	LiveMotion from Adobe, Adobe's entry into Web animation development.
www.beatware.com	e-Picture Pro and eZ-Motion from Beatware, Inc., highly rated Web animation tools.

Design Basics

The "design" of a Web page—its "look and feel"—is created in a process that, when done well, merges techniques and skills from both graphic design and computer interface design. The terms "look" and "feel," as applied to Web pages, are often clumped together, but for our purposes, this book will consider "look" to mean the graphic design of a Web page and "feel" to mean the organization of the site and the relationships among all the pages.

Look affects how easy it is to read a page, and feel affects how easy it is to navigate and, hence, find the correct information. We've talked a lot in this chapter and others about planning your site to achieve the best feel. The feel of your site is largely responsible for your site's success at keeping visitors and making them happy.

The look of your site accomplishes different but complementary roles. The look is the first impression your site makes on a visitor. Your site's look can suggest the level of professionalism of your company, the your site's hipness factor, or the attention you've paid to your own Web site. Over the longer term, the look of your site can make visitors feel comfortable, can help you build name and brand recognition for your site, or can irritate visitors with gratuitous animation and perplexing navigation and send them fleeing to other sites.

Graphic design for the Web is a topic that, once again, I am not going to pretend I can cover in one section of a chapter. There are numerous books on the subject, and if you are truly serious about your site's design, this is a task best left to professionals. What I can provide are some rules of thumb that will help those of you who aren't graphic designers keep your site looking professional with a minimum of fuss.

Web Colors

A lot of your site's design can be accomplished with the basic HTML tags and attributes that allow you to control the color of the background, text, links, and other components of your pages. With more advanced HTML tags, you can control the color of individual letters, phrases, or sections of text, as well as tables or table cells. The goal in changing colors from the browser defaults is to create an attractive and distinctive page that is easy to read. The first trick is performing an honest assessment of whether or not *you* can choose attractive colors that match. The second trick is to find colors that not only make the text easy to read, but also appear the same across many browsers and platforms.

Colors in HTML are specified by a six-digit hexadecimal (base 16) value. If you do not know hexadecimal numbering, the sixteen digits are 0–9 and A–F, with A=10, B=11, and so on, to F=15. The color format is then six digits 0–F in the format *#rrggbb,* where *rr, gg,* and *bb* are the hexadecimal values for the red, green, and blue components of the color, respectively. The term "Web-safe palette" is used to describe the set of 216 colors that display consistently across most platforms. Web-safe colors are those defined by mixing and matching 00, 33, 66, 99, CC, and FF as the red, green, and blue values (6 × 6 × 6 = 216).

If you stick with these colors, you can be sure that your page colors will look the same across platforms. (But other elements of the design may change!) Table 15-13 lists some sites that help you choose color schemes for your Web pages. If you stray from the 216 Web-safe colors, be aware that what appears as a great color scheme on one display may be unreadable on another type of display.

Browsers or client displays may "round" other values to the nearest Web-safe color, which may alter the effect you are looking for. For example, a page may look fine on a color monitor but be unreadable on a laptop display with the standard 256-color laptop palette.

Because hexadecimal numbers are not always easy to remember, Internet Explorer and Netscape Navigator both support named colors. Initially, Explorer recognized 16 named colors, but Netscape soon upped the ante, supporting several hundred named colors, from "aliceblue" to "lavenderblush" to "yellowgreen." However, very few of the named colors come from the 216 Web-safe colors. Use these other colors with care.

As a rule, test your Web pages on as many display types and as many Web browsers as possible to ensure they are readable before releasing them to the world.

Basic Design Guidelines

In this section, I'll provide a list of guidelines that I have found useful in designing Web pages. If you forget all the items on this list, just remember that your ultimate goal is to transfer the maximum amount of information in the most effective way. If a design feature does not transfer any information, you should seriously ask yourself why it is necessary.

Table 15-13. Choosing Web-Safe Colors

Location	Description
www.hidaho.com/colorcenter	ColorCenter JavaScript application to sample color combinations from a palette or specify colors in hexadecimal, decimal, or percentage form.
www.imagitek.com/bcs.html	A basic form for entering hexadecimal colors and previewing a page's color scheme from Imagitek Network Graphic Design.
www.autek.com/pub_html/colors.html	More than 470 named colors and codes, provided by Jack Holden. Slow to download, since each color sample is an image.
nuthinbutlinks.com/colors.htm	Links to color-choosing tools from Nuthin' but Links.

As a reminder, before starting the design process, you should have planned how to organize the information. First, you need to understand your intended audience, as described in Chapter 3. How are visitors to your site going to want to view this information? How will they likely discover the components that they are interested in? Once you have contemplated the answers to these questions, you need to relate those answers to the following practical questions:

- What are the logical chunks of information I should be serving?
- How should those chunks be referenced: as static HTML files, in a forum or other interactive service, as data served from a database, or in some other format?
- What links should I establish between those chunks of information? In other words, what are the various views that people seeking the information are going to want, and therefore, what pathways should I set up for them to follow?

Once you've considered these preliminary factors, you can design your pages. Again, this may be a step best left to a professional, but if you can't afford to hire a designer, I've included some basic tips to set you on the path to a neatly designed site.

Color, Text, and Images

- Use a white background and black body text. Don't even think about other combinations. You won't be pushing the design envelope, but no one will complain either. Perhaps you can get away with colored headlines, but use them sparingly.
- Keep a rein on your color choices. Aside from full-color photographs, limit your color palette to two or three matching colors for highlights.
- Once you choose a design, stick with it. Don't change the colors, font faces, and font sizes from page to page. Style sheets are useful in maintaining a consistent look throughout your site.
- Keep your site accessible. Remember that not everyone will visit your site from a Mac or PC with a 21-inch monitor and millions of screen colors. For text-only browsers such as those in personal digital organizers or those used by visually impaired persons, provide alternative

text for images, avoid image-only navigation links, and don't use color as the only clue in providing information.

- Be selective in using images. Fewer images mean faster download times for visitors on slow connections. Fewer images also mean a less cluttered look.
- No image is better than a bad image. Don't kill yourself looking for cheesy clip art. This also applies to text presented as an image. If the text isn't properly anti-aliased and well designed, you're better off sticking with HTML-based text.
- Don't rely on icons as navigation clues. In fact, unless you're a professional designer, you're much better off not creating or using icons at all. Icon-only navigation presents too many opportunities for miscommunication. Text-based navigation (whether that text is in HTML or in a graphic) offers a much greater chance of success.
- Stick to basic image formats. Unless your goal is to showcase a new image format or cutting-edge Web techniques, go with JPEG or GIF images.

Navigation Aids

- Make your home page self-explanatory, yet concise, and insert links to all the major sections of your site. Add links back to the home page from pages lower in the hierarchy. A common convention is to have a home page link in the upper left corner of every page.
- Conventional publishing techniques remain very effective navigation guides—an index (or site map), a table of contents, and so forth.
- Don't forget the page title. Make the title as informative as possible, since this is what users will see in their lists of bookmarks or favorites. To avoid confusion, be sure that the page title in the <title> tag is consistent with the headline on the page itself.
- Avoid using the header tags <h1> through <h7> for anything other than headings. Using header tags for other purposes, such as changing the font size, destroys the logical structure of the document that headers were intended to preserve. This will come back to haunt you as XHTML becomes the norm and in large documents in which the

header levels are useful markers and are likely to be used later, for example, by a tool that automatically generates a table of contents for a fast-growing document.

- Avoid the phrase "Click here." Browsing does not necessarily require a mouse, and so the term may be meaningless. More importantly, the phrase is redundant, does not add useful information, and draws attention away from the description of where you might go, since you have to read back to figure out why to "click here."
- Don't turn off the underlines for text links in the Web browser display. Although it's possible to turn off underlined links with style sheets, underlined text is the convention most widely used to identify links. Removing the underlines removes a powerful visual cue.
- In long pages, use named links and anchors to navigate backward and forward to appropriate points in the page. For example, named links supplement scrolling by immediately taking you backward or forward to appropriate sections in the document.

Web Design and Style Guides

I realize that my ad hoc list of tips is not going to win you any Webby awards. But without going into another book's worth of information, I've given you about all the information I have right now. After all, I'm not a designer. I just pretend I'm one every once in a while. For more detailed treatments on Web style and design, you should consult some of the references in Table 15-14.

Table 15-14. Web Style Guides

Location	Description
www.w3.org/Provider/Style	The style guide from the W3 Consortium.
www.useit.com	Useit.com, Jakob Nielsen's Web site on useable information technology.
www.webeditor.org	WebEditor.org, by Alexander J. Storey.
www.wpdfd.com	*Web Page Design for Designers,* by Joe Gillespie.
info.med.yale.edu/caim/manual	*Web Style Guide,* by Patrick J. Lynch and Sarah Horton.

How *Not* to Do It

The most important advice I can offer for the amateur Web page designer is this: Just because you *can* do something on a Web page doesn't mean you *should*. For example, you *can* use yellow text on a magenta background, but for crying out loud, *don't*. The same goes for blinking text, animated GIF icons, background images, and scrolling marquees. Gone are the days when people would be impressed with your extensive knowledge of HTML tags. These days, it's just plain annoying.

So if the *only* reason you're adding a design feature to your Web site is either (1) you can or (2) it's cool, take a deep breath, count to 10, and save the feature for the bloopers page. Table 15-15 points you to some Web sites that will introduce you to bad Web design, so you won't inflict it upon others.

Table 15-15. How Not to Design Web Pages

Location	Description
www.webpagesthatsuck.com	*Web Pages That Suck*, a Web site and book by Vincent Flanders.
webdevelopersjournal.com/columns/perpend1.html	"How to Build Lame Sites," by Charlie Morris, at *Web Developer's Journal.*
www.users.nac.net/falken/annoying	"How to Make an Annoying Web Page," by Stevyn Falken.
jeffglover.com/ss.php	"Sucky to Savvy," by Jeffrey M. Glover.

CHAPTER 16

FUTURE WEB

I feel obligated to include this chapter on where the Web is heading so that it sounds like I have the ability to extract patterns from the seemingly chaotic sprawl of technologies on today's Web. Well, I don't. Based on a similar chapter in my previous book, *Mac OS 8 Web Server Cookbook,* my predictive powers are no better than random chance—about 50-50.

In that book I predicted correctly that Mac OS X would be the future of Mac Web serving and that vanilla HTML would be superseded by DHTML, CSS, and XML. Granted, I wasn't really going out on a limb with those predictions. On the other hand, I also wrote that you should watch out for push technology and Web channels. I also promised that we'd all soon be collaborating in virtual classrooms and conference rooms. Instead, push technology fizzled completely, and companies latched onto portals, which are still evolving, and business-to-business (B2B), which is having a rough time of it. As for collaboration, it hasn't happened yet, but Web forums, chat rooms, and Internet telephony continue to move us in that direction. It may be too early to tell what form collaboration will eventually take.

For this book, I debated whether to take another stab at prognostication. Part of my frustration lies in the realization that no matter how hard I try, the Web will keep evolving out my of reach. And not just slightly beyond my grasp. There's the very real possibility that I could wake up one morning to find that the Web has transmogrified into some completely different creature, with HTML consigned to the digital dustbin of history, GIF and JPEG two archaic graphic formats, and dot-com businesses that actually turn a profit.

In the not too distant future, you may find yourself creating Web pages that incorporate the Mind Reading Markup Language (MRML), an incredibly useful if not currently usable HTML extension (*www.oxy.edu/~ashes/mrml.html*). Laugh now, but the Web is taking steps in this direction.

Cookies and customizable portals let Web pages "remember" who you are. Online directories, mapping services, grocery club card profiles, and information brokers have all sorts of data about you. One day, you'll be passing through a brand new online mall looking for a pair of water skis, and the Web site will ask you, "Hey, have you bought anything for your mom's birthday? She wants a pair of inline skates." There are already sites that will let you set reminders like that. It won't be long before you get a reminder whether you want one or not.

WEB ANYWHERE AND EVERYWHERE

I don't have to worry about this prediction coming true. It's almost here. For those of you who have digital personal communications services (PCS) or cellular phones, handheld personal digital assistants (PDAs), or Ricochet modems for your laptops, you're already experiencing the beginnings of Web anywhere and everywhere. More and more, webmasters will have to worry about how their sites appear on a wide variety of displays, often just an inch or two across.

As a webmaster or Web designer, you might be thinking to yourself, "How do I design a Web site for a screen that's half a dozen text lines high and maybe 20 characters across?" As a sometime Web designer myself, I was close to believing that, finally, everyone who is anyone will soon have a screen resolution of at least 800 pixels wide by 600 pixels high. Those are dimensions I can work with. But now, do webmasters have to worry about screens the size of postage stamps? The answer is yes and no.

You may not have to worry about wireless devices right away, and certainly, not all information is relevant to wireless users. Eventually, though, the wireless Web will become a force to be reckoned with. Some sources estimate there are 300 million mobile phone users worldwide today—about double the number of current Internet users—with some predictions calling for 530 million wireless subscribers by the end of 2001, when wireless industry analysts are predicting there could be as many as 21 million mobile data users in the United States alone.

Wireless Data Transmission

The first step in creating the wireless Web is to connect wireless devices to the wired Web. At the start of the 21st century, a number of wireless data network providers were competing to become the standard bearers for the wireless Web infrastructure.

Let me clarify that I'm talking here about wireless wide-area networks. Don't confuse this discussion with wireless local-area networks, which are becoming common in offices and homes through technologies such as Apple's AirPort, or wireless personal-area networks, which the Bluetooth technology is working toward. If you're not familiar with these technologies, I'll elaborate briefly.

AirPort and similar technologies replace the cables that run from network routers and other access points to individual computers with a base station with which each computer communicates via radio waves. A wireless base station has a range of about 50 meters.

Bluetooth technology works over shorter distances. You can think of Bluetooth as the replacement for the annoying tangle of cables required to link your computer, mouse, keyboard, printer, external drives, PDAs, and other peripherals. For example, instead of needing a USB cradle to sync your iMac with your Palm OS–based organizer, you would simply bring your PDA near your iMac and they would be connected. Bluetooth works over a distance of up to 10 meters.

The wireless Web, however, requires the ability for devices (and their owners) to roam over distances measured in miles or even entire countries. Instead of wires, these companies provide antennas and relay points—the wireless network equivalent of fiber-optic cables—that allow wireless devices to be online anywhere. Each technology requires its own wireless modems and antennas. It's likely that at some point there will be a convergence, but in the meantime, the following technologies are part of the mix:

- Global Systems for Mobile (GSM) communications is a digital cellular or PCS standard used throughout the world and the de facto standard in Europe.
- Cellular Digital Packet Data (CDPD) is a packet data protocol designed to work over the original cellular network or as a protocol for Time Division Multiple Access (TDMA) cellular networks. CDPD and TDMA are sometimes used interchangeably.
- Code Division Multiple Access (CDMA), developed by Qualcomm, is a spread-spectrum air-interface technology used in some digital cellular, PCS, and other wireless networks.
- Other entries include Mobitex networks, used in 23 countries, including in the United States by BellSouth Wireless Data, and Metricom's U.S.-based Ricochet network.

Table 16-1 contains pointers to further information on the various options. How do you choose your wireless network connection? Good question. In some areas you may not have a choice. Since the growth of these networks is focused on urban areas, you may not have any choice if you live in a more rural area. In other areas, you may only have one choice. In some cases, your choice of wireless device may automatically select your wireless network.

For example, if you purchase a Palm VII organizer, you can connect to Palm.net, which is a service that runs over the BellSouth Wireless Data network. If you want to connect other Palm or Handspring organizers, you need to purchase a wireless modem, such as those available for OmniSky, which connects to AT&T Wireless Services' CDPD network. If you need a wireless connection to your PowerBook or other laptop, Metricom's Ricochet network is the primary provider of services for portable computers as well as handhelds.

Table 16-1. Wireless Data Transmission Networks

Location	Description
www.wirelessdata.org	Wireless Data Forum.
www.wow-com.com	World of Wireless Communications from the Cellular Telecommunications Industry Association.
www.mdi-ng.org	Mobile Data Initiative, next generation (MDI-ng), information on GSM and PCS.
www.attws.com	AT&T Wireless Services, a major CDPD provider.
www.cdg.org	CDMA Development Group.
www.ricochet.net	Ricochet by Metricom, Inc.
www.mobitex.org	Mobitex Operators Association.
www.wirelessweek.com	Wireless Week from Cahners Business Information.

WAP and WML

No matter which wireless network technology your visitors use, the wireless Web introduces further issues for webmasters. To handle both users of computing devices with "normal" screens—including desktops, laptops, and Web-surfing appliances—and users of wireless devices, the trick is to limit the data you send to different categories of devices. And there is another significant reason to be selective in what you send to wireless Web surfers: bandwidth. If a household cable modem is comparable to a fire hose of data, wireless devices are listening at the business end of an eyedropper.

Faced with these discrepancies, the Web industry seems to have converged on a rather sensible conclusion: The tools used to communicate with traditional Web devices are not sufficient for wireless devices. Enter WAP, the Wireless Application Protocol. WAP, in essence, is the wireless replacement for not only Web interactions (normally conducted via HTTP) but also lower-level networking protocols when TCP/IP does not make sense. WAP is a standard backed by the WAP Forum, whose members represent more than 95 percent of the global handset market and include Palm Computing, Motorola, Qualcomm, and Sprint PCS.

But WAP is only half the answer. The other half is the wireless parallel to HTML, the language of Web pages. In a fit of creativity, the WAP community christened the new language the Wireless Markup Language (WML). WML is based on XML and is intended to specify content and user interface for wireless devices that are constrained by a small display and limited user input facilities, a low-bandwidth network connection, and limited memory and computational resources. The specification for WML, currently at version 1.2, is available from the WAP Forum site, listed in Table 16-2.

WML introduces a new metaphor for organizing your information. In contrast to the "pages" of information viewed from a Web browser, WML uses "cards" that are collected into "decks." A WML deck is similar to an HTML page in that it is identified by a URL and is the unit of data delivered in response to a single request. A card specifies one or more units of user interaction, such as a choice menu, a screen of text, or a text entry field. Logically, a user navigates through a series of WML cards, enters requested information or makes choices, and moves on to another card. Choosing an option that links to another URL will load another deck. There's even a wireless subset of JavaScript called WMLScript.

WAP and WML present an opportunity for Mac webmasters to reach new audiences (or old audiences connecting to the Web in new ways). The efforts of the WAP Forum seem to be on track to provide standard protocols and languages for wireless Web browsing. Late last year, for example, the WAP Forum and the W3 Consortium announced a formal liaison relationship to define next-generation Web specifications that support the full participation of wireless devices on the Web. In large part, this will be accomplished by including WML features into XHTML. Table 16-2 lists further resources for information on WAP and WML.

In short, the number of wireless users is growing rapidly, as people make use of even the limited bandwidth to wireless devices to make Internet connectivity an integral part of their lives. If you're not quite ready to leap into this world yet, you can still take away an important message: Millions of people find the Web useful even when pages are presented as plain text on a screen two inches square. This fact should clearly tell you that the information you are serving and its organization are just as important as, if not more important than, its presentation.

Table 16-2. WAP and WML Resources

Location	Description
www.wapforum.org	The WAP Forum.
www.w3.org/Mobile	The W3 Consortium's mobile access activity.
www.wirelessdevnet.com	Wireless Developer Network.
allnetdevices.com/faq	The Wireless FAQ from allNetDevices.com.
builder.cnet.com/Authoring/WAPUp	"WAP Up Your Site" by Jacob McKee at CNET's Builder.com.

COLLABORATION AND CONTROL

Developers are continuing to extend the Web for collaborating among groups. A *collaborative environment* tries to replicate the feel and interactions of a face-to-face meeting from a collection of remote groups and the Internet. In a very broad sense, the Web is, by definition and original intent, a collaboration environment developed to allow physicists to exchange information. When you add the capabilities of forums, chat rooms, and Web cams, you have a collaboration environment that's virtually equivalent to getting a group of people together for a meeting in the same room. Well, almost, but not quite.

The difference between the Web and a meeting in a conference room (or even a videoconference or conference call) lies in the nature of the interaction. With meetings and phone calls, the interaction is immediate. One person's question, statement, or overhead transparency generates responses—questions, nods of agreement, or quizzical looks, for example—from the other participants.

Initially, many Web collaboration projects attempted to define Web forms, pages, and processes that mimic as closely as possible the methods by which groups of people work on the same task. However, these environments lack immediate feedback. A message would be posted to a threaded message area, or a document would be made available in a restricted download area for comments. These sorts of environments can provide useful collaboration for some tasks, such as joint editing of documents, and may be the most cost-effective solution for a large, geographically dispersed group.

But the Web marches on. In the two years since the *Mac OS 8 Web Server Cookbook* was published, there have been many advances in Web-based collaboration. Several companies are now providing commercial software and services to make it possible. In addition, many research projects continue to push the boundaries of Internet-based collaboration.

Collaboration Today

Web collaboration today does, in fact, combine many of the capabilities that are provided by chat rooms, the cross-platform Java technology, instant messaging, and other existing Web technologies. Several companies are making commercial ventures of Web-based collaboration, either hosting collaboration servers or providing software to establish a company's own collaboration server. Table 16-3 lists some of today's Web collaboration options.

Commercial Options

DocuShare from Xerox, as the name suggests, is a document sharing system rather than a real-time collaboration environment, but DocuShare offers a Web-based interface to a company's shared documents. Documents can be made publicly available or restricted to viewing and editing by certain registered users. A key feature of DocuShare is its version-control and history-tracking system, which allows many persons to collaborate on editing a single document without overwriting others' changes. It also lets you extract older versions of a document for comparison or a global Undo back through several editing steps.

Table 16-3. Web Collaboration Today

Location	Description
www.carracho.com	Carracho, freeware from Carracho Communications GbR.
docushare.xerox.com	DocuShare by Xerox Corporation.
www.evoke.com	Evoke Communications, Inc.
www.bigredh.com	Hotline Connect, freeware from Hotline Communications, Ltd.
www.webwisdom.com	TANGO Interactive from WebWisdom.com, Inc.
www.w3.org/Collaboration	W3C pages on Web-based collaboration.
www.webex.com	WebEx Communications, Inc.

Evoke Communications and WebEx Communications offer various types of virtual meetings, hosted through their own servers. Meeting capabilities range from displaying presentations to Web audiences in concert with a phone-based conference call, leading tours of a Web site, demonstrating software live, and sharing an application on your system to synchronizing slides with streaming video and creating an online video library. TANGO Interactive (with related products from WebWisdom.com) is a product that lets you create your own Web collaboration environment by assembling modules that provide many of the same features.

Carracho

For those on a budget, there are two freeware options that provide a lower-tech, but still interesting, subset of the Web meeting environment. Hotline Connect and Carracho use their own Internet application protocols to provide real-time chat rooms, messaging, forums, and file exchange. Instead of adding capabilities to your Web server, Hotline Connect and Carracho have their own servers through which your Web audience interacts with dedicated client software.

While Hotline Connect is the older of the two freeware community and collaboration servers, I present Carracho here because it was the first available for Mac OS X. (Hotline Connect had client and server applications only for the Classic Mac OS at the time of writing.) As mentioned above, Carracho requires its own server software *and* its own client software. This requirement can be both an advantage and a disadvantage. On the plus side, you don't have to establish a Web server with FTP, news, chat, and forum capabilities to get all the capabilities offered by a Carracho server. On the down side, your viewers have to download special client software instead of using their Web browsers to access your virtual community.

Figure 16-1 shows some of the features of a Carracho server, as seen through the Carracho client. The client presents windows for each activity—not all of which have to be viewed at once, as is the case in this image. You can view the users who are connected to the server, participate in public chats, start private conferences, send person-to-person messages, explore a file archive, post messages to newsgroups, and transfer files between the client and server.

Carracho and Hotline Connect do not have some of the features available through the commercial Web meeting options. You can't make a PowerPoint presentation to an audience of Carracho viewers, incorporate video, or share

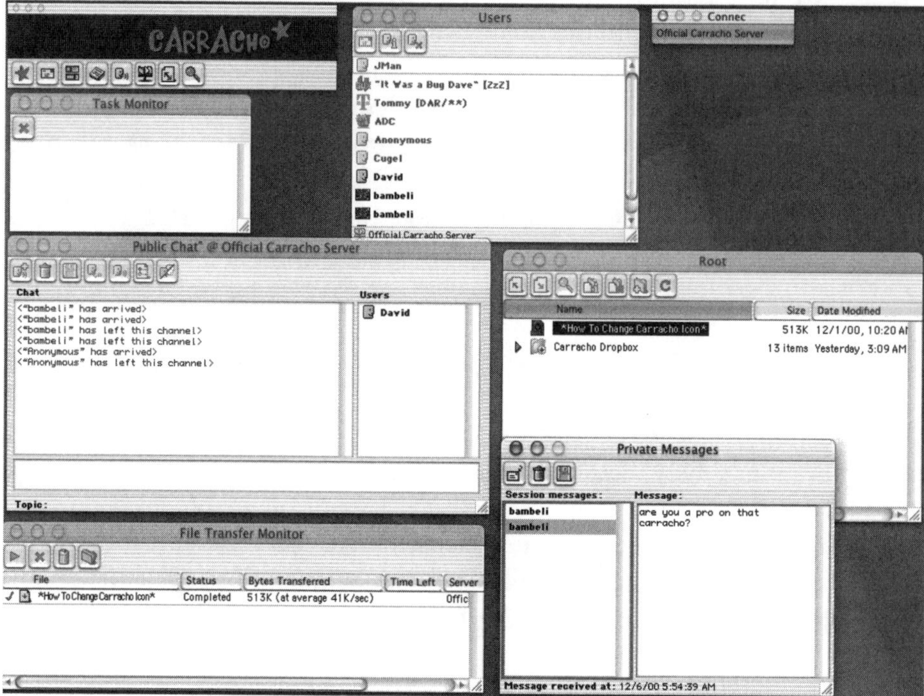

Figure 16-1. Collaboration with Carracho.

your desktop or a working application. However, by connecting to a Carracho server, you automatically can participate in a surprisingly wide range of community activities. On the server side, you can provide these capabilities to your own community by double-clicking on a single application icon rather than installing a Web server and a half-dozen server add-ons or additional servers. Ease of use is one of the major advantages of Carracho and Hotline Connect.

Collaboration Tomorrow

Since I know a number of the groups working on the projects that I've categorized as tomorrow's Web collaboration in Table 16-4, let me state for the record that these efforts do work today. However, the reason I've classified them as projects to watch is because they're not yet for everybody. The efforts below are research projects that have a limited number of users or that require a great deal of technical support to ensure their successful operation. You'll have to wait a

Table 16-4. Web Collaboration Tomorrow

Location	Description
www.accessgrid.org	Access Grid, developed and coordinated by Argonne National Laboratory.
www-ncmir.ucsd.edu/CMDA	Collaboratory for Microscopic Digital Anatomy (CMDA) at UC San Diego.
www.cerc.wvu.edu	Concurrent Engineering Research Center at West Virginia University.
vision.lbl.gov	DeepView from the Imaging and Collaborative Computing Group at Lawrence Berkeley National Laboratory.
mice.sdsc.edu	Molecular Interactive Collaborative Environment (MICE) project at SDSC.

few years before you can buy these products at your neighborhood discount electronics superstore.

These projects are exploring such future capabilities as collaboration in 3-D worlds, interaction with online data collections, remote control of scientific instrumentation, and multisite, two-way, audio-video-data conferencing.

Access Grid

The Access Grid, developed by Argonne National Laboratory and its partners, takes Internet meetings to another level. Whereas today's Web meeting capabilities focus on bringing individuals (or individual desktop computers) together, the Access Grid emphasizes group-to-group collaboration. In addition, the Access Grid permits real-time interaction not only with computer presentations but also with high-end research software and hardware.

Large-scale scientific and technical collaborations often involve multiple teams working together, and the Access Grid is exploring and supporting the more complex requirements and needs of such groups. Each group in an Access Grid event participates through a "node," which is a room or similar space that is designed to handle the high-end audio and video technology needed. An Access Grid node consists of a large-format multimedia display, presentation and interaction software environments, several high-resolution projectors, remotely controlled digital video cameras, microphones and speakers, high-speed network connections, interfaces to remote application and visualization environments, and usually several technicians standing by.

Each group in an Access Grid event views the same large display on which all the other participant groups are seen and heard, as well as the relevant presentations or software windows. With these resources, the Access Grid supports large-scale distributed meetings, collaborative teamwork sessions, seminars, lectures, tutorials, and training. At the SC2001 conference, the annual conference of high-end computing and networking, the Access Grid will be used (or was used, if you're reading this after November 2001) to make this sort of group-to-group collaboration part of a major scientific conference.

Telescience

Two projects listed in Table 16-4 are extending Web collaboration beyond the realm of networked computers. The Collaboratory for Microscopic Digital Anatomy (CMDA) at the University of California, San Diego, and DeepView at Lawrence Berkeley National Laboratory's Imaging and Collaborative Computing Group are environments that allow researchers to collaborate in real time not only with one another, but also with a computer-controlled electron microscope.

While the projects differ in their implementation details, both accomplish similar goals. Because high-voltage electron microscopes are expensive and relatively scarce scientific instruments, researchers must often schedule time to examine their specimens and travel to the site of the microscope to view the high-resolution images. When researchers are collaborating on a project, they must all travel to the microscope.

CMDA and DeepView are designed to make it possible to eliminate the need for researchers to travel to and from the same location in order to work together. Through software, geographically separated researchers can control the specimen stage of the electron microscope and capture detailed images over the network.

In other words, the collaborative environments created by these projects include not only the human researchers but also the necessary real-world instruments. The same concepts will also likely be extended to other expensive, scarce instruments, such as telescopes or particle accelerators.

Worldwide Computing

Another step beyond collaboration and Web serving is to combine the computing power of all these computers on the Internet to tackle complex problems or work together in some organized fashion. Web servers are very independent creatures; no Web server depends on the existence of any other Web server to do its job. In the same way, Web clients are also independent, with no single Web surfer's activities impinging on any others, aside from perhaps the effect of too many surfers bogging down a particular Web server.

The concept of a *computing grid* is based on the idea that every server and every client connected to the Internet is a potential source of computing power. In some sense, the situation is analogous to that of the electrical power grid, in which electrical power plants contribute their generated power to the grid rather than sending a particular watt of energy to a particular consumer. For computing grids the trick is to get a computer to contribute its unused processing cycles to the collective grid.

Distributed Computing

The most common approach for accessing this collective computing power is often called *distributed computing*. The distributed.net organization was one of the first to harness this power to crack supposedly unbreakable encryption schemes. The simplest way to break an encryption scheme is to try every possible key, which could mean trying billions or trillions of numbers. A time-consuming task, to be sure, but it becomes less daunting if you can apply hundreds of thousands of computers to the task.

After several successes, the SETI@home project put distributed computing in the headlines. Cracking esoteric codes is one thing, but searching for signs of alien communication is something else entirely. SETI@home, which also works as a screen saver, produces visually appealing, if unintelligible, graphics as it works.

Today, a number of companies are trying to turn such volunteer efforts into profitable ventures. By providing computing client software and offering incentives to participate, companies such as Entropia and Parabon are trying to make distributed computing a more generally useful tool for solving complex scientific problems. The grassroots distributed.net and SETI@home projects are much more ecumenical, and volunteers with those projects have created clients for virtually any operating system you can name, including Mac OS X. The commercial Entropia and Parabon efforts only ran under Windows at the time of writing, although Parabon noted that Macintosh, Linux, and UNIX versions were under development.

Computing Grids

The advantages of distributed computing techniques include their ability to enlist many computers to tackle a single problem. There are disadvantages, however. Two major ones include the inability to know how long it will take to solve a given problem and the difficulty of breaking a complex problem into bite-sized pieces that can be farmed out to a computing collective.

But the disadvantages don't mean that computing grids can't be used in such cases. Research projects, such as Globus and Legion, and related tools make it possible to treat large numbers of computers as a giant, unified virtual computer. In particular, with Globus and Legion you can get dedicated access to the power of supercomputers (as opposed to spare cycles from desktop systems) that are located across the country or around the world. This solution addresses the two major concerns. You can guarantee or specify the amount of computing power that must be brought to bear on a given problem, and you don't have to chop the computation into microscopic chunks.

If you'll pardon the simplification, both Globus and Legion aim to become the "operating system" for a group of supercomputers in much the same way that Mac OS X is the operating system for a single iMac or Power Mac computer. Globus and Legion are undertaking the task of hiding the geographic distance, software differences, and operating system idiosyncrasies that a scientist might face in attempting to use an arbitrary collection of supercomputers for his or her research.

In the most advanced form of grid computing, all the details of the underlying hardware could be hidden from the computer user. A scientist could focus on science, or a businessperson on business, without having to worry about how to use a particular computer or even what computer is being used. The SDSC GridPort project and other tools listed in Table 16-5 are being created to help application developers create such interfaces to complex scientific programs.

Table 16-5. Computing Grids and Distributed Computing Information

Location	Description
www.computefarm.com	Compute Farms from Blackstone Technology Group.
distributed.net	Distributed.net, a grassroots organization that cracks encryption schemes.
www.entropia.com	Entropia 2000 from Entropia, Inc.
www.gridforum.org	Global Grid Forum.
www.globus.org	The Globus Project.
legion.virginia.edu	The Legion Worldwide Virtual Computer.
hotpage.paci.org	The PACI HotPage, a portal to National Science Foundation–supported computing resources.
www.parabon.com	Pioneer from Parabon Computation.
gridport.sdsc.edu	SDSC GridPort, a toolkit for developing grid-based interfaces to scientific applications.
setiathome.ssl.berkeley.edu	SETI@home, a screen saver that analyzes data from the Search for Extraterrestrial Intelligence.

Out on a Limb

So far I haven't really gone out on a limb with my predictions. My impossible dream is to get ahead of the Web. I've got a Web server running. I can serve up data from a database, put some dynamic information on pages, and even create simple polls. I also scan through a couple of Internet weeklies, file away Web monthlies to read when I get a spare minute, keep abreast of Mac-related news, and subscribe to a half-dozen mailing lists telling me about this morning's revolutionary change. And still, it frightens me to think about the information I'm missing.

But at the same time, I like to think that I have at least a passing familiarity with what's going on. (If you've bought this book, I'm sure you'd like to think that I do as well.) So here's what I'm going to do. I'm going way out on a limb to take some wild stabs at what we should be watching for in the Web world. I'm putting these predictions down for posterity, so that in a few years, I may have some predictions to boast about and, more likely, some predictions to make us all laugh.

Prediction 1. Plan on XML sticking around. This is a pretty safe bet. XML is great for exchanging and analyzing semistructured data, which describes most information on the Internet. Computers prefer the structure imposed by XML over the stylistic trappings that Web designers have attached to HTML, which leads to my next prediction.

Prediction 2. Face it. The Internet is about computers talking to computers, whether those computers are the machines in a high-end data warehouse, your iMac, your Palm organizer, a cell phone, or your refrigerator. You can almost think of the Web as the makeup that the Internet puts on so humans can look at it. That's why e-commerce will never quite displace real-world shopping. People *like* going to stores, touching what they're about to buy, and returning clothes that don't fit. This is not to say that e-commerce or person-to-person Web communication will disappear. All I'm saying is that, in the final analysis, people like dealing with people, and computers like dealing with computers.

Prediction 3. At some point, people will push back against computers and the endless flood of information. Between cell phones, pagers, handheld computers, intelligent appliances nagging you to buy milk or put the clothes in the dryer, e-mail stations in the toilet stall, interactive television, always-on wireless networking, and wearable computers, people will decide that they *can* be too connected. Somewhere we have to squeeze in a little bit of real life and personal time. Here's a moneymaking proposition for a few years down the road: Come up with a way to prevent information from reaching a person—a digital "cone of silence," if you will, "push back" technology instead of "push."

Prediction 4. Someone will figure out the Internet business model, and some dot-coms will start making money in a sustainable way. There's obviously money to be made out there. The prize will go to the companies that perform in the long-term. Banner ads will not be the answer.

Prediction 5. Something will happen to force the Internet to adopt a security and privacy model that works. Denial-of-service attacks are just the beginning. Factor in companies that will sell you a person's Social Security number for $29.95. Factor in intelligent refrigerators and wireless mobile networks. Throw in Web caching and the merger between AOL and Time Warner. Who knows what will turn up? Here's another moneymaking idea whose time will soon come: a Web "shredder," or anti-search-engine. I suspect plenty of people would pay to have their personal information removed from the Web or scrambled into oblivion.

Prediction 6. Now I'll really go out on a limb. HTML (or XHTML), GIF, and JPEG will stick around longer than you might think. Why? They're simple and they work. People take in information sequentially, one word at a time and one image at a time, and HTML and bitmapped images work well to present information quickly. You can scan a text-based page and extract the highlights; try that with video. And 3-D won't really take off until the primary computer interface is not a 2-D screen controlled with a mouse rolling on a 2-D pad.

I thought I'd conclude with some suggestions for how you can act on these predictions. First, you don't have to be out on the cutting edge to have a successful and useful Web server. Maybe you won't strike it rich overnight, but you probably won't be left bleeding either. Second, although the Web is changing by the minute, the parts that work stick around longer than you'd expect. HTTP is still at version 1.1, after all. Finally, if you can present information in a usable and accessible way, serve it and they will come.

APPENDIX A

MAC OS X RESOURCES

This book is not intended to be a definitive source of information about administering, maintaining, or using Mac OS X. Although Mac OS X retains many of the usability features Mac users have grown familiar with over the years, it also represents an entirely new system on many levels. For further information, I've included some online and off-line resources in this appendix.

APPLE AND MAC OS X

Table A-1 lists some of the official Apple Web sites for Mac OS X and other software information. If you need a quick answer to a software issue or question, these are the best places to start. The Tech Info Library has the official word on the current state of the Mac OS and any problems, as well as documentation on software components.

Table A-1. Apple and Mac OS X Resources

Location	Description
www.apple.com/macosx	The official Mac OS X site.
developer.apple.com/macosx	Mac OS X technical information for developers.
www.apple.com/quicktime	The official QuickTime site.
asu.info.apple.com	Apple Software Updates.
til.info.apple.com	Apple's Tech Info Library.

Software and Updates

Table A-2 presets a few useful sites where you can learn about software, updates, and other products available for or compatible with Mac OS X. Apple's Macintosh Product Guide lists peripherals, software, and just about everything else available for the Macintosh. Pure Mac is one of my favorite sites for browsing Mac OS and Mac OS X software by category. Freeware, shareware, and commercial software are all listed here. Finally, VersionTracker will help you make sure you have the latest and greatest version of the software you need or already have.

Table A-2. Resources for Mac OS X Software and Products

Location	Description
guide.apple.com	Apple's Macintosh Product Guide.
www.macosx.com	MacOSX.com, a collection of forums on Mac OS X topics from Express Media, Inc.
www.pure-mac.com	Pure Mac, "All the software you really need."
www.versiontracker.com	VersionTracker, "The #1 resource for Macintosh software."

News and Reference

Just in case you don't have your personal favorite site or magazine for Apple- and Macintosh-related news, Table A-3 lists some of the stalwarts of the Mac publishing world. Most of the online sites have news, forums, and reference areas to help you sort out your problems. MacFixIt is a great resource to find out exactly why your Mac is doing what it's doing and whether anyone else has had the same problem—and how they fixed it. Stepwise.com comes from another perspective as a site originally focused on NeXTStep and OpenStep, the precursors to Mac OS X.

Table A-3. Mac OS News Sources

Location	Description
www.applelinks.com	AppleLinks.com, "The ultimate Macintosh resource."
www.insanely-great.com	Insanely Great Mac.
www.macaddict.com	*MacAddict,* print magazine and online resource.
www.maccentral.com	*MacCentral Online.*
www.macfixit.com	MacFixIt, "Troubleshooting Solutions for the Macintosh."
www.machome.com	*MacHome,* a print magazine and online resource.
www.macnn.com	Macintosh News Network.
www.maclaunch.com	MacLaunch, the Macintosh Portal.
www.mactech.com	*MacTech* magazine.
www.macworld.com	*Macworld*, a print magazine and online resource.
www.tidbits.com	TidBITS, "All the news that's fit to byte."
www.stepwise.com	Stepwise.com by Scott Anguish.

Books

A number of books were slated to be published at or around the same time as the final release of Mac OS X. The list below was taken from an online bookseller during late 2000. I can't speak on the merits of any of these titles since none of them existed as I was writing this book.

- *The Complete Idiot's Guide to Mac OS X* by Kate Binder (Que, 2001).
- *Mac OS X Clearly Explained* by John Rizzo (Morgan Kaufmann Publishers, 2000).

- *Mac OS X for Dummies* by Bob Levitus et al. (IDG Books Worldwide, 2000).
- *Mac OS X: The Complete Reference* by Jesse Feiler (Osborne McGraw-Hill, 2000).
- *Mac OS X Black Book: The Reference Guide for Power Users* by Mark Bell et al. (The Coriolis Group, 2001).
- *The Mac OS X Book* by Mark Bell (The Coriolis Group, 2001).
- *The Mac OS X Guide* by Brad Miser (Que Education & Training, 2001).
- *Mac OS X Little Black Book* by Gene Steinberg (Coriolis Group, 2000).
- *Mac OS X Power User's Guide* by Rita Lewis (Prima Publishing, 2001).
- *Mac OS X: Visual QuickStart Guide* by Maria Langer (Peachpit Press, 2001).
- *MacWorld Mac OS X Bible* by Lon Poole (IDG Books Worldwide, 2000).
- *Mastering Mac OS X* by Todd Stauffer (Sybex, 2001).

UNIX Guides and Tutorials

Since using the Terminal application and working from the command line may be a new experience for many Mac webmasters, I've included in Table A-4 a few resources where you can learn about basic UNIX commands. For this book, the commands you'll need to use most often will be "cd" (for changing directories), "ls" (for listing files in a directory), and "chmod" (for changing file permissions). There are plenty of other commands, variations, and combinations.

Table A-4. UNIX Guides and Tutorials

Location	Description
www.bsd.org	A large list of UNIX commands at BSD.org.
www.msoe.edu/~taylor/4ltrwrd	"Unix is a Four-Letter Word" by Christopher C. Taylor.
www.unix-manuals.com	Unix Manuals, a site for UNIX guides and references.
www.geek-girl.com/unix.html	*The UNIX Reference Desk,* by Jennifer Myers.

APPENDIX B

WEB REFERENCE GUIDES

Just as this book can't be the last word on Mac OS X, it can't be the definitive resource for Web development and the various Web standards you might encounter in the development process. Besides, there are a number of Web sites that make it their business to keep you up to date on the latest Web news.

Here are some of the sites I turn to for the official word on Web standards and a steady stream of articles on Web development tips and techniques.

INTERNET AND WEB STANDARDS

It's virtually impossible to predict where the Web and the Internet might be heading, but at least you can track down the current status of most Internet and Web standards at the sites listed in Table B-1. From the latest version of HTML to the progress and plans for new top-level domains, a handful of organizations are tasked with maintaining the basic infrastructure of the Internet. What that means for the future is left as an exercise for the reader.

If all you have is an acronym and you don't know if you're looking at something related to the Web, networking, or software, you should start at Whatis?com or the Free On-Line Dictionary of Computing. Once you've got the basics, you can move to one of the standards organizations.

For Web-related standards the W3 Consortium is the place to start. The site is regularly updated, and it's easy to navigate the site even if all you have is an acronym.

Table B-1. Internet and Web Standards Organizations

Location	Description
www.foldoc.org	*Free On-Line Dictionary of Computing,* from the Imperial College Department of Computing.
www.iana.org	Internet Assigned Numbers Authority.
www.icann.org	Internet Corporation for Assigned Numbers and Names.
www.ietf.org	Internet Engineering Task Force.
www.isoc.org	Internet Society.
www.isc.org	Internet Software Consortium.
whatis.com	Whatis?com, from TechTarget.com, "the IT-specific encyclopedia."
www.w3.org	World Wide Web (W3) Consortium.

General Development Guides

If you still don't understand the difference between HTML, XHTML, and XML or want to learn more about what cascading style sheets can do for you, a half-dozen or so sites have emerged as the major sites for developers. These sites provide comprehensive overviews; for in-depth information on a specific standard or language, use the index to find the relevant sections of this book for more pointers.

Whether you're a beginner feeling your way around or an expert looking for tips and tricks, one of the sites listed in Table B-2 should have the information you need. You'll also find useful information such as browser compatibility charts and sample JavaScript goodies to try out on your site.

All of the sites cover many of the same topics, from the basics to advanced techniques. If you can't find what you're looking for at your favorite site, try the others, because someone is sure to have covered it.

Table B-2. General Web Development Guides

Location	Description
www.builder.com	CNET Builder.com, "Solutions for Site Builders."
www.wdvl.com	Web Developer's Virtual Library from internet.com.
www.webreview.com	Web Review from CMP, Inc., "Cross-Training for Web Teams."
www.webtechniques.com	*Web Techniques,* a magazine and online resource from CMP Media, Inc.
www.webdeveloper.com	WebDeveloper.com, from internet.com.
hotwired.lycos.com/webmonkey	WebMonkey from Wired Digital and Lycos, "The Web Developer's Resource."
www.webreference.com	WebReference.com, the Webmaster's Reference Library, from internet.com.

INDEX

B

C

D